What is Property?

An Inquiry into the Principle of Right and of Government

by P. J. Proudhon

Copyright©2018 by Ashed Phoenix Library

All rights reserved.

Ashed Phoenix Library

All Rights Reserved ©2018 Ashed Phoenix.
First Printing: 2018.

The editorial arrangement, analysis, professional commentary and glossary are subject to this copyright notice. No portion of this book may be copied, retransmitted, reposted, duplicated, or otherwise used without the express written approval of the author, except by reviewers who may quote brief excerpts in connection with a review.

United States laws and regulations are public domain and not subject to copyright. Any unauthorized copying, reproduction, translation, or distribution of any part of this material without permission by the author is prohibited and against the law.

Disclaimer and Terms of Use: No information contained in this book should be considered as financial, tax, or legal advice. Your reliance upon information and content obtained by you at or through this publication is solely at your own risk. Teumessian Fox Library or the authors assume no liability or responsibility for damage or injury to you, other persons, or property arising from any use of any product, information, idea, or instruction contained in the content or services provided to you through this book. Reliance upon information contained in this material is solely at the reader's own risk. The authors have no financial interest in and receive no compensation from manufacturers of products or websites mentioned in this book.

Created in the United States of America

WHAT IS PROPERTY?

AN INQUIRY INTO THE PRINCIPLE OF RIGHT AND OF GOVERNMENT

By P. J. Proudhon

DETAILED CONTENTS

P. J. PROUDHON: HIS LIFE AND HIS WORKS

PREFACE

FIRST MEMOIR

CHAPTER I.

METHOD PURSUED IN THIS WORK.—THE IDEA OF A REVOLUTION

CHAPTER II.

PROPERTY CONSIDERED AS A NATURAL RIGHT.—OCCUPATION AND CIVIL LAW AS EFFICIENT BASES OF PROPERTY.—DEFINITIONS
% 1. Property as a Natural Right.
% 2. Occupation as the Title to Property.
% 3. Civil Law as the Foundation and Sanction of Property.

CHAPTER III.

LABOR AS THE EFFICIENT CAUSE OF THE DOMAIN OF PROPERTY
% 1. The Land cannot be appropriated.
% 2. Universal Consent no Justification of Property.
% 3. Prescription gives no Title to Property.
% 4. Labor.—That Labor has no Inherent Power to appropriate Natural Wealth.
% 5. That Labor leads to Equality of Property.
% 6. That in Society all Wages are Equal.
% 7. That Inequality of Powers is the Necessary Condition of Equality of Fortunes.
% 8. That, from the stand-point of Justice, Labor destroys Property.

CHAPTER IV.

THAT PROPERTY IS IMPOSSIBLE

DEMONSTRATION. AXIOM.

Property is the Right of Increase claimed by the Proprietor over any thing which he has stamped as his own.

FIRST PROPOSITION.
Property is Impossible, because it demands Something for Nothing.

SECOND PROPOSITION.
Property is Impossible, because, wherever it exists, Production costs more than it is worth.

THIRD PROPOSITION.
Property is Impossible, because, with a given Capital, Production is proportional to Labor, not to Property.

FOURTH PROPOSITION.
Property is Impossible, because it is Homicide.

FIFTH PROPOSITION.
Property is Impossible, because, if it exists, Society devours itsel

Appendix to the Fifth Proposition.

SIXTH PROPOSITION.
Property is Impossible, because it is the Mother of Tyranny.

SEVENTH PROPOSITION.
Property is Impossible, because, in consuming its Receipts, it loses them; in hoarding them, it nullifies them; and, in using them as Capital, it turns them against Production.

EIGHTH PROPOSITION.
Property is Impossible, because its Power of Accumulation is infinite, and is exercised only over Finite Quantities.

NINTH PROPOSITION
Property is Impossible, because it is powerless against Property.

TENTH PROPOSITION.
Property is Impossible, because it is the Negation of Equality.

CHAPTER V.
PSYCHOLOGICAL EXPOSITION OF THE IDEA OF JUSTICE AND IN JUSTICE, AND A DETERMINATION OF THE PRINCIPLE OF GOVERNMENT AND OF RIGHT.

PART 1.

% 1. Of the Moral Sense in Man and the Animals.
% 2. Of the First and Second Degrees of Sociability.
% 3. Of the Third Degree of Sociability.

PART I 1.
% 1. Of the Causes of our Mistakes. The Origin of Property.
% 2. Characteristics of Communism and of Property.
% 3. Determination of the Third Form of Society. Conclusion.

SECOND MEMOIR
LETTER TO M. BLANQUI ON PROPERTY

Linked Contents

P. J. PROUDHON: HIS LIFE AND HIS WORKS.

PREFACE.

WHAT IS PROPERTY? OR,

FIRST MEMOIR.

CHAPTER I. METHOD PURSUED IN THIS WORK.—THE IDEA OF A REVOLUTION.

CHAPTER II. PROPERTY CONSIDERED AS A NATURAL RIGHT

CHAPTER III. LABOR AS THE EFFICIENT CAUSE OF THE DOMAIN OF PROPERTY.

CHAPTER IV. THAT PROPERTY IS IMPOSSIBLE.

APPENDIX TO THE FIFTH PROPOSITION.

CHAPTER V. PSYCHOLOGICAL EXPOSITION OF THE IDEA OF JUSTICE

PART FIRST.

PART SECOND.

WHAT IS PROPERTY?

SECOND MEMOIR.

Conclusion.—"The results of the labor performed by this generation are

FOOTNOTES:

P. J. PROUDHON: HIS LIFE AND HIS WORKS.

The correspondence [1] of P. J. Proudhon, the first volumes of which we publish to-day, has been collected since his death by the faithful and intelligent labors of his daughter, aided by a few friends. It was incomplete when submitted to Sainte Beuve, but the portion with which the illustrious academician became acquainted was sufficient to allow him to estimate it as a whole with that soundness of judgment which characterized him as a literary critic.

He would, however, caution readers against accepting the biographer's interpretation of the author's views as in any sense authoritative; advising them, rather, to await the publication of the remainder of Proudhon's writings, that they may form an opinion for themselves.—Translator.

In an important work, which his habitual readers certainly have not forgotten, although death did not allow him to finish it, Sainte Beuve thus judges the correspondence of the great publicist:—

"The letters of Proudhon, even outside the circle of his particular friends, will always be of value; we can always learn something from them, and here is the proper place to determine the general character of his correspondence.

"It has always been large, especially since he became so celebrated; and, to tell the truth, I am persuaded that, in the future, the correspondence of Proudhon will be his principal, vital work, and that most of his books will be only accessory to and corroborative of this. At any rate, his books can be well understood only by the aid of his letters and the continual explanations which he makes to those who consult him in their doubt, and request him to define more clearly his position.

"There are, among celebrated people, many methods of correspondence. There are those to whom letter-writing is a bore, and who, assailed with questions and compliments, reply in the greatest haste, solely that the job may be over with, and who return politeness for politeness, mingling it with more or less wit. This kind of correspondence, though coming from celebrated people, is insignificant and unworthy of collection and classification.

"After those who write letters in performance of a disagreeable duty, and almost side by side with them in point of insignificance, I should put those who write in a manner wholly external, wholly superficial, devoted only to flattery, lavishing praise like gold, without counting it; and those also who weigh every word, who reply formally and pompously, with a view to fine phrases and effects. They exchange words only, and choose them solely for their brilliancy and show. You think it is you, individually, to whom they speak; but they are addressing themselves in your person to the four corners of Europe. Such letters are empty, and teach us nothing but theatrical execution and the favorite pose of their writers.

"I will not class among the latter the more prudent and sagacious authors who, when writing to individuals, keep one eye on posterity. We know that many who pursue this method have written long, finished, charming, flattering, and tolerably natural letters. Beranger furnishes us with the best example of this class.

"Proudhon, however, is a man of entirely different nature and habits. In writing, he thinks of nothing but his idea and the person whom he addresses: ad rem et ad hominem. A man of conviction and doctrine, to write does not weary him; to be questioned does not annoy him. When approached, he cares only to know that your motive is not one of futile curiosity, but the love of truth; he assumes you to be serious, he replies, he examines your objections, sometimes verbally, sometimes in writing; for, as he remarks, 'if there be some points which correspondence can never settle, but which can be made clear by conversation in two minutes, at other times just the opposite is the case: an objection clearly stated in writing, a doubt well expressed, which elicits a direct and positive reply, helps things along more than ten hours of oral intercourse!' In writing to you he does not hesitate to treat the subject anew; he unfolds to you the foundation and superstructure of his thought: rarely does he confess himself defeated—it is not his way; he holds to his position, but admits the breaks, the variations, in short, the EVOLUTION of his mind. The history of his mind is in his letters; there it must be sought.

"Proudhon, whoever addresses him, is always ready; he quits the page of the book on which he is at work to answer you with the same pen, and that without losing patience, without getting confused, without sparing or complaining of his ink; he is a public man, devoted to the propagation of his idea by all methods, and the best method, with him, is always the present one, the latest one. His very handwriting, bold, uniform, legible, even in the most tiresome passages, betrays no haste, no hurry to finish. Each line is accurate: nothing is left to chance; the punctuation, very correct and a little emphatic and decided, indicates with precision and delicate distinction all the links in the chain of his argument. He is devoted entirely to you, to his business and yours, while writing to you, and never to anything else. All the letters of his which I have seen are serious: not one is commonplace.

"But at the same time he is not at all artistic or affected; he does not CONSTRUCT his letters, he does not revise them, he spends no time in reading them over; we have a first draught, excellent and clear, a jet from the fountain-head, but that is all. The new arguments, which he discovers in support of his ideas and which opposition suggests to him, are an agreeable surprise, and shed a light which we should vainly search for even in his works. His correspondence differs essentially from his books, in that it gives you no uneasiness; it places you in the very heart of the man, explains him to you, and leaves you with an impression of moral esteem and almost of intellectual security. We feel his sincerity. I know of no one to whom he can be more fitly compared in this respect than George Sand, whose correspondence is large, and at the same time full of sincerity. His role and his nature correspond. If he is writing to a young man who unbosoms himself to him in sceptical anxiety, to a young woman who asks him to decide delicate questions of conduct for her, his letter takes the form of a short moral essay, of a father-confessor's advice. Has he perchance attended the theatre (a rare thing for him) to witness one of Ponsart's comedies, or a drama of Charles Edmond's, he feels bound to give an account of his impressions to the friend to whom he is indebted for this pleasure, and his letter becomes a literary and philosophical criticism, full of sense, and like no other. His familiarity is suited to his correspondent; he affects no rudeness. The terms of civility or affection which he employs towards his correspondents are sober, measured, appropriate to each, and honest in their simplicity and cordiality. When he speaks of morals and the family, he seems at times like the patriarchs of the Bible. His command of language is complete, and he never fails to avail himself of it. Now and then a coarse word, a few personalities, too bitter and quite unjust or injurious, will have to be suppressed in printing; time, however, as it passes away, permits many things and renders them inoffensive. Am I right in saying that Proudhon's correspondence, always substantial, will one day be the most accessible and attractive portion of his works?"

Almost the whole of Proudhon's real biography is included in his correspondence. Up to 1837, the date of the first letter which we have been able to collect, his life, narrated by Sainte Beuve, from whom we make numerous extracts, may be summed up in a few pages.

Pierre Joseph Proudhon was born on the 15th of January, 1809, in a suburb of Besancon, called Mouillere. His father and mother were employed in the great brewery belonging to M. Renaud. His father, though a cousin of the jurist Proudhon, the celebrated professor in the faculty of Dijon, was a journeyman brewer. His mother, a genuine peasant, was a common servant. She was an orderly person of great good sense; and, as they who knew her say, a superior woman of HEROIC character,—to use the expression of the venerable M. Weiss, the librarian at Besancon. She it was especially that Proudhon resembled: she and his grandfather Tournesi, the soldier peasant of whom his mother told him, and whose courageous deeds he has described in his work on "Justice." Proudhon, who always felt a great veneration for his mother Catharine, gave her name to the elder of his daughters. In 1814, when Besancon was blockaded, Mouillere, which stood in front of the walls of the town, was destroyed in the defence of the place, and Proudhon's father established a cooper's shop in a suburb of Battant, called Vignerons. Very honest, but simple-minded and short-sighted, this cooper, the father of five children, of whom Pierre Joseph was the eldest, passed his life in poverty. At eight years of age, Proudhon either made himself useful in the house, or tended the cattle out of doors. No one should fail to read that beautiful and precious page of his work on "Justice," in which he describes the rural sports which he enjoyed when a neatherd. At the age of twelve, he was a cellar-boy in an inn. This, however, did not prevent him from studying.

His mother was greatly aided by M. Renaud, the former owner of the brewery, who had at that time retired from business, and was engaged in the education of his children.

Proudhon entered school as a day-scholar in the sixth class. He was necessarily irregular in his attendance; domestic cares and restraints sometimes kept him from his classes. He succeeded nevertheless in his studies; he showed great perseverance. His family were so poor that they could not afford to furnish him with books; he was obliged to borrow them from his comrades, and copy the text of his lessons. He has himself told us that he was obliged to leave his wooden shoes outside the door, that he might not disturb the classes with his noise; and that, having no hat, he went to school bareheaded. One day, towards the close of his studies, on returning from the distribution of the prizes, loaded with crowns, he found nothing to eat in the house.

"In his eagerness for labor and his thirst for knowledge, Proudhon," says Sainte Beuve, "was not content with the instruction of his teachers. From his twelfth to his fourteenth year, he was a constant frequenter of the town library. One curiosity led to another, and he called for book after book, sometimes eight or ten at one sitting. The learned librarian, the friend and almost the brother of Charles Nodier, M. Weiss, approached him one day, and said, smiling, 'But, my little friend, what do you wish to do with all these books?' The child raised his head, eyed his questioner, and replied: 'What's that to you?' And the good M. Weiss remembers it to this day."

Forced to earn his living, Proudhon could not continue his studies. He entered a printing-office in Besancon as a proof-reader. Becoming, soon after, a compositor, he made a tour of France in this capacity. At Toulon, where he found himself without money and without work, he had a scene with the mayor, which he describes in his work on "Justice."

Sainte Beuve says that, after his tour of France, his service book being filled with good certificates, Proudhon was promoted to the position of foreman. But he does not tell us, for the reason that he had no knowledge of a letter written by Fallot, of which we never heard until six months since, that the printer at that time contemplated quitting his trade in order to become a teacher.

Towards 1829, Fallot, who was a little older than Proudhon, and who, after having obtained the Suard pension in 1832, died in his twenty-ninth year, while filling the position of assistant librarian at the Institute, was charged, Protestant though he was, with the revisal of a "Life of the Saints," which was published at Besancon. The book was in Latin, and Fallot added some notes which also were in Latin.

"But," says Sainte Beuve, "it happened that some errors escaped his attention, which Proudhon, then proof-reader in the printing office, did not fail to point out to him. Surprised at finding so good a Latin scholar in a workshop, he desired to make his acquaintance; and soon there sprung up between them a most earnest and intimate friendship: a friendship of the intellect and of the heart."

Addressed to a printer between twenty-two and twenty-three years of age, and predicting in formal terms his future fame, Fallot's letter seems to us so interesting that we do not hesitate to reproduce it entire.

"PARIS, December 5, 1831.

"MY DEAR PROUDHON,—YOU have a right to be surprised at, and even dissatisfied with, my long delay in replying to your kind letter; I will tell you the cause of it. It became necessary to forward an account of your ideas to M. J. de Gray; to hear his objections, to reply to them, and to await his definitive response, which reached me but a short time ago; for M. J. is a sort of financial king, who takes no pains to be punctual in dealing with poor devils like ourselves. I, too, am careless in matters of business; I sometimes push my negligence even to disorder, and the metaphysical musings which continually occupy my mind, added to the amusements of Paris, render me the most incapable man in the world for conducting a negotiation with despatch.

"I have M. Jobard's decision; here it is: In his judgment, you are too learned and clever for his children; he fears that you could not accommodate your mind and character to the childish notions common to their age and station. In short, he is what the world calls a good father; that is, he wants to spoil his children, and, in order to do this easily, he thinks fit to retain his present instructor, who is not very learned, but who takes part in their games and joyous sports with wonderful facility, who points out the letters of the alphabet to the little girl, who takes the little boys to mass, and who, no less obliging than the worthy Abbe P. of our acquaintance, would readily dance for Madame's amusement. Such a profession would not suit you, you who have a free, proud, and manly soul: you are refused; let us dismiss the matter from our minds. Perhaps another time my solicitude will be less unfortunate. I can only ask your pardon for having thought of thus disposing of you almost without consulting you. I find my excuse in the motives which guided me; I had in view your well-being and advancement in the ways of this world.

"I see in your letter, my comrade, through its brilliant witticisms and beneath the frank and artless gayety with which you have sprinkled it, a tinge of sadness and despondency which pains me. You are unhappy, my friend: your present situation does not suit you; you cannot remain in it, it was not made for you, it is beneath you; you ought, by all means, to leave it, before its injurious influence begins to affect your faculties, and before you become settled, as they say, in the ways of your profession, were it possible that such a thing could ever happen, which I flatly deny. You are unhappy; you have not yet entered upon the path which Nature has marked out for you. But, faint-hearted soul, is that a cause for despondency? Ought you to feel discouraged? Struggle, morbleu, struggle persistently, and you will triumph. J. J. Rousseau groped about for forty years before his genius was revealed to him. You are not J. J Rousseau; but listen: I know not whether I should have divined the author of "Emile" when he was twenty years of age, supposing that I had been his contemporary, and had enjoyed the honor of his acquaintance. But I have known you, I have loved you, I have divined your future, if I may venture to say so; for the first time in my life, I am going to risk a prophecy. Keep this letter, read it again fifteen or twenty years hence, perhaps twenty-five, and if at that time the prediction which I am about to make has not been fulfilled, burn it as a piece of folly out of charity and respect for my memory. This is my prediction: you will be, Proudhon, in spite of yourself, inevitably, by the fact of your destiny, a writer, an author; you will be a philosopher; you will be one of the lights of the century, and your name will occupy a place in the annals of the nineteenth century, like those of Gassendi, Descartes, Malebranche, and Bacon in the seventeenth, and those of Diderot, Montesquieu, Helvetius, Locke, Hume, and Holbach in the eighteenth. Such will be your lot! Do now what you will, set type in a printing-office, bring up children, bury yourself in deep seclusion, seek obscure and lonely villages, it is all one to me; you cannot escape your destiny; you cannot divest yourself of your noblest feature, that active, strong, and inquiring mind, with which you are endowed; your place in the world has been appointed, and it cannot remain empty. Go where you please, I expect you in Paris, talking philosophy and the doctrines of Plato; you will have to come, whether you want to or not. I, who say this to you, must feel very sure of it in order to be willing to put it upon paper, since, without reward for my prophetic skill,—to which, I assure you, I make not the slightest claim,—I run the risk of passing for a hare-brained fellow, in case I prove to be mistaken: he plays a bold game who risks his good sense upon his cards, in return for the very trifling and insignificant merit of having divined a young man's future.

"When I say that I expect you in Paris, I use only a proverbial phrase which you must not allow to mislead you as to my projects and plans. To reside in Paris is disagreeable to me, very much so; and when this fine-art fever which possesses me has left me, I shall abandon the place without regret to seek a more peaceful residence in a provincial town, provided always the town shall afford me the means of living, bread, a bed, books, rest, and solitude. How I miss, my good Proudhon, that dark, obscure, smoky chamber in which I dwelt in Besancon, and where we spent so many pleasant hours in the discussion of philosophy! Do you remember it? But that is now far away. Will that happy time ever return? Shall we one day meet again? Here my life is restless, uncertain, precarious, and, what is worse, indolent, illiterate, and vagrant. I do no work, I live in idleness, I ramble about; I do not read, I no longer study; my books are forsaken; now and then I glance over a few metaphysical works, and after a days walk through dirty, filthy, crowded streets. I lie down with empty head and tired body, to repeat the performance on the following day. What is the object of these walks, you will ask. I make visits, my friend; I hold interviews with stupid people. Then a fit of curiosity seizes me, the least inquisitive of beings: there are museums, libraries, assemblies, churches, palaces, gardens, and theatres to visit. I am fond of pictures, fond of music, fond of sculpture; all these are beautiful and good, but they cannot appease hunger, nor take the place of my pleasant readings of Bailly, Hume, and Tennemann, which I used to enjoy by my fireside when I was able to read.

"But enough of complaints. Do not allow this letter to affect you too much, and do not think that I give way to dejection or despondency; no, I am a fatalist, and I believe in my star. I do not know yet what my calling is, nor for what branch of polite literature I am best fitted; I do not even know whether I am, or ever shall be, fitted for any: but what matters it? I suffer, I labor, I dream, I enjoy, I think; and, in a word, when my last hour strikes, I shall have lived.

"Proudhon, I love you, I esteem you; and, believe me, these are not mere phrases. What interest could I have in flattering and praising a poor printer? Are you rich, that you may pay for courtiers? Have you a sumptuous table, a dashing wife, and gold to scatter, in order to attract them to your suite? Have you the glory, honors, credit, which would render your acquaintance pleasing to their vanity and pride? No; you are poor, obscure, abandoned; but, poor, obscure, and abandoned, you have a friend, and a friend who knows all the obligations which that word imposes upon honorable people, when they venture to assume it. That friend is myself: put me to the test.

"GUSTAVE FALLOT."

It appears from this letter that if, at this period, Proudhon had already exhibited to the eyes of a clairvoyant friend his genius for research and investigation, it was in the direction of philosophical, rather than of economical and social, questions.

Having become foreman in the house of Gauthier & Co., who carried on a large printing establishment at Besancon, he corrected the proofs of ecclesiastical writers, the Fathers of the Church. As they were printing a Bible, a Vulgate, he was led to compare the Latin with the original Hebrew.

"In this way," says Sainte Beuve, "he learned Hebrew by himself, and, as everything was connected in his mind, he was led to the study of comparative philology. As the house of Gauthier published many works on Church history and theology, he came also to acquire, through this desire of his to investigate everything, an extensive knowledge of theology, which afterwards caused misinformed persons to think that he had been in an ecclesiastical seminary."

Towards 1836, Proudhon left the house of Gauthier, and, in company with an associate, established a small printing-office in Besancon. His contribution to the partnership consisted, not so much in capital, as in his knowledge of the trade. His partner committing suicide in 1838, Proudhon was obliged to wind up the business, an operation which he did not accomplish as quickly and as easily as he hoped. He was then urged by his friends to enter the ranks of the competitors for the Suard pension. This pension consisted of an income of fifteen hundred francs bequeathed to the Academy of Besancon by Madame Suard, the widow of the academician, to be given once in three years to the young man residing in the department of Doubs, a bachelor of letters or of science, and not possessing a fortune, whom the Academy of Besancon SHOULD DEEM BEST FITTED FOR A LITERARY OR SCIENTIFIC CAREER, OR FOR THE STUDY OF LAW OR OF MEDICINE. The first to win the Suard pension was Gustave Fallot. Mauvais, who was a distinguished astronomer in the Academy of Sciences, was the second. Proudhon aspired to be the third. To qualify himself, he had to be received as a bachelor of letters, and was obliged to write a letter to the Academy of Besancon. In a phrase of this letter, the terms of which he had to modify, though he absolutely refused to change its spirit, Proudhon expressed his firm resolve to labor for the amelioration of the condition of his brothers, the working-men.

The only thing which he had then published was an "Essay on General Grammar," which appeared without the author's signature. While reprinting, at Besancon, the "Primitive Elements of Languages, Discovered by the Comparison of Hebrew roots with those of the Latin and French," by the Abbe Bergier, Proudhon had enlarged the edition of his "Essay on General Grammar."

The date of the edition, 1837, proves that he did not at that time think of competing for the Suard pension. In this work, which continued and completed that of the Abbe Bergier, Proudhon adopted the same point of view, that of Moses and of Biblical tradition. Two years later, in February, 1839, being already in possession of the Suard pension, he addressed to the Institute, as a competitor for the Volney prize, a memoir entitled: "Studies in Grammatical Classification and the Derivation of some French words." It was his first work, revised and presented in another form. Four memoirs only were sent to the Institute, none of which gained the prize. Two honorable mentions were granted, one of them to memoir No. 4; that is, to P. J. Proudhon, printer at Besancon. The judges were MM. Amedde Jaubert, Reinaud, and Burnouf.

"The committee," said the report presented at the annual meeting of the five academies on Thursday, May 2, 1839, "has paid especial attention to manuscripts No. 1 and No. 4. Still, it does not feel able to grant the prize to either of these works, because they do not appear to be sufficiently elaborated. The committee, which finds in No. 4 some ingenious analyses, particularly in regard to the mechanism of the Hebrew language, regrets that the author has resorted to hazardous conjectures, and has sometimes forgotten the special recommendation of the committee to pursue the experimental and comparative method."

Proudhon remembered this. He attended the lectures of Eugene Burnouf, and, as soon as he became acquainted with the labors and discoveries of Bopp and his successors, he definitively abandoned an hypothesis which had been condemned by the Academy of Inscriptions and Belles-lettres. He then sold, for the value of the paper, the remaining copies of the "Essay" published by him in 1837. In 1850, they were still lying in a grocer's back-shop.

A neighboring publisher then placed the edition on the market, with the attractive name of Proudhon upon it. A lawsuit ensued, in which the author was beaten. His enemies, and at that time there were many of them, would have been glad to have proved him a renegade and a recanter. Proudhon, in his work on "Justice," gives some interesting details of this lawsuit.

In possession of the Suard pension, Proudhon took part in the contest proposed by the Academy of Besancon on the question of the utility of the celebration of Sunday. His memoir obtained honorable mention, together with a medal which was awarded him, in open session, on the 24th of August, 1839. The reporter of the committee, the Abbe Doney, since made Bishop of Montauban, called attention to the unquestionable superiority of his talent.

"But," says Sainte Beuve, "he reproached him with having adopted dangerous theories, and with having touched upon questions of practical politics and social organization, where upright intentions and zeal for the public welfare cannot justify rash solutions."

Was it policy, we mean prudence, which induced Proudhon to screen his ideas of equality behind the Mosaic law? Sainte Beuve, like many others, seems to think so. But we remember perfectly well that, having asked Proudhon, in August, 1848, if he did not consider himself indebted in some respects to his fellow-countryman, Charles Fourier, we received from him the following reply: "I have certainly read Fourier, and have spoken of him more than once in my works; but, upon the whole, I do not think that I owe anything to him. My real masters, those who have caused fertile ideas to spring up in my mind, are three in number: first, the Bible; next, Adam Smith; and last, Hegel."

Freely confessed in the "Celebration of Sunday," the influence of the Bible on Proudhon is no less manifest in his first memoir on property. Proudhon undoubtedly brought to this work many ideas of his own; but is not the very foundation of ancient Jewish law to be found in its condemnation of usurious interest and its denial of the right of personal appropriation of land?

The first memoir on property appeared in 1840, under the title, "What is Property? or an Inquiry into the Principle of Right and of Government." Proudhon dedicated it, in a letter which served as the preface, to the Academy of Besancon. The latter, finding itself brought to trial by its pensioner, took the affair to heart, and evoked it, says Sainte Beuve, with all possible haste.

The pension narrowly escaped being immediately withdrawn from the bold defender of the principle of equality of conditions. M. Vivien, then Minister of Justice, who was earnestly solicited to prosecute the author, wished first to obtain the opinion of the economist, Blanqui, a member of the Academy of Moral and Political Sciences. Proudhon having presented to this academy a copy of his book, M. Blanqui was appointed to review it. This review, though it opposed Proudhon's views, shielded him. Treated as a savant by M. Blanqui, the author was not prosecuted. He was always grateful to MM. Blanqui and Vivien for their handsome conduct in the matter.

the 7th of September, 1840, naturally led Proudhon to address to him, in the form of a letter, his second memoir on property, which appeared in April, 1841. Proudhon had endeavored, in his first memoir, to demonstrate that the pursuit of equality of conditions is the true principle of right and of government. In the "Letter to M. Blanqui," he passes in review the numerous and varied methods by which this principle gradually becomes realized in all societies, especially in modern society.

In 1842, a third memoir appeared, entitled, "A Notice to Proprietors, or a Letter to M. Victor Considerant, Editor of 'La Phalange,' in Reply to a Defence of Property." Here the influence of Adam Smith manifested itself, and was frankly admitted. Did not Adam Smith find, in the principle of equality, the first of all the laws which govern wages? There are other laws, undoubtedly; but Proudhon considers them all as springing from the principle of property, as he defined it in his first memoir. Thus, in humanity, there are two principles,—one which leads us to equality, another which separates us from it. By the former, we treat each other as associates; by the latter, as strangers, not to say enemies. This distinction, which is constantly met with throughout the three memoirs, contained already, in germ, the idea which gave birth to the "System of Economical Contradictions," which appeared in 1846, the idea of antinomy or contre-loi.

The "Notice to Proprietors" was seized by the magistrates of Besancon; and Proudhon was summoned to appear before the assizes of Doubs within a week. He read his written defence to the jurors in person, and was acquitted. The jury, like M. Blanqui, viewed him only as a philosopher, an inquirer, a savant.

In 1843, Proudhon published the "Creation of Order in Humanity," a large volume, which does not deal exclusively with questions of social economy. Religion, philosophy, method, certainty, logic, and dialectics are treated at considerable length.

Released from his printing-office on the 1st of March of the same year, Proudhon had to look for a chance to earn his living. Messrs. Gauthier Bros., carriers by water between Mulhouse and Lyons, the eldest of whom was Proudhon's companion in childhood, conceived the happy thought of employing him, of utilizing his ability in their business, and in settling the numerous points of difficulty which daily arose. Besides the large number of accounts which his new duties required him to make out, and which retarded the publication of the "System of Economical Contradictions," until October, 1846, we ought to mention a work, which, before it appeared in pamphlet form, was published in the "Revue des Economistes,"—"Competition between Railroads and Navigable Ways."

"Le Miserere, or the Repentance of a King," which he published in March, 1845, in the "Revue Independante," during that Lenten season when Lacordaire was preaching in Lyons, proves that, though devoting himself with ardor to the study of economical problems, Proudhon had not lost his interest in questions of religious history. Among his writings on these questions, which he was unfortunately obliged to leave unfinished, we may mention a nearly completed history of the early Christian heresies, and of the struggle of Christianity against Caesarism.

We have said that, in 1848, Proudhon recognized three masters. Having no knowledge of the German language, he could not have read the works of Hegel, which at that time had not been translated into French. It was Charles Grun, a German, who had come to France to study the various philosophical and socialistic systems, who gave him the substance of the Hegelian ideas. During the winter of 1844-45, Charles Grun had some long conversations with Proudhon, which determined, very decisively, not the ideas, which belonged exclusively to the bisontin thinker, but the form of the important work on which he labored after 1843, and which was published in 1846 by Guillaumin.

Hegel's great idea, which Proudhon appropriated, and which he demonstrates with wonderful ability in the "System of Economical Contradictions," is as follows: Antinomy, that is, the existence of two laws or tendencies which are opposed to each other, is possible, not only with two different things, but with one and the same thing. Considered in their thesis, that is, in the law or tendency which created them, all the economical categories are rational,—competition, monopoly, the balance of trade, and property, as well as the division of labor, machinery, taxation, and credit. But, like communism and population, all these categories are antinomical; all are opposed, not only to each other, but to themselves. All is opposition, and disorder is born of this system of opposition. Hence, the sub-title of the work,—"Philosophy of Misery." No category can be suppressed; the opposition, antinomy, or contre-tendance, which exists in each of them, cannot be suppressed.

Where, then, lies the solution of the social problem? Influenced by the Hegelian ideas, Proudhon began to look for it in a superior synthesis, which should reconcile the thesis and antithesis. Afterwards, while at work upon his book on "Justice," he saw that the antinomical terms do not cancel each other, any more than the opposite poles of an electric pile destroy each other; that they are the procreative cause of motion, life, and progress; that the problem is to discover, not their fusion, which would be death, but their equilibrium,—an equilibrium for ever unstable, varying with the development of society.

On the cover of the "System of Economical Contradictions," Proudhon announced, as soon to appear, his "Solution of the Social Problem." This work, upon which he was engaged when the Revolution of 1848 broke out, had to be cut up into pamphlets and newspaper articles. The two pamphlets, which he published in March, 1848, before he became editor of "Le Representant du Peuple," bear the same title,—"Solution of the Social Problem." The first, which is mainly a criticism of the early acts of the provisional government, is notable from the fact that in it Proudhon, in advance of all others, energetically opposed the establishment of national workshops. The second, "Organization of Credit and Circulation," sums up in a few pages his idea of economical progress: a gradual reduction of interest, profit, rent, taxes, and wages. All progress hitherto has been made in this manner; in this manner it must continue to be made. Those workingmen who favor a nominal increase of wages are, unconsciously following a back-track, opposed to all their interests.

After having published in "Le Representant du Peuple," the statutes of the Bank of Exchange,—a bank which was to make no profits, since it was to have no stockholders, and which, consequently, was to discount commercial paper without interest, charging only a commission sufficient to defray its running expenses,—Proudhon endeavored, in a number of articles, to explain its mechanism and necessity. These articles have been collected in one volume, under the double title, "Resume of the Social Question; Bank of Exchange." His other articles, those which up to December, 1848, were inspired by the progress of events, have been collected in another volume,—"Revolutionary Ideas."

Almost unknown in March, 1848, and struck off in April from the list of candidates for the Constituent Assembly by the delegation of workingmen which sat at the Luxembourg, Proudhon had but a very small number of votes at the general elections of April. At the complementary elections, which were held in the early days of June, he was elected in Paris by seventy-seven thousand votes.

After the fatal days of June, he published an article on le terme, which caused the first suspension of "Le Representant du Peuple." It was at that time that he introduced a bill into the Assembly, which, being referred to the Committee on the Finances, drew forth, first, the report of M. Thiers, and then the speech which Proudhon delivered, on the 31st of July, in reply to this report. "Le Representant du Peuple," reappearing a few days later, he wrote, a propos of the law requiring journals to give bonds, his famous article on "The Malthusians" (August 10, 1848).

Ten days afterwards, "Le Representant du Peuple," again suspended, definitively ceased to appear. "Le Peuple," of which he was the editor-in-chief, and the first number of which was issued in the early part of September, appeared weekly at first, for want of sufficient bonds; it afterwards appeared daily, with a double number once a week. Before "Le Peuple" had obtained its first bond, Proudhon published a remarkable pamphlet on the "Right to Labor,"—a right which he denied in the form in which it was then affirmed. It was during the same period that he proposed, at the Poissonniere banquet, his Toast to the Revolution.

Proudhon, who had been asked to preside at the banquet, refused, and proposed in his stead, first, Ledru-Rollin, and then, in view of the reluctance of the organizers of the banquet, the illustrious president of the party of the Mountain, Lamennais. It was evidently his intention to induce the representatives of the Extreme Left to proclaim at last with him the Democratic and Social Republic. Lamennais being accepted by the organizers, the Mountain promised to be present at the banquet. The night before, all seemed right, when General Cavaignac replaced Minister Senart by Minister Dufaure-Vivien. The Mountain, questioning the government, proposed a vote of confidence in the old minister, and, tacitly, of want of confidence in the new. Proudhon abstained from voting on this proposition. The Mountain declared that it would not attend the banquet, if Proudhon was to be present. Five Montagnards, Mathieu of Drome at their head, went to the temporary office of "Le Peuple" to notify him of this. "Citizen Proudhon," said they to the organizers in his presence, "in abstaining from voting to-day on the proposition of the Mountain, has betrayed the Republican cause." Proudhon, vehemently questioned, began his defence by recalling, on the one hand, the treatment which he had received from the dismissed minister; and, on the other, the impartial conduct displayed towards him in 1840 by M. Vivien, the new minister. He then attacked the Mountain by telling its delegates that it sought only a private conversation, whether with him or with the organizers of the banquet, it had not the courage to publicly declare itself Socialist.

On the following day, in his Toast to the Revolution, a toast which was filled with allusions to the exciting scene of the night before, Proudhon commenced his struggle against the Mountain. His duel with Felix Pyat was one of the episodes of this struggle, which became less bitter on Proudhon's side after the Mountain finally decided to publicly proclaim the Democratic and Social Republic. The campaign for the election of a President of the Republic had just begun. Proudhon made a very sharp attack on the candidacy of Louis Bonaparte in a pamphlet which is regarded as one of his literary chefs-d'oeuvre: the "Pamphlet on the Presidency." An opponent of this institution, against which he had voted in the Constituent Assembly, he at first decided to take no part in the campaign. But soon seeing that he was thus increasing the chances of

Louis Bonaparte, and that if, as was not at all probable, the latter should not obtain an absolute majority of the votes, the Assembly would not fail to elect General Cavaignac, he espoused, for the sake of form, the candidacy of Raspail, who was supported by his friends in the Socialist Committee. Charles Delescluze, the editor-in-chief of "La Revolution Democratique et Sociale," who could not forgive him for having preferred Raspail to Ledru-Rollin, the candidate of the Mountain, attacked him on the day after the election with a violence which overstepped all bounds. At first, Proudhon had the wisdom to refrain from answering him. At length, driven to an extremity, he became aggressive himself, and Delescluze sent him his seconds. This time, Proudhon positively refused to fight; he would not have fought with Felix Pyat, had not his courage been called in question.

On the 25th of January, 1849, Proudhon, rising from a sick bed, saw that the existence of the Constituent Assembly was endangered by the coalition of the monarchical parties with Louis Bonaparte, who was already planning his coup d'Etat. He did not hesitate to openly attack the man who had just received five millions of votes. He wanted to break the idol; he succeeded only in getting prosecuted and condemned himself. The prosecution demanded against him was authorized by a majority of the Constituent Assembly, in spite of the speech which he delivered on that occasion. Declared guilty by the jury, he was sentenced, in March, 1849, to three years' imprisonment and the payment of a fine of ten thousand francs.

Proudhon had not abandoned for a single moment his project of a Bank of Exchange, which was to operate without capital with a sufficient number of merchants and manufacturers for adherents. This bank, which he then called the Bank of the People, and around which he wished to gather the numerous working-people's associations which had been formed since the 24th of February, 1848, had already obtained a certain number of subscribers and adherents, the latter to the number of thirty-seven thousand. It was about to commence operations, when Proudhon's sentence forced him to choose between imprisonment and exile. He did not hesitate to abandon his project and return the money to the subscribers. He explained the motives which led him to this decision in an article in "Le Peuple."

Having fled to Belgium, he remained there but a few days, going thence to Paris, under an assumed name, to conceal himself in a house in the Rue de Chabrol. From his hiding-place he sent articles almost every day, signed and unsigned, to "Le Peuple." In the evening, dressed in a blouse, he went to some secluded spot to take the air. Soon, emboldened by habit, he risked an evening promenade upon the Boulevards, and afterwards carried his imprudence so far as to take a stroll by daylight in the neighborhood of the Gare du Nord. It was not long before he was recognized by the police, who arrested him on the 6th of June, 1849, in the Rue du Faubourg-Poissonniere.

Taken to the office of the prefect of police, then to Sainte-Pelagie, he was in the Conciergerie on the day of the 13th of June, 1849, which ended with the violent suppression of "Le Peuple." He then began to write the "Confessions of a Revolutionist," published towards the end of the year. He had been again transferred to Sainte-Pelagie, when he married, in December, 1849, Mlle. Euphrasie Piegard, a young working girl whose hand he had requested in 1847. Madame Proudhon bore him four daughters, of whom but two, Catherine and Stephanie, survived their father. Stephanie died in 1873.

In October, 1849, "Le Peuple" was replaced by a new journal, "La Voix du Peuple," which Proudhon edited from his prison cell. In it were published his discussions with Pierre Leroux and Bastiat.

The political articles which he sent to "La Voix du Peuple" so displeased the government finally, that it transferred him to Doullens, where he was secretly confined for some time. Afterwards taken back to Paris, to appear before the assizes of the Seine in reference to an article in "La Voix du Peuple," he was defended by M. Cremieux and acquitted. From the Conciergerie he went again to Sainte-Pelagie, where he ended his three years in prison on the 6th of June, 1852.

"La Voix du Peuple," suppressed before the promulgation of the law of the 31st of May, had been replaced by a weekly sheet, "Le Peuple" of 1850. Established by the aid of the principal members of the Mountain, this journal soon met with the fate of its predecessors.

In 1851, several months before the coup d'Etat, Proudhon published the "General Idea of the Revolution of the Nineteenth Century," in which, after having shown the logical series of unitary governments,—from monarchy, which is the first term, to the direct government of the people, which is the last,—he opposes the ideal of an-archy or self-government to the communistic or governmental ideal.

At this period, the Socialist party, discouraged by the elections of 1849, which resulted in a greater conservative triumph than those of 1848, and justly angry with the national representative body which had just passed the law of the 31st of May, 1850, demanded direct legislation and direct government. Proudhon, who did not want, at any price, the plebiscitary system which he had good reason to regard as destructive of liberty, did not hesitate to point out, to those of his friends who expected every thing from direct legislation, one of the antinomies of universal suffrage. In so far as it is an institution intended to achieve, for the benefit of the greatest number, the social reforms to which landed suffrage is opposed, universal suffrage is powerless; especially if it pretends to legislate or govern directly. For, until the social reforms are accomplished, the greatest number is of necessity the least enlightened, and consequently the least capable of understanding and effecting reforms. In regard to the antinomy, pointed out by him, of liberty and government,—whether the latter be monarchic, aristocratic, or democratic in form,—Proudhon, whose chief desire was to preserve liberty, naturally sought the solution in the free contract. But though the free contract may be a practical solution of purely economical questions, it cannot be made use of in politics. Proudhon recognized this ten years later, when his beautiful study on "War and Peace" led him to find in the FEDERATIVE PRINCIPLE the exact equilibrium of liberty and government.

"The Social Revolution Demonstrated by the Coup d'Etat" appeared in 1852, a few months after his release from prison. At that time, terror prevailed to such an extent that no one was willing to publish his book without express permission from the government. He succeeded in obtaining this permission by writing to Louis Bonaparte a letter which he published at the same time with the work. The latter being offered for sale, Proudhon was warned that he would not be allowed to publish any more books of the same character. At that time he entertained the idea of writing a universal history entitled "Chronos." This project was never fulfilled.

Already the father of two children, and about to be presented with a third, Proudhon was obliged to devise some immediate means of gaining a living; he resumed his labors, and published, at first anonymously, the "Manual of a Speculator in the Stock-Exchange." Later, in 1857, after having completed the work, he did not hesitate to sign it, acknowledging in the preface his indebtedness to his collaborator, G. Duchene.

Meantime, he vainly sought permission to establish a journal, or review. This permission was steadily refused him. The imperial government always suspected him after the publication of the "Social Revolution Demonstrated by the Coup d'Etat."

Towards the end of 1853, Proudhon issued in Belgium a pamphlet entitled "The Philosophy of Progress." Entirely inoffensive as it was, this pamphlet, which he endeavored to send into France, was seized on the frontier. Proudhon's complaints were of no avail.

The empire gave grants after grants to large companies. A financial society, having asked for the grant of a railroad in the east of France, employed Proudhon to write several memoirs in support of this demand. The grant was given to another company. The author was offered an indemnity as compensation, to be paid (as was customary in such cases) by the company which received the grant. It is needless to say that Proudhon would accept nothing. Then, wishing to explain to the public, as well as to the government, the end which he had in view, he published the work entitled "Reforms to be Effected in the Management of Railroads."

Towards the end of 1854, Proudhon had already begun his book on "Justice," when he had a violent attack of cholera, from which he recovered with great difficulty. Ever afterwards his health was delicate.

At last, on the 22d of April, 1858, he published, in three large volumes, the important work upon which he had labored since 1854. This work had two titles: the first, "Justice in the Revolution and in the Church;" the second, "New Principles of Practical Philosophy, addressed to His Highness Monseigneur Mathieu, Cardinal-Archbishop of Besancon." On the 27th of April, when there had scarcely been time to read the work, an order was issued by the magistrate for its seizure; on the 28th the seizure was effected. To this first act of the magistracy, the author of the incriminated book replied on the 11th of May in a strongly-motived petition, demanding a revision of the concordat of 1802; or, in other words, a new adjustment of the relations between Church and State. At bottom, this petition was but the logical consequence of the work itself. An edition of a thousand copies being published on the 17th of May, the "Petition to the Senate" was regarded by the public prosecutor as an aggravation of the offence or offences discovered in the body of the work to which it was an appendix, and was seized in its turn on the 23d. On the first of June, the author appealed to the Senate in a second "Petition," which was deposited with the first in the office of the Secretary of the Assembly, the guardian and guarantee, according to the constitution of 1852, of the principles of '89. On the 2d of June, the two processes being united, Proudhon appeared at the bar with his publisher, the printer of the book, and the printer of the petition, to receive the sentence of the police magistrate, which condemned him to three years' imprisonment, a fine of four thousand francs, and the suppression of his work. It is needless to say that the publisher and printers were also condemned by the sixth chamber.

Proudhon lodged an appeal; he wrote a memoir which the law of 1819, in the absence of which he would have been liable to a new prosecution, gave him the power to publish previous to the hearing. Having decided to make use of the means which the law permitted, he urged in vain the printers who were prosecuted with him to lend him their aid. He then demanded of Attorney-General Chaix d'Est Ange a statement to the effect that the twenty-third article of the law of the 17th of May, 1819, allows a written defence, and that a printer runs no risk in printing it. The attorney-general flatly refused. Proudhon then started for Belgium, where he printed his defence, which could not, of course, cross the French frontier. This memoir is entitled to rank with the best of Beaumarchais's; it is entitled: "Justice prosecuted by the Church; An Appeal from the Sentence passed upon P. J. Proudhon by the Police Magistrate of the Seine, on the 2d of June, 1858." A very close discussion of the grounds of the judgment of the sixth chamber, it was at the same time an excellent resume of his great work.

Once in Belgium, Proudhon did not fail to remain there. In 1859, after the general amnesty which followed the Italian war, he at first thought himself included in it. But the imperial government, consulted by his friends, notified him that, in its opinion, and in spite of the contrary advice of M. Faustin Helie, his condemnation was not of a political character. Proudhon, thus classed by the government with the authors of immoral works, thought it beneath his dignity to protest, and waited patiently for the advent of 1863 to allow him to return to France.

In Belgium, where he was not slow in forming new friendships, he published in 1859-60, in separate parts, a new edition of his great work on "Justice." Each number contained, in addition to the original text carefully reviewed and corrected, numerous explanatory notes and some "Tidings of the Revolution." In these tidings, which form a sort of review of the progress of ideas in Europe, Proudhon sorrowfully asserts that after having for a long time marched at the head of the progressive nations, France has become, without appearing to suspect it, the most retrogressive of nations; and he considers her more than once as seriously threatened with moral death.

The Italian war led him to write a new work, which he published in 1861, entitled "War and Peace." This work, in which, running counter to a multitude of ideas accepted until then without examination, he pronounced for the first time against the restoration of an aristocratic and priestly Poland, and against the establishment of a unitary government in Italy, created for him a multitude of enemies. Most of his friends, disconcerted by his categorical affirmation of a right of force, notified him that they decidedly disapproved of his new publication. "You see," triumphantly cried those whom he had always combated, "this man is only a sophist."

Led by his previous studies to test every thing by the question of right, Proudhon asks, in his "War and Peace," whether there is a real right of which war is the vindication, and victory the demonstration. This right, which he roughly calls the right of the strongest or the right of force, and which is, after all, only the right of the most worthy to the preference in certain definite cases, exists, says Proudhon, independently of war. It cannot be legitimately vindicated except where necessity clearly demands the subordination of one will to another, and within the limits in which it exists; that is, without ever involving the enslavement of one by the other. Among nations, the right of the majority, which is only a corollary of the right of force, is as unacceptable as universal monarchy. Hence, until equilibrium is established and recognized between States or national forces, there must be war. War, says Proudhon, is not always necessary to determine which side is the strongest; and he has no trouble in proving this by examples drawn from the family, the workshop, and elsewhere. Passing then to the study of war, he proves that it by no means corresponds in practice to that which it ought to be according to his theory of the right of force. The systematic horrors of war naturally lead him to seek a cause for it other than the vindication of this right; and then only does the economist take it upon himself to denounce this cause to those who, like himself, want peace. The necessity of finding abroad a compensation for the misery resulting in every nation from the absence of economical equilibrium, is, according to Proudhon, the ever real, though ever concealed, cause of war. The pages devoted to this demonstration and to his theory of poverty, which he clearly distinguishes from misery and pauperism, shed entirely new light upon the philosophy of history. As for the author's conclusion, it is a very simple one. Since the treaty of Westphalia, and especially since the treaties of 1815, equilibrium has been the international law of Europe. It remains now, not to destroy it, but, while maintaining it, to labor peacefully, in every nation protected by it, for the equilibrium of economical forces. The last line of the book, evidently written to check imperial ambition, is: "Humanity wants no more war."

In 1861, after Garibaldi's expedition and the battle of Castelfidardo, Proudhon immediately saw that the establishment of Italian unity would be a severe blow to European equilibrium. It was chiefly in order to maintain this equilibrium that he pronounced so energetically in favor of Italian federation, even though it should be at first only a federation of monarchs. In vain was it objected that, in being established by France, Italian unity would break European equilibrium in our favor. Proudhon, appealing to history, showed that every State which breaks the equilibrium in its own favor only causes the other States to combine against it, and thereby diminishes its influence and power. He added that, nations being essentially selfish, Italy would not fail, when opportunity offered, to place her interest above her gratitude.

To maintain European equilibrium by diminishing great States and multiplying small ones; to unite the latter in organized federations, not for attack, but for defence; and with these federations, which, if they were not republican already, would quickly become so, to hold in check the great military monarchies,—such, in the beginning of 1861, was the political programme of Proudhon.

The object of the federations, he said, will be to guarantee, as far as possible, the beneficent reign of peace; and they will have the further effect of securing in every nation the triumph of liberty over despotism. Where the largest unitary State is, there liberty is in the greatest danger; further, if this State be democratic, despotism without the counterpoise of majorities is to be feared. With the federation, it is not so. The universal suffrage of the federal State is checked by the universal suffrage of the federated States; and the latter is offset in its turn by PROPERTY, the stronghold of liberty, which it tends, not to destroy, but to balance with the institutions of MUTUALISM.

All these ideas, and many others which were only hinted at in his work on "War and Peace," were developed by Proudhon in his subsequent publications, one of which has for its motto, "Reforms always, Utopias never." The thinker had evidently finished his evolution.

The Council of State of the canton of Vaud having offered prizes for essays on the question of taxation, previously discussed at a congress held at Lausanne, Proudhon entered the ranks and carried off the first prize. His memoir was published in 1861 under the title of "The Theory of Taxation."

About the same time, he wrote at Brussels, in "L'Office de Publicite," some remarkable articles on the question of literary property, which was discussed at a congress held in Belgium, These articles must not be confounded with "Literary Majorats," a more complete work on the same subject, which was published in 1863, soon after his return to France.

Arbitrarily excepted from the amnesty in 1859, Proudhon was pardoned two years later by a special act. He did not wish to take advantage of this favor, and seemed resolved to remain in Belgium until the 2d of June, 1863, the time when he was to acquire the privilege of prescription, when an absurd and ridiculous riot, excited in Brussels by an article published by him on federation and unity in Italy, induced him to hasten his return to France. Stones were thrown against the house in which he lived, in the Faubourg d'Ixelles. After having placed his wife and daughters in safety among his friends at Brussels, he arrived in Paris in September, 1862, and published there, "Federation and Italian Unity," a pamphlet which rioters in Brussels.

Among the works begun by Proudhon while in Belgium, which death did not allow him to finish, we ought to mention a "History of Poland," which will be published later; and, "The Theory of Property," which appeared in 1865, before "The Gospels Annotated," and after the volume entitled "The Principle of Art and its Social Destiny."

The publications of Proudhon, in 1863, were: 1. "Literary Majorats: An Examination of a Bill having for its object the Creation of a Perpetual Monopoly for the Benefit of Authors, Inventors, and Artists;" 2. "The Federative Principle and the Necessity of Re-establishing the Revolutionary party;" 3. "The Sworn Democrats and the Refractories;" 4. "Whether the Treaties of 1815 have ceased to exist? Acts of the Future Congress."

The disease which was destined to kill him grew worse and worse; but Proudhon labored constantly!... A series of articles, published in 1864 in "Le Messager de Paris," have been collected in a pamphlet under the title of "New Observations on Italian Unity." He hoped to publish during the same year his work on "The Political Capacity of the Working Classes," but was unable to write the last chapter.... He grew weaker continually. His doctor prescribed rest. In the month of August he went to Franche-Comte, where he spent a month. Having returned to Paris, he resumed his labor with difficulty.... From the month of December onwards, the heart disease made rapid progress; the oppression became insupportable, his legs were swollen, and he could not sleep....

On the 19th of January, 1865, he died, towards two o'clock in the morning, in the arms of his wife, his sister-in-law, and the friend who writes these lines....

The publication of his correspondence, to which his daughter Catherine is faithfully devoted, will tend, no doubt, to increase his reputation as a thinker, as a writer, and as an honest man.

PREFACE.

The following letter served as a preface to the first edition of this memoir:—

"To the Members of the Academy of Besancon

"PARIS, June 30, 1840.

"GENTLEMEN,—In the course of your debate of the 9th of May, 1833, in regard to the triennial pension established by Madame Suard, you expressed the following wish:—

"'The Academy requests the titulary to present it annually, during the first fortnight in July, with a succinct and logical statement of the various studies which he has pursued during the year which has just expired.'

"I now propose, gentlemen, to discharge this duty.

"When I solicited your votes, I boldly avowed my intention to bend my efforts to the discovery of some means of AMELIORATING THE PHYSICAL, MORAL, AND INTELLECTUAL CONDITION OF THE MERE NUMEROUS AND POORER CLASSES. This idea, foreign as it may have seemed to the object of my candidacy, you received favorably; and, by the precious distinction with which it has been your pleasure to honor me, you changed this formal offer into an inviolable and sacred obligation. Thenceforth I understood with how worthy and honorable a society I had to deal: my regard for its enlightenment, my recognition of its benefits, my enthusiasm for its glory, were unbounded.

"Convinced at once that, in order to break loose from the beaten paths of opinions and systems, it was necessary to proceed in my study of man and society by scientific methods, and in a rigorous manner, I devoted one year to philology and grammar; linguistics, or the natural history of speech, being, of all the sciences, that which was best suited to the character of my mind, seemed to bear the closest relation to the researches which I was about to commence. A treatise, written at this period upon one of the most interesting questions of comparative grammar[2] if it did not reveal the astonishing success, at least bore witness to the thoroughness, of my labors.

"Since that time, metaphysics and moral science have been my only studies; my perception of the fact that these sciences, though badly defined as to their object and not confined to their sphere, are, like the natural sciences, susceptible of demonstration and certainty, has already rewarded my efforts.

"But, gentlemen, of all the masters whom I have followed, to none do I owe so much as to you. Your co-operation, your programmes, your instructions, in agreement with my secret wishes and most cherished hopes, have at no time failed to enlighten me and to point out my road; this memoir on property is the child of your thought.

"In 1838, the Academy of Besancon proposed the following question: TO WHAT CAUSES MUST WE ATTRIBUTE THE CONTINUALLY INCREASING NUMBER OF SUICIDES, AND WHAT ARE THE PROPER MEANS FOR ARRESTING THE EFFECTS OF THIS MORAL CONTAGION?

"Thereby it asked, in less general terms, what was the cause of the social evil, and what was its remedy? You admitted that yourselves, gentlemen when your committee reported that the competitors had enumerated with exactness the immediate and particular causes of suicide, as well as the means of preventing each of them; but that from this enumeration, chronicled with more or less skill, no positive information had been gained, either as to the primary cause of the evil, or as to its remedy.

"In 1839, your programme, always original and varied in its academical expression, became more exact. The investigations of 1838 had pointed out, as the causes or rather as the symptoms of the social malady, the neglect of the principles of religion and morality, the desire for wealth, the passion for enjoyment, and political disturbances. All these data were embodied by you in a single proposition: THE UTILITY OF THE CELEBRATION OF SUNDAY AS REGARDS HYGIENE, MORALITY, AND SOCIAL AND POLITICAL RELATION.

"In a Christian tongue you asked, gentlemen, what was the true system of society. A competitor [3] dared to maintain, and believed that he had proved, that the institution of a day of rest at weekly intervals is inseparably bound up with a political system based on the equality of conditions; that without equality this institution is an anomaly and an impossibility: that equality alone can revive this ancient and mysterious keeping of the seventh day. This argument did not meet with your approbation, since, without denying the relation pointed out by the competitor, you judged, and rightly gentlemen, that the principle of equality of conditions not being demonstrated, the ideas of the author were nothing more than hypotheses.

"Finally, gentlemen, this fundamental principle of equality you presented for competition in the following terms: THE ECONOMICAL AND MORAL CONSEQUENCES IN FRANCE UP TO THE PRESENT TIME, AND THOSE WHICH SEEM LIKELY TO APPEAR IN FUTURE, OF THE LAW CONCERNING THE EQUAL DIVISION OF HEREDITARY PROPERTY BETWEEN THE CHILDREN.

"Instead of confining one to common places without breadth or significance, it seems to me that your question should be developed as follows:—

"If the law has been able to render the right of heredity common to all the children of one father, can it not render it equal for all his grandchildren and great-grandchildren?

"If the law no longer heeds the age of any member of the family, can it not, by the right of heredity, cease to heed it in the race, in the tribe, in the nation?

"Can equality, by the right of succession, be preserved between citizens, as well as between cousins and brothers? In a word, can the principle of succession become a principle of equality?

"To sum up all these ideas in one inclusive question: What is the principle of heredity? What are the foundations of inequality? What is property?

"Such, gentlemen, is the object of the memoir that I offer you to day.

"If I have rightly grasped the object of your thought; if I succeed in bringing to light a truth which is indisputable, but, from causes which I am bold enough to claim to have explained, has always been misunderstood; if by an infallible method of investigation, I establish the dogma of equality of conditions; if I determine the principle of civil law, the essence of justice, and the form of society; if I annihilate property forever,—to you, gentlemen, will redound all the glory, for it is to your aid and your inspiration that I owe it.

"My purpose in this work is the application of method to the problems of philosophy; every other intention is foreign to and even abusive of it.

"I have spoken lightly of jurisprudence: I had the right; but I should be unjust did I not distinguish between this pretended science and the men who practise it. Devoted to studies both laborious and severe, entitled in all respects to the esteem of their fellow-citizens by their knowledge and eloquence our legists deserve but one reproach, that of an excessive deference to arbitrary laws.

"I have been pitiless in my criticism of the economists: for them I confess that, in general, I have no liking. The arrogance and the emptiness of their writings, their impertinent pride and their unwarranted blunders, have disgusted me. Whoever, knowing them, pardons them, may read them.

"I have severely blamed the learned Christian Church: it was my duty. This blame results from the facts which I call attention to: why has the Church decreed concerning things which it does not understand? The Church has erred in dogma and in morals; physics and mathematics testify against her. It may be wrong for me to say it, but surely it is unfortunate for Christianity that it is true. To restore religion, gentlemen, it is necessary to condemn the Church.

"Perhaps you will regret, gentlemen, that, in giving all my attention to method and evidence, I have too much neglected form and style: in vain should I have tried to do better. Literary hope and faith I have none. The nineteenth century is, in my eyes, a genesic era, in which new principles are elaborated, but in which nothing that is written shall endure. That is the reason, in my opinion, why, among so many men of talent, France to-day counts not one great writer. In a society like ours, to seek for literary glory seems to me an anachronism. Of what use is it to invoke an ancient sibyl when a muse is on the eve of birth? Pitiable actors in a tragedy nearing its end, that which it behooves us to do is to precipitate the catastrophe. The most deserving among us is he who plays best this part. Well, I no longer aspire to this sad success!

"Why should I not confess it, gentlemen? I have aspired to your suffrages and sought the title of your pensioner, hating all which exists and full of projects for its destruction; I shall finish this investigation in a spirit of calm and philosophical resignation. I have derived more peace from the knowledge of the truth, than anger from the feeling of oppression; and the most precious fruit that I could wish to gather from this memoir would be the inspiration of my readers with that tranquillity of soul which arises from the clear perception of evil and its cause, and which is much more powerful than passion and enthusiasm. My hatred of privilege and human authority was unbounded; perhaps at times I have been guilty, in my indignation, of confounding persons and things; at present I can only despise and complain; to cease to hate I only needed to know.

"It is for you now, gentlemen, whose mission and character are the proclamation of the truth, it is for you to instruct the people, and to tell them for what they ought to hope and what they ought to fear. The people, incapable as yet of sound judgment as to what is best for them, applaud indiscriminately the most opposite ideas, provided that in them they get a taste of flattery: to them the laws of thought are like the confines of the possible; to-day they can no more distinguish between a savant and a sophist, than formerly they could tell a physician from a sorcerer. 'Inconsiderately accepting, gathering together, and accumulating everything that is new, regarding all reports as true and indubitable, at the breath or ring of novelty they assemble like bees at the sound of a basin.' [4]

"May you, gentlemen, desire equality as I myself desire it; may you, for the eternal happiness of our country, become its propagators and its heralds; may I be the last of your pensioners! Of all the wishes that I can frame, that, gentlemen, is the most worthy of you and the most honorable for me.

"I am, with the profoundest respect and the most earnest gratitude,

"Your pensioner,

"P. J. PROUDHON."

Two months after the receipt of this letter, the Academy, in its debate of August 24th, replied to the address of its pensioner by a note, the text of which I give below:—

"A member calls the attention of the Academy to a pamphlet, published last June by the titulary of the Suard pension, entitled, "What is property?" and dedicated by the author to the Academy. He is of the opinion that the society owes it to justice, to example, and to its own dignity, to publicly disavow all responsibility for the anti-social doctrines contained in this publication. In consequence he demands:

"1. That the Academy disavow and condemn, in the most formal manner, the work of the Suard pensioner, as having been published without its assent, and as attributing to it opinions diametrically opposed to the principles of each of its members;

"2. That the pensioner be charged, in case he should publish a second edition of his book, to omit the dedication;

"3. That this judgment of the Academy be placed upon the records.

"These three propositions, put to vote, are adopted."

After this ludicrous decree, which its authors thought to render powerful by giving it the form of a contradiction, I can only beg the reader not to measure the intelligence of my compatriots by that of our Academy.

While my patrons in the social and political sciences were fulminating anathemas against my brochure, a man, who was a stranger to Franche-Comte, who did not know me, who might even have regarded himself as personally attacked by the too sharp judgment which I had passed upon the economists, a publicist as learned as he was modest, loved by the people whose sorrows he felt, honored by the power which he sought to enlighten without flattering or disgracing it, M. Blanqui—member of the Institute, professor of political economy, defender of property—took up my defence before his associates and before the ministry, and saved me from the blows of a justice which is always blind, because it is always ignorant.

It seems to me that the reader will peruse with pleasure the letter which M. Blanqui did me the honor to write to me upon the publication of my second memoir, a letter as honorable to its author as it is flattering to him to whom it is addressed.

"PARIS, May 1, 1841.

"MONSIEUR,—I hasten to thank you for forwarding to me your second memoir upon property. I have read it with all the interest that an acquaintance with the first would naturally inspire. I am very glad that you have modified somewhat the rudeness of form which gave to a work of such gravity the manner and appearance of a pamphlet; for you quite frightened me, sir, and your talent was needed to reassure me in regard to your intentions. One does not expend so much real knowledge with the purpose of inflaming his country. This proposition, now coming into notice—PROPERTY IS ROBBERY!—was of a nature to repel from your book even those serious minds who do not judge by appearances, had you persisted in maintaining it in its rude simplicity. But if you have softened the form, you are none the less faithful to the ground-work of your doctrines; and although you have done me the honor to give me a share in this perilous teaching, I cannot accept a partnership which, as far as talent goes, would surely be a credit to me, but which would compromise me in all other respects.

"I agree with you in one thing only; namely, that all kinds of property get too frequently abused in this world. But I do not reason from the abuse to the abolition,—an heroic remedy too much like death, which cures all evils. I will go farther: I will confess that, of all abuses, the most hateful to me are those of property; but once more, there is a remedy for this evil without violating it, all the more without destroying it. If the present laws allow abuse, we can reconstruct them. Our civil code is not the Koran; it is not wrong to examine it. Change, then, the laws which govern the use of property, but be sparing of anathemas; for, logically, where is the honest man whose hands are entirely clean? Do you think that one can be a robber without knowing it, without wishing it, without suspecting it? Do you not admit that society in its present state, like every man, has in its constitution all kinds of virtues and vices inherited from our ancestors? Is property, then, in your eyes a thing so simple and so abstract that you can re-knead and equalize it, if I may so speak, in your metaphysical mill? One who has said as many excellent and practical things as occur in these two beautiful and paradoxical improvisations of yours cannot be a pure and unwavering utopist. You are too well acquainted with the economical and academical phraseology to play with the hard words of revolutions. I believe, then, that you have handled property as Rousseau, eighty years ago, handled letters, with a magnificent and poetical display of wit and knowledge. Such, at least, is my opinion.

"That is what I said to the Institute at the time when I presented my report upon your book. I knew that they wished to proceed against you in the courts; you perhaps do not know by how narrow a chance I succeeded in preventing them. 5 What chagrin I should always have felt, if the king's counsel, that is to say, the intellectual executioner, had followed in my very tracks to attack your book and annoy your person! I actually passed two terrible nights, and I succeeded in restraining the secular arm only by showing that your book was an academical dissertation, and not the manifesto of an incendiary. Your style is too lofty ever to be of service to the madmen who in discussing the gravest questions of our social order, use paving-stones as their weapons. But see to it, sir, that ere long they do not come, in spite of you, to seek for ammunition in this formidable arsenal, and that your vigorous metaphysics falls not into the hands of some sophist of the market-place, who might discuss the question in the presence of a starving audience: we should have pillage for conclusion and peroration.

"I feel as deeply as you, sir, the abuses which you point out; but I have so great an affection for order,—not that common and strait-laced order with which the police are satisfied, but the majestic and imposing order of human societies,—that I sometimes find myself embarrassed in attacking certain abuses. I like to rebuild with one hand when I am compelled to destroy with the other. In pruning an old tree, we guard against destruction of the buds and fruit. You know that as well as any one. You are a wise and learned man; you have a thoughtful mind. The terms by which you characterize the fanatics of our day are strong enough to reassure the most suspicious imaginations as to your intentions; but you conclude in favor of the abolition of property! You wish to abolish the most powerful motor of the human mind; you attack the paternal sentiment in its sweetest illusions; with one word you arrest the formation of capital, and we build henceforth upon the sand instead of on a rock. That I cannot agree to; and for that reason I have criticised your book, so full of beautiful pages, so brilliant with knowledge and fervor!

"I wish, sir, that my impaired health would permit me to examine with you, page by page, the memoir which you have done me the honor to address to me publicly and personally; I think I could offer some important criticisms. For the moment, I must content myself with thanking you for the kind words in which you have seen fit to speak of me. We each possess the merit of sincerity; I desire also the merit of prudence. You know how deep-seated is the disease under which the working-people are suffering; I know how many noble hearts beat under those rude garments, and I feel an irresistible and fraternal sympathy with the thousands of brave people who rise early in the morning to labor, to pay their taxes, and to make our country strong. I try to serve and enlighten them, whereas some endeavor to mislead them. You have not written directly for them. You have issued two magnificent manifestoes, the second more guarded than the first; issue a third more guarded than the second, and you will take high rank in science, whose first precept is calmness and impartiality.

"Farewell, sir! No man's esteem for another can exceed mine for you.

"BLANQUI."

I should certainly take some exceptions to this noble and eloquent letter; but I confess that I am more inclined to realize the prediction with which it terminates than to augment needlessly the number of my antagonists. So much controversy fatigues and wearies me. The intelligence expended in the warfare of words is like that employed in battle: it is intelligence wasted. M. Blanqui acknowledges that property is abused in many harmful ways; I call PROPERTY the sum these abuses exclusively. To each of us property seems a polygon whose angles need knocking off; but, the operation performed, M. Blanqui maintains that the figure will still be a polygon (an hypothesis admitted in mathematics, although not proven), while I consider that this figure will be a circle. Honest people can at least understand one another.

For the rest, I allow that, in the present state of the question, the mind may legitimately hesitate before deciding in favor of the abolition of property. To gain the victory for one's cause, it does not suffice simply to overthrow a principle generally recognized, which has the indisputable merit of systematically recapitulating our political theories; it is also necessary to establish the opposite principle, and to formulate the system which must proceed from it. Still further, it is necessary to show the method by which the new system will satisfy all the moral and political needs which induced the establishment of the first. On the following conditions, then, of subsequent evidence, depends the correctness of my preceding arguments:—

The discovery of a system of absolute equality in which all existing institutions, save property, or the sum of the abuses of property, not only may find a place, but may themselves serve as instruments of equality: individual liberty, the division of power, the public ministry, the jury system, administrative and judicial organization, the unity and completeness of instruction, marriage, the family, heredity in direct and collateral succession, the right of sale and exchange, the right to make a will, and even birthright,—a system which, better than property, guarantees the formation of capital and keeps up the courage of all; which, from a superior point of view, explains, corrects, and completes the theories of association hitherto proposed, from Plato and Pythagoras to Babeuf, Saint Simon, and Fourier; a system, finally, which, serving as a means of transition, is immediately applicable.

A work so vast requires, I am aware, the united efforts of twenty Montesquieus; nevertheless, if it is not given to a single man to finish, a single one can commence, the enterprise. The road that he shall traverse will suffice to show the end and assure the result.

WHAT IS PROPERTY? OR,

AN INQUIRY INTO THE PRINCIPLE OF RIGHT AND OF GOVERNMENT.

FIRST MEMOIR.

Adversus hostem aeterna auctertas esto.

Against the enemy, revendication is eternal. LAW OF THE
TWELVE TABLES.

CHAPTER I. METHOD PURSUED IN THIS WORK.—THE IDEA OF A REVOLUTION.

If I were asked to answer the following question: WHAT IS SLAVERY? and I should answer in one word, IT IS MURDER, my meaning would be understood at once. No extended argument would be required to show that the power to take from a man his thought, his will, his personality, is a power of life and death; and that to enslave a man is to kill him. Why, then, to this other question: WHAT IS PROPERTY! may I not likewise answer, IT IS ROBBERY, without the certainty of being misunderstood; the second proposition being no other than a transformation of the first?

I undertake to discuss the vital principle of our government and our institutions, property: I am in my right. I may be mistaken in the conclusion which shall result from my investigations: I am in my right. I think best to place the last thought of my book first: still am I in my right.

Such an author teaches that property is a civil right, born of occupation and sanctioned by law; another maintains that it is a natural right, originating in labor,—and both of these doctrines, totally opposed as they may seem, are encouraged and applauded. I contend that neither labor, nor occupation, nor law, can create property; that it is an effect without a cause: am I censurable?

But murmurs arise!

PROPERTY IS ROBBERY! That is the war-cry of '93! That is the signal of revolutions!

Reader, calm yourself: I am no agent of discord, no firebrand of sedition. I anticipate history by a few days; I disclose a truth whose development we may try in vain to arrest; I write the preamble of our future constitution. This proposition which seems to you blasphemous—PROPERTY IS ROBBERY—would, if our prejudices allowed us to consider it, be recognized as the lightning-rod to shield us from the coming thunderbolt; but too many interests stand in the way!... Alas! philosophy will not change the course of events: destiny will fulfill itself regardless of prophecy. Besides, must not justice be done and our education be finished?

PROPERTY IS ROBBERY!... What a revolution in human ideas! PROPRIETOR and ROBBER have been at all times expressions as contradictory as the beings whom they designate are hostile; all languages have perpetuated this opposition. On what authority, then, do you venture to attack universal consent, and give the lie to the human race? Who are you, that you should question the judgment of the nations and the ages?

Of what consequence to you, reader, is my obscure individuality? I live, like you, in a century in which reason submits only to fact and to evidence. My name, like yours, is TRUTH-SEEKER. [6] My mission is written in these words of the law: SPEAK WITHOUT HATRED AND WITHOUT FEAR; TELL THAT WHICH THOU KNOWEST! The work of our race is to build the temple of science, and this science includes man and Nature. Now, truth reveals itself to all; to-day to Newton and Pascal, tomorrow to the herdsman in the valley and the journeyman in the shop. Each one contributes his stone to the edifice; and, his task accomplished, disappears. Eternity precedes us, eternity follows us: between two infinites, of what account is one poor mortal that the century should inquire about him?

Disregard then, reader, my title and my character, and attend only to my arguments. It is in accordance with universal consent that I undertake to correct universal error; from the OPINION of the human race I appeal to its FAITH. Have the courage to follow me; and, if your will is untrammelled, if your conscience is free, if your mind can unite two propositions and deduce a third therefrom, my ideas will inevitably become yours. In beginning by giving you my last word, it was my purpose to warn you, not to defy you; for I am certain that, if you read me, you will be compelled to assent. The things of which I am to speak are so simple and clear that you will be astonished at not having perceived them before, and you will say: "I have neglected to think." Others offer you the spectacle of genius wresting Nature's secrets from her, and unfolding before you her sublime messages; you will find here only a series of experiments upon JUSTICE and RIGHT a sort of verification of the weights and measures of your conscience. The operations shall be conducted under your very eyes; and you shall weigh the result.

Nevertheless, I build no system. I ask an end to privilege, the abolition of slavery, equality of rights, and the reign of law. Justice, nothing else; that is the alpha and omega of my argument: to others I leave the business of governing the world.

One day I asked myself: Why is there so much sorrow and misery in society? Must man always be wretched? And not satisfied with the explanations given by the reformers,—these attributing the general distress to governmental cowardice and incapacity, those to conspirators and emeutes, still others to ignorance and general corruption,—and weary of the interminable quarrels of the tribune and the press, I sought to fathom the matter myself. I have consulted the masters of science; I have read a hundred volumes of philosophy, law, political economy, and history: would to God that I had lived in a century in which so much reading had been useless! I have made every effort to obtain exact information, comparing doctrines, replying to objections, continually constructing equations and reductions from arguments, and weighing thousands of syllogisms in the scales of the most rigorous logic. In this laborious work, I have collected many interesting facts which I shall share with my friends and the public as soon as I have leisure. But I must say that I recognized at once that we had never understood the meaning of these words, so common and yet so sacred: JUSTICE, EQUITY, LIBERTY; that concerning each of these principles our ideas have been utterly obscure; and, in fact, that this ignorance was the sole cause, both of the poverty that devours us, and of all the calamities that have ever afflicted the human race.

My mind was frightened by this strange result: I doubted my reason. What! said I, that which eye has not seen, nor ear heard, nor insight penetrated, you have discovered! Wretch, mistake not the visions of your diseased brain for the truths of science! Do you not know (great philosophers have said so) that in points of practical morality universal error is a contradiction?

I resolved then to test my arguments; and in entering upon this new labor I sought an answer to the following questions: Is it possible that humanity can have been so long and so universally mistaken in the application of moral principles? How and why could it be mistaken? How can its error, being universal, be capable of correction?

These questions, on the solution of which depended the certainty of my conclusions, offered no lengthy resistance to analysis. It will be seen, in chapter V. of this work, that in morals, as in all other branches of knowledge, the gravest errors are the dogmas of science; that, even in works of justice, to be mistaken is a privilege which ennobles man; and that whatever philosophical merit may attach to me is infinitely small. To name a thing is easy: the difficulty is to discern it before its appearance. In giving expression to the last stage of an idea,—an idea which permeates all minds, which to-morrow will be proclaimed by another if I fail to announce it to-day,—I can claim no merit save that of priority of utterance. Do we eulogize the man who first perceives the dawn?

Yes: all men believe and repeat that equality of conditions is identical with equality of rights; that PROPERTY and ROBBERY are synonymous terms; that every social advantage accorded, or rather usurped, in the name of superior talent or service, is iniquity and extortion. All men in their hearts, I say, bear witness to these truths; they need only to be made to understand it.

Before entering directly upon the question before me, I must say a word of the road that I shall traverse. When Pascal approached a geometrical problem, he invented a method of solution; to solve a problem in philosophy a method is equally necessary. Well, by how much do the problems of which philosophy treats surpass in the gravity of their results those discussed by geometry! How much more imperatively, then, do they demand for their solution a profound and rigorous analysis!

It is a fact placed for ever beyond doubt, say the modern psychologists, that every perception received by the mind is determined by certain general laws which govern the mind; is moulded, so to speak, in certain types pre-existing in our understanding, and which constitutes its original condition. Hence, say they, if the mind has no innate IDEAS, it has at least innate FORMS. Thus, for example, every phenomenon is of necessity conceived by us as happening in TIME and SPACE,—that compels us to infer a CAUSE of its occurrence; every thing which exists implies the ideas of SUBSTANCE, MODE, RELATION, NUMBER, &c.; in a word, we form no idea which is not related to some one of the general principles of reason, independent of which nothing exists.

These axioms of the understanding, add the psychologists, these fundamental types, by which all our judgments and ideas are inevitably shaped, and which our sensations serve only to illuminate, are known in the schools as CATEGORIES. Their primordial existence in the mind is to-day demonstrated; they need only to be systematized and catalogued. Aristotle recognized ten; Kant increased the number to fifteen; M. Cousin has reduced it to three, to two, to one; and the indisputable glory of this professor will be due to the fact that, if he has not discovered the true theory of categories, he has, at least, seen more clearly than any one else the vast importance of this question,—the greatest and perhaps the only one with which metaphysics has to deal.

I confess that I disbelieve in the innateness, not only of IDEAS, but also of FORMS or LAWS of our understanding; and I hold the metaphysics of Reid and Kant to be still farther removed from the truth than that of Aristotle. However, as I do not wish to enter here into a discussion of the mind, a task which would demand much labor and be of no interest to the public, I shall admit the hypothesis that our most general and most necessary ideas—such as time, space, substance, and cause—exist originally in the mind; or, at least, are derived immediately from its constitution.

But it is a psychological fact none the less true, and one to which the philosophers have paid too little attention, that habit, like a second nature, has the power of fixing in the mind new categorical forms derived from the appearances which impress us, and by them usually stripped of objective reality, but whose influence over our judgments is no less predetermining than that of the original categories. Hence we reason by the ETERNAL and ABSOLUTE laws of our mind, and at the same time by the secondary rules, ordinarily faulty, which are suggested to us by imperfect observation. This is the most fecund source of false prejudices, and the permanent and often invincible cause of a multitude of errors. The bias resulting from these prejudices is so strong that often, even when we are fighting against a principle which our mind thinks false, which is repugnant to our reason, and which our conscience disapproves, we defend it without knowing it, we reason in accordance with it, and we obey it while attacking it. Enclosed within a circle, our mind revolves about itself, until a new observation, creating within us new ideas, brings to view an external principle which delivers us from the phantom by which our imagination is possessed.

Thus, we know to-day that, by the laws of a universal magnetism whose cause is still unknown, two bodies (no obstacle intervening) tend to unite by an accelerated impelling force which we call GRAVITATION. It is gravitation which causes unsupported bodies to fall to the ground, which gives them weight, and which fastens us to the earth on which we live. Ignorance of this cause was the sole obstacle which prevented the ancients from believing in the antipodes. "Can you not see," said St. Augustine after Lactantius, "that, if there were men under our feet, their heads would point downward, and that they would fall into the sky?" The bishop of Hippo, who thought the earth flat because it appeared so to the eye, supposed in consequence that, if we should connect by straight lines the zenith with the nadir in different places, these lines would be parallel with each other; and in the direction of these lines he traced every movement from above to below. Thence he naturally concluded that the stars were rolling torches set in the vault of the sky; that, if left to themselves, they would fall to the earth in a shower of fire; that the earth was one vast plain, forming the lower portion of the world, &c. If he had been asked by what the world itself was sustained, he would have answered that he did not know, but that to God nothing is impossible. Such were the ideas of St. Augustine in regard to space and movement, ideas fixed within him by a prejudice derived from an appearance, and which had become with him a general and categorical rule of judgment. Of the reason why bodies fall his mind knew nothing; he could only say that a body falls because it falls.

With us the idea of a fall is more complex: to the general ideas of space and movement which it implies, we add that of attraction or direction towards a centre, which gives us the higher idea of cause. But if physics has fully corrected our judgment in this respect, we still make use of the prejudice of St. Augustine; and when we say that a thing has FALLEN, we do not mean simply and in general that there has been an effect of gravitation, but specially and in particular that it is towards the earth, and FROM ABOVE TO BELOW, that this movement has taken place. Our mind is enlightened in vain; the imagination prevails, and our language remains forever incorrigible. To DESCEND FROM HEAVEN is as incorrect an expression as to MOUNT TO HEAVEN; and yet this expression will live as long as men use language.

All these phrases—FROM ABOVE TO BELOW; TO DESCEND FROM HEAVEN; TO FALL FROM THE CLOUDS, &c.—are henceforth harmless, because we know how to rectify them in practice; but let us design to consider for a moment how much they have retarded the progress of science. If, indeed, it be a matter of little importance to statistics, mechanics, hydrodynamics, and ballistics, that the true cause of the fall of bodies should be known, and that our ideas of the general movements in space should be exact, it is quite otherwise when we undertake to explain the system of the universe, the cause of tides, the shape of the earth, and its position in the heavens: to understand these things we must leave the circle of appearances. In all ages there have been ingenious mechanicians, excellent architects, skilful artillerymen: any error, into which it was possible for them to fall in regard to the rotundity of the earth and gravitation, in no wise retarded the development of their art; the solidity of their buildings and accuracy of their aim was not affected by it. But sooner or later they were forced to grapple with phenomena, which the supposed parallelism of all perpendiculars erected from the earth's surface rendered inexplicable: then also commenced a struggle between the prejudices, which for centuries had sufficed in daily practice, and the unprecedented opinions which the testimony of the eyes seemed to contradict.

Thus, on the one hand, the falsest judgments, whether based on isolated facts or only on appearances, always embrace some truths whose sphere, whether large or small, affords room for a certain number of inferences, beyond which we fall into absurdity. The ideas of St. Augustine, for example, contained the following truths: that bodies fall towards the earth, that they fall in a straight line, that either the sun or the earth moves, that either the sky or the earth turns, &c. These general facts always have been true; our science has added nothing to them. But, on the other hand, it being necessary to account for every thing, we are obliged to seek for principles more and more comprehensive: that is why we have had to abandon successively, first the opinion that the world was flat, then the theory which regards it as the stationary centre of the universe, &c.

If we pass now from physical nature to the moral world, we still find ourselves subject to the same deceptions of appearance, to the same influences of spontaneity and habit. But the distinguishing feature of this second division of our knowledge is, on the one hand, the good or the evil which we derive from our opinions; and, on the other, the obstinacy with which we defend the prejudice which is tormenting and killing us.

Whatever theory we embrace in regard to the shape of the earth and the cause of its weight, the physics of the globe does not suffer; and, as for us, our social economy can derive therefrom neither profit nor damage. But it is in us and through us that the laws of our moral nature work; now, these laws cannot be executed without our deliberate aid, and, consequently, unless we know them. If, then, our science of moral laws is false, it is evident that, while desiring our own good, we are accomplishing our own evil; if it is only incomplete, it may suffice for a time for our social progress, but in the long run it will lead us into a wrong road, and will finally precipitate us into an abyss of calamities.

Then it is that we need to exercise our highest judgments; and, be it said to our glory, they are never found wanting: but then also commences a furious struggle between old prejudices and new ideas. Days of conflagration and anguish! We are told of the time when, with the same beliefs, with the same institutions, all the world seemed happy: why complain of these beliefs; why banish these institutions? We are slow to admit that that happy age served the precise purpose of developing the principle of evil which lay dormant in society; we accuse men and gods, the powers of earth and the forces of Nature. Instead of seeking the cause of the evil in his mind and heart, man blames his masters, his rivals, his neighbors, and himself; nations arm themselves, and slay and exterminate each other, until equilibrium is restored by the vast depopulation, and peace again arises from the ashes of the combatants. So loath is humanity to touch the customs of its ancestors, and to change the laws framed by the founders of communities, and confirmed by the faithful observance of the ages.

Nihil motum ex antiquo probabile est. Distrust all innovations, wrote Titus Livius. Undoubtedly it would be better were man not compelled to change: but what! because he is born ignorant, because he exists only on condition of gradual self-instruction, must he abjure the light, abdicate his reason, and abandon himself to fortune? Perfect health is better than convalescence: should the sick man, therefore, refuse to be cured? Reform, reform! cried, ages since, John the Baptist and Jesus Christ. Reform, reform! cried our fathers, fifty years ago; and for a long time to come we shall shout, Reform, reform!

Seeing the misery of my age, I said to myself: Among the principles that support society, there is one which it does not understand, which its ignorance has vitiated, and which causes all the evil that exists. This principle is the most ancient of all; for it is a characteristic of revolutions to tear down the most modern principles, and to respect those of long-standing. Now the evil by which we suffer is anterior to all revolutions. This principle, impaired by our ignorance, is honored and cherished; for if it were not cherished it would harm nobody, it would be without influence.

But this principle, right in its purpose, but misunderstood: this principle, as old as humanity, what is it? Can it be religion?

All men believe in God: this dogma belongs at once to their conscience and their mind. To humanity God is a fact as primitive, an idea as inevitable, a principle as necessary as are the categorical ideas of cause, substance, time, and space to our understanding. God is proven to us by the conscience prior to any inference of the mind; just as the sun is proven to us by the testimony of the senses prior to all the arguments of physics. We discover phenomena and laws by observation and experience; only this deeper sense reveals to us existence. Humanity believes that God is; but, in believing in God, what does it believe? In a word, what is God?

The nature of this notion of Divinity,—this primitive, universal notion, born in the race,—the human mind has not yet fathomed. At each step that we take in our investigation of Nature and of causes, the idea of God is extended and exalted; the farther science advances, the more God seems to grow and broaden. Anthropomorphism and idolatry constituted of necessity the faith of the mind in its youth, the theology of infancy and poesy. A harmless error, if they had not endeavored to make it a rule of conduct, and if they had been wise enough to respect the liberty of thought. But having made God in his own image, man wished to appropriate him still farther; not satisfied with disfiguring the Almighty, he treated him as his patrimony, his goods, his possessions. God, pictured in monstrous forms, became throughout the world the property of man and of the State. Such was the origin of the corruption of morals by religion, and the source of pious feuds and holy wars. Thank Heaven! we have learned to allow every one his own beliefs; we seek for moral laws outside the pale of religion. Instead of legislating as to the nature and attributes of God, the dogmas of theology, and the destiny of our souls, we wisely wait for science to tell us what to reject and what to accept. God, soul, religion,—eternal objects of our unwearied thought and our most fatal aberrations, terrible problems whose solution, for ever attempted, for ever remains unaccomplished,—concerning all these questions we may still be mistaken, but at least our error is harmless. With liberty in religion, and the separation of the spiritual from the temporal power, the influence of religious ideas upon the progress of society is purely negative; no law, no political or civil institution being founded on religion. Neglect of duties imposed by religion may increase the general corruption, but it is not the primary cause; it is only an auxiliary or result. It is universally admitted, and especially in the matter which now engages our attention, that the cause of the inequality of conditions among men—of pauperism, of universal misery, and of governmental embarrassments—can no longer be traced to religion: we must go farther back, and dig still deeper.

But what is there in man older and deeper than the religious sentiment?

There is man himself; that is, volition and conscience, free-will and law, eternally antagonistic. Man is at war with himself: why?

"Man," say the theologians, "transgressed in the beginning; our race is guilty of an ancient offence. For this transgression humanity has fallen; error and ignorance have become its sustenance. Read history, you will find universal proof of this necessity for evil in the permanent misery of nations. Man suffers and always will suffer; his disease is hereditary and constitutional. Use palliatives, employ emollients; there is no remedy."

Nor is this argument peculiar to the theologians; we find it expressed in equivalent language in the philosophical writings of the materialists, believers in infinite perfectibility. Destutt de Tracy teaches formally that poverty, crime, and war are the inevitable conditions of our social state; necessary evils, against which it would be folly to revolt. So, call it NECESSITY OF EVIL or ORIGINAL DEPRAVITY, it is at bottom the same philosophy.

"The first man transgressed." If the votaries of the Bible interpreted it faithfully, they would say: MAN ORIGINALLY TRANSGRESSED, that is, made a mistake; for TO TRANSGRESS, TO FAIL, TO MAKE A MISTAKE, all mean the same thing.

"The consequences of Adam's transgression are inherited by the race; the first is ignorance." Truly, the race, like the individual, is born ignorant; but, in regard to a multitude of questions, even in the moral and political spheres, this ignorance of the race has been dispelled: who says that it will not depart altogether? Mankind makes continual progress toward truth, and light ever triumphs over darkness. Our disease is not, then, absolutely incurable, and the theory of the theologians is worse than inadequate; it is ridiculous, since it is reducible to this tautology: "Man errs, because he errs." While the true statement is this: "Man errs, because he learns."

Now, if man arrives at a knowledge of all that he needs to know, it is reasonable to believe that, ceasing to err, he will cease to suffer.

But if we question the doctors as to this law, said to be engraved upon the heart of man, we shall immediately see that they dispute about a matter of which they know nothing; that, concerning the most important questions, there are almost as many opinions as authors; that we find no two agreeing as to the best form of government, the principle of authority, and the nature of right; that all sail hap-hazard upon a shoreless and bottomless sea, abandoned to the guidance of their private opinions which they modestly take to be right reason. And, in view of this medley of contradictory opinions, we say: "The object of our investigations is the law, the determination of the social principle. Now, the politicians, that is, the social scientists, do not understand each other; then the error lies in themselves; and, as every error has a reality for its object, we must look in their books to find the truth which they have unconsciously deposited there."

Now, of what do the lawyers and the publicists treat? Of JUSTICE, EQUITY, LIBERTY, NATURAL LAW, CIVIL LAWS, &c. But what is justice? What is its principle, its character, its formula? To this question our doctors evidently have no reply; for otherwise their science, starting with a principle clear and well defined, would quit the region of probabilities, and all disputes would end.

What is justice? The theologians answer: "All justice comes from God." That is true; but we know no more than before.

The philosophers ought to be better informed: they have argued so much about justice and injustice! Unhappily, an examination proves that their knowledge amounts to nothing, and that with them—as with the savages whose every prayer to the sun is simply O! O!—it is a cry of admiration, love, and enthusiasm; but who does not know that the sun attaches little meaning to the interjection O! That is exactly our position toward the philosophers in regard to justice. Justice, they say, is a DAUGHTER OF HEAVEN; A LIGHT WHICH ILLUMINES EVERY MAN THAT COMES INTO THE WORLD; THE MOST BEAUTIFUL PREROGATIVE OF OUR NATURE; THAT WHICH DISTINGUISHES US FROM THE BEASTS AND LIKENS US TO GOD—and a thousand other similar things. What, I ask, does this pious litany amount to? To the prayer of the savages: O!

All the most reasonable teachings of human wisdom concerning justice are summed up in that famous adage: DO UNTO OTHERS THAT WHICH YOU WOULD THAT OTHERS SHOULD DO UNTO YOU; DO NOT UNTO OTHERS THAT WHICH YOU WOULD NOT THAT OTHERS SHOULD DO UNTO YOU. But this rule of moral practice is unscientific: what have I a right to wish that others should do or not do to me? It is of no use to tell me that my duty is equal to my right, unless I am told at the same time what my right is.

Let us try to arrive at something more precise and positive.

Justice is the central star which governs societies, the pole around which the political world revolves, the principle and the regulator of all transactions. Nothing takes place between men save in the name of RIGHT; nothing without the invocation of justice. Justice is not the work of the law: on the contrary, the law is only a declaration and application of JUSTICE in all circumstances where men are liable to come in contact. If, then, the idea that we form of justice and right were ill-defined, if it were imperfect or even false, it is clear that all our legislative applications would be wrong, our institutions vicious, our politics erroneous: consequently there would be disorder and social chaos.

This hypothesis of the perversion of justice in our minds, and, as a necessary result, in our acts, becomes a demonstrated fact when it is shown that the opinions of men have not borne a constant relation to the notion of justice and its applications; that at different periods they have undergone modifications: in a word, that there has been progress in ideas. Now, that is what history proves by the most overwhelming testimony.

Eighteen Hundred years ago, the world, under the rule of the Caesars, exhausted itself in slavery, superstition, and voluptuousness. The people—intoxicated and, as it were, stupefied by their long-continued orgies—had lost the very notion of right and duty: war and dissipation by turns swept them away; usury and the labor of machines (that is of slaves), by depriving them of the means of subsistence, hindered them from continuing the species. Barbarism sprang up again, in a hideous form, from this mass of corruption, and spread like a devouring leprosy over the depopulated provinces. The wise foresaw the downfall of the empire, but could devise no remedy. What could they think indeed? To save this old society it would have been necessary to change the objects of public esteem and veneration, and to abolish the rights affirmed by a justice purely secular; they said: "Rome has conquered through her politics and her gods; any change in theology and public opinion would be folly and sacrilege. Rome, merciful toward conquered nations, though binding them in chains, spared their lives; slaves are the most fertile source of her wealth; freedom of the nations would be the negation of her rights and the ruin of her finances. Rome, in fact, enveloped in the pleasures and gorged with the spoils of the universe, is kept alive by victory and government; her luxury and her pleasures are the price of her conquests: she can neither abdicate nor dispossess herself." Thus Rome had the facts and the law on her side. Her pretensions were justified by universal custom and the law of nations. Her institutions were based upon idolatry in religion, slavery in the State, and epicurism in private life; to touch those was to shake society to its foundations, and, to use our modern expression, to open the abyss of revolutions. So the idea occurred to no one; and yet humanity was dying in blood and luxury.

All at once a man appeared, calling himself The Word of God. It is not known to this day who he was, whence he came, nor what suggested to him his ideas. He went about proclaiming everywhere that the end of the existing society was at hand, that the world was about to experience a new birth; that the priests were vipers, the lawyers ignoramuses, and the philosophers hypocrites and liars; that master and slave were equals, that usury and every thing akin to it was robbery, that proprietors and idlers would one day burn, while the poor and pure in heart would find a haven of peace.

This man—The Word of God—was denounced and arrested as a public enemy by the priests and the lawyers, who well understood how to induce the people to demand his death. But this judicial murder, though it put the finishing stroke to their crimes, did not destroy the doctrinal seeds which The Word of God had sown. After his death, his original disciples travelled about in all directions, preaching what they called the GOOD NEWS, creating in their turn millions of missionaries; and, when their task seemed to be accomplished, dying by the sword of Roman justice. This persistent agitation, the war of the executioners and martyrs, lasted nearly three centuries, ending in the conversion of the world. Idolatry was destroyed, slavery abolished, dissolution made room for a more austere morality, and the contempt for wealth was sometimes pushed almost to privation.

Society was saved by the negation of its own principles, by a revolution in its religion, and by violation of its most sacred rights. In this revolution, the idea of justice spread to an extent that had not before been dreamed of, never to return to its original limits. Heretofore justice had existed only for the masters; 7 it then commenced to exist for the slaves.

Nevertheless, the new religion at that time had borne by no means all its fruits. There was a perceptible improvement of the public morals, and a partial release from oppression; but, other than that, the SEEDS SOWN BY THE SON OF MAN, having fallen into idolatrous hearts, had produced nothing save innumerable discords and a quasi-poetical mythology. Instead of developing into their practical consequences the principles of morality and government taught by The Word of God, his followers busied themselves in speculations as to his birth, his origin, his person, and his actions; they discussed his parables, and from the conflict of the most extravagant opinions upon unanswerable questions and texts which no one understood, was born THEOLOGY,—which may be defined as the SCIENCE OF THE INFINITELY ABSURD.

The truth of CHRISTIANITY did not survive the age of the apostles; the GOSPEL, commented upon and symbolized by the Greeks and Latins, loaded with pagan fables, became literally a mass of contradictions; and to this day the reign of the INFALLIBLE CHURCH has been a long era of darkness. It is said that the GATES OF HELL will not always prevail, that THE WORD OF GOD will return, and that one day men will know truth and justice; but that will be the death of Greek and Roman Catholicism, just as in the light of science disappeared the caprices of opinion.

The monsters which the successors of the apostles were bent on destroying, frightened for a moment, reappeared gradually, thanks to the crazy fanaticism, and sometimes the deliberate connivance, of priests and theologians. The history of the enfranchisement of the French communes offers constantly the spectacle of the ideas of justice and liberty spreading among the people, in spite of the combined efforts of kings, nobles, and clergy. In the year 1789 of the Christian era, the French nation, divided by caste, poor and oppressed, struggled in the triple net of royal absolutism, the tyranny of nobles and parliaments, and priestly intolerance. There was the right of the king and the right of the priest, the right of the patrician and the right of the plebeian; there were the privileges of birth, province, communes, corporations, and trades; and, at the bottom of all, violence, immorality, and misery. For some time they talked of reformation; those who apparently desired it most favoring it only for their own profit, and the people who were to be the gainers expecting little and saying nothing. For a long time these poor people, either from distrust, incredulity, or despair, hesitated to ask for their rights: it is said that the habit of serving had taken the courage away from those old communes, which in the middle ages were so bold.

Finally a book appeared, summing up the whole matter in these two propositions: WHAT IS THE THIRD ESTATE? —NOTHING. WHAT OUGHT IT TO BE?—EVERY THING. Some one added by way of comment: WHAT IS THE KING?—THE SERVANT OF THE PEOPLE.

This was a sudden revelation: the veil was torn aside, a thick bandage fell from all eyes. The people commenced to reason thus:—

If the king is our servant, he ought to report to us;
If he ought to report to us, he is subject to control;
If he can be controlled, he is responsible;
If he is responsible, he is punishable;
If he is punishable, he ought to be punished according to his merits;
If he ought to be punished according to his merits, he can be punished with death.

Five years after the publication of the brochure of Sieyes, the third estate was every thing; the king, the nobility, the clergy, were no more. In 1793, the nation, without stopping at the constitutional fiction of the inviolability of the sovereign, conducted Louis XVI. to the scaffold; in 1830, it accompanied Charles X. to Cherbourg. In each case, it may have erred, in fact, in its judgment of the offence; but, in right, the logic which led to its action was irreproachable. The people, in punishing their sovereign, did precisely that which the government of July was so severely censured for failing to do when it refused to execute Louis Bonaparte after the affair of Strasburg: they struck the true culprit. It was an application of the common law, a solemn decree of justice enforcing the penal laws. [8]

The spirit which gave rise to the movement of '89 was a spirit of negation; that, of itself, proves that the order of things which was substituted for the old system was not methodical or well-considered; that, born of anger and hatred, it could not have the effect of a science based on observation and study; that its foundations, in a word, were not derived from a profound knowledge of the laws of Nature and society. Thus the people found that the republic, among the so-called new institutions, was acting on the very principles against which they had fought, and was swayed by all the prejudices which they had intended to destroy. We congratulate ourselves, with inconsiderate enthusiasm, on the glorious French Revolution, the regeneration of 1789, the great changes that have been effected, and the reversion of institutions: a delusion, a delusion!

When our ideas on any subject, material, intellectual, or social, undergo a thorough change in consequence of new observations, I call that movement of the mind REVOLUTION. If the ideas are simply extended or modified, there is only PROGRESS. Thus the system of Ptolemy was a step in astronomical progress, that of Copernicus was a revolution. So, in 1789, there was struggle and progress; revolution there was none. An examination of the reforms which were attempted proves this.

The nation, so long a victim of monarchical selfishness, thought to deliver itself for ever by declaring that it alone was sovereign. But what was monarchy? The sovereignty of one man. What is democracy? The sovereignty of the nation, or, rather, of the national majority. But it is, in both cases, the sovereignty of man instead of the sovereignty of the law, the sovereignty of the will instead of the sovereignty of the reason; in one word, the passions instead of justice. Undoubtedly, when a nation passes from the monarchical to the democratic state, there is progress, because in multiplying the sovereigns we increase the opportunities of the reason to substitute itself for the will; but in reality there is no revolution in the government, since the principle remains the same. Now, we have the proof to-day that, with the most perfect democracy, we cannot be free. [9]

Nor is that all. The nation-king cannot exercise its sovereignty itself; it is obliged to delegate it to agents: this is constantly reiterated by those who seek to win its favor. Be these agents five, ten, one hundred, or a thousand, of what consequence is the number; and what matters the name? It is always the government of man, the rule of will and caprice. I ask what this pretended revolution has revolutionized?

We know, too, how this sovereignty was exercised; first by the Convention, then by the Directory, afterwards confiscated by the Consul. As for the Emperor, the strong man so much adored and mourned by the nation, he never wanted to be dependent on it; but, as if intending to set its sovereignty at defiance, he dared to demand its suffrage: that is, its abdication, the abdication of this inalienable sovereignty; and he obtained it.

But what is sovereignty? It is, they say, the POWER TO MAKE LAW. [10] Another absurdity, a relic of despotism. The nation had long seen kings issuing their commands in this form: FOR SUCH IS OUR PLEASURE; it wished to taste in its turn the pleasure of making laws. For fifty years it has brought them forth by myriads; always, be it understood, through the agency of representatives. The play is far from ended.

The definition of sovereignty was derived from the definition of the law. The law, they said, is THE EXPRESSION OF THE WILL OF THE SOVEREIGN: then, under a monarchy, the law is the expression of the will of the king; in a republic, the law is the expression of the will of the people. Aside from the difference in the number of wills, the two systems are exactly identical: both share the same error, namely, that the law is the expression of a will; it ought to be the expression of a fact. Moreover they followed good leaders: they took the citizen of Geneva for their prophet, and the contrat social for their Koran.

Bias and prejudice are apparent in all the phrases of the new legislators. The nation had suffered from a multitude of exclusions and privileges; its representatives issued the following declaration: ALL MEN ARE EQUAL BY NATURE AND BEFORE THE LAW; an ambiguous and redundant declaration. MEN ARE EQUAL BY NATURE: does that mean that they are equal in size, beauty, talents, and virtue? No; they meant, then, political and civil equality. Then it would have been sufficient to have said: ALL MEN ARE EQUAL BEFORE THE LAW.

But what is equality before the law? Neither the constitution of 1790, nor that of '93, nor the granted charter, nor the accepted charter, have defined it accurately. All imply an inequality in fortune and station incompatible with even a shadow of equality in rights. In this respect it may be said that all our constitutions have been faithful expressions of the popular will: I am going, to prove it.

Formerly the people were excluded from civil and military offices; it was considered a wonder when the following high-sounding article was inserted in the Declaration of Rights: "All citizens are equally eligible to office; free nations know no qualifications in their choice of officers save virtues and talents."

They certainly ought to have admired so beautiful an idea: they admired a piece of nonsense. Why! the sovereign people, legislators, and reformers, see in public offices, to speak plainly, only opportunities for pecuniary advancement. And, because it regards them as a source of profit, it decrees the eligibility of citizens. For of what use would this precaution be, if there were nothing to gain by it? No one would think of ordaining that none but astronomers and geographers should be pilots, nor of prohibiting stutterers from acting at the theatre and the opera. The nation was still aping the kings: like them it wished to award the lucrative positions to its friends and flatterers. Unfortunately, and this last feature completes the resemblance, the nation did not control the list of livings; that was in the hands of its agents and representatives. They, on the other hand, took care not to thwart the will of their gracious sovereign.

This edifying article of the Declaration of Rights, retained in the charters of 1814 and 1830, implies several kinds of civil inequality; that is, of inequality before the law: inequality of station, since the public functions are sought only for the consideration and emoluments which they bring; inequality of wealth, since, if it had been desired to equalize fortunes, public service would have been regarded as a duty, not as a reward; inequality of privilege, the law not stating what it means by TALENTS and VIRTUES. Under the empire, virtue and talent consisted simply in military bravery and devotion to the emperor; that was shown when Napoleon created his nobility, and attempted to connect it with the ancients. To-day, the man who pays taxes to the amount of two hundred francs is virtuous; the talented man is the honest pickpocket: such truths as these are accounted trivial.

The people finally legalized property. God forgive them, for they knew not what they did! For fifty years they have suffered for their miserable folly. But how came the people, whose voice, they tell us, is the voice of God, and whose conscience is infallible,—how came the people to err? How happens it that, when seeking liberty and equality, they fell back into privilege and slavery? Always through copying the ancient regime.

Formerly, the nobility and the clergy contributed towards the expenses of the State only by voluntary aid and gratuitous gift; their property could not be seized even for debt,—while the plebeian, overwhelmed by taxes and statute-labor, was continually tormented, now by the king's tax-gatherers, now by those of the nobles and clergy. He whose possessions were subject to mortmain could neither bequeath nor inherit property; he was treated like the animals, whose services and offspring belong to their master by right of accession. The people wanted the conditions of OWNERSHIP to be alike for all; they thought that every one should ENJOY AND FREELY DISPOSE OF HIS POSSESSIONS HIS INCOME AND THE FRUIT OF HIS LABOR AND INDUSTRY. The people did not invent property; but as they had not the same privileges in regard to it, which the nobles and clergy possessed, they decreed that the right should be exercised by all under the same conditions. The more obnoxious forms of property—statute-labor, mortmain, maitrise, and exclusion from public office—have disappeared; the conditions of its enjoyment have been modified: the principle still remains the same. There has been progress in the regulation of the right; there has been no revolution.

These, then, are the three fundamental principles of modern society, established one after another by the movements of 1789 and 1830: 1. SOVEREIGNTY OF THE HUMAN WILL; in short, DESPOTISM. 2. INEQUALITY OF WEALTH AND RANK. 3. PROPERTY—above JUSTICE, always invoked as the guardian angel of sovereigns, nobles, and proprietors; JUSTICE, the general, primitive, categorical law of all society.

We must ascertain whether the ideas of DESPOTISM, CIVIL INEQUALITY and PROPERTY, are in harmony with the primitive notion of JUSTICE, and necessarily follow from it,—assuming various forms according to the condition, position, and relation of persons; or whether they are not rather the illegitimate result of a confusion of different things, a fatal association of ideas. And since justice deals especially with the questions of government, the condition of persons, and the possession of things, we must ascertain under what conditions, judging by universal opinion and the progress of the human mind, government is just, the condition of citizens is just, and the possession of things is just; then, striking out every thing which fails to meet these conditions, the result will at once tell us what legitimate government is, what the legitimate condition of citizens is, and what the legitimate possession of things is; and finally, as the last result of the analysis, what JUSTICE is.

Is the authority of man over man just?

Everybody answers, "No; the authority of man is only the authority of the law, which ought to be justice and truth." The private will counts for nothing in government, which consists, first, in discovering truth and justice in order to make the law; and, second, in superintending the execution of this law. I do not now inquire whether our constitutional form of government satisfies these conditions; whether, for example, the will of the ministry never influences the declaration and interpretation of the law; or whether our deputies, in their debates, are more intent on conquering by argument than by force of numbers: it is enough for me that my definition of a good government is allowed to be correct. This idea is exact. Yet we see that nothing seems more just to the Oriental nations than the despotism of their sovereigns; that, with the ancients and in the opinion of the philosophers themselves, slavery was just; that in the middle ages the nobles, the priests, and the bishops felt justified in holding slaves; that Louis XIV. thought that he was right when he said, "The State! I am the State;" and that Napoleon deemed it a crime for the State to oppose his will. The idea of justice, then, applied to sovereignty and government, has not always been what it is to-day; it has gone on developing and shaping itself by degrees, until it has arrived at its present state. But has it reached its last phase? I think not: only, as the last obstacle to be overcome arises from the institution of property which we have kept intact, in order to finish the reform in government and consummate the revolution, this very institution we must attack.

Is political and civil inequality just?

Some say yes; others no. To the first I would reply that, when the people abolished all privileges of birth and caste, they did it, in all probability, because it was for their advantage; why then do they favor the privileges of fortune more than those of rank and race? Because, say they, political inequality is a result of property; and without property society is impossible: thus the question just raised becomes a question of property. To the second I content myself with this remark: If you wish to enjoy political equality, abolish property; otherwise, why do you complain?

Is property just?

Everybody answers without hesitation, "Yes, property is just." I say everybody, for up to the present time no one who thoroughly understood the meaning of his words has answered no. For it is no easy thing to reply understandingly to such a question; only time and experience can furnish an answer. Now, this answer is given; it is for us to understand it. I undertake to prove it.

We are to proceed with the demonstration in the following order:—

I. We dispute not at all, we refute nobody, we deny nothing; we accept as sound all the arguments alleged in favor of property, and confine ourselves to a search for its principle, in order that we may then ascertain whether this principle is faithfully expressed by property. In fact, property being defensible on no ground save that of justice, the idea, or at least the intention, of justice must of necessity underlie all the arguments that have been made in defence of property; and, as on the other hand the right of property is only exercised over those things which can be appreciated by the senses, justice, secretly objectifying itself, so to speak, must take the shape of an algebraic formula.

By this method of investigation, we soon see that every argument which has been invented in behalf of property, WHATEVER IT MAY BE, always and of necessity leads to equality; that is, to the negation of property.

The first part covers two chapters: one treating of occupation, the foundation of our right; the other, of labor and talent, considered as causes of property and social inequality.

The first of these chapters will prove that the right of occupation OBSTRUCTS property; the second that the right of labor DESTROYS it.

II. Property, then, being of necessity conceived as existing only in connection with equality, it remains to find out why, in spite of this necessity of logic, equality does not exist. This new investigation also covers two chapters: in the first, considering the fact of property in itself, we inquire whether this fact is real, whether it exists, whether it is possible; for it would imply a contradiction, were these two opposite forms of society, equality and inequality, both possible. Then we discover, singularly enough, that property may indeed manifest itself accidentally; but that, as an institution and principle, it is mathematically impossible. So that the axiom of the school—ab actu ad posse valet consecutio: from the actual to the possible the inference is good—is given the lie as far as property is concerned.

Finally, in the last chapter, calling psychology to our aid, and probing man's nature to the bottom, we shall disclose the principle of JUSTICE—its formula and character; we shall state with precision the organic law of society; we shall explain the origin of property, the causes of its establishment, its long life, and its approaching death; we shall definitively establish its identity with robbery. And, after having shown that these three prejudices—THE SOVEREIGNTY OF MAN, THE INEQUALITY OF CONDITIONS, AND PROPERTY—are one and the same; that they may be taken for each other, and are reciprocally convertible,—we shall have no trouble in inferring therefrom, by the principle of contradiction, the basis of government and right. There our investigations will end, reserving the right to continue them in future works.

The importance of the subject which engages our attention is recognized by all minds.

"Property," says M. Hennequin, "is the creative and conservative principle of civil society. Property is one of those basic institutions, new theories concerning which cannot be presented too soon; for it must not be forgotten, and the publicist and statesman must know, that on the answer to the question whether property is the principle or the result of social order, whether it is to be considered as a cause or an effect, depends all morality, and, consequently, all the authority of human institutions."

These words are a challenge to all men of hope and faith; but, although the cause of equality is a noble one, no one has yet picked up the gauntlet thrown down by the advocates of property; no one has been courageous enough to enter upon the struggle. The spurious learning of haughty jurisprudence, and the absurd aphorisms of a political economy controlled by property have puzzled the most generous minds; it is a sort of password among the most influential friends of liberty and the interests of the people that EQUALITY IS A CHIMERA! So many false theories and meaningless analogies influence minds otherwise keen, but which are unconsciously controlled by popular prejudice. Equality advances every day—fit aequalitas. Soldiers of liberty, shall we desert our flag in the hour of triumph?

A defender of equality, I shall speak without bitterness and without anger; with the independence becoming a philosopher, with the courage and firmness of a free man. May I, in this momentous struggle, carry into all hearts the light with which I am filled; and show, by the success of my argument, that equality failed to conquer by the sword only that it might conquer by the pen!

CHAPTER II. PROPERTY CONSIDERED AS A NATURAL RIGHT

PROPERTY CONSIDERED AS A NATURAL RIGHT.—OCCUPATION AND CIVIL LAW AS EFFICIENT BASES OF PROPERTY. DEFINITIONS.

The Roman law defined property as the right to use and abuse one's own within the limits of the law—jus utendi et abutendi re sua, quatenus juris ratio patitur. A justification of the word ABUSE has been attempted, on the ground that it signifies, not senseless and immoral abuse, but only absolute domain. Vain distinction! invented as an excuse for property, and powerless against the frenzy of possession, which it neither prevents nor represses. The proprietor may, if he chooses, allow his crops to rot under foot; sow his field with salt; milk his cows on the sand; change his vineyard into a desert, and use his vegetable-garden as a park: do these things constitute abuse, or not? In the matter of property, use and abuse are necessarily indistinguishable.

According to the Declaration of Rights, published as a preface to the Constitution of '93, property is "the right to enjoy and dispose at will of one's goods, one's income, and the fruit of one's labor and industry."

Code Napoleon, article 544: "Property is the right to enjoy and dispose of things in the most absolute manner, provided we do not overstep the limits prescribed by the laws and regulations."

These two definitions do not differ from that of the Roman law: all give the proprietor an absolute right over a thing; and as for the restriction imposed by the code,—PROVIDED WE DO NOT OVERSTEP THE LIMITS PRESCRIBED BY THE LAWS AND REGULATIONS,—its object is not to limit property, but to prevent the domain of one proprietor from interfering with that of another. That is a confirmation of the principle, not a limitation of it.

There are different kinds of property: 1. Property pure and simple, the dominant and seigniorial power over a thing; or, as they term it, NAKED PROPERTY. 2. POSSESSION. "Possession," says Duranton, "is a matter of fact, not of right." Toullier: "Property is a right, a legal power; possession is a fact." The tenant, the farmer, the commandite, the usufructuary, are possessors; the owner who lets and lends for use, the heir who is to come into possession on the death of a usufructuary, are proprietors. If I may venture the comparison: a lover is a possessor, a husband is a proprietor.

This double definition of property—domain and possession—is of the highest importance; and it must be clearly understood, in order to comprehend what is to follow.

From the distinction between possession and property arise two sorts of rights: the jus in re, the right in a thing, the right by which I may reclaim the property which I have acquired, in whatever hands I find it; and the jus ad rem, the right TO a thing, which gives me a claim to become a proprietor. Thus the right of the partners to a marriage over each other's person is the jus in re; that of two who are betrothed is only the jus ad rem. In the first, possession and property are united; the second includes only naked property. With me who, as a laborer, have a right to the possession of the products of Nature and my own industry,—and who, as a proletaire, enjoy none of them,—it is by virtue of the jus ad rem that I demand admittance to the jus in re.

This distinction between the jus in re and the jus ad rem is the basis of the famous distinction between possessoire and petitoire,—actual categories of jurisprudence, the whole of which is included within their vast boundaries. Petitoire refers to every thing relating to property; possessoire to that relating to possession. In writing this memoir against property, I bring against universal society an action petitoire: I prove that those who do not possess to-day are proprietors by the same title as those who do possess; but, instead of inferring therefrom that property should be shared by all, I demand, in the name of general security, its entire abolition. If I fail to win my case, there is nothing left for us (the proletarian class and myself) but to cut our throats: we can ask nothing more from the justice of nations; for, as the code of procedure (art 26) tells us in its energetic style, THE PLAINTIFF WHO HAS BEEN NON-SUITED IN AN ACTION PETITOIRE, IS DEBARRED THEREBY FROM BRINGING AN ACTION POSSESSOIRE. If, on the contrary, I gain the case, we must then commence an action possessoire, that we may be reinstated in the enjoyment of the wealth of which we are deprived by property. I hope that we shall not be forced to that extremity; but these two actions cannot be prosecuted at once, such a course being prohibited by the same code of procedure.

Before going to the heart of the question, it will not be useless to offer a few preliminary remarks.

% 1.—Property as a Natural Right.

The Declaration of Rights has placed property in its list of the natural and inalienable rights of man, four in all: LIBERTY, EQUALITY, PROPERTY, SECURITY. What rule did the legislators of '93 follow in compiling this list? None. They laid down principles, just as they discussed sovereignty and the laws; from a general point of view, and according to their own opinion. They did every thing in their own blind way.

If we can believe Toullier: "The absolute rights can be reduced to three: SECURITY, LIBERTY, PROPERTY." Equality is eliminated by the Rennes professor; why? Is it because LIBERTY implies it, or because property prohibits it? On this point the author of "Droit Civil Explique" is silent: it has not even occurred to him that the matter is under discussion.

Nevertheless, if we compare these three or four rights with each other, we find that property bears no resemblance whatever to the others; that for the majority of citizens it exists only potentially, and as a dormant faculty without exercise; that for the others, who do enjoy it, it is susceptible of certain transactions and modifications which do not harmonize with the idea of a natural right; that, in practice, governments, tribunals, and laws do not respect it; and finally that everybody, spontaneously and with one voice, regards it as chimerical.

Liberty is inviolable. I can neither sell nor alienate my liberty; every contract, every condition of a contract, which has in view the alienation or suspension of liberty, is null: the slave, when he plants his foot upon the soil of liberty, at that moment becomes a free man. When society seizes a malefactor and deprives him of his liberty, it is a case of legitimate defence: whoever violates the social compact by the commission of a crime declares himself a public enemy; in attacking the liberty of others, he compels them to take away his own. Liberty is the original condition of man; to renounce liberty is to renounce the nature of man: after that, how could we perform the acts of man?

Likewise, equality before the law suffers neither restriction nor exception. All Frenchmen are equally eligible to office: consequently, in the presence of this equality, condition and family have, in many cases, no influence upon choice. The poorest citizen can obtain judgment in the courts against one occupying the most exalted station. Let the millionaire, Ahab, build a chateau upon the vineyard of Naboth: the court will have the power, according to the circumstances, to order the destruction of the chateau, though it has cost millions; and to force the trespasser to restore the vineyard to its original state, and pay the damages. The law wishes all property, that has been legitimately acquired, to be kept inviolate without regard to value, and without respect for persons.

The charter demands, it is true, for the exercise of certain political rights, certain conditions of fortune and capacity; but all publicists know that the legislator's intention was not to establish a privilege, but to take security. Provided the conditions fixed by law are complied with, every citizen may be an elector, and every elector eligible. The right, once acquired, is the same for all; the law compares neither persons nor votes. I do not ask now whether this system is the best; it is enough that, in the opinion of the charter and in the eyes of every one, equality before the law is absolute, and, like liberty, admits of no compromise.

It is the same with the right of security. Society promises its members no half-way protection, no sham defence; it binds itself to them as they bind themselves to it. It does not say to them, "I will shield you, provided it costs me nothing; I will protect you, if I run no risks thereby." It says, "I will defend you against everybody; I will save and avenge you, or perish myself."

The whole strength of the State is at the service of each citizen; the obligation which binds them together is absolute.

How different with property! Worshipped by all, it is acknowledged by none: laws, morals, customs, public and private conscience, all plot its death and ruin.

To meet the expenses of government, which has armies to support, tasks to perform, and officers to pay, taxes are needed. Let all contribute to these expenses: nothing more just. But why should the rich pay more than the poor? That is just, they say, because they possess more. I confess that such justice is beyond my comprehension.

Why are taxes paid? To protect all in the exercise of their natural rights—liberty, equality, security, and property; to maintain order in the State; to furnish the public with useful and pleasant conveniences.

Now, does it cost more to defend the rich man's life and liberty than the poor man's? Who, in time of invasion, famine, or plague, causes more trouble,—the large proprietor who escapes the evil without the assistance of the State, or the laborer who sits in his cottage unprotected from danger?

Is public order endangered more by the worthy citizen, or by the artisan and journeyman? Why, the police have more to fear from a few hundred laborers, out of work, than from two hundred thousand electors!

Does the man of large income appreciate more keenly than the poor man national festivities, clean streets, and beautiful monuments?

Why, he prefers his country-seat to all the popular pleasures; and when he wants to enjoy himself, he does not wait for the greased pole!

One of two things is true: either the proportional tax affords greater security to the larger tax-payers, or else it is a wrong.

Because, if property is a natural right, as the Declaration of '93 declares, all that belongs to me by virtue of this right is as sacred as my person; it is my blood, my life, myself: whoever touches it offends the apple of my eye. My income of one hundred thousand francs is as inviolable as the grisette's daily wage of seventy-five centimes; her attic is no more sacred than my suite of apartments. The tax is not levied in proportion to strength, size, or skill: no more should it be levied in proportion to property.

If, then, the State takes more from me, let it give me more in return, or cease to talk of equality of rights; for otherwise, society is established, not to defend property, but to destroy it. The State, through the proportional tax, becomes the chief of robbers; the State sets the example of systematic pillage: the State should be brought to the bar of justice at the head of those hideous brigands, that execrable mob which it now kills from motives of professional jealousy.

But, they say, the courts and the police force are established to restrain this mob; government is a company, not exactly for insurance, for it does not insure, but for vengeance and repression. The premium which this company exacts, the tax, is divided in proportion to property; that is, in proportion to the trouble which each piece of property occasions the avengers and repressers paid by the government.

This is any thing but the absolute and inalienable right of property. Under this system the poor and the rich distrust, and make war upon, each other. But what is the object of the war? Property. So that property is necessarily accompanied by war upon property. The liberty and security of the rich do not suffer from the liberty and security of the poor; far from that, they mutually strengthen and sustain each other. The rich man's right of property, on the contrary, has to be continually defended against the poor man's desire for property. What a contradiction! In England they have a poor-rate: they wish me to pay this tax. But what relation exists between my natural and inalienable right of property and the hunger from which ten million wretched people are suffering? When religion commands us to assist our fellows, it speaks in the name of charity, not in the name of law. The obligation of benevolence, imposed upon me by Christian morality, cannot be imposed upon me as a political tax for the benefit of any person or poor-house. I will give alms when I see fit to do so, when the sufferings of others excite in me that sympathy of which philosophers talk, and in which I do not believe: I will not be forced to bestow them. No one is obliged to do more than comply with this injunction: IN THE EXERCISE OF YOUR OWN RIGHTS DO NOT ENCROACH UPON THE RIGHTS OF ANOTHER; an injunction which is the exact definition of liberty. Now, my possessions are my own; no one has a claim upon them: I object to the placing of the third theological virtue in the order of the day.

Everybody, in France, demands the conversion of the five per cent. bonds; they demand thereby the complete sacrifice of one species of property. They have the right to do it, if public necessity requires it; but where is the just indemnity promised by the charter? Not only does none exist, but this indemnity is not even possible; for, if the indemnity were equal to the property sacrificed, the conversion would be useless.

The State occupies the same position to-day toward the bondholders that the city of Calais did, when besieged by Edward III, toward its notables. The English conqueror consented to spare its inhabitants, provided it would surrender to him its most distinguished citizens to do with as he pleased. Eustache and several others offered themselves; it was noble in them, and our ministers should recommend their example to the bondholders. But had the city the right to surrender them? Assuredly not. The right to security is absolute; the country can require no one to sacrifice himself. The soldier standing guard within the enemy's range is no exception to this rule. Wherever a citizen stands guard, the country stands guard with him: to-day it is the turn of the one, to-morrow of the other. When danger and devotion are common, flight is parricide. No one has the right to flee from danger; no one can serve as a scapegoat. The maxim of Caiaphas—IT IS RIGHT THAT A MAN SHOULD DIE FOR HIS NATION—is that of the populace and of tyrants; the two extremes of social degradation.

It is said that all perpetual annuities are essentially redeemable. This maxim of civil law, applied to the State, is good for those who wish to return to the natural equality of labor and wealth; but, from the point of view of the proprietor, and in the mouth of conversionists, it is the language of bankrupts. The State is not only a borrower, it is an insurer and guardian of property; granting the best of security, it assures the most inviolable possession. How, then, can it force open the hands of its creditors, who have confidence in it, and then talk to them of public order and security of property? The State, in such an operation, is not a debtor who discharges his debt; it is a stock-company which allures its stockholders into a trap, and there, contrary to its authentic promise, exacts from them twenty, thirty, or forty per cent. of the interest on their capital.

That is not all. The State is a university of citizens joined together under a common law by an act of society. This act secures all in the possession of their property; guarantees to one his field, to another his vineyard, to a third his rents, and to the bondholder, who might have bought real estate but who preferred to come to the assistance of the treasury, his bonds. The State cannot demand, without offering an equivalent, the sacrifice of an acre of the field or a corner of the vineyard; still less can it lower rents: why should it have the right to diminish the interest on bonds? This right could not justly exist, unless the bondholder could invest his funds elsewhere to equal advantage; but being confined to the State, where can he find a place to invest them, since the cause of conversion, that is, the power to borrow to better advantage, lies in the State? That is why a government, based on the principle of property, cannot redeem its annuities without the consent of their holders.

The money deposited with the republic is property which it has no right to touch while other kinds of property are respected; to force their redemption is to violate the social contract, and outlaw the bondholders.

The whole controversy as to the conversion of bonds finally reduces itself to this:—

QUESTION. Is it just to reduce to misery forty-five thousand families who derive an income from their bonds of one hundred francs or less?

ANSWER. Is it just to compel seven or eight millions of tax-payers to pay a tax of five francs, when they should pay only three? It is clear, in the first place, that the reply is in reality no reply; but, to make the wrong more apparent, let us change it thus: Is it just to endanger the lives of one hundred thousand men, when we can save them by surrendering one hundred heads to the enemy? Reader, decide!

All this is clearly understood by the defenders of the present system. Yet, nevertheless, sooner or later, the conversion will be effected and property be violated, because no other course is possible; because property, regarded as a right, and not being a right, must of right perish; because the force of events, the laws of conscience, and physical and mathematical necessity must, in the end, destroy this illusion of our minds.

To sum up: liberty is an absolute right, because it is to man what impenetrability is to matter,—a sine qua non of existence; equality is an absolute right, because without equality there is no society; security is an absolute right, because in the eyes of every man his own liberty and life are as precious as another's. These three rights are absolute; that is, susceptible of neither increase nor diminution; because in society each associate receives as much as he gives,—liberty for liberty, equality for equality, security for security, body for body, soul for soul, in life and in death.

But property, in its derivative sense, and by the definitions of law, is a right outside of society; for it is clear that, if the wealth of each was social wealth, the conditions would be equal for all, and it would be a contradiction to say: PROPERTY IS A MAN'S RIGHT TO DISPOSE AT WILL OF SOCIAL PROPERTY. Then if we are associated for the sake of liberty, equality, and security, we are not associated for the sake of property; then if property is a NATURAL right, this natural right is not SOCIAL, but ANTI-SOCIAL. Property and society are utterly irreconcilable institutions. It is as impossible to associate two proprietors as to join two magnets by their opposite poles. Either society must perish, or it must destroy property.

If property is a natural, absolute, imprescriptible, and inalienable right, why, in all ages, has there been so much speculation as to its origin?—for this is one of its distinguishing characteristics. The origin of a natural right! Good God! who ever inquired into the origin of the rights of liberty, security, or equality? They exist by the same right that we exist; they are born with us, they live and die with us. With property it is very different, indeed. By law, property can exist without a proprietor, like a quality without a subject. It exists for the human being who as yet is not, and for the octogenarian who is no more. And yet, in spite of these wonderful prerogatives which savor of the eternal and the infinite, they have never found the origin of property; the doctors still disagree. On one point only are they in harmony: namely, that the validity of the right of property depends upon the authenticity of its origin. But this harmony is their condemnation. Why have they acknowledged the right before settling the question of origin?

Certain classes do not relish investigation into the pretended titles to property, and its fabulous and perhaps scandalous history. They wish to hold to this proposition: that property is a fact; that it always has been, and always will be. With that proposition the savant Proudhon 11 commenced his "Treatise on the Right of Usufruct," regarding the origin of property as a useless question. Perhaps I would subscribe to this doctrine, believing it inspired by a commendable love of peace, were all my fellow-citizens in comfortable circumstances; but, no! I will not subscribe to it.

The titles on which they pretend to base the right of property are two in number: OCCUPATION and LABOR. I shall examine them successively, under all their aspects and in detail; and I remind the reader that, to whatever authority we appeal, I shall prove beyond a doubt that property, to be just and possible, must necessarily have equality for its condition.

% 2.—Occupation, as the Title to Property.

It is remarkable that, at those meetings of the State Council at which the Code was discussed, no controversy arose as to the origin and principle of property. All the articles of Vol. II., Book 2, concerning property and the right of accession, were passed without opposition or amendment. Bonaparte, who on other questions had given his legists so much trouble, had nothing to say about property. Be not surprised at it: in the eyes of that man, the most selfish and wilful person that ever lived, property was the first of rights, just as submission to authority was the most holy of duties.

The right of OCCUPATION, or of the FIRST OCCUPANT, is that which results from the actual, physical, real possession of a thing. I occupy a piece of land; the presumption is, that I am the proprietor, until the contrary is proved. We know that originally such a right cannot be legitimate unless it is reciprocal; the jurists say as much.

Cicero compares the earth to a vast theatre: *Quemadmodum theatrum cum commune sit, recte tamen dici potest ejus esse eum locum quem quisque occuparit.*

This passage is all that ancient philosophy has to say about the origin of property.

The theatre, says Cicero, is common to all; nevertheless, the place that each one occupies is called HIS OWN; that is, it is a place POSSESSED, not a place APPROPRIATED. This comparison annihilates property; moreover, it implies equality. Can I, in a theatre, occupy at the same time one place in the pit, another in the boxes, and a third in the gallery?

Not unless I have three bodies, like Geryon, or can exist in different places at the same time, as is related of the magician Apollonius.

According to Cicero, no one has a right to more than he needs: such is the true interpretation of his famous axiom —*suum quidque cujusque sit*, to each one that which belongs to him—an axiom that has been strangely applied. That which belongs to each is not that which each MAY possess, but that which each HAS A RIGHT to possess. Now, what have we a right to possess? That which is required for our labor and consumption; Cicero's comparison of the earth to a theatre proves it. According to that, each one may take what place he will, may beautify and adorn it, if he can; it is allowable: but he must never allow himself to overstep the limit which separates him from another. The doctrine of Cicero leads directly to equality; for, occupation being pure toleration, if the toleration is mutual (and it cannot be otherwise) the possessions are equal.

Grotius rushes into history; but what kind of reasoning is that which seeks the origin of a right, said to be natural, elsewhere than in Nature? This is the method of the ancients: the fact exists, then it is necessary, then it is just, then its antecedents are just also. Nevertheless, let us look into it.

"Originally, all things were common and undivided; they were the property of all." Let us go no farther. Grotius tells us how this original communism came to an end through ambition and cupidity; how the age of gold was followed by the age of iron, &c. So that property rested first on war and conquest, then on treaties and agreements. But either these treaties and agreements distributed wealth equally, as did the original communism (the only method of distribution with which the barbarians were acquainted, and the only form of justice of which they could conceive; and then the question of origin assumes this form: how did equality afterwards disappear?)—or else these treaties and agreements were forced by the strong upon the weak, and in that case they are null; the tacit consent of posterity does not make them valid, and we live in a permanent condition of iniquity and fraud.

We never can conceive how the equality of conditions, having once existed, could afterwards have passed away. What was the cause of such degeneration? The instincts of the animals are unchangeable, as well as the differences of species; to suppose original equality in human society is to admit by implication that the present inequality is a degeneration from the nature of this society,—a thing which the defenders of property cannot explain. But I infer therefrom that, if Providence placed the first human beings in a condition of equality, it was an indication of its desires, a model that it wished them to realize in other forms; just as the religious sentiment, which it planted in their hearts, has developed and manifested itself in various ways. Man has but one nature, constant and unalterable: he pursues it through instinct, he wanders from it through reflection, he returns to it through judgment; who shall say that we are not returning now? According to Grotius, man has abandoned equality; according to me, he will yet return to it. How came he to abandon it? Why will he return to it? These are questions for future consideration.

Reid writes as follows:—

"The right of property is not innate, but acquired. It is not grounded upon the constitution of man, but upon his actions. Writers on jurisprudence have explained its origin in a manner that may satisfy every man of common understanding.

"The earth is given to men in common for the purposes of life, by the bounty of Heaven. But to divide it, and appropriate one part of its produce to one, another part to another, must be the work of men who have power and understanding given them, by which every man may accommodate himself, WITHOUT HURT TO ANY OTHER.

"This common right of every man to what the earth produces, before it be occupied and appropriated by others, was, by ancient moralists, very properly compared to the right which every citizen had to the public theatre, where every man that came might occupy an empty seat, and thereby acquire a right to it while the entertainment lasted; but no man had a right to dispossess another.

"The earth is a great theatre, furnished by the Almighty, with perfect wisdom and goodness, for the entertainment and employment of all mankind. Here every man has a right to accommodate himself as a spectator, and to perform his part as an actor; but without hurt to others."

Consequences of Reid's doctrine.

1. That the portion which each one appropriates may wrong no one, it must be equal to the quotient of the total amount of property to be shared, divided by the number of those who are to share it;

2. The number of places being of necessity equal at all times to that of the spectators, no spectator can occupy two places, nor can any actor play several parts;

3. Whenever a spectator comes in or goes out, the places of all contract or enlarge correspondingly: for, says Reid, "THE RIGHT OF PROPERTY IS NOT INNATE, BUT ACQUIRED;" consequently, it is not absolute; consequently, the occupancy on which it is based, being a conditional fact, cannot endow this right with a stability which it does not possess itself. This seems to have been the thought of the Edinburgh professor when he added:—

"A right to life implies a right to the necessary means of life; and that justice, which forbids the taking away the life of an innocent man, forbids no less the taking from him the necessary means of life. He has the same right to defend the one as the other. To hinder another man's innocent labor, or to deprive him of the fruit of it, is an injustice of the same kind, and has the same effect as to put him in fetters or in prison, and is equally a just object of resentment."

Thus the chief of the Scotch school, without considering at all the inequality of skill or labor, posits a priori the equality of the means of labor, abandoning thereafter to each laborer the care of his own person, after the eternal axiom: WHOSO DOES WELL, SHALL FARE WELL.

The philosopher Reid is lacking, not in knowledge of the principle, but in courage to pursue it to its ultimate. If the right of life is equal, the right of labor is equal, and so is the right of occupancy. Would it not be criminal, were some islanders to repulse, in the name of property, the unfortunate victims of a shipwreck struggling to reach the shore? The very idea of such cruelty sickens the imagination. The proprietor, like Robinson Crusoe on his island, wards off with pike and musket the proletaire washed overboard by the wave of civilization, and seeking to gain a foothold upon the rocks of property. "Give me work!" cries he with all his might to the proprietor: "don't drive me away, I will work for you at any price." "I do not need your services," replies the proprietor, showing the end of his pike or the barrel of his gun. "Lower my rent at least." "I need my income to live upon." "How can I pay you, when I can get no work?" "That is your business." Then the unfortunate proletaire abandons himself to the waves; or, if he attempts to land upon the shore of property, the proprietor takes aim, and kills him.

We have just listened to a spiritualist; we will now question a materialist, then an eclectic: and having completed the circle of philosophy, we will turn next to law.

According to Destutt de Tracy, property is a necessity of our nature. That this necessity involves unpleasant consequences, it would be folly to deny. But these consequences are necessary evils which do not invalidate the principle; so that it is as unreasonable to rebel against property on account of the abuses which it generates, as to complain of life because it is sure to end in death. This brutal and pitiless philosophy promises at least frank and close reasoning. Let us see if it keeps its promise.

"We talk very gravely about the conditions of property,... as if it was our province to decide what constitutes property.... It would seem, to hear certain philosophers and legislators, that at a certain moment, spontaneously and without cause, people began to use the words THINE and MINE; and that they might have, or ought to have, dispensed with them. But THINE and MINE were never invented."

A philosopher yourself, you are too realistic. THINE and MINE do not necessarily refer to self, as they do when I say your philosophy, and my equality; for your philosophy is you philosophizing, and my equality is I professing equality. THINE and MINE oftener indicate a relation,—YOUR country, YOUR parish, YOUR tailor, YOUR milkmaid; MY chamber, MY seat at the theatre, MY company and MY battalion in the National Guard. In the former sense, we may sometimes say MY labor, MY skill, MY virtue; never MY grandeur nor MY majesty: in the latter sense only, MY field, MY house, MY vineyard, MY capital,—precisely as the banker's clerk says MY cash-box. In short, THINE and MINE are signs and expressions of personal, but equal, rights; applied to things outside of us, they indicate possession, function, use, not property.

It does not seem possible, but, nevertheless, I shall prove, by quotations, that the whole theory of our author is based upon this paltry equivocation.

"Prior to all covenants, men are, not exactly, as Hobbes says, in a state of HOSTILITY, but of ESTRANGEMENT. In this state, justice and injustice are unknown; the rights of one bear no relation to the rights of another. All have as many rights as needs, and all feel it their duty to satisfy those needs by any means at their command."

Grant it; whether true or false, it matters not. Destutt de Tracy cannot escape equality. On this theory, men, while in a state of ESTRANGEMENT, are under no obligations to each other; they all have the right to satisfy their needs without regard to the needs of others, and consequently the right to exercise their power over Nature, each according to his strength and ability. That involves the greatest inequality of wealth. Inequality of conditions, then, is the characteristic feature of estrangement or barbarism: the exact opposite of Rousseau's idea.

But let us look farther:—

"Restrictions of these rights and this duty commence at the time when covenants, either implied or expressed, are agreed upon. Then appears for the first time justice and injustice; that is, the balance between the rights of one and the rights of another, which up to that time were necessarily equal."

Listen: RIGHTS WERE EQUAL; that means that each individual had the right to SATISFY HIS NEEDS WITHOUT REFERENCE TO THE NEEDS OF OTHERS. In other words, that all had the right to injure each other; that there was no right save force and cunning. They injured each other, not only by war and pillage, but also by usurpation and appropriation. Now, in order to abolish this equal right to use force and stratagem,—this equal right to do evil, the sole source of the inequality of benefits and injuries,—they commenced to make COVENANTS EITHER IMPLIED OR EXPRESSED, and established a balance. Then these agreements and this balance were intended to secure to all equal comfort; then, by the law of contradictions, if isolation is the principle of inequality, society must produce equality. The social balance is the equalization of the strong and the weak; for, while they are not equals, they are strangers; they can form no associations,—they live as enemies. Then, if inequality of conditions is a necessary evil, so is isolation, for society and inequality are incompatible with each other. Then, if society is the true condition of man's existence, so is equality also. This conclusion cannot be avoided.

This being so, how is it that, ever since the establishment of this balance, inequality has been on the increase? How is it that justice and isolation always accompany each other? Destutt de Tracy shall reply:—

"NEEDS and MEANS, RIGHTS and DUTIES, are products of the will. If man willed nothing, these would not exist. But to have needs and means, rights and duties, is to HAVE, to POSSESS, something. They are so many kinds of property, using the word in its most general sense: they are things which belong to us."

Shameful equivocation, not justified by the necessity for generalization! The word PROPERTY has two meanings: 1. It designates the quality which makes a thing what it is; the attribute which is peculiar to it, and especially distinguishes it. We use it in this sense when we say THE PROPERTIES OF THE TRIANGLE or of NUMBERS; THE PROPERTY OF THE MAGNET, &c. 2. It expresses the right of absolute control over a thing by a free and intelligent being. It is used in this sense by writers on jurisprudence. Thus, in the phrase, IRON ACQUIRES THE PROPERTY OF A MAGNET, the word PROPERTY does not convey the same idea that it does in this one: *I HAVE ACQUIRED THIS MAGNET AS MY PROPERTY.* To tell a poor man that he HAS property because he HAS arms and legs,—that the hunger from which he suffers, and his power to sleep in the open air are his property,—is to play upon words, and to add insult to injury.

"The sole basis of the idea of property is the idea of personality. As soon as property is born at all, it is born, of necessity, in all its fulness. As soon as an individual knows HIMSELF,—his moral personality, his capacities of enjoyment, suffering, and action,—he necessarily sees also that this SELF is exclusive proprietor of the body in which it dwells, its organs, their powers, faculties, &c.... Inasmuch as artificial and conventional property exists, there must be natural property also; for nothing can exist in art without its counterpart in Nature."

We ought to admire the honesty and judgment of philosophers! Man has properties; that is, in the first acceptation of the term, faculties. He has property; that is, in its second acceptation, the right of domain. He has, then, the property of being proprietor. How ashamed I should be to notice such foolishness, were I here considering only the authority of Destutt de Tracy! But the entire human race, since the origination of society and language, when metaphysics and dialectics were first born, has been guilty of this puerile confusion of thought. All which man could call his own was identified in his mind with his person. He considered it as his property, his wealth; a part of himself, a member of his body, a faculty of his mind. The possession of things was likened to property in the powers of the body and mind; and on this false analogy was based the right of property,—THE IMITATION OF NATURE BY ART, as Destutt de Tracy so elegantly puts it.

But why did not this ideologist perceive that man is not proprietor even of his own faculties? Man has powers, attributes, capacities; they are given him by Nature that he may live, learn, and love: he does not own them, but has only the use of them; and he can make no use of them that does not harmonize with Nature's laws. If he had absolute mastery over his faculties, he could avoid hunger and cold; he could eat unstintedly, and walk through fire; he could move mountains, walk a hundred leagues in a minute, cure without medicines and by the sole force of his will, and could make himself immortal. He could say, "I wish to produce," and his tasks would be finished with the words; he could say, "I wish to know," and he would know; "I love," and he would enjoy. What then? Man is not master of himself, but may be of his surroundings. Let him use the wealth of Nature, since he can live only by its use; but let him abandon his pretensions to the title of proprietor, and remember that he is called so only metaphorically.

To sum up: Destutt de Tracy classes together the external PRODUCTIONS of nature and art, and the POWERS or FACULTIES of man, making both of them species of property; and upon this equivocation he hopes to establish, so firmly that it can never be disturbed, the right of property. But of these different kinds of property some are INNATE, as memory, imagination, strength, and beauty; while others are ACQUIRED, as land, water, and forests. In the state of Nature or isolation, the strongest and most skilful (that is, those best provided with innate property) stand the best chance of obtaining acquired property. Now, it is to prevent this encroachment and the war which results therefrom, that a balance (justice) has been employed, and covenants (implied or expressed) agreed upon: it is to correct, as far as possible, inequality of innate property by equality of acquired property. As long as the division remains unequal, so long the partners remain enemies; and it is the purpose of the covenants to reform this state of things. Thus we have, on the one hand, isolation, inequality, enmity, war, robbery, murder; on the other, society, equality, fraternity, peace, and love. Choose between them!

M. Joseph Dutens—a physician, engineer, and geometrician, but a very poor legist, and no philosopher at all—is the author of a "Philosophy of Political Economy," in which he felt it his duty to break lances in behalf of property. His reasoning seems to be borrowed from Destutt de Tracy. He commences with this definition of property, worthy of Sganarelle: "Property is the right by which a thing is one's own." Literally translated: Property is the right of property.

After getting entangled a few times on the subjects of will, liberty, and personality; after having distinguished between IMMATERIAL-NATURAL property, and MATERIAL-NATURAL property, a distinction similar to Destutt de Tracy's of innate and acquired property,—M. Joseph Dutens concludes with these two general propositions: 1. Property is a natural and inalienable right of every man; 2. Inequality of property is a necessary result of Nature,—which propositions are convertible into a simpler one: All men have an equal right of unequal property.

He rebukes M. de Sismondi for having taught that landed property has no other basis than law and conventionality; and he says himself, speaking of the respect which people feel for property, that "their good sense reveals to them the nature of the ORIGINAL CONTRACT made between society and proprietors."

He confounds property with possession, communism with equality, the just with the natural, and the natural with the possible. Now he takes these different ideas to be equivalents; now he seems to distinguish between them, so much so that it would be infinitely easier to refute him than to understand him. Attracted first by the title of the work, "Philosophy of Political Economy," I have found, among the author's obscurities, only the most ordinary ideas. For that reason I will not speak of him.

M. Cousin, in his "Moral Philosophy," page 15, teaches that all morality, all laws, all rights are given to man with this injunction: "FREE BEING, REMAIN FREE." Bravo! master; I wish to remain free if I can. He continues:—

"Our principle is true; it is good, it is social. Do not fear to push it to its ultimate.

"1. If the human person is sacred, its whole nature is sacred; and particularly its interior actions, its feelings, its thoughts, its voluntary decisions. This accounts for the respect due to philosophy, religion, the arts industry, commerce, and to all the results of liberty. I say respect, not simply toleration; for we do not tolerate a right, we respect it."

I bow my head before this philosophy.

"2. My liberty, which is sacred, needs for its objective action an instrument which we call the body: the body participates then in the sacredness of liberty; it is then inviolable. This is the basis of the principle of individual liberty.

"3. My liberty needs, for its objective action, material to work upon; in other words, property or a thing. This thing or property naturally participates then in the inviolability of my person. For instance, I take possession of an object which has become necessary and useful in the outward manifestation of my liberty. I say, 'This object is mine since it belongs to no one else; consequently, I possess it legitimately.' So the legitimacy of possession rests on two conditions. First, I possess only as a free being. Suppress free activity, you destroy my power to labor. Now it is only by labor that I can use this property or thing, and it is only by using it that I possess it. Free activity is then the principle of the right of property. But that alone does not legitimate possession. All men are free; all can use property by labor. Does that mean that all men have a right to all property? Not at all. To possess legitimately, I must not only labor and produce in my capacity of a free being, but I must also be the first to occupy the property. In short, if labor and production are the principle of the right of property, the fact of first occupancy is its indispensable condition.

"4. I possess legitimately: then I have the right to use my property as I see fit. I have also the right to give it away. I have also the right to bequeath it; for if I decide to make a donation, my decision is as valid after my death as during my life."

In fact, to become a proprietor, in M. Cousin's opinion, one must take possession by occupation and labor. I maintain that the element of time must be considered also; for if the first occupants have occupied everything, what are the new comers to do? What will become of them, having an instrument with which to work, but no material to work upon? Must they devour each other? A terrible extremity, unforeseen by philosophical prudence; for the reason that great geniuses neglect little things.

Notice also that M. Cousin says that neither occupation nor labor, taken separately, can legitimate the right of property; and that it is born only from the union of the two. This is one of M. Cousin's eclectic turns, which he, more than any one else, should take pains to avoid. Instead of proceeding by the method of analysis, comparison, elimination, and reduction (the only means of discovering the truth amid the various forms of thought and whimsical opinions), he jumbles all systems together, and then, declaring each both right and wrong, exclaims: "There you have the truth."

But, adhering to my promise, I will not refute him. I will only prove, by all the arguments with which he justifies the right of property, the principle of equality which kills it. As I have already said, my sole intent is this: to show at the bottom of all these positions that inevitable major, EQUALITY; hoping hereafter to show that the principle of property vitiates the very elements of economical, moral, and governmental science, thus leading it in the wrong direction.

Well, is it not true, from M. Cousin's point of view, that, if the liberty of man is sacred, it is equally sacred in all individuals; that, if it needs property for its objective action, that is, for its life, the appropriation of material is equally necessary for all; that, if I wish to be respected in my right of appropriation, I must respect others in theirs; and, consequently, that though, in the sphere of the infinite, a person's power of appropriation is limited only by himself, in the sphere of the finite this same power is limited by the mathematical relation between the number of persons and the space which they occupy? Does it not follow that if one individual cannot prevent another—his fellow-man—from appropriating an amount of material equal to his own, no more can he prevent individuals yet to come; because, while individuality passes away, universality persists, and eternal laws cannot be determined by a partial view of their manifestations? Must we not conclude, therefore, that whenever a person is born, the others must crowd closer together; and, by reciprocity of obligation, that if the new comer is afterwards to become an heir, the right of succession does not give him the right of accumulation, but only the right of choice?

I have followed M. Cousin so far as to imitate his style, and I am ashamed of it. Do we need such high-sounding terms, such sonorous phrases, to say such simple things? Man needs to labor in order to live; consequently, he needs tools to work with and materials to work upon. His need to produce constitutes his right to produce. Now, this right is guaranteed him by his fellows, with whom he makes an agreement to that effect. One hundred thousand men settle in a large country like France with no inhabitants: each man has a right to 1/100,000 of the land. If the number of possessors increases, each one's portion diminishes in consequence; so that, if the number of inhabitants rises to thirty-four millions, each one will have a right only to 1/34,000,000. Now, so regulate the police system and the government, labor, exchange, inheritance, &c., that the means of labor shall be shared by all equally, and that each individual shall be free; and then society will be perfect.

Of all the defenders of property, M. Cousin has gone the farthest. He has maintained against the economists that labor does not establish the right of property unless preceded by occupation, and against the jurists that the civil law can determine and apply a natural right, but cannot create it. In fact, it is not sufficient to say, "The right of property is demonstrated by the existence of property; the function of the civil law is purely declaratory." To say that, is to confess that there is no reply to those who question the legitimacy of the fact itself. Every right must be justifiable in itself, or by some antecedent right; property is no exception. For this reason, M. Cousin has sought to base it upon the SANCTITY of the human personality, and the act by which the will assimilates a thing. "Once touched by man," says one of M. Cousin's disciples, "things receive from him a character which transforms and humanizes them." I confess, for my part, that I have no faith in this magic, and that I know of nothing less holy than the will of man. But this theory, fragile as it seems to psychology as well as jurisprudence, is nevertheless more philosophical and profound than those theories which are based upon labor or the authority of the law. Now, we have just seen to what this theory of which we are speaking leads,—to the equality implied in the terms of its statement.

But perhaps philosophy views things from too lofty a standpoint, and is not sufficiently practical; perhaps from the exalted summit of speculation men seem so small to the metaphysician that he cannot distinguish between them; perhaps, indeed, the equality of conditions is one of those principles which are very true and sublime as generalities, but which it would be ridiculous and even dangerous to attempt to rigorously apply to the customs of life and to social transactions. Undoubtedly, this is a case which calls for imitation of the wise reserve of moralists and jurists, who warn us against carrying things to extremes, and who advise us to suspect every definition; because there is not one, they say, which cannot be utterly destroyed by developing its disastrous results—*Omnis definitio in jure civili periculosa est: parum est enim ut non subverti possit.* Equality of conditions,—a terrible dogma in the ears of the proprietor, a consoling truth at the poor-man's sick-bed, a frightful reality under the knife of the anatomist,—equality of conditions, established in the political, civil, and industrial spheres, is only an alluring impossibility, an inviting bait, a satanic delusion.

It is never my intention to surprise my reader. I detest, as I do death, the man who employs subterfuge in his words and conduct. From the first page of this book, I have expressed myself so plainly and decidedly that all can see the tendency of my thought and hopes; and they will do me the justice to say, that it would be difficult to exhibit more frankness and more boldness at the same time. I do not hesitate to declare that the time is not far distant when this reserve, now so much admired in philosophers—this happy medium so strongly recommended by professors of moral and political science—will be regarded as the disgraceful feature of a science without principle, and as the seal of its reprobation. In legislation and morals, as well as in geometry, axioms are absolute, definitions are certain; and all the results of a principle are to be accepted, provided they are logically deduced. Deplorable pride! We know nothing of our nature, and we charge our blunders to it; and, in a fit of unaffected ignorance, cry out, "The truth is in doubt, the best definition defines nothing!" We shall know some time whether this distressing uncertainty of jurisprudence arises from the nature of its investigations, or from our prejudices; whether, to explain social phenomena, it is not enough to change our hypothesis, as did Copernicus when he reversed the system of Ptolemy.

But what will be said when I show, as I soon shall, that this same jurisprudence continually tries to base property upon equality? What reply can be made?

% 3.—Civil Law as the Foundation and Sanction of Property.

Pothier seems to think that property, like royalty, exists by divine right. He traces back its origin to God himself—ab Jove principium. He begins in this way:—

"God is the absolute ruler of the universe and all that it contains: *Domini est terra et plenitudo ejus, orbis et universi qui habitant in eo*. For the human race he has created the earth and all its creatures, and has given it a control over them subordinate only to his own. 'Thou madest him to have dominion over the works of thy hands; thou hast put all things under his feet,' says the Psalmist. God accompanied this gift with these words, addressed to our first parents after the creation: 'Be fruitful, and multiply and replenish the earth,'" &c.

After this magnificent introduction, who would refuse to believe the human race to be an immense family living in brotherly union, and under the protection of a venerable father? But, heavens! are brothers enemies? Are fathers unnatural, and children prodigal?

GOD GAVE THE EARTH TO THE HUMAN RACE: why then have I received none? HE HAS PUT ALL THINGS UNDER MY FEET,—and I have not where to lay my head! MULTIPLY, he tells us through his interpreter, Pothier. Ah, learned Pothier! that is as easy to do as to say; but you must give moss to the bird for its nest.

"The human race having multiplied, men divided among themselves the earth and most of the things upon it; that which fell to each, from that time exclusively belonged to him. That was the origin of the right of property."

Say, rather, the right of possession. Men lived in a state of communism; whether positive or negative it matters little. Then there was no property, not even private possession. The genesis and growth of possession gradually forcing people to labor for their support, they agreed either formally or tacitly,—it makes no difference which,—that the laborer should be sole proprietor of the fruit of his labor; that is, they simply declared the fact that thereafter none could live without working. It necessarily followed that, to obtain equality of products, there must be equality of labor; and that, to obtain equality of labor, there must be equality of facilities for labor. Whoever without labor got possession, by force or by strategy, of another's means of subsistence, destroyed equality, and placed himself above or outside of the law. Whoever monopolized the means of production on the ground of greater industry, also destroyed equality. Equality being then the expression of right, whoever violated it was UNJUST.

Thus, labor gives birth to private possession; the right in a thing—jus in re. But in what thing? Evidently IN THE PRODUCT, not IN THE SOIL. So the Arabs have always understood it; and so, according to Caesar and Tacitus, the Germans formerly held. "The Arabs," says M. de Sismondi, "who admit a man's property in the flocks which he has raised, do not refuse the crop to him who planted the seed; but they do not see why another, his equal, should not have a right to plant in his turn. The inequality which results from the pretended right of the first occupant seems to them to be based on no principle of justice; and when all the land falls into the hands of a certain number of inhabitants, there results a monopoly in their favor against the rest of the nation, to which they do not wish to submit."

Well, they have shared the land. I admit that therefrom results a more powerful organization of labor; and that this method of distribution, fixed and durable, is advantageous to production: but how could this division give to each a transferable right of property in a thing to which all had an inalienable right of possession? In the terms of jurisprudence, this metamorphosis from possessor to proprietor is legally impossible; it implies in the jurisdiction of the courts the union of possessoire and petitoire; and the mutual concessions of those who share the land are nothing less than traffic in natural rights. The original cultivators of the land, who were also the original makers of the law, were not as learned as our legislators, I admit; and had they been, they could not have done worse: they did not foresee the consequences of the transformation of the right of private possession into the right of absolute property. But why have not those, who in later times have established the distinction between jus in re and jus ad rem, applied it to the principle of property itself?

Let me call the attention of the writers on jurisprudence to their own maxims.

The right of property, provided it can have a cause, can have but one—*Dominium non potest nisi ex una causa contingere*. I can possess by several titles; I can become proprietor by only one—*Non ut ex pluribus causis idem nobis deberi potest, ita ex pluribus causis idem potest nostrum esse*. The field which I have cleared, which I cultivate, on which I have built my house, which supports myself, my family, and my livestock, I can possess: 1st. As the original occupant; 2d. As a laborer; 3d. By virtue of the social contract which assigns it to me as my share.

But none of these titles confer upon me the right of property. For, if I attempt to base it upon occupancy, society can reply, "I am the original occupant." If I appeal to my labor, it will say, "It is only on that condition that you possess." If I speak of agreements, it will respond, "These agreements establish only your right of use." Such, however, are the only titles which proprietors advance. They never have been able to discover any others. Indeed, every right—it is Pothier who says it—supposes a producing cause in the person who enjoys it; but in man who lives and dies, in this son of earth who passes away like a shadow, there exists, with respect to external things, only titles of possession, not one title of property. Why, then, has society recognized a right injurious to itself, where there is no producing cause? Why, in according possession, has it also conceded property? Why has the law sanctioned this abuse of power?

The German Ancillon replies thus:—

"Some philosophers pretend that man, in employing his forces upon a natural object,—say a field or a tree,—acquires a right only to the improvements which he makes, to the form which he gives to the object, not to the object itself. Useless distinction! If the form could be separated from the object, perhaps there would be room for question; but as this is almost always impossible, the application of man's strength to the different parts of the visible world is the foundation of the right of property, the primary origin of riches."

property from possession, possession must be shared; in any case, society reserves the right to fix the conditions of property. Let us suppose that an appropriated farm yields a gross income of ten thousand francs; and, as very seldom happens, that this farm cannot be divided. Let us suppose farther that, by economical calculation, the annual expenses of a family are three thousand francs: the possessor of this farm should be obliged to guard his reputation as a good father of a family, by paying to society ten thousand francs,—less the total costs of cultivation, and the three thousand francs required for the maintenance of his family. This payment is not rent, it is an indemnity.

What sort of justice is it, then, which makes such laws as this:—

"Whereas, since labor so changes the form of a thing that the form and substance cannot be separated without destroying the thing itself, either society must be disinherited, or the laborer must lose the fruit of his labor; and

"Whereas, in every other case, property in raw material would give a title to added improvements, minus their cost; and whereas, in this instance, property in improvements ought to give a title to the principal;

"Therefore, the right of appropriation by labor shall never be admitted against individuals, but only against society."

In such a way do legislators always reason in regard to property.

The law is intended to protect men's mutual rights,—that is, the rights of each against each, and each against all; and, as if a proportion could exist with less than four terms, the law-makers always disregard the latter. As long as man is opposed to man, property offsets property, and the two forces balance each other; as soon as man is isolated, that is, opposed to the society which he himself represents, jurisprudence is at fault: Themis has lost one scale of her balance.

Listen to the professor of Rennes, the learned Toullier:—

"How could this claim, made valid by occupation, become stable and permanent property, which might continue to stand, and which might be reclaimed after the first occupant had relinquished possession?

"Agriculture was a natural consequence of the multiplication of the human race, and agriculture, in its turn, favors population, and necessitates the establishment of permanent property; for who would take the trouble to plough and sow, if he were not certain that he would reap?"

To satisfy the husbandman, it was sufficient to guarantee him possession of his crop; admit even that he should have been protected in his right of occupation of land, as long as he remained its cultivator. That was all that he had a right to expect; that was all that the advance of civilization demanded. But property, property! the right of escheat over lands which one neither occupies nor cultivates,—who had authority to grant it? who pretended to have it?

"Agriculture alone was not sufficient to establish permanent property; positive laws were needed, and magistrates to execute them; in a word, the civil State was needed.

"The multiplication of the human race had rendered agriculture necessary; the need of securing to the cultivator the fruit of his labor made permanent property necessary, and also laws for its protection. So we are indebted to property for the creation of the civil State."

Yes, of our civil State, as you have made it; a State which, at first, was despotism, then monarchy, then aristocracy, today democracy, and always tyranny.

"Without the ties of property it never would have been possible to subordinate men to the wholesome yoke of the law; and without permanent property the earth would have remained a vast forest. Let us admit, then, with the most careful writers, that if transient property, or the right of preference resulting from occupation, existed prior to the establishment of civil society, permanent property, as we know it to-day, is the work of civil law. It is the civil law which holds that, when once acquired, property can be lost only by the action of the proprietor, and that it exists even after the proprietor has relinquished possession of the thing, and it has fallen into the hands of a third party.

"Thus property and possession, which originally were confounded, became through the civil law two distinct and independent things; two things which, in the language of the law, have nothing whatever in common. In this we see what a wonderful change has been effected in property, and to what an extent Nature has been altered by the civil laws."

Thus the law, in establishing property, has not been the expression of a psychological fact, the development of a natural law, the application of a moral principle. It has literally CREATED a right outside of its own province. It has realized an abstraction, a metaphor, a fiction; and that without deigning to look at the consequences, without considering the disadvantages, without inquiring whether it was right or wrong.

It has sanctioned selfishness; it has indorsed monstrous pretensions; it has received with favor impious vows, as if it were able to fill up a bottomless pit, and to satiate hell! Blind law; the law of the ignorant man; a law which is not a law; the voice of discord, deceit, and blood! This it is which, continually revived, reinstated, rejuvenated, restored, re-enforced—as the palladium of society—has troubled the consciences of the people, has obscured the minds of the masters, and has induced all the catastrophes which have befallen nations.

This it is which Christianity has condemned, but which its ignorant ministers deify; who have as little desire to study Nature and man, as ability to read their Scriptures.

But, indeed, what guide did the law follow in creating the domain of property? What principle directed it? What was its standard?

Would you believe it? It was equality.

Agriculture was the foundation of territorial possession, and the original cause of property. It was of no use to secure to the farmer the fruit of his labor, unless the means of production were at the same time secured to him. To fortify the weak against the invasion of the strong, to suppress spoliation and fraud, the necessity was felt of establishing between possessors permanent lines of division, insuperable obstacles. Every year saw the people multiply, and the cupidity of the husbandman increase: it was thought best to put a bridle on ambition by setting boundaries which ambition would in vain attempt to overstep. Thus the soil came to be appropriated through need of the equality which is essential to public security and peaceable possession. Undoubtedly the division was never geographically equal; a multitude of rights, some founded in Nature, but wrongly interpreted and still more wrongly applied, inheritance, gift, and exchange; others, like the privileges of birth and position, the illegitimate creations of ignorance and brute force,—all operated to prevent absolute equality. But, nevertheless, the principle remained the same: equality had sanctioned possession; equality sanctioned property.

The husbandman needed each year a field to sow; what more convenient and simple arrangement for the barbarians,—instead of indulging in annual quarrels and fights, instead of continually moving their houses, furniture, and families from spot to spot,—than to assign to each individual a fixed and inalienable estate?

It was not right that the soldier, on returning from an expedition, should find himself dispossessed on account of the services which he had just rendered to his country; his estate ought to be restored to him. It became, therefore, customary to retain property by intent alone—*nudo animo;* it could be sacrificed only with the consent and by the action of the proprietor.

It was necessary that the equality in the division should be kept up from one generation to another, without a new distribution of the land upon the death of each family; it appeared therefore natural and just that children and parents, according to the degree of relationship which they bore to the deceased, should be the heirs of their ancestors. Thence came, in the first place, the feudal and patriarchal custom of recognizing only one heir; then, by a quite contrary application of the principle of equality, the admission of all the children to a share in their father's estate, and, very recently also among us, the definitive abolition of the right of primogeniture.

But what is there in common between these rude outlines of instinctive organization and the true social science? How could these men, who never had the faintest idea of statistics, valuation, or political economy, furnish us with principles of legislation?

"The law," says a modern writer on jurisprudence, "is the expression of a social want, the declaration of a fact: the legislator does not make it, he declares it. 'This definition is not exact. The law is a method by which social wants must be satisfied; the people do not vote it, the legislator does not express it: the savant discovers and formulates it." But in fact, the law, according to M. Ch. Comte, who has devoted half a volume to its definition, was in the beginning only the EXPRESSION OF A WANT, and the indication of the means of supplying it; and up to this time it has been nothing else. The legists—with mechanical fidelity, full of obstinacy, enemies of philosophy, buried in literalities—have always mistaken for the last word of science that which was only the inconsiderate aspiration of men who, to be sure, were well-meaning, but wanting in foresight.

They did not foresee, these old founders of the domain of property, that the perpetual and absolute right to retain one's estate,—a right which seemed to them equitable, because it was common,—involves the right to transfer, sell, give, gain, and lose it; that it tends, consequently, to nothing less than the destruction of that equality which they established it to maintain. And though they should have foreseen it, they disregarded it; the present want occupied their whole attention, and, as ordinarily happens in such cases, the disadvantages were at first scarcely perceptible, and they passed unnoticed.

They did not foresee, these ingenuous legislators, that if property is retainable by intent alone—*nudo animo*—it carries with it the right to let, to lease, to loan at interest, to profit by exchange, to settle annuities, and to levy a tax on a field which intent reserves, while the body is busy elsewhere.

They did not foresee, these fathers of our jurisprudence, that, if the right of inheritance is any thing other than Nature's method of preserving equality of wealth, families will soon become victims of the most disastrous exclusions; and society, pierced to the heart by one of its most sacred principles, will come to its death through opulence and misery. 12

Under whatever form of government we live, it can always be said that *le mort saisit le vif;* that is, that inheritance and succession will last for ever, whoever may be the recognized heir. But the St. Simonians wish the heir to be designated by the magistrate; others wish him to be chosen by the deceased, or assumed by the law to be so chosen: the essential point is that Nature's wish be satisfied, so far as the law of equality allows.

To-day the real controller of inheritance is chance or caprice; now, in matters of legislation, chance and caprice cannot be accepted as guides. It is for the purpose of avoiding the manifold disturbances which follow in the wake of chance that Nature, after having created us equal, suggests to us the principle of heredity; which serves as a voice by which society asks us to choose, from among all our brothers, him whom we judge best fitted to complete our unfinished work.

They did not foresee.... But why need I go farther?

The consequences are plain enough, and this is not the time to criticise the whole Code.

The history of property among the ancient nations is, then, simply a matter of research and curiosity. It is a rule of jurisprudence that the fact does not substantiate the right. Now, property is no exception to this rule: then the universal recognition of the right of property does not legitimate the right of property. Man is mistaken as to the constitution of society, the nature of right, and the application of justice; just as he was mistaken regarding the cause of meteors and the movement of the heavenly bodies. His old opinions cannot be taken for articles of faith. Of what consequence is it to us that the Indian race was divided into four classes; that, on the banks of the Nile and the Ganges, blood and position formerly determined the distribution of the land; that the Greeks and Romans placed property under the protection of the gods; that they accompanied with religious ceremonies the work of partitioning the land and appraising their goods? The variety of the forms of privilege does not sanction injustice. The faith of Jupiter, the proprietor, 13 proves no more against the equality of citizens, than do the mysteries of Venus, the wanton, against conjugal chastity.

The authority of the human race is of no effect as evidence in favor of the right of property, because this right, resting of necessity upon equality, contradicts its principle; the decision of the religions which have sanctioned it is of no effect, because in all ages the priest has submitted to the prince, and the gods have always spoken as the politicians desired; the social advantages, attributed to property, cannot be cited in its behalf, because they all spring from the principle of equality of possession.

What means, then, this dithyramb upon property?

"The right of property is the most important of human institutions."...

Yes; as monarchy is the most glorious.

"The original cause of man's prosperity upon earth."

Because justice was supposed to be its principle.

"Property became the legitimate end of his ambition, the hope of his existence, the shelter of his family; in a word, the corner-stone of the domestic dwelling, of communities, and of the political State."

Possession alone produced all that.

"Eternal principle,—"

Property is eternal, like every negation,—

"Of all social and civil institutions."

For that reason, every institution and every law based on property will perish.

"It is a boon as precious as liberty."

For the rich proprietor.

"In fact, the cause of the cultivation of the habitable earth."

If the cultivator ceased to be a tenant, would the land be worse cared for?

"The guarantee and the morality of labor."

Under the regime of property, labor is not a condition, but a privilege.

"The application of justice."

What is justice without equality of fortunes? A balance with false weights.

"All morality,—"

A famished stomach knows no morality,—

"All public order,—"

Certainly, the preservation of property,—

"Rest on the right of property." 14

Corner-stone of all which is, stumbling-block of all which ought to be,—such is property.

To sum up and conclude:—

Not only does occupation lead to equality, it PREVENTS property. For, since every man, from the fact of his existence, has the right of occupation, and, in order to live, must have material for cultivation on which he may labor; and since, on the other hand, the number of occupants varies continually with the births and deaths,—it follows that the quantity of material which each laborer may claim varies with the number of occupants; consequently, that occupation is always subordinate to population. Finally, that, inasmuch as possession, in right, can never remain fixed, it is impossible, in fact, that it can ever become property.

Every occupant is, then, necessarily a possessor or usufructuary,—a function which excludes proprietorship. Now, this is the right of the usufructuary: he is responsible for the thing entrusted to him; he must use it in conformity with general utility, with a view to its preservation and development; he has no power to transform it, to diminish it, or to change its nature; he cannot so divide the usufruct that another shall perform the labor while he receives the product. In a word, the usufructuary is under the supervision of society, submitted to the condition of labor and the law of equality.

Thus is annihilated the Roman definition of property—THE RIGHT OF USE AND ABUSE—an immorality born of violence, the most monstrous pretension that the civil laws ever sanctioned. Man receives his usufruct from the hands of society, which alone is the permanent possessor. The individual passes away, society is deathless.

What a profound disgust fills my soul while discussing such simple truths! Do we doubt these things to-day? Will it be necessary to again take arms for their triumph? And can force, in default of reason, alone introduce them into our laws?

ALL HAVE AN EQUAL RIGHT OF OCCUPANCY.

THE AMOUNT OCCUPIED BEING MEASURED, NOT BY THE WILL, BUT BY THE VARIABLE CONDITIONS OF SPACE AND NUMBER, PROPERTY CANNOT EXIST.

This no code has ever expressed; this no constitution can admit! These are axioms which the civil law and the law of nations deny!.....

But I hear the exclamations of the partisans of another system: "Labor, labor! that is the basis of property!"

Reader, do not be deceived. This new basis of property is worse than the first, and I shall soon have to ask your pardon for having demonstrated things clearer, and refuted pretensions more unjust, than any which we have yet considered.

CHAPTER III. LABOR AS THE EFFICIENT CAUSE OF THE DOMAIN OF PROPERTY.

Nearly all the modern writers on jurisprudence, taking their cue from the economists, have abandoned the theory of first occupancy as a too dangerous one, and have adopted that which regards property as born of labor. In this they are deluded; they reason in a circle. To labor it is necessary to occupy, says M. Cousin.

Consequently, I have added in my turn, all having an equal right of occupancy, to labor it is necessary to submit to equality. "The rich," exclaims Jean Jacques, "have the arrogance to say, 'I built this wall; I earned this land by my labor.' Who set you the tasks? we may reply, and by what right do you demand payment from us for labor which we did not impose upon you?" All sophistry falls to the ground in the presence of this argument.

But the partisans of labor do not see that their system is an absolute contradiction of the Code, all the articles and provisions of which suppose property to be based upon the fact of first occupancy. If labor, through the appropriation which results from it, alone gives birth to property, the Civil Code lies, the charter is a falsehood, our whole social system is a violation of right. To this conclusion shall we come, at the end of the discussion which is to occupy our attention in this chapter and the following one, both as to the right of labor and the fact of property. We shall see, on the one hand, our legislation in opposition to itself; and, on the other hand, our new jurisprudence in opposition both to its own principle and to our legislation.

I have asserted that the system which bases property upon labor implies, no less than that which bases it upon occupation, the equality of fortunes; and the reader must be impatient to learn how I propose to deduce this law of equality from the inequality of skill and faculties: directly his curiosity shall be satisfied. But it is proper that I should call his attention for a moment to this remarkable feature of the process; to wit, the substitution of labor for occupation as the principle of property; and that I should pass rapidly in review some of the prejudices to which proprietors are accustomed to appeal, which legislation has sanctioned, and which the system of labor completely overthrows.

Reader, were you ever present at the examination of a criminal? Have you watched his tricks, his turns, his evasions, his distinctions, his equivocations? Beaten, all his assertions overthrown, pursued like a fallow deer by the inexorable judge, tracked from hypothesis to hypothesis,—he makes a statement, he corrects it, retracts it, contradicts it, he exhausts all the tricks of dialectics, more subtle, more ingenious a thousand times than he who invented the seventy-two forms of the syllogism. So acts the proprietor when called upon to defend his right. At first he refuses to reply, he exclaims, he threatens, he defies; then, forced to accept the discussion, he arms himself with chicanery, he surrounds himself with formidable artillery,—crossing his fire, opposing one by one and all together occupation, possession, limitation, covenants, immemorial custom, and universal consent. Conquered on this ground, the proprietor, like a wounded boar, turns on his pursuers. "I have done more than occupy," he cries with terrible emotion; "I have labored, produced, improved, transformed, CREATED. This house, these fields, these trees are the work of my hands; I changed these brambles into a vineyard, and this bush into a fig-tree; and to-day I reap the harvest of my labors. I have enriched the soil with my sweat; I have paid those men who, had they not had the work which I gave them, would have died of hunger. No one shared with me the trouble and expense; no one shall share with me the benefits."

You have labored, proprietor! why then do you speak of original occupancy? What, were you not sure of your right, or did you hope to deceive men, and make justice an illusion? Make haste, then, to acquaint us with your mode of defence, for the judgment will be final; and you know it to be a question of restitution.

You have labored! but what is there in common between the labor which duty compels you to perform, and the appropriation of things in which there is a common interest? Do you not know that domain over the soil, like that over air and light, cannot be lost by prescription?

You have labored! have you never made others labor? Why, then, have they lost in laboring for you what you have gained in not laboring for them?

You have labored! very well; but let us see the results of your labor. We will count, weigh, and measure them. It will be the judgment of Balthasar; for I swear by balance, level, and square, that if you have appropriated another's labor in any way whatsoever, you shall restore it every stroke.

Thus, the principle of occupation is abandoned; no longer is it said, "The land belongs to him who first gets possession of it." Property, forced into its first intrenchment, repudiates its old adage; justice, ashamed, retracts her maxims, and sorrow lowers her bandage over her blushing cheeks. And it was but yesterday that this progress in social philosophy began: fifty centuries required for the extirpation of a lie! During this lamentable period, how many usurpations have been sanctioned, how many invasions glorified, how many conquests celebrated! The absent dispossessed, the poor banished, the hungry excluded by wealth, which is so ready and bold in action! Jealousies and wars, incendiarism and bloodshed, among the nations! But henceforth, thanks to the age and its spirit, it is to be admitted that the earth is not a prize to be won in a race; in the absence of any other obstacle, there is a place for everybody under the sun. Each one may harness his goat to the bearn, drive his cattle to pasture, sow a corner of a field, and bake his bread by his own fireside.

But, no; each one cannot do these things. I hear it proclaimed on all sides, "Glory to labor and industry! to each according to his capacity; to each capacity according to its results!" And I see three-fourths of the human race again despoiled, the labor of a few being a scourge to the labor of the rest.

"The problem is solved," exclaims M. Hennequin. "Property, the daughter of labor, can be enjoyed at present and in the future only under the protection of the laws. It has its origin in natural law; it derives its power from civil law; and from the union of these two ideas, LABOR and PROTECTION, positive legislation results."...

Ah! THE PROBLEM IS SOLVED! PROPERTY IS THE DAUGHTER OF LABOR! What, then, is the right of accession, and the right of succession, and the right of donation, &c., if not the right to become a proprietor by simple occupancy? What are your laws concerning the age of majority, emancipation, guardianship, and interdiction, if not the various conditions by which he who is already a laborer gains or loses the right of occupancy; that is, property?

Being unable, at this time, to enter upon a detailed discussion of the Code, I shall content myself with examining the three arguments oftenest resorted to in support of property. 1. APPROPRIATION, or the formation of property by possession; 2. THE CONSENT OF MANKIND; 3. PRESCRIPTION. I shall then inquire into the effects of labor upon the relative condition of the laborers and upon property.

% 1.—The Land cannot be Appropriated.

"It would seem that lands capable of cultivation ought to be regarded as natural wealth, since they are not of human creation, but Nature's gratuitous gift to man; but inasmuch as this wealth is not fugitive, like the air and water,—inasmuch as a field is a fixed and limited space which certain men have been able to appropriate, to the exclusion of all others who in their turn have consented to this appropriation,—the land, which was a natural and gratuitous gift, has become social wealth, for the use of which we ought to pay."—SAY: POLITICAL ECONOMY.

Was I wrong in saying, at the beginning of this chapter, that the economists are the very worst authorities in matters of legislation and philosophy? It is the FATHER of this class of men who clearly states the question, How can the supplies of Nature, the wealth created by Providence, become private property? and who replies by so gross an equivocation that we scarcely know which the author lacks, sense or honesty. What, I ask, has the fixed and solid nature of the earth to do with the right of appropriation? I can understand that a thing LIMITED and STATIONARY, like the land, offers greater chances for appropriation than the water or the sunshine; that it is easier to exercise the right of domain over the soil than over the atmosphere: but we are not dealing with the difficulty of the thing, and Say confounds the right with the possibility. We do not ask why the earth has been appropriated to a greater extent than the sea and the air; we want to know by what right man has appropriated wealth WHICH HE DID NOT CREATE, AND WHICH NATURE GAVE TO HIM GRATUITOUSLY.

Say, then, did not solve the question which he asked. But if he had solved it, if the explanation which he has given us were as satisfactory as it is illogical, we should know no better than before who has a right to exact payment for the use of the soil, of this wealth which is not man's handiwork. Who is entitled to the rent of the land? The producer of the land, without doubt. Who made the land? God. Then, proprietor, retire!

But the creator of the land does not sell it: he gives it; and, in giving it, he is no respecter of persons. Why, then, are some of his children regarded as legitimate, while others are treated as bastards? If the equality of shares was an original right, why is the inequality of conditions a posthumous right?

Say gives us to understand that if the air and the water were not of a FUGITIVE nature, they would have been appropriated. Let me observe in passing that this is more than an hypothesis; it is a reality. Men have appropriated the air and the water, I will not say as often as they could, but as often as they have been allowed to.

The Portuguese, having discovered the route to India by the Cape of Good Hope, pretended to have the sole right to that route; and Grotius, consulted in regard to this matter by the Dutch who refused to recognize this right, wrote expressly for this occasion his treatise on the "Freedom of the Seas," to prove that the sea is not liable to appropriation.

The right to hunt and fish used always to be confined to lords and proprietors; to-day it is leased by the government and communes to whoever can pay the license-fee and the rent. To regulate hunting and fishing is an excellent idea, but to make it a subject of sale is to create a monopoly of air and water.

What is a passport? A universal recommendation of the traveller's person; a certificate of security for himself and his property. The treasury, whose nature it is to spoil the best things, has made the passport a means of espionage and a tax. Is not this a sale of the right to travel?

Finally, it is permissible neither to draw water from a spring situated in another's grounds without the permission of the proprietor, because by the right of accession the spring belongs to the possessor of the soil, if there is no other claim; nor to pass a day on his premises without paying a tax; nor to look at a court, a garden, or an orchard, without the consent of the proprietor; nor to stroll in a park or an enclosure against the owner's will: every one is allowed to shut himself up and to fence himself in. All these prohibitions are so many positive interdictions, not only of the land, but of the air and water. We who belong to the proletaire class: property excommunicates us! *Terra, et aqua, et aere, et igne interdicti sumus.*

Men could not appropriate the most fixed of all the elements without appropriating the three others; since, by French and Roman law, property in the surface carries with it property from zenith to nadir—*Cujus est solum, ejus est usque ad caelum.* Now, if the use of water, air, and fire excludes property, so does the use of the soil. This chain of reasoning seems to have been presented by M. Ch. Comte, in his "Treatise on Property," chap. 5.

"If a man should be deprived of air for a few moments only, he would cease to exist, and a partial deprivation would cause him severe suffering; a partial or complete deprivation of food would produce like effects upon him though less suddenly; it would be the same, at least in certain climates! were he deprived of all clothing and shelter.... To sustain life, then, man needs continually to appropriate many different things. But these things do not exist in like proportions. Some, such as the light of the stars, the atmosphere of the earth, the water composing the seas and oceans, exist in such large quantities that men cannot perceive any sensible increase or diminution; each one can appropriate as much as his needs require without detracting from the enjoyment of others, without causing them the least harm. Things of this sort are, so to speak, the common property of the human race; the only duty imposed upon each individual in this regard is that of infringing not at all upon the rights of others."

Let us complete the argument of M. Ch. Comte. A man who should be prohibited from walking in the highways, from resting in the fields, from taking shelter in caves, from lighting fires, from picking berries, from gathering herbs and boiling them in a bit of baked clay,—such a man could not live. Consequently the earth—like water, air, and light—is a primary object of necessity which each has a right to use freely, without infringing another's right. Why, then, is the earth appropriated? M. Ch. Comte's reply is a curious one. Say pretends that it is because it is not FUGITIVE; M. Ch. Comte assures us that it is because it is not INFINITE. The land is limited in amount. Then, according to M. Ch. Comte, it ought to be appropriated. It would seem, on the contrary, that he ought to say, Then it ought not to be appropriated. Because, no matter how large a quantity of air or light any one appropriates, no one is damaged thereby; there always remains enough for all. With the soil, it is very different. Lay hold who will, or who can, of the sun's rays, the passing breeze, or the sea's billows; he has my consent, and my pardon for his bad intentions. But let any living man dare to change his right of territorial possession into the right of property, and I will declare war upon him, and wage it to the death!

M. Ch. Comte's argument disproves his position. "Among the things necessary to the preservation of life," he says, "there are some which exist in such large quantities that they are inexhaustible; others which exist in lesser quantities, and can satisfy the wants of only a certain number of persons. The former are called COMMON, the latter PRIVATE."

This reasoning is not strictly logical. Water, air, and light are COMMON things, not because they are INEXHAUSTIBLE, but because they are INDISPENSABLE; and so indispensable that for that very reason Nature has created them in quantities almost infinite, in order that their plentifulness might prevent their appropriation. Likewise the land is indispensable to our existence,—consequently a common thing, consequently insusceptible of appropriation; but land is much scarcer than the other elements, therefore its use must be regulated, not for the profit of a few, but in the interest and for the security of all.

In a word, equality of rights is proved by equality of needs. Now, equality of rights, in the case of a commodity which is limited in amount, can be realized only by equality of possession. An agrarian law underlies M. Ch. Comte's arguments.

From whatever point we view this question of property—provided we go to the bottom of it—we reach equality. I will not insist farther on the distinction between things which can, and things which cannot, be appropriated. On this point, economists and legists talk worse than nonsense. The Civil Code, after having defined property, says nothing about susceptibility of appropriation; and if it speaks of things which are in THE MARKET, it always does so without enumerating or describing them. However, light is not wanting. There are some few maxims such as these: *Ad reges potestas omnium pertinet, ad singulos proprietas; Omnia rex imperio possidet, singula dominio.* Social sovereignty opposed to private property!—might not that be called a prophecy of equality, a republican oracle? Examples crowd upon us: once the possessions of the church, the estates of the crown, the fiefs of the nobility were inalienable and imprescriptible. If, instead of abolishing this privilege, the Constituent had extended it to every individual; if it had declared that the right of labor, like liberty, can never be forfeited,—at that moment the revolution would have been consummated, and we could now devote ourselves to improvement in other directions.

% 2.—Universal Consent no Justification of Property.

In the extract from Say, quoted above, it is not clear whether the author means to base the right of property on the stationary character of the soil, or on the consent which he thinks all men have granted to this appropriation. His language is such that it may mean either of these things, or both at once; which entitles us to assume that the author intended to say, "The right of property resulting originally from the exercise of the will, the stability of the soil permitted it to be applied to the land, and universal consent has since sanctioned this application."

However that may be, can men legitimate property by mutual consent? I say, no. Such a contract, though drafted by Grotius, Montesquieu, and J. J. Rousseau, though signed by the whole human race, would be null in the eyes of justice, and an act to enforce it would be illegal. Man can no more give up labor than liberty. Now, to recognize the right of territorial property is to give up labor, since it is to relinquish the means of labor; it is to traffic in a natural right, and divest ourselves of manhood.

But I wish that this consent, of which so much is made, had been given, either tacitly or formally. What would have been the result? Evidently, the surrenders would have been reciprocal; no right would have been abandoned without the receipt of an equivalent in exchange. We thus come back to equality again,—the sine qua non of appropriation; so that, after having justified property by universal consent, that is, by equality, we are obliged to justify the inequality of conditions by property. Never shall we extricate ourselves from this dilemma. Indeed, if, in the terms of the social compact, property has equality for its condition, at the moment when equality ceases to exist, the compact is broken and all property becomes usurpation. We gain nothing, then, by this pretended consent of mankind.

% 3.—Prescription Gives No Title to Property.

The right of property was the origin of evil on the earth, the first link in the long chain of crimes and misfortunes which the human race has endured since its birth. The delusion of prescription is the fatal charm thrown over the intellect, the death sentence breathed into the conscience, to arrest man's progress towards truth, and bolster up the worship of error.

The Code defines prescription thus: "The process of gaining and losing through the lapse of time." In applying this definition to ideas and beliefs, we may use the word PRESCRIPTION to denote the everlasting prejudice in favor of old superstitions, whatever be their object; the opposition, often furious and bloody, with which new light has always been received, and which makes the sage a martyr. Not a principle, not a discovery, not a generous thought but has met, at its entrance into the world, with a formidable barrier of preconceived opinions, seeming like a conspiracy of all old prejudices. Prescriptions against reason, prescriptions against facts, prescriptions against every truth hitherto unknown,—that is the sum and substance of the *statu quo* philosophy, the watchword of conservatives throughout the centuries.

When the evangelical reform was broached to the world, there was prescription in favor of violence, debauchery, and selfishness; when Galileo, Descartes, Pascal, and their disciples reconstructed philosophy and the sciences, there was prescription in favor of the Aristotelian philosophy; when our fathers of '89 demanded liberty and equality, there was prescription in favor of tyranny and privilege. "There always have been proprietors and there always will be:" it is with this profound utterance, the final effort of selfishness dying in its last ditch, that the friends of social inequality hope to repel the attacks of their adversaries; thinking undoubtedly that ideas, like property, can be lost by prescription.

Enlightened to-day by the triumphal march of science, taught by the most glorious successes to question our own opinions, we receive with favor and applause the observer of Nature, who, by a thousand experiments based upon the most profound analysis, pursues a new principle, a law hitherto that abler men than ourselves lived in former days, who did not notice the same phenomena, nor grasp the same analogies. Why do we not preserve a like attitude towards political and philosophical questions? Why this ridiculous mania for affirming that every thing has been said, which means that we know all about mental and moral science? Why is the proverb, THERE IS NOTHING NEW UNDER THE SUN, applied exclusively to metaphysical investigations?

Because we still study philosophy with the imagination, instead of by observation and method; because fancy and will are universally regarded as judges, in the place of arguments and facts,—it has been impossible to this day to distinguish the charlatan from the philosopher, the savant from the impostor. Since the days of Solomon and Pythagoras, imagination has been exhausted in guessing out social and psychological laws; all systems have been proposed. Looked at in this light, it is probably true that EVERY THING HAS BEEN SAID; but it is no less true that EVERY THING REMAINS TO BE PROVED. In politics (to take only this branch of philosophy), in politics every one is governed in his choice of party by his passion and his interests; the mind is submitted to the impositions of the will,—there is no knowledge, there is not even a shadow of certainty. In this way, general ignorance produces general tyranny; and while liberty of thought is written in the charter, slavery of thought, under the name of MAJORITY RULE, is decreed by the charter.

In order to confine myself to the civil prescription of which the Code speaks, I shall refrain from beginning a discussion upon this worn-out objection brought forward by proprietors; it would be too tiresome and declamatory. Everybody knows that there are rights which cannot be prescribed; and, as for those things which can be gained through the lapse of time, no one is ignorant of the fact that prescription requires certain conditions, the omission of one of which renders it null. If it is true, for example, that the proprietor's possession has been CIVIL, PUBLIC, PEACEABLE, and UNINTERRUPTED, it is none the less true that it is not based on a just title; since the only titles which it can show—occupation and labor—prove as much for the proletaire who demands, as for the proprietor who defends. Further, this possession is DISHONEST, since it is founded on a violation of right, which prevents prescription, according to the saying of St. Paul—*Nunquam in usucapionibus juris error possessori prodest.* The violation of right lies either in the fact that the holder possesses as proprietor, while he should possess only as usufructuary; or in the fact that he has purchased a thing which no one had a right to transfer or sell.

Another reason why prescription cannot be adduced in favor of property (a reason borrowed from jurisprudence) is that the right to possess real estate is a part of a universal right which has never been totally destroyed even at the most critical periods; and the proletaire, in order to regain the power to exercise it fully, has only to prove that he has always exercised it in part.

He, for example, who has the universal right to possess, give, exchange, loan, let, sell, transform, or destroy a thing, preserves the integrity of this right by the sole act of loaning, though he has never shown his authority in any other manner. Likewise we shall see that EQUALITY OF POSSESSIONS, EQUALITY OF RIGHTS, LIBERTY, WILL, PERSONALITY, are so many identical expressions of one and the same idea,—the RIGHT OF PRESERVATION and DEVELOPMENT; in a word, the right of life, against which there can be no prescription until the human race has vanished from the face of the earth.

Finally, as to the time required for prescription, it would be superfluous to show that the right of property in general cannot be acquired by simple possession for ten, twenty, a hundred, a thousand, or one hundred thousand years; and that, so long as there exists a human head capable of understanding and combating the right of property, this right will never be prescribed. For principles of jurisprudence and axioms of reason are different from accidental and contingent facts. One man's possession can prescribe against another man's possession; but just as the possessor cannot prescribe against himself, so reason has always the faculty of change and reformation. Past error is not binding on the future. Reason is always the same eternal force. The institution of property, the work of ignorant reason, may be abrogated by a more enlightened reason. Consequently, property cannot be established by prescription. This is so certain and so true, that on it rests the maxim that in the matter of prescription a violation of right goes for nothing.

But I should be recreant to my method, and the reader would have the right to accuse me of charlatanism and bad faith, if I had nothing further to advance concerning prescription. I showed, in the first place, that appropriation of land is illegal; and that, supposing it to be legal, it must be accompanied by equality of property. I have shown, in the second place, that universal consent proves nothing in favor of property; and that, if it proves any thing, it proves equality of property. I have yet to show that prescription, if admissible at all, presupposes equality of property.

This demonstration will be neither long nor difficult. I need only to call attention to the reasons why prescription was introduced.

"Prescription," says Dunod, "seems repugnant to natural equity, which permits no one either to deprive another of his possessions without his knowledge and consent, or to enrich himself at another's expense. But as it might often happen, in the absence of prescription, that one who had honestly earned would be ousted after long possession; and even that he who had received a thing from its rightful owner, or who had been legitimately relieved from all obligations, would, on losing his title, be liable to be dispossessed or subjected again,—the public welfare demanded that a term should be fixed, after the expiration of which no one should be allowed to disturb actual possessors, or reassert rights too long neglected.... The civil law, in regulating prescription, has aimed, then, only to perfect natural law, and to supplement the law of nations; and as it is founded on the public good, which should always be considered before individual welfare,—*bono publico usucapio introducta est*, —it should be regarded with favor, provided the conditions required by the law are fulfilled."

Toullier, in his "Civil Law," says: "In order that the question of proprietorship may not remain too long unsettled, and thereby injure the public welfare, disturbing the peace of families and the stability of social transactions, the law has fixed a time when all claims shall be cancelled, and possession shall regain its ancient prerogative through its transformation into property."

Cassiodorus said of property, that it was the only safe harbor in which to seek shelter from the tempests of chicanery and the gales of avarice—*Hic unus inter humanas pro cellas portus, quem si homines fervida voluntate praeterierint; in undosis semper jurgiis errabunt.*

Thus, in the opinion of the authors, prescription is a means of preserving public order; a restoration in certain cases of the original mode of acquiring property; a fiction of the civil law which derives all its force from the necessity of settling differences which otherwise would never end. For, as Grotius says, time has no power to produce effects; all things happen in time, but nothing is done by time. Prescription, or the right of acquisition through the lapse of time, is, therefore, a fiction of the law, conventionally adopted.

But all property necessarily originated in prescription, or, as the Latins say, in *usucapion;* that is, in continued possession.

I ask, then, in the first place, how possession can become property by the lapse of time? Continue possession as long as you wish, continue it for years and for centuries, you never can give duration—which of itself creates nothing, changes nothing, modifies nothing—the power to change the usufructuary into a proprietor. Let the civil law secure against chance-comers the honest possessor who has held his position for many years,—that only confirms a right already respected; and prescription, applied in this way, simply means that possession which has continued for twenty, thirty, or a hundred years shall be retained by the occupant. But when the law declares that the lapse of time changes possessor into proprietor, it supposes that a right can be created without a producing cause; it unwarrantably alters the character of the subject; it legislates on a matter not open to legislation; it exceeds its own powers. Public order and private security ask only that possession shall be protected. Why has the law created property? Prescription was simply security for the future; why has the law made it a matter of privilege?

Thus the origin of prescription is identical with that of property itself, and since the latter can legitimate itself only when accompanied by equality, prescription is but another of the thousand forms which the necessity of maintaining this precious equality has taken. And this is no vain induction, no far-fetched inference. The proof is written in all the codes.

And, indeed, if all nations, through their instinct of justice and their conservative nature, have recognized the utility and the necessity of prescription; and if their design has been to guard thereby the interests of the possessor,—could they not do something for the absent citizen, separated from his family and his country by commerce, war, or captivity, and in no position to exercise his right of possession? No. Also, at the same time that prescription was introduced into the laws, it was admitted that property is preserved by intent alone,—*nudo animo*. Now, if property is preserved by intent alone, if it can be lost only by the action of the proprietor, what can be the use of prescription? How does the law dare to presume that the proprietor, who preserves by intent alone, intended to abandon that which he has allowed to be prescribed? What lapse of time can warrant such a conjecture; and by what right does the law punish the absence of the proprietor by depriving him of his goods? What then! we found but a moment since that prescription and property were identical; and now we find that they are mutually destructive!

Grotius, who perceived this difficulty, replied so singularly that his words deserve to be quoted: *Bene sperandum de hominibus, ac propterea non putandum eos hoc esse animo ut, rei caducae causa, hominem alterum velint in perpetuo peccato versari, quod evitari saepe non poterit sine tali derelictione.*

"Where is the man," he says, "with so unchristian a soul that, for a trifle, he would perpetuate the trespass of a possessor, which would inevitably be the result if he did not consent to abandon his right?" By the Eternal! I am that man. Though a million proprietors should burn for it in hell, I lay the blame on them for depriving me of my portion of this world's goods. To this powerful consideration Grotius rejoins, that it is better to abandon a disputed right than to go to law, disturb the peace of nations, and stir up the flames of civil war. I accept, if you wish it, this argument, provided you indemnify me. But if this indemnity is refused me, what do I, a proletaire, care for the tranquillity and security of the rich? I care as little for PUBLIC ORDER as for the proprietor's safety. I ask to live a laborer; otherwise I will die a warrior.

Whichever way we turn, we shall come to the conclusion that prescription is a contradiction of property; or rather that prescription and property are two forms of the same principle, but two forms which serve to correct each other; and ancient and modern jurisprudence did not make the least of its blunders in pretending to reconcile them. Indeed, if we see in the institution of property only a desire to secure to each individual his share of the soil and his right to labor; in the distinction between naked property and possession only an asylum for absentees, orphans, and all who do not know, or cannot maintain, their rights; in prescription only a means, either of defence against unjust pretensions and encroachments, or of settlement of the differences caused by the removal of possessors,—we shall recognize in these various forms of human justice the spontaneous efforts of the mind to come to the aid of the social instinct; we shall see in this protection of all rights the sentiment of equality, a constant levelling tendency. And, looking deeper, we shall find in the very exaggeration of these principles the confirmation of our doctrine; because, if equality of conditions and universal association are not soon realized, it will be owing to the obstacle thrown for the time in the way of the common sense of the people by the stupidity of legislators and judges; and also to the fact that, while society in its original state was illuminated with a flash of truth, the early speculations of its leaders could bring forth nothing but darkness.

After the first covenants, after the first draughts of laws and constitutions, which were the expression of man's primary needs, the legislator's duty was to reform the errors of legislation; to complete that which was defective; to harmonize, by superior definitions, those things which seemed to conflict. Instead of that, they halted at the literal meaning of the laws, content to play the subordinate part of commentators and scholiasts. Taking the inspirations of the human mind, at that time necessarily weak and faulty, for axioms of eternal and unquestionable truth,—influenced by public opinion, enslaved by the popular religion,—they have invariably started with the principle (following in this respect the example of the theologians) that that is infallibly true which has been admitted by all persons, in all places, and at all times—*quod ab omnibus, quod ubique, quod semper;* as if a general but spontaneous opinion was any thing more than an indication of the truth. Let us not be deceived: the opinion of all nations may serve to authenticate the perception of a fact, the vague sentiment of a law; it can teach us nothing about either fact or law. The consent of mankind is an indication of Nature; not, as Cicero says, a law of Nature. Under the indication is hidden the truth, which faith can believe, but only thought can know. Such has been the constant progress of the human mind in regard to physical phenomena and the creations of genius: how can it be otherwise with the facts of conscience and the rules of human conduct?

% 4.—Labor—That Labor Has No Inherent Power to Appropriate Natural Wealth.

We shall show by the maxims of political economy and law, that is, by the authorities recognized by property,—

1. That labor has no inherent power to appropriate natural wealth.

2. That, if we admit that labor has this power, we are led directly to equality of property,—whatever the kind of labor, however scarce the product, or unequal the ability of the laborers.

3. That, in the order of justice, labor DESTROYS property.

Following the example of our opponents, and that we may leave no obstacles in the path, let us examine the question in the strongest possible light.

M. Ch. Comte says, in his "Treatise on Property:"—

"France, considered as a nation, has a territory which is her own."

France, as an individuality, possesses a territory which she cultivates; it is not her property. Nations are related to each other as individuals are: they are commoners and workers; it is an abuse of language to call them proprietors. The right of use and abuse belongs no more to nations than to men; and the time will come when a war waged for the purpose of checking a nation in its abuse of the soil will be regarded as a holy war.

Thus, M. Ch. Comte—who undertakes to explain how property comes into existence, and who starts with the supposition that a nation is a proprietor—falls into that error known as BEGGING THE QUESTION; a mistake which vitiates his whole argument.

If the reader thinks it is pushing logic too far to question a nation's right of property in the territory which it possesses, I will simply remind him of the fact that at all ages the results of the fictitious right of national property have been pretensions to suzerainty, tributes, monarchical privileges, statute-labor, quotas of men and money, supplies of merchandise, &c.; ending finally in refusals to pay taxes, insurrections, wars, and depopulations.

"Scattered through this territory are extended tracts of land, which have not been converted into individual property. These lands, which consist mainly of forests, belong to the whole population, and the government, which receives the revenues, uses or ought to use them in the interest of all."

OUGHT TO USE is well said: a lie is avoided thereby.

"Let them be offered for sale...."

Why offered for sale? Who has a right to sell them? Even were the nation proprietor, can the generation of to-day dispossess the generation of to-morrow? The nation, in its function of usufructuary, possesses them; the government rules, superintends, and protects them. If it also granted lands, it could grant only their use; it has no right to sell them or transfer them in any way whatever. Not being a proprietor, how can it transmit property?

"Suppose some industrious man buys a portion, a large swamp for example. This would be no usurpation, since the public would receive the exact value through the hands of the government, and would be as rich after the sale as before."

How ridiculous! What! because a prodigal, imprudent, incompetent official sells the State's possessions, while I, a ward of the State,—I who have neither an advisory nor a deliberative voice in the State councils,—while I am allowed to make no opposition to the sale, this sale is right and legal! The guardians of the nation waste its substance, and it has no redress! I have received, you tell me, through the hands of the government my share of the proceeds of the sale: but, in the first place, I did not wish to sell; and, had I wished to, I could not have sold. I had not the right. And then I do not see that I am benefited by the sale. My guardians have dressed up some soldiers, repaired an old fortress, erected in their pride some costly but worthless monument,—then they have exploded some fireworks and set up a greased pole! What does all that amount to in comparison with my loss?

The purchaser draws boundaries, fences himself in, and says, "This is mine; each one by himself, each one for himself." Here, then, is a piece of land upon which, henceforth, no one has a right to step, save the proprietor and his friends; which can benefit nobody, save the proprietor and his servants. Let these sales multiply, and soon the people—who have been neither able nor willing to sell, and who have received none of the proceeds of the sale—will have nowhere to rest, no place of shelter, no ground to till. They will die of hunger at the proprietor's door, on the edge of that property which was their birthright; and the proprietor, watching them die, will exclaim, "So perish idlers and vagrants!"

To reconcile us to the proprietor's usurpation, M. Ch. Comte assumes the lands to be of little value at the time of sale.

"The importance of these usurpations should not be exaggerated: they should be measured by the number of men which the occupied land would support, and by the means which it would furnish them.

"It is evident, for instance, that if a piece of land which is worth to-day one thousand francs was worth only five centimes when it was usurped, we really lose only the value of five centimes. A square league of earth would be hardly sufficient to support a savage in distress; to-day it supplies one thousand persons with the means of existence. Nine hundred and ninety-nine parts of this land is the legitimate property of the possessors; only one-thousandth of the value has been usurped."

A peasant admitted one day, at confession, that he had destroyed a document which declared him a debtor to the amount of three hundred francs. Said the father confessor, "You must return these three hundred francs." "No," replied the peasant, "I will return a penny to pay for the paper."

M. Ch. Comte's logic resembles this peasant's honesty. The soil has not only an integrant and actual value, it has also a potential value,—a value of the future,—which depends on our ability to make it valuable, and to employ it in our work. Destroy a bill of exchange, a promissory note, an annuity deed,—as a paper you destroy almost no value at all; but with this paper you destroy your title, and, in losing your title, you deprive yourself of your goods. Destroy the land, or, what is the same thing, sell it,—you not only transfer one, two, or several crops, but you annihilate all the products that you could derive from it; you and your children and your children's children.

When M. Ch. Comte, the apostle of property and the eulogist of labor, supposes an alienation of the soil on the part of the government, we must not think that he does so without reason and for no purpose; it is a necessary part of his position. As he rejected the theory of occupancy, and as he knew, moreover, that labor could not constitute the right in the absence of a previous permission to occupy, he was obliged to connect this permission with the authority of the government, which means that property is based upon the sovereignty of the people; in other words, upon universal consent. This theory we have already considered.

To say that property is the daughter of labor, and then to give labor material on which to exercise itself, is, if I am not mistaken, to reason in a circle. Contradictions will result from it.

"A piece of land of a certain size produces food enough to supply a man for one day. If the possessor, through his labor, discovers some method of making it produce enough for two days, he doubles its value. This new value is his work, his creation: it is taken from nobody; it is his property."

I maintain that the possessor is paid for his trouble and industry in his doubled crop, but that he acquires no right to the land. "Let the laborer have the fruits of his labor." Very good; but I do not understand that property in products carries with it property in raw material. Does the skill of the fisherman, who on the same coast can catch more fish than his fellows, make him proprietor of the fishing-grounds? Can the expertness of a hunter ever be regarded as a property-title to a game-forest? The analogy is perfect,—the industrious cultivator finds the reward of his industry in the abundancy and superiority of his crop. If he has made improvements in the soil, he has the possessor's right of preference. Never, under any circumstances, can he be allowed to claim a property-title to the soil which he cultivates, on the ground of his skill as a cultivator.

To change possession into property, something is needed besides labor, without which a man would cease to be proprietor as soon as he ceased to be a laborer. Now, the law bases property upon immemorial, unquestionable possession; that is, prescription. Labor is only the sensible sign, the physical act, by which occupation is manifested. If, then, the cultivator remains proprietor after he has ceased to labor and produce; if his possession, first conceded, then tolerated, finally becomes inalienable,—it happens by permission of the civil law, and by virtue of the principle of occupancy. So true is this, that there is not a bill of sale, not a farm lease, not an annuity, but implies it. I will quote only one example.

How do we measure the value of land? By its product. If a piece of land yields one thousand francs, we say that at five per cent. it is worth twenty thousand francs; at four per cent. twenty-five thousand francs, &c.; which means, in other words, that in twenty or twenty-five years' time the purchaser would recover in full the amount originally paid for the land. If, then, after a certain length of time, the price of a piece of land has been wholly recovered, why does the purchaser continue to be proprietor? Because of the right of occupancy, in the absence of which every sale would be a redemption.

The theory of appropriation by labor is, then, a contradiction of the Code; and when the partisans of this theory pretend to explain the laws thereby, they contradict themselves.

"If men succeed in fertilizing land hitherto unproductive, or even death-producing, like certain swamps, they create thereby property in all its completeness."

What good does it do to magnify an expression, and play with equivocations, as if we expected to change the reality thereby? THEY CREATE PROPERTY IN ALL ITS COMPLETENESS. You mean that they create a productive capacity which formerly did not exist; but this capacity cannot be created without material to support it. The substance of the soil remains the same; only its qualities and modifications are changed. Man has created every thing—every thing save the material itself. Now, I maintain that this material he can only possess and use, on condition of permanent labor,—granting, for the time being, his right of property in things which he has produced.

This, then, is the first point settled: property in product, if we grant so much, does not carry with it property in the means of production; that seems to me to need no further demonstration. There is no difference between the soldier who possesses his arms, the mason who possesses the materials committed to his care, the fisherman who possesses the water, the hunter who possesses the fields and forests, and the cultivator who possesses the lands: all, if you say so, are proprietors of their products—not one is proprietor of the means of production. The right to product is exclusive—jus in re; the right to means is common—jus ad rem.

% 5.—*That Labor leads to Equality of Property.*

Admit, however, that labor gives a right of property in material.

Why is not this principle universal? Why is the benefit of this pretended law confined to a few and denied to the mass of laborers? A philosopher, arguing that all animals sprang up formerly out of the earth warmed by the rays of the sun, almost like mushrooms, on being asked why the earth no longer yielded crops of that nature, replied: "Because it is old, and has lost its fertility." Has labor, once so fecund, likewise become sterile? Why does the tenant no longer acquire through his labor the land which was formerly acquired by the labor of the proprietor?

"Because," they say, "it is already appropriated." That is no answer. A farm yields fifty bushels per hectare; the skill and labor of the tenant double this product: the increase is created by the tenant. Suppose the owner, in a spirit of moderation rarely met with, does not go to the extent of absorbing this product by raising the rent, but allows the cultivator to enjoy the results of his labor; even then justice is not satisfied. The tenant, by improving the land, has imparted a new value to the property; he, therefore, has a right to a part of the property. If the farm was originally worth one hundred thousand francs, and if by the labor of the tenant its value has risen to one hundred and fifty thousand francs, the tenant, who produced this extra value, is the legitimate proprietor of one-third of the farm. M. Ch. Comte could not have pronounced this doctrine false, for it was he who said:—

"Men who increase the fertility of the earth are no less useful to their fellow-men, than if they should create new land."

Why, then, is not this rule applicable to the man who improves the land, as well as to him who clears it? The labor of the former makes the land worth one; that of the latter makes it worth two: both create equal values. Why not accord to both equal property? I defy any one to refute this argument, without again falling back on the right of first occupancy.

"But," it will be said, "even if your wish should be granted, property would not be distributed much more evenly than now. Land does not go on increasing in value for ever; after two or three seasons it attains its maximum fertility. That which is added by the agricultural art results rather from the progress of science and the diffusion of knowledge, than from the skill of the cultivator. Consequently, the addition of a few laborers to the mass of proprietors would be no argument against property."

This discussion would, indeed, prove a well-nigh useless one, if our labors culminated in simply extending land-privilege and industrial monopoly; in emancipating only a few hundred laborers out of the millions of proletaires. But this also is a misconception of our real thought, and does but prove the general lack of intelligence and logic.

If the laborer, who adds to the value of a thing, has a right of property in it, he who maintains this value acquires the same right. For what is maintenance? It is incessant addition,—continuous creation. What is it to cultivate? It is to give the soil its value every year; it is, by annually renewed creation, to prevent the diminution or destruction of the value of a piece of land. Admitting, then, that property is rational and legitimate,—admitting that rent is equitable and just,—I say that he who cultivates acquires property by as good a title as he who clears, or he who improves; and that every time a tenant pays his rent, he obtains a fraction of property in the land entrusted to his care, the denominator of which is equal to the proportion of rent paid. Unless you admit this, you fall into absolutism and tyranny; you recognize class privileges; you sanction slavery.

Whoever labors becomes a proprietor—this is an inevitable deduction from the acknowledged principles of political economy and jurisprudence. And when I say proprietor, I do not mean simply (as do our hypocritical economists) proprietor of his allowance, his salary, his wages,—I mean proprietor of the value which he creates, and by which the master alone profits.

As all this relates to the theory of wages and of the distribution of products,—and as this matter never has been even partially cleared up,—I ask permission to insist on it: this discussion will not be useless to the work in hand. Many persons talk of admitting working-people to a share in the products and profits; but in their minds this participation is pure benevolence: they have never shown—perhaps never suspected—that it was a natural, necessary right, inherent in labor, and inseparable from the function of producer, even in the lowest forms of his work.

This is my proposition: THE LABORER RETAINS, EVEN AFTER HE HAS RECEIVED HIS WAGES, A NATURAL RIGHT OF PROPERTY IN THE THING WHICH HE HAS PRODUCED.

I again quote M. Ch. Comte:—

"Some laborers are employed in draining marshes, in cutting down trees and brushwood,—in a word, in cleaning up the soil. They increase the value, they make the amount of property larger; they are paid for the value which they add in the form of food and daily wages: it then becomes the property of the capitalist."

The price is not sufficient: the labor of the workers has created a value; now this value is their property. But they have neither sold nor exchanged it; and you, capitalist, you have not earned it. That you should have a partial right to the whole, in return for the materials that you have furnished and the provisions that you have supplied, is perfectly just. You contributed to the production, you ought to share in the enjoyment. But your right does not annihilate that of the laborers, who, in spite of you, have been your colleagues in the work of production. Why do you talk of wages? The money with which you pay the wages of the laborers remunerates them for only a few years of the perpetual possession which they have abandoned to you. Wages is the cost of the daily maintenance and refreshment of the laborer. You are wrong in calling it the price of a sale. The workingman has sold nothing; he knows neither his right, nor the extent of the concession which he has made to you, nor the meaning of the contract which you pretend to have made with him. On his side, utter ignorance; on yours, error and surprise, not to say deceit and fraud.

Let us make this clearer by another and more striking example.

No one is ignorant of the difficulties that are met with in the conversion of untilled land into arable and productive land. These difficulties are so great, that usually an isolated man would perish before he could put the soil in a condition to yield him even the most meagre living. To that end are needed the united and combined efforts of society, and all the resources of industry. M. Ch. Comte quotes on this subject numerous and well-authenticated facts, little thinking that he is amassing testimony against his own system.

Let us suppose that a colony of twenty or thirty families establishes itself in a wild district, covered with underbrush and forests; and from which, by agreement, the natives consent to withdraw. Each one of these families possesses a moderate but sufficient amount of capital, of such a nature as a colonist would be apt to choose,—animals, seeds, tools, and a little money and food. The land having been divided, each one settles himself as comfortably as possible, and begins to clear away the portion allotted to him. But after a few weeks of fatigue, such as they never before have known, of inconceivable suffering, of ruinous and almost useless labor, our colonists begin to complain of their trade; their condition seems hard to them; they curse their sad existence.

Suddenly, one of the shrewdest among them kills a pig, cures a part of the meat; and, resolved to sacrifice the rest of his provisions, goes to find his companions in misery. "Friends," he begins in a very benevolent tone, "how much trouble it costs you to do a little work and live uncomfortably! A fortnight of labor has reduced you to your last extremity!... Let us make an arrangement by which you shall all profit. I offer you provisions and wine: you shall get so much every day; we will work together, and, zounds! my friends, we will be happy and contented!"

Would it be possible for empty stomachs to resist such an invitation? The hungriest of them follow the treacherous tempter. They go to work; the charm of society, emulation, joy, and mutual assistance double their strength; the work can be seen to advance. Singing and laughing, they subdue Nature. In a short time, the soil is thoroughly changed; the mellowed earth waits only for the seed. That done, the proprietor pays his laborers, who, on going away, return him their thanks, and grieve that the happy days which they have spent with him are over.

Others follow this example, always with the same success. Then, these installed, the rest disperse,—each one returns to his grubbing. But, while grubbing, it is necessary to live. While they have been clearing away for their neighbor, they have done no clearing for themselves. One year's seed-time and harvest is already gone. They had calculated that in lending their labor they could not but gain, since they would save their own provisions; and, while living better, would get still more money. False calculation! they have created for another the means wherewith to produce, and have created nothing for themselves. The difficulties of clearing remain the same; their clothing wears out, their provisions give out; soon their purse becomes empty for the profit of the individual for whom they have worked, and who alone can furnish the provisions which they need, since he alone is in a position to produce them. Then, when the poor grubber has exhausted his resources, the man with the provisions (like the wolf in the fable, who scents his victim from afar) again comes forward. One he offers to employ again by the day; from another he offers to buy at a favorable price a piece of his bad land, which is not, and never can be, of any use to him: that is, he uses the labor of one man to cultivate the field of another for his own benefit. So that at the end of twenty years, of thirty individuals originally equal in point of wealth, five or six have become proprietors of the whole district, while the rest have been philanthropically dispossessed!

In this century of bourgeoisie morality, in which I have had the honor to be born, the moral sense is so debased that I should not be at all surprised if I were asked, by many a worthy proprietor, what I see in this that is unjust and illegitimate? Debased creature! galvanized corpse! how can I expect to convince you, if you cannot tell robbery when I show it to you? A man, by soft and insinuating words, discovers the secret of taxing others that he may establish himself; then, once enriched by their united efforts, he refuses, on the very conditions which he himself dictated, to advance the well-being of those who made his fortune for him: and you ask laborers, that he owes them nothing more, that he has nothing to gain by putting himself at the service of others, while his own occupations claim his attention,—he refuses, I say, to aid others in getting a foothold, as he was aided in getting his own; and when, in the impotence of their isolation, these poor laborers are compelled to sell their birthright, he—this ungrateful proprietor, this knavish upstart—stands ready to put the finishing touch to their deprivation and their ruin. And you think that just? Take care!

I read in your startled countenance the reproach of a guilty conscience, much more clearly than the innocent astonishment of involuntary ignorance.

"The capitalist," they say, "has paid the laborers their DAILY WAGES." To be accurate, it must be said that the capitalist has paid as many times one day's wage as he has employed laborers each day,—which is not at all the same thing. For he has paid nothing for that immense power which results from the union and harmony of laborers, and the convergence and simultaneousness of their efforts. Two hundred grenadiers stood the obelisk of Luxor upon its base in a few hours; do you suppose that one man could have accomplished the same task in two hundred days? Nevertheless, on the books of the capitalist, the amount of wages paid would have been the same. Well, a desert to prepare for cultivation, a house to build, a factory to run,—all these are obelisks to erect, mountains to move. The smallest fortune, the most insignificant establishment, the setting in motion of the lowest industry, demand the concurrence of so many different kinds of labor and skill, that one man could not possibly execute the whole of them. It is astonishing that the economists never have called attention to this fact. Strike a balance, then, between the capitalist's receipts and his payments.

The laborer needs a salary which will enable him to live while he works; for unless he consumes, he cannot produce. Whoever employs a man owes him maintenance and support, or wages enough to procure the same. That is the first thing to be done in all production. I admit, for the moment, that in this respect the capitalist has discharged his duty.

It is necessary that the laborer should find in his production, in addition to his present support, a guarantee of his future support; otherwise the source of production would dry up, and his productive capacity would become exhausted: in other words, the labor accomplished must give birth perpetually to new labor—such is the universal law of reproduction. In this way, the proprietor of a farm finds: 1. In his crops, means, not only of supporting himself and his family, but of maintaining and improving his capital, of feeding his live-stock—in a word, means of new labor and continual reproduction; 2. In his ownership of a productive agency, a permanent basis of cultivation and labor.

But he who lends his services,—what is his basis of cultivation?

The proprietor's presumed need of him, and the unwarranted supposition that he wishes to employ him. Just as the commoner once held his land by the munificence and condescension of the lord, so to-day the working-man holds his labor by the condescension and necessities of the master and proprietor: that is what is called possession by a precarious [15] title. But this precarious condition is an injustice, for it implies an inequality in the bargain. The laborer's wages exceed but little his running expenses, and do not assure him wages for to-morrow; while the independence and security for the future.

Now, this reproductive leaven—this eternal germ of life, this preparation of the land and manufacture of implements for production—constitutes the debt of the capitalist to the producer, which he never pays; and it is this fraudulent denial which causes the poverty of the laborer, the luxury of idleness, and the inequality of conditions. This it is, above all other things, which has been so fitly named the exploitation of man by man.

One of three things must be done. Either the laborer must be given a portion of the product in addition to his wages; or the employer must render the laborer an equivalent in productive service; or else he must pledge himself to employ him for ever. Division of the product, reciprocity of service, or guarantee of perpetual labor,—from the adoption of one of these courses the capitalist cannot escape. But it is evident that he cannot satisfy the second and third of these conditions—he can neither put himself at the service of the thousands of working-men who, directly or indirectly, have aided him in establishing himself, nor employ them all for ever. He has no other course left him, then, but a division of the property. But if the property is divided, all conditions will be equal—there will be no more large capitalists or large proprietors.

Consequently, when M. Ch. Comte—following out his hypothesis—shows us his capitalist acquiring one after another the products of his employees' labor, he sinks deeper and deeper into the mire; and, as his argument does not change, our reply of course remains the same.

"Other laborers are employed in building: some quarry the stone, others transport it, others cut it, and still others put it in place. Each of them adds a certain value to the material which passes through his hands; and this value, the product of his labor, is his property. He sells it, as fast as he creates it, to the proprietor of the building, who pays him for it in food and wages."

Divide et impera—divide, and you shall command; divide, and you shall grow rich; divide, and you shall deceive men, you shall daze their minds, you shall mock at justice! Separate laborers from each other, perhaps each one's daily wage exceeds the value of each individual's product; but that is not the question under consideration. A force of one thousand men working twenty days has been paid the same wages that one would be paid for working fifty-five years; but this force of one thousand has done in twenty days what a single man could not have accomplished, though he had labored for a million centuries. Is the exchange an equitable one? Once more, no; when you have paid all the individual forces, the collective force still remains to be paid.

Consequently, there remains always a right of collective property which you have not acquired, and which you enjoy unjustly.

Admit that twenty days' wages suffice to feed, lodge, and clothe this multitude for twenty days: thrown out of employment at the end of that time, what will become of them, if, as fast as they create, they abandon their creations to the proprietors who will soon discharge them? While the proprietor, firm in his position (thanks to the aid of all the laborers), dwells in security, and fears no lack of labor or bread, the laborer's only dependence is upon the benevolence of this same proprietor, to whom he has sold and surrendered his liberty. If, then, the proprietor, shielding himself behind his comfort and his rights, refuses to employ the laborer, how can the laborer live? He has ploughed an excellent field, and cannot sow it; he has built an elegant and commodious house, and cannot live in it; he has produced all, and can enjoy nothing.

Labor leads us to equality. Every step that we take brings us nearer to it; and if laborers had equal strength, diligence, and industry, clearly their fortunes would be equal also. Indeed, if, as is pretended,—and as we have admitted,—the laborer is proprietor of the value which he creates, it follows:—

1. That the laborer acquires at the expense of the idle proprietor;
2. That all production being necessarily collective, the laborer is entitled to a share of the products and profits commensurate with his labor;
3. That all accumulated capital being social property, no one can be its exclusive proprietor.

These inferences are unavoidable; these alone would suffice to revolutionize our whole economical system, and change our institutions and our laws. Why do the very persons, who laid down this principle, now refuse to be guided by it? Why do the Says, the Comtes, the Hennequins, and others—after having said that property is born of labor—seek to fix it by occupation and prescription?

But let us leave these sophists to their contradictions and blindness. The good sense of the people will do justice to their equivocations. Let us make haste to enlighten it, and show it the true path. Equality approaches; already between it and us but a short distance intervenes: to-morrow even this distance will have been traversed.

% 6.—That in Society all Wages are Equal.

When the St. Simonians, the Fourierists, and, in general, all who in our day are connected with social economy and reform, inscribe upon their banner,—

"TO EACH ACCORDING TO HIS CAPACITY, TO EACH CAPACITY ACCORDING TO ITS RESULTS" (St. Simon);

"TO EACH ACCORDING TO HIS CAPITAL, HIS LABOR, AND HIS SKILL" (Fourier),—

they mean—although they do not say so in so many words—that the products of Nature procured by labor and industry are a reward, a palm, a crown offered to all kinds of preeminence and superiority. They regard the land as an immense arena in which prizes are contended for,—no longer, it is true, with lances and swords, by force and by treachery; but by acquired wealth, by knowledge, talent, and by virtue itself. In a word, they mean—and everybody agrees with them—that the greatest capacity is entitled to the greatest reward; and, to use the mercantile phraseology,—which has, at least, the merit of being straightforward,—that salaries must be governed by capacity and its results.

The disciples of these two self-styled reformers cannot deny that such is their thought; for, in doing so, they would contradict their official interpretations, and would destroy the unity of their systems. Furthermore, such a denial on their part is not to be feared. The two sects glory in laying down as a principle inequality of conditions,—reasoning from Nature, who, they say, intended the inequality of capacities. They boast only of one thing; namely, that their political system is so perfect, that the social inequalities always correspond with the natural inequalities. They no more trouble themselves to inquire whether inequality of conditions—I mean of salaries—is possible, than they do to fix a measure of capacity.[*]

```
    * In St. Simon's system, the St.-Simonian priest determines the
    capacity of each by virtue of his pontifical infallibility, in imitation
    of the Roman Church: in Fourier's, the ranks and merits are decided by
    vote, in imitation of the constitutional regime.
```

Clearly, the great man is an object of ridicule to the reader; he did not mean to tell his secret.

"To each according to his capacity, to each capacity according to its results."

"To each according to his capital, his labor, and his skill."

Since the death of St. Simon and Fourier, not one among their numerous disciples has attempted to give to the public a scientific demonstration of this grand maxim; and I would wager a hundred to one that no Fourierist even suspects that this biform aphorism is susceptible of two interpretations.

"To each according to his capacity, to each capacity according to its results."

"To each according to his capital, his labor, and his skill."

This proposition, taken, as they say, *in sensu obvio*—in the sense usually attributed to it—is false, absurd, unjust, contradictory, hostile to liberty, friendly to tyranny, anti-social, and was unluckily framed under the express influence of the property idea.

And, first, CAPITAL must be crossed off the list of elements which are entitled to a reward. The Fourierists—as far as I have been able to learn from a few of their pamphlets—deny the right of occupancy, and recognize no basis of property save labor. Starting with a like premise, they would have seen—had they reasoned upon the matter—that capital is a source of production to its proprietor only by virtue of the right of occupancy, and that this production is therefore illegitimate. Indeed, if labor is the sole basis of property, I cease to be proprietor of my field as soon as I receive rent for it from another. This we have shown beyond all cavil. It is the same with all capital; so that to put capital in an enterprise, is, by the law's decision, to exchange it for an equivalent sum in products. I will not enter again upon this now useless discussion, since I propose, in the following chapter, to exhaust the subject of PRODUCTION BY CAPITAL.

Thus, capital can be exchanged, but cannot be a source of income.

LABOR and SKILL remain; or, as St. Simon puts it, RESULTS and CAPACITIES. I will examine them successively.

Should wages be governed by labor? In other words, is it just that he who does the most should get the most? I beg the reader to pay the closest attention to this point.

To solve the problem with one stroke, we have only to ask ourselves the following question: "Is labor a CONDITION or a STRUGGLE?" The reply seems plain.

God said to man, "In the sweat of thy face shalt thou eat bread,"—that is, thou shalt produce thy own bread: with more or less ease, according to thy skill in directing and combining thy efforts, thou shalt labor. God did not say, "Thou shalt quarrel with thy neighbor for thy bread;" but, "Thou shalt labor by the side of thy neighbor, and ye shall dwell together in harmony." Let us develop the meaning of this law, the extreme simplicity of which renders it liable to misconstruction.

In labor, two things must be noticed and distinguished: ASSOCIATION and AVAILABLE MATERIAL.

In so far as laborers are associated, they are equal; and it involves a contradiction to say that one should be paid more than another. For, as the product of one laborer can be paid for only in the product of another laborer, if the two products are unequal, the remainder—or the difference between the greater and the smaller—will not be acquired by society; and, therefore, not being exchanged, will not affect the equality of wages. There will result, it is true, in favor of the stronger laborer a natural inequality, but not a social inequality; no one having suffered by his strength and productive energy. In a word, society exchanges only equal products—that is, rewards no labor save that performed for her benefit; consequently, she pays all laborers equally: with what they produce outside of her sphere she has no more to do, than with the difference in their voices and their hair.

I seem to be positing the principle of inequality: the reverse of this is the truth. The total amount of labor which can be performed for society (that is, of labor susceptible of exchange), being, within a given space, as much greater as the laborers are more numerous, and as the task assigned to each is less in magnitude,—it follows that natural inequality neutralizes itself in proportion as association extends, and as the quantity of consumable values produced thereby increases. So that in society the only thing which could bring back the inequality of labor would be the right of occupancy,—the right of property.

Now, suppose that this daily social task consists in the ploughing, hoeing, or reaping of two square decameters, and that the average time required to accomplish it is seven hours: one laborer will finish it in six hours, another will require eight; the majority, however, will work seven. But provided each one furnishes the quantity of labor demanded of him, whatever be the time he employs, they are entitled to equal wages.

Shall the laborer who is capable of finishing his task in six hours have the right, on the ground of superior strength and activity, to usurp the task of the less skilful laborer, and thus rob him of his labor and bread? Who dares maintain such a proposition? He who finishes before the others may rest, if he chooses; he may devote himself to useful exercise and labors for the maintenance of his strength, and the culture of his mind, and the pleasure of his life. This he can do without injury to any one: but let him confine himself to services which affect him solely. Vigor, genius, diligence, and all the personal advantages which result therefrom, are the work of Nature and, to a certain extent, of the individual; society awards them the esteem which they merit: but the wages which it pays them is measured, not by their power, but by their production. Now, the product of each is limited by the right of all.

If the soil were infinite in extent, and the amount of available material were exhaustless, even then we could not accept this maxim,—TO EACH ACCORDING TO HIS LABOR. And why? Because society, I repeat, whatever be the number of its subjects, is forced to pay them all the same wages, since she pays them only in their own products. Only, on the hypothesis just made, inasmuch as the strong cannot be prevented from using all their advantages, the inconveniences of natural inequality would reappear in the very bosom of social equality. But the land, considering the productive power of its inhabitants and their ability to multiply, is very limited; further, by the immense variety of products and the extreme division of labor, the social task is made easy of accomplishment. Now, through this limitation of things producible, and through the ease of producing them, the law of absolute equality takes effect.

Yes, life is a struggle. But this struggle is not between man and man—it is between man and Nature; and it is each one's duty to take his share in it. If, in the struggle, the strong come to the aid of the weak, their kindness deserves praise and love; but their aid must be accepted as a free gift,—not imposed by force, nor offered at a price. All have the same career before them, neither too long nor too difficult; whoever finishes it finds his reward at the end: it is not necessary to get there first.

In printing-offices, where the laborers usually work by the job, the compositor receives so much per thousand letters set; the pressman so much per thousand sheets printed. There, as elsewhere, inequalities of talent and skill are to be found. When there is no prospect of dull times (for printing and typesetting, like all other trades, sometimes come to a stand-still), every one is free to work his hardest, and exert his faculties to the utmost: he who does more gets more; he who does less gets less. When business slackens, compositors and pressmen divide up their labor; all monopolists are detested as no better than robbers or traitors.

There is a philosophy in the action of these printers, to which neither economists nor legists have ever risen. If our legislators had introduced into their codes the principle of distributive justice which governs printing-offices; if they had observed the popular instincts,—not for the sake of servile imitation, but in order to reform and generalize them,—long ere this liberty and equality would have been established on an immovable basis, and we should not now be disputing about the right of property and the necessity of social distinctions.

It has been calculated that if labor were equally shared by the whole number of able-bodied individuals, the average working-day of each individual, in France, would not exceed five hours. This being so, how can we presume to talk of the inequality of laborers? It is the LABOR of Robert Macaire that causes inequality.

The principle, TO EACH ACCORDING TO HIS LABOR, interpreted to mean, WHO WORKS MOST SHOULD RECEIVE MOST, is based, therefore, on two palpable errors: one, an error in economy, that in the labor of society tasks must necessarily be unequal; the other, an error in physics, that there is no limit to the amount of producible things.

"But," it will be said, "suppose there are some people who wish to perform only half of their task?"... Is that very embarrassing? Probably they are satisfied with half of their salary. Paid according to the labor that they had performed, of what could they complain? and what injury would they do to others? In this sense, it is fair to apply the maxim,—TO EACH ACCORDING TO HIS RESULTS. It is the law of equality itself.

Further, numerous difficulties, relative to the police system and the organization of industry, might be raised here. I will reply to them all with this one sentence,—that they must all be solved by the principle of equality. Thus, some one might observe, "Here is a task which cannot be postponed without detriment to production. Ought society to suffer from the negligence of a few? and will she not venture—out of respect for the right of labor—to assure with her own hands the product which they refuse her? In such a case, to whom will the salary belong?"

To society; who will be allowed to perform the labor, either herself, or through her representatives, but always in such a way that the general equality shall never be violated, and that only the idler shall be punished for his idleness. Further, if society may not use excessive severity towards her lazy members, she has a right, in self-defence, to guard against abuses.

But every industry needs—they will add—leaders, instructors, superintendents, &c. Will these be engaged in the general task? No; since their task is to lead, instruct, and superintend. But they must be chosen from the laborers by the laborers themselves, and must fulfil the conditions of eligibility. It is the same with all public functions, whether of administration or instruction.

Then, article first of the universal constitution will be:—

"The limited quantity of available material proves the necessity of dividing the labor among the whole number of laborers. The capacity, given to all, of accomplishing a social task,—that is, an equal task,—and the impossibility of paying one laborer save in the products of another, justify the equality of wages."

% 7.—That Inequality of Powers is the Necessary Condition of Equality of Fortunes.

It is objected,—and this objection constitutes the second part of the St. Simonian, and the third part of the Fourieristic, maxims,—

"That all kinds of labor cannot be executed with equal ease. Some require great superiority of skill and intelligence; and on this superiority is based the price. The artist, the savant, the poet, the statesman, are esteemed only because of their excellence; and this excellence destroys all similitude between them and other men: in the presence of these heights of science and genius the law of equality disappears. Now, if equality is not absolute, there is no equality. From the poet we descend to the novelist; from the sculptor to the stonecutter; from the architect to the mason; from the chemist to the cook, &c. Capacities are classified and subdivided into orders, genera, and species. The extremes of talent are connected by intermediate talents. Humanity is a vast hierarchy, in which the individual estimates himself by comparison, and fixes his price by the value placed upon his product by the public."

This objection always has seemed a formidable one. It is the stumbling-block of the economists, as well as of the defenders of equality. It has led the former into egregious blunders, and has caused the latter to utter incredible platitudes. Gracchus Babeuf wished all superiority to be STRINGENTLY REPRESSED, and even PERSECUTED AS A SOCIAL CALAMITY. To establish his communistic edifice, he lowered all citizens to the stature of the smallest. Ignorant eclectics have been known to object to the inequality of knowledge, and I should not be surprised if some one should yet rebel against the inequality of virtue. Aristotle was banished, Socrates drank the hemlock, Epaminondas was called to account, for having proved superior in intelligence and virtue to some dissolute and foolish demagogues. Such follies will be re-enacted, so long as the inequality of fortunes justifies a populace, blinded and oppressed by the wealthy, in fearing the elevation of new tyrants to power.

Nothing seems more unnatural than that which we examine too closely, and often nothing seems less like the truth than the truth itself. On the other hand, according to J. J. Rousseau, "it takes a great deal of philosophy to enable us to observe once what we see every day;" and, according to d'Alembert, "the ordinary truths of life make but little impression on men, unless their attention is especially called to them." The father of the school of economists (Say), from whom I borrow these two quotations, might have profited by them; but he who laughs at the blind should wear spectacles, and he who notices him is near-sighted.

Strange! that which has frightened so many minds is not, after all, an objection to equality—it is the very condition on which equality exists!...

Natural inequality the condition of equality of fortunes!... What a paradox!... I repeat my assertion, that no one may think I have blundered—inequality of powers is the sine qua non of equality of fortunes.

There are two things to be considered in society—FUNCTIONS and RELATIONS.

I. FUNCTIONS. Every laborer is supposed to be capable of performing the task assigned to him; or, to use a common expression, "every workman must know his trade." The workman equal to his work,—there is an equation between functionary and function.

In society, functions are not alike; there must be, then, different capacities. Further,—certain functions demand greater intelligence and powers; then there are people of superior mind and talent. For the performance of work necessarily involves a workman: from the need springs the idea, and the idea makes the producer. We only know what our senses long for and our intelligence demands; we have no keen desire for things of which we cannot conceive, and the greater our powers of conception, the greater our capabilities of production.

Thus, functions arising from needs, needs from desires, and desires from spontaneous perception and imagination, the same intelligence which imagines can also produce; consequently, no labor is superior to the laborer. In a word, if the function calls out the functionary, it is because the functionary exists before the function.

Let us admire Nature's economy. With regard to these various needs which she has given us, and which the isolated man cannot satisfy unaided, Nature has granted to the race a power refused to the individual. This gives rise to the principle of the DIVISION OF LABOR,—a principle founded on the SPECIALITY OF VOCATIONS.

The satisfaction of some needs demands of man continual creation; while others can, by the labor of a single individual, be satisfied for millions of men through thousands of centuries. For example, the need of clothing and food requires perpetual reproduction; while a knowledge of the system of the universe may be acquired for ever by two or three highly-gifted men. The perpetual current of rivers supports our commerce, and runs our machinery; but the sun, alone in the midst of space, gives light to the whole world. Nature, who might create Platos and Virgils, Newtons and Cuviers, as she creates husbandmen and shepherds, does not see fit to do so; choosing rather to proportion the rarity of genius to the duration of its products, and to balance the number of capacities by the competency of each one of them.

I do not inquire here whether the distance which separates one man from another, in point of talent and intelligence, arises from the deplorable condition of civilization, nor whether that which is now called the INEQUALITY OF POWERS would be in an ideal society any thing more than a DIVERSITY OF POWERS. I take the worst view of the matter; and, that I may not be accused of tergiversation and evasion of difficulties, I acknowledge all the inequalities that any one can desire. [16]

Certain philosophers, in love with the levelling idea, maintain that all minds are equal, and that all differences are the result of education. I am no believer, I confess, in this doctrine; which, even if it were true, would lead to a result directly opposite to that desired. For, if capacities are equal, whatever be the degree of their power (as no one can be coerced), there are functions deemed coarse, low, and degrading, which deserve higher pay,—a result no less repugnant to equality than to the principle, TO EACH CAPACITY ACCORDING TO ITS RESULTS. Give me, on the contrary, a society in which every kind of talent bears a proper numerical relation to the needs of the society, and which demands from each producer only that which his special function requires him to produce; and, without impairing in the least the hierarchy of functions, I will deduce the equality of fortunes.

This is my second point.

II. RELATIONS. In considering the element of labor, I have shown that in the same class of productive services, the capacity to perform a social task being possessed by all, no inequality of reward can be based upon an inequality of individual powers. However, it is but fair to say that certain capacities seem quite incapable of certain services; so that, if human industry were entirely confined to one class of products, numerous incapacities would arise, and, consequently, the greatest social inequality. But every body sees, without any hint from me, that the variety of industries avoids this difficulty; so clear is this that I shall not stop to discuss it. We have only to prove, then, that functions are equal to each other; just as laborers, who perform the same function, are equal to each other.

Property makes man a eunuch, and then reproaches him for being nothing but dry wood, a decaying tree.

Are you astonished that I refuse to genius, to knowledge, to courage,—in a word, to all the excellences admired by the world,—the homage of dignities, the distinctions of power and wealth? It is not I who refuse it: it is economy, it is justice, it is liberty. Liberty! for the first time in this discussion I appeal to her. Let her rise in her own defence, and achieve her victory.

Every transaction ending in an exchange of products or services may be designated as a COMMERCIAL OPERATION.

Whoever says commerce, says exchange of equal values; for, if the values are not equal, and the injured party perceives it, he will not consent to the exchange, and there will be no commerce.

Commerce exists only among free men. Transactions may be effected between other people by violence or fraud, but there is no commerce.

A free man is one who enjoys the use of his reason and his faculties; who is neither blinded by passion, nor hindered or driven by oppression, nor deceived by erroneous opinions.

So, in every exchange, there is a moral obligation that neither of the contracting parties shall gain at the expense of the other; that is, that, to be legitimate and true, commerce must be exempt from all inequality. This is the first condition of commerce. Its second condition is, that it be voluntary; that is, that the parties act freely and openly.

I define, then, commerce or exchange as an act of society.

The negro who sells his wife for a knife, his children for some bits of glass, and finally himself for a bottle of brandy, is not free. The dealer in human flesh, with whom he negotiates, is not his associate; he is his enemy.

The civilized laborer who bakes a loaf that he may eat a slice of bread, who builds a palace that he may sleep in a stable, who weaves rich fabrics that he may dress in rags, who produces every thing that he may dispense with every thing,—is not free. His employer, not becoming his associate in the exchange of salaries or services which takes place between them, is his enemy.

The soldier who serves his country through fear instead of through love is not free; his comrades and his officers, the ministers or organs of military justice, are all his enemies.

The peasant who hires land, the manufacturer who borrows capital, the tax-payer who pays tolls, duties, patent and license fees, personal and property taxes, &c., and the deputy who votes for them,—all act neither intelligently nor freely. Their enemies are the proprietors, the capitalists, the government.

Give men liberty, enlighten their minds that they may know the meaning of their contracts, and you will see the most perfect equality in exchanges without regard to superiority of talent and knowledge; and you will admit that in commercial affairs, that is, in the sphere of society, the word superiority is void of sense.

Let Homer sing his verse. I listen to this sublime genius in comparison with whom I, a simple herdsman, an humble farmer, am as nothing. What, indeed,—if product is to be compared with product,—are my cheeses and my beans in the presence of his "Iliad"? But, if Homer wishes to take from me all that I possess, and make me his slave in return for his inimitable poem, I will give up the pleasure of his lays, and dismiss him. I can do without his "Iliad," and wait, if necessary, for the "AEneid."

Homer cannot live twenty-four hours without my products. Let him accept, then, the little that I have to offer; and then his muse may instruct, encourage, and console me.

"What! do you say that such should be the condition of one who sings of gods and men? Alms, with the humiliation and suffering which they bring with them!—what barbarous generosity!"... Do not get excited, I beg of you. Property makes of a poet either a Croesus or a beggar; only equality knows how to honor and to praise him. What is its duty? To regulate the right of the singer and the duty of the listener. Now, notice this point, which is a very important one in the solution of this question: both are free, the one to sell, the other to buy. Henceforth their respective pretensions go for nothing; and the estimate, whether fair or unfair, that they place, the one upon his verse, the other upon his liberality, can have no influence upon the conditions of the contract. We must no longer, in making our bargains, weigh talent; we must consider products only.

In order that the bard of Achilles may get his due reward, he must first make himself wanted: that done, the exchange of his verse for a fee of any kind, being a free act, must be at the same time a just act; that is, the poet's fee must be equal to his product. Now, what is the value of this product?

Let us suppose, in the first place, that this "Iliad"—this chef-d' oeuvre that is to be equitably rewarded—is really above price, that we do not know how to appraise it. If the public, who are free to purchase it, refuse to do so, it is clear that, the poem being unexchangeable, its intrinsic value will not be diminished; but that its exchangeable value, or its productive utility, will be reduced to zero, will be nothing at all. Then we must seek the amount of wages to be paid between infinity on the one hand and nothing on the other, at an equal distance from each, since all rights and liberties are entitled to equal respect; in other words, it is not the intrinsic value, but the relative value, of the thing sold that needs to be fixed. The question grows simpler: what is this relative value? To what reward does a poem like the "Iliad" entitle its author?

The first business of political economy, after fixing its definitions, was the solution of this problem; now, not only has it not been solved, but it has been declared insoluble. According to the economists, the relative or exchangeable value of things cannot be absolutely determined; it necessarily varies.

"The value of a thing," says Say, "is a positive quantity, but only for a given moment. It is its nature to perpetually vary, to change from one point to another. Nothing can fix it absolutely, because it is based on needs and means of production which vary with every moment. These variations complicate economical phenomena, and often render them very difficult of observation and solution. I know no remedy for this; it is not in our power to change the nature of things."

Elsewhere Say says, and repeats, that value being based on utility, and utility depending entirely on our needs, whims, customs, &c., value is as variable as opinion. Now, political economy being the science of values, of their production, distribution, exchange, and consumption,—if exchangeable value cannot be absolutely determined, how is political economy possible? How can it be a science? How can two economists look each other in the face without laughing? How dare they insult metaphysicians and psychologists? What! that fool of a Descartes imagined that philosophy needed an immovable base —an *aliquid inconcussum*—on which the edifice of science might be built, and he was simple enough to search for it! And the Hermes of economy, Trismegistus Say, devoting half a volume to the amplification of that solemn text, *political economy is a science*, has the courage to affirm immediately afterwards that this science cannot determine its object,—which is equivalent to saying that it is without a principle or foundation! He does not know, then, the illustrious Say, the nature of a science; or rather, he knows nothing of the subject which he discusses.

Say's example has borne its fruits. Political economy, as it exists at present, resembles ontology: discussing effects and causes, it knows nothing, explains nothing, decides nothing. The ideas honored with the name of economic laws are nothing more than a few trifling generalities, to which the economists thought to give an appearance of depth by clothing them in high-sounding words. As for the attempts that have been made by the economists to solve social problems, all that can be said of them is, that, if a glimmer of sense occasionally appears in their lucubrations, they immediately fall back into absurdity. For twenty-five years political economy, like a heavy fog, has weighed upon France, checking the efforts of the mind, and setting limits to liberty.

Has every creation of industry a venal, absolute, unchangeable, and consequently legitimate and true value?—Yes.

Can every product of man be exchanged for some other product of man?—Yes, again.

How many nails is a pair of shoes worth?

If we can solve this appalling problem, we shall have the key of the social system for which humanity has been searching for six thousand years. In the presence of this problem, the economist recoils confused; the peasant who can neither read nor write replies without hesitation: "As many as can be made in the same time, and with the same expense."

The absolute value of a thing, then, is its cost in time and expense. How much is a diamond worth which costs only the labor of picking it up?—Nothing; it is not a product of man. How much will it be worth when cut and mounted?—The time and expense which it has cost the laborer. Why, then, is it sold at so high a price?—Because men are not free. Society must regulate the exchange and distribution of the rarest things, as it does that of the most common ones, in such a way that each may share in the enjoyment of them. What, then, is that value which is based upon opinion?—Delusion, injustice, and robbery.

By this rule, it is easy to reconcile every body. If the mean term, which we are searching for, between an infinite value and no value at all is expressed in the case of every product, by the amount of time and expense which the product cost, a poem which has cost its author thirty years of labor and an outlay of ten thousand francs in journeys, books, &c., must be paid for by the ordinary wages received by a laborer during thirty years, PLUS ten thousand francs indemnity for expense incurred. Suppose the whole amount to be fifty thousand francs; if the society which gets the benefit of the production include a million of men, my share of the debt is five centimes.

This gives rise to a few observations.

1. The same product, at different times and in different places, may cost more or less of time and outlay; in this view, it is true that value is a variable quantity. But this variation is not that of the economists, who place in their list of the causes of the variation of values, not only the means of production, but taste, caprice, fashion, and opinion. In short, the true value of a thing is invariable in its algebraic expression, although it may vary in its monetary expression.

2. The price of every product in demand should be its cost in time and outlay—neither more nor less: every product not in demand is a loss to the producer—a commercial non-value.

3. The ignorance of the principle of evaluation, and the difficulty under many circumstances of applying it, is the source of commercial fraud, and one of the most potent causes of the inequality of fortunes.

4. To reward certain industries and pay for certain products, a society is needed which corresponds in size with the rarity of talents, the costliness of the products, and the variety of the arts and sciences. If, for example, a society of fifty farmers can support a schoolmaster, it requires one hundred for a shoemaker, one hundred and fifty for a blacksmith, two hundred for a tailor, &c. If the number of farmers rises to one thousand, ten thousand, one hundred thousand, &c., as fast as their number increases, that of the functionaries which are earliest required must increase in the same proportion; so that the highest functions become possible only in the most powerful societies. [17] That is the peculiar feature of capacities; the character of genius, the seal of its glory, cannot arise and develop itself, except in the bosom of a great nation. But this physiological condition, necessary to the existence of genius, adds nothing to its social rights: far from that,—the delay in its appearance proves that, in economical and civil affairs, the loftiest intelligence must submit to the equality of possessions; an equality which is anterior to it, and of which it constitutes the crown.

This is severe on our pride, but it is an inexorable truth. And here psychology comes to the aid of social economy, giving us to understand that talent and material recompense have no common measure; that, in this respect, the condition of all producers is equal: consequently, that all comparison between them, and all distinction in fortunes, is impossible.

In fact, every work coming from the hands of man—compared with the raw material of which it is composed—is beyond price. In this respect, the distance is as great between a pair of wooden shoes and the trunk of a walnut-tree, as between a statue by Scopas and a block of marble. The genius of the simplest mechanic exerts as much influence over the materials which he uses, as does the mind of a Newton over the inert spheres whose distances, volumes, and revolutions he calculates. You ask for talent and genius a corresponding degree of honor and reward. Fix for me the value of a woodcutter's talent, and I will fix that of Homer. If any thing can reward intelligence, it is intelligence itself. That is what happens, when various classes of producers pay to each other a reciprocal tribute of admiration and praise. But if they contemplate an exchange of products with a view to satisfying mutual needs, this exchange must be effected in accordance with a system of economy which is indifferent to considerations of talent and genius, and whose laws are deduced, not from vague and meaningless admiration, but from a just balance between DEBIT and CREDIT; in short, from commercial accounts.

Now, that no one may imagine that the liberty of buying and selling is the sole basis of the equality of wages, and that society's sole protection against superiority of talent lies in a certain force of inertia which has nothing in common with right, I shall proceed to explain why all capacities are entitled to the same reward, and why a corresponding difference in wages would be an injustice. I shall prove that the obligation to stoop to the social level is inherent in talent; and on this very superiority of genius I will found the equality of fortunes. I have just given the negative argument in favor of rewarding all capacities alike; I will now give the direct and positive argument.

Listen, first, to the economist: it is always pleasant to see how he reasons, and how he understands justice. Without him, moreover, without his amusing blunders and his wonderful arguments, we should learn nothing. Equality, so odious to the economist, owes every thing to political economy.

"When the parents of a physician [the text says a lawyer, which is not so good an example] have expended on his education forty thousand francs, this sum may be regarded as so much capital invested in his head. It is therefore permissible to consider it as yielding an annual income of four thousand francs. If the physician earns thirty thousand, there remains an income of twenty-six thousand francs due to the personal talents given him by Nature. This natural capital, then, if we assume ten per cent. as the rate of interest, amounts to two hundred and sixty thousand francs; and the capital given him by his parents, in defraying the expenses of his education, to forty thousand francs. The union of these two kinds of capital constitutes his fortune."—Say: Complete Course, &c.

Say divides the fortune of the physician into two parts: one is composed of the capital which went to pay for his education, the other represents his personal talents. This division is just; it is in conformity with the nature of things; it is universally admitted; it serves as the major premise of that grand argument which establishes the inequality of capacities. I accept this premise without qualification; let us look at the consequences.

1. Say CREDITS the physician with forty thousand francs,—the cost of his education. This amount should be entered upon the DEBIT side of the account. For, although this expense was incurred for him, it was not incurred by him. Then, instead of appropriating these forty thousand francs, the physician should add them to the price of his product, and repay them to those who are entitled to them. Notice, further, that Say speaks of INCOME instead of REIMBURSEMENT; reasoning on the false principle of the productivity of capital. The expense of educating a talent is a debt contracted by this talent. From the very fact of its existence, it becomes a debtor to an amount equal to the cost of its production. This is so true and simple that, if the education of some one child in a family has cost double or triple that of its brothers, the latter are entitled to a proportional amount of the property previous to its division. There is no difficulty about this in the case of guardianship, when the estate is administered in the name of the minors.

2. That which I have just said of the obligation incurred by talent of repaying the cost of its education does not embarrass the economist. The man of talent, he says, inheriting from his family, inherits among other things a claim to the forty thousand francs which his education costs; and he becomes, in consequence, its proprietor. But this is to abandon the right of talent, and to fall back upon the right of occupancy; which again calls up all the questions asked in Chapter II. What is the right of occupancy? what is inheritance? Is the right of succession a right of accumulation or only a right of choice? how did the physician's father get his fortune? was he a proprietor, or only a usufructuary? If he was rich, let him account for his wealth; if he was poor, how could he incur so large an expense? If he received aid, what right had he to use that aid to the disadvantage of his benefactors, &c.?

3. "There remains an income of twenty-six thousand francs due to the personal talents given him by Nature." (Say,—as above quoted.) Reasoning from this premise, Say concludes that our physician's talent is equivalent to a capital of two hundred and sixty thousand francs. This skilful calculator mistakes a consequence for a principle. The talent must not be measured by the gain, but rather the gain by the talent; for it may happen, that, notwithstanding his merit, the physician in question will gain nothing at all, in which case will it be necessary to conclude that his talent or fortune is equivalent to zero? To such a result, however, would Say's reasoning lead; a result which is clearly absurd.

Now, it is impossible to place a money value on any talent whatsoever, since talent and money have no common measure. On what plausible ground can it be maintained that a physician should be paid two, three, or a hundred times as much as a peasant? An unavoidable difficulty, which has never been solved save by avarice, necessity, and oppression. It is not thus that the right of talent should be determined. But how is it to be determined?

4. I say, first, that the physician must be treated with as much favor as any other producer, that he must not be placed below the level of others. This I will not stop to prove. But I add that neither must he be lifted above that level; because his talent is collective property for which he did not pay, and for which he is ever in debt.

Just as the creation of every instrument of production is the result of collective force, so also are a man's talent and knowledge the product of universal intelligence and of general knowledge slowly accumulated by a number of masters, and through the aid of many inferior industries. When the physician has paid for his teachers, his books, his diplomas, and all the other items of his educational expenses, he has no more paid for his talent than the capitalist pays for his house and land when he gives his employees their wages. The man of talent has contributed to the production in himself of a useful instrument. He has, then, a share in its possession; he is not its proprietor. There exist side by side in him a free laborer and an accumulated social capital. As a laborer, he is charged with the use of an instrument, with the superintendence of a machine; namely, his capacity. As capital, he is not his own master; he uses himself, not for his own benefit, but for that of others.

Even if talent did not find in its own excellence a reward for the sacrifices which it costs, still would it be easier to find reasons for lowering its reward than for raising it above the common level. Every producer receives an education; every laborer is a talent, a capacity,—that is, a piece of collective property. But all talents are not equally costly. It takes but few teachers, but few years, and but little study, to make a farmer or a mechanic: the generative effort and—if I may venture to use such language—the period of social gestation are proportional to the loftiness of the capacity. But while the physician, the poet, the artist, and the savant produce but little, and that slowly, the productions of the farmer are much less uncertain, and do not require so long a time. Whatever be then the capacity of a man,—when this capacity is once created,—it does not belong to him. Like the material fashioned by an industrious hand, it had the power of BECOMING, and society has given it BEING. Shall the vase say to the potter, "I am that I am, and I owe you nothing"?

The artist, the savant, and the poet find their just recompense in the permission that society gives them to devote themselves exclusively to science and to art: so that in reality they do not labor for themselves, but for society, which creates them, and requires of them no other duty. Society can, if need be, do without prose and verse, music and painting, and the knowledge of the movements of the moon and stars; but it cannot live a single day without food and shelter.

Undoubtedly, man does not live by bread alone; he must, also (according to the Gospel), LIVE BY THE WORD OF GOD; that is, he must love the good and do it, know and admire the beautiful, and study the marvels of Nature. But in order to cultivate his mind, he must first take care of his body,—the latter duty is as necessary as the former is noble. If it is glorious to charm and instruct men, it is honorable as well to feed them. When, then, society—faithful to the principle of the division of labor—intrusts a work of art or of science to one of its members, allowing him to abandon ordinary labor, it owes him an indemnity for all which it prevents him from producing industrially; but it owes him nothing more. If he should demand more, society should, by refusing his services, annihilate his pretensions. Forced, then, in order to live, to devote himself to labor repugnant to his nature, the man of genius would feel his weakness, and would live the most distasteful of lives.

They tell of a celebrated singer who demanded of the Empress of Russia (Catherine II) twenty thousand roubles for his services: "That is more than I give my field-marshals," said Catherine. "Your majesty," replied the other, "has only to make singers of her field-marshals."

If France (more powerful than Catherine II) should say to Mademoiselle Rachel, "You must act for one hundred louis, or else spin cotton;" to M. Duprez, "You must sing for two thousand four hundred francs, or else work in the vineyard,"—do you think that the actress Rachel, and the singer Duprez, would abandon the stage? If they did, they would be the first to repent it.

Mademoiselle Rachel receives, they say, sixty thousand francs annually from the Comedie-Francaise. For a talent like hers, it is a slight fee. Why not one hundred thousand francs, two hundred thousand francs? Why! not a civil list? What meanness! Are we really guilty of chaffering with an artist like Mademoiselle Rachel?

It is said, in reply, that the managers of the theatre cannot give more without incurring a loss; that they admit the superior talent of their young associate; but that, in fixing her salary, they have been compelled to take the account of the company's receipts and expenses into consideration also.

That is just, but it only confirms what I have said; namely, that an artist's talent may be infinite, but that its mercenary claims are necessarily limited,—on the one hand, by its usefulness to the society which rewards it; on the other, by the resources of this society: in other words, that the demand of the seller is balanced by the right of the buyer.

Mademoiselle Rachel, they say, brings to the treasury of the Theatre-Francais more than sixty thousand francs. I admit it; but then I blame the theatre. From whom does the Theatre-Francais take this money? From some curious people who are perfectly free. Yes; but the workingmen, the lessees, the tenants, those who borrow by pawning their possessions, from whom these curious people recover all that they pay to the theatre,—are they free? And when the better part of their products are consumed by others at the play, do you assure me that their families are not in want? Until the French people, reflecting on the salaries paid to all artists, savants, and public functionaries, have plainly expressed their wish and judgment as to the matter, the salaries of Mademoiselle Rachel and all her fellow-artists will be a compulsory tax extorted by violence, to reward pride, and support libertinism.

It is because we are neither free nor sufficiently enlightened, that we submit to be cheated in our bargains; that the laborer pays the duties levied by the prestige of power and the selfishness of talent upon the curiosity of the idle, and that we are perpetually scandalized by these monstrous inequalities which are encouraged and applauded by public opinion.

The whole nation, and the nation only, pays its authors, its savants, its artists, its officials, whatever be the hands through which their salaries pass. On what basis should it pay them? On the basis of equality. I have proved it by estimating the value of talent. I shall confirm it in the following chapter, by proving the impossibility of all social inequality.

What have we shown so far? Things so simple that really they seem silly:—

That, as the traveller does not appropriate the route which he traverses, so the farmer does not appropriate the field which he sows;

That if, nevertheless, by reason of his industry, a laborer may appropriate the material which he employs, every employer of material becomes, by the same title, a proprietor;

That all capital, whether material or mental, being the result of collective labor, is, in consequence, collective property;

That the strong have no right to encroach upon the labor of the weak, nor the shrewd to take advantage of the credulity of the simple;

Finally, that no one can be forced to buy that which he does not want, still less to pay for that which he has not bought; and, consequently, that the exchangeable value of a product, being measured neither by the opinion of the buyer nor that of the seller, but by the amount of time and outlay which it has cost, the property of each always remains the same.

Are not these very simple truths? Well, as simple as they seem to you, reader, you shall yet see others which surpass them in dullness and simplicity. For our course is the reverse of that of the geometricians: with them, the farther they advance, the more difficult their problems become; we, on the contrary, after having commenced with the most abstruse propositions, shall end with the axioms.

But I must close this chapter with an exposition of one of those startling truths which never have been dreamed of by legists or economists.

% 8.—*That, from the Stand-point of Justice, Labor destroys Property.*

This proposition is the logical result of the two preceding sections, which we have just summed up.

The isolated man can supply but a very small portion of his wants; all his power lies in association, and in the intelligent combination of universal effort. The division and co-operation of labor multiply the quantity and the variety of products; the individuality of functions improves their quality.

There is not a man, then, but lives upon the products of several thousand different industries; not a laborer but receives from society at large the things which he consumes, and, with these, the power to reproduce. Who, indeed, would venture the assertion, "I produce, by my own effort, all that I consume; I need the aid of no one else"? The farmer, whom the early economists regarded as the only real producer—the farmer, housed, furnished, clothed, fed, and assisted by the mason, the carpenter, the tailor, the miller, the baker, the butcher, the grocer, the blacksmith, &c.,—the farmer, I say, can he boast that he produces by his own unaided effort?

The various articles of consumption are given to each by all; consequently, the production of each involves the production of all. One product cannot exist without another; an isolated industry is an impossible thing. What would be the harvest of the farmer, if others did not manufacture for him barns, wagons, ploughs, clothes, &c.? Where would be the savant without the publisher; the printer without the typecaster and the machinist; and these, in their turn, without a multitude of other industries?... Let us not prolong this catalogue—so easy to extend—lest we be accused of uttering commonplaces. All industries are united by mutual relations in a single group; all productions do reciprocal service as means and end; all varieties of talent are but a series of changes from the inferior to the superior.

Now, this undisputed and indisputable fact of the general participation in every species of product makes all individual productions common; so that every product, coming from the hands of the producer, is mortgaged in advance by society. The producer himself is entitled to only that portion of his product, which is expressed by a fraction whose denominator is equal to the number of individuals of which society is composed. It is true that in return this same producer has a share in all the products of others, so that he has a claim upon all, just as all have a claim upon him; but is it not clear that this reciprocity of mortgages, far from authorizing property, destroys even possession? The laborer is not even possessor of his product; scarcely has he finished it, when society claims it.

"But," it will be answered, "even if that is so—even if the product does not belong to the producer—still society gives each laborer an equivalent for his product; and this equivalent, this salary, this reward, this allowance, becomes his property. Do you deny that this property is legitimate? And if the laborer, instead of consuming his entire wages, chooses to economize,—who dare question his right to do so?"

The laborer is not even proprietor of the price of his labor, and cannot absolutely control its disposition. Let us not be blinded by a spurious justice. That which is given the laborer in exchange for his product is not given him as a reward for past labor, but to provide for and secure future labor. We consume before we produce. The laborer may say at the end of the day, "I have paid yesterday's expenses; to-morrow I shall pay those of today." At every moment of his life, the member of society is in debt; he dies with the debt unpaid:—how is it possible for him to accumulate?

They talk of economy—it is the proprietor's hobby. Under a system of equality, all economy which does not aim at subsequent reproduction or enjoyment is impossible—why? Because the thing saved, since it cannot be converted into capital, has no object, and is without a FINAL CAUSE. This will be explained more fully in the next chapter.

To conclude:—

The laborer, in his relation to society, is a debtor who of necessity dies insolvent. The proprietor is an unfaithful guardian who denies the receipt of the deposit committed to his care, and wishes to be paid for his guardianship down to the last day.

Lest the principles just set forth may appear to certain readers too metaphysical, I shall reproduce them in a more concrete form, intelligible to the dullest brains, and pregnant with the most important consequences.

Hitherto, I have considered property as a power of EXCLUSION; hereafter, I shall examine it as a power of INVASION.

CHAPTER IV. THAT PROPERTY IS IMPOSSIBLE.

The last resort of proprietors,—the overwhelming argument whose invincible potency reassures them,—is that, in their opinion, equality of conditions is impossible. "Equality of conditions is a chimera," they cry with a knowing air; "distribute wealth equally to-day—to-morrow this equality will have vanished."

To this hackneyed objection, which they repeat everywhere with the most marvellous assurance, they never fail to add the following comment, as a sort of GLORY BE TO THE FATHER: "If all men were equal, nobody would work." This anthem is sung with variations.

"If all were masters, nobody would obey."

"If nobody were rich, who would employ the poor?"

And, "If nobody were poor, who would labor for the rich?"

But let us have done with invective—we have better arguments at our command.

If I show that property itself is impossible—that it is property which is a contradiction, a chimera, a utopia; and if I show it no longer by metaphysics and jurisprudence, but by figures, equations, and calculations,—imagine the fright of the astounded proprietor! And you, reader; what do you think of the retort?

Numbers govern the world—mundum regunt numeri. This proverb applies as aptly to the moral and political, as to the sidereal and molecular, world. The elements of justice are identical with those of algebra; legislation and government are simply the arts of classifying and balancing powers; all jurisprudence falls within the rules of arithmetic. This chapter and the next will serve to lay the foundations of this extraordinary doctrine. Then will be unfolded to the reader's vision an immense and novel career; then shall we commence to see in numerical relations the synthetic unity of philosophy and the sciences; and, filled with admiration and enthusiasm for this profound and majestic simplicity of Nature, we shall shout with the apostle: "Yes, the Eternal has made all things by number, weight, and measure!" We shall understand not only that equality of conditions is possible, but that all else is impossible; that this seeming impossibility which we charge upon it arises from the fact that we always think of it in connection either with the proprietary or the communistic regime,—political systems equally irreconcilable with human nature. We shall see finally that equality is constantly being realized without our knowledge, even at the very moment when we are pronouncing it incapable of realization; that the time draws near when, without any effort or even wish of ours, we shall have it universally established; that with it, in it, and by it, the natural and true political order must make itself manifest.

It has been said, in speaking of the blindness and obstinacy of the passions, that, if man had any thing to gain by denying the truths of arithmetic, he would find some means of unsettling their certainty: here is an opportunity to try this curious experiment. I attack property, no longer with its own maxims, but with arithmetic. Let the proprietors prepare to verify my figures; for, if unfortunately for them the figures prove accurate, the proprietors are lost.

In proving the impossibility of property, I complete the proof of its injustice. In fact,—

That which is JUST must be USEFUL;

That which is useful must be TRUE;

That which is true must be POSSIBLE;

Therefore, every thing which is impossible is untrue, useless, unjust. Then,—a priori,—we may judge of the justice of any thing by its possibility; so that if the thing were absolutely impossible, it would be absolutely unjust.

PROPERTY IS PHYSICALLY AND MATHEMATICALLY IMPOSSIBLE. DEMONSTRATION.

AXIOM.—Property is the Right of Increase claimed by the Proprietor over any thing which he has stamped as his own.

This proposition is purely an axiom, because,—

1. It is not a definition, since it does not express all that is included in the right of property—the right of sale, of exchange, of gift; the right to transform, to alter, to consume, to destroy, to use and abuse, &c. All these rights are so many different powers of property, which we may consider separately; but which we disregard here, that we may devote all our attention to this single one,—the right of increase.

2. It is universally admitted. No one can deny it without denying the facts, without being instantly belied by universal custom.

3. It is self-evident, since property is always accompanied (either actually or potentially) by the fact which this axiom expresses; and through this fact, mainly, property manifests, establishes, and asserts itself.

4. Finally, its negation involves a contradiction. The right of increase is really an inherent right, so essential a part of property, that, in its absence, property is null and void.

OBSERVATIONS.—Increase receives different names according to the thing by which it is yielded: if by land, FARM-RENT; if by houses and furniture, RENT; if by life-investments, REVENUE; if by money, INTEREST; if by exchange, ADVANTAGE, GAIN, PROFIT (three things which must not be confounded with the wages or legitimate price of labor).

Increase—a sort of royal prerogative, of tangible and consumable homage—is due to the proprietor on account of his nominal and metaphysical occupancy. His seal is set upon the thing; that is enough to prevent any one else from occupying it without HIS permission.

This permission to use his things the proprietor may, if he chooses, freely grant. Commonly he sells it. This sale is really a stellionate and an extortion; but by the legal fiction of the right of property, this same sale, severely punished, we know not why, in other cases, is a source of profit and value to the proprietor.

The amount demanded by the proprietor, in payment for this permission, is expressed in monetary terms by the dividend which the supposed product yields in nature. So that, by the right of increase, the proprietor reaps and does not plough; gleans and does not till; consumes and does not produce; enjoys and does not labor. Very different from the idols of the Psalmist are the gods of property: the former had hands and felt not; the latter, on the contrary, *manus habent et palpabunt*. The right of increase is conferred in a very mysterious and supernatural manner. The inauguration of a proprietor is accompanied by the awful ceremonies of an ancient initiation. First, comes the CONSECRATION of the article; a consecration which makes known to all that they must offer up a suitable sacrifice to the proprietor, whenever they wish, by his permission obtained and signed, to use his article.

Second, comes the ANATHEMA, which prohibits—except on the conditions aforesaid—all persons from touching the article, even in the proprietor's absence; and pronounces every violator of property sacrilegious, infamous, amenable to the secular power, and deserving of being handed over to it.

Finally, the DEDICATION, which enables the proprietor or patron saint—the god chosen to watch over the article—to inhabit it mentally, like a divinity in his sanctuary. By means of this dedication, the substance of the article—so to speak—becomes converted into the person of the proprietor, who is regarded as ever present in its form.

This is exactly the doctrine of the writers on jurisprudence. "Property," says Toullier, "is a MORAL QUALITY inherent in a thing; AN ACTUAL BOND which fastens it to the proprietor, and which cannot be broken save by his act." Locke humbly doubted whether God could make matter INTELLIGENT. Toullier asserts that the proprietor renders it MORAL. How much does he lack of being a God? These are by no means exaggerations.

PROPERTY IS THE RIGHT OF INCREASE; that is, the power to produce without labor. Now, to produce without labor is to make something from nothing; in short, to create. Surely it is no more difficult to do this than to moralize matter. The jurists are right, then, in applying to proprietors this passage from the Scriptures,—*Ego dixi: Dii estis et filii Excelsi omnes*,—"I have said, Ye are gods; and all of you are children of the Most High."

PROPERTY IS THE RIGHT OF INCREASE. To us this axiom shall be like the name of the beast in the Apocalypse,—a name in which is hidden the complete explanation of the whole mystery of this beast. It was known that he who should solve the mystery of this name would obtain a knowledge of the whole prophecy, and would succeed in mastering the beast. Well! by the most careful interpretation of our axiom we shall kill the sphinx of property.

Starting from this eminently characteristic fact—the RIGHT OF INCREASE—we shall pursue the old serpent through his coils; we shall count the murderous entwinings of this frightful taenia, whose head, with its thousand suckers, is always hidden from the sword of its most violent enemies, though abandoning to them immense fragments of its body. It requires something more than courage to subdue this monster. It was written that it should not die until a proletaire, armed with a magic wand, had fought with it.

COROLLARIES.—1. THE AMOUNT OF INCREASE IS PROPORTIONAL TO THE THING INCREASED. Whatever be the rate of interest,—whether it rise to three, five, or ten per cent., or fall to one-half, one-fourth, one-tenth,—it does not matter; the law of increase remains the same. The law is as follows:—

All capital—the cash value of which can be estimated—may be considered as a term in an arithmetical series which progresses in the ratio of one hundred, and the revenue yielded by this capital as the corresponding term of another arithmetical series which progresses in a ratio equal to the rate of interest. Thus, a capital of five hundred francs being the fifth term of the arithmetical progression whose ratio is one hundred, its revenue at three per cent. will be indicated by the fifth term of the arithmetical progression whose ratio is three:—

$$100 \ . \ 200 \ . \ 300 \ . \ 400 \ . \ 500.$$
$$3 \ . \ 6 \ . \ 9 \ . \ 12 \ . \ 15.$$

An acquaintance with this sort of LOGARITHMS—tables of which, calculated to a very high degree, are possessed by proprietors—will give us the key to the most puzzling problems, and cause us to experience a series of surprises.

By this LOGARITHMIC theory of the right of increase, a piece of property, together with its income, may be defined as A NUMBER WHOSE LOGARITHM IS EQUAL TO THE SUM OF ITS UNITS DIVIDED BY ONE HUNDRED, AND MULTIPLIED BY THE RATE OF INTEREST. For instance; a house valued at one hundred thousand francs, and leased at five per cent., yields a revenue of five thousand francs, according to the formula 100,000 x 5 / 100 = five thousand. Vice versa, a piece of land which yields, at two and a half per cent., a revenue of three thousand francs is worth one hundred and twenty thousand francs, according to this other formula; 3,000 x 100/ 2 1/2 = one hundred and twenty thousand.

In the first case, the ratio of the progression which marks the increase of interest is five; in the second, it is two and a half.

OBSERVATION.—The forms of increase known as farm-rent, income, and interest are paid annually; rent is paid by the week, the month, or the year; profits and gains are paid at the time of exchange. Thus, the amount of increase is proportional both to the thing increased, and the time during which it increases; in other words, usury grows like a cancer —*foenus serpit sicut cancer*.

2. THE INCREASE PAID TO THE PROPRIETOR BY THE OCCUPANT IS A DEAD LOSS TO THE LATTER. For if the proprietor owed, in exchange for the increase which he receives, some thing more than the permission which he grants, his right of property would not be perfect—he would not possess *jure optimo, jure perfecto;* that is, he would not be in reality a proprietor. Then, all which passes from the hands of the occupant into those of the proprietor in the name of increase, and as the price of the permission to occupy, is a permanent gain for the latter, and a dead loss and annihilation for the former; to whom none of it will return, save in the forms of gift, alms, wages paid for his services, or the price of merchandise which he has delivered. In a word, increase perishes so far as the borrower is concerned; or to use the more energetic Latin phrase,—*res perit solventi*.

3. THE RIGHT OF INCREASE OPPRESSES THE PROPRIETOR AS WELL AS THE STRANGER. The master of a thing, as its proprietor, levies a tax for the use of his property upon himself as its possessor, equal to that which he would receive from a third party; so that capital bears interest in the hands of the capitalist, as well as in those of the borrower and the commandite. If, indeed, rather than accept a rent of five hundred francs for my apartment, I prefer to occupy and enjoy it, it is clear that I shall become my own debtor for a rent equal to that which I deny myself. This principle is universally practised in business, and is regarded as an axiom by the economists. Manufacturers, also, who have the advantage of being proprietors of their floating capital, although they owe no interest to any one, in calculating their profits subtract from them, not only their running expenses and the wages of their employees, but also the interest on their capital. For the same reason, money-lenders retain in their own possession as little money as possible; for, since all capital necessarily bears interest, if this interest is supplied by no one, it comes out of the capital, which is to that extent diminished. Thus, by the right of increase, capital eats itself up. This is, doubtless, the idea that Papinius intended to convey in the phrase, as elegant as it is forcible—*Foenus mordet solidam*. I beg pardon for using Latin so frequently in discussing this subject; it is an homage which I pay to the most usurious nation that ever existed.

FIRST PROPOSITION.

Property is impossible, because it demands Something for Nothing.

The discussion of this proposition covers the same ground as that of the origin of farm-rent, which is so much debated by the economists. When I read the writings of the greater part of these men, I cannot avoid a feeling of contempt mingled with anger, in view of this mass of nonsense, in which the detestable vies with the absurd. It would be a repetition of the story of the elephant in the moon, were it not for the atrocity of the consequences. To seek a rational and legitimate origin of that which is, and ever must be, only robbery, extortion, and plunder—that must be the height of the proprietor's folly; the last degree of bedevilment into which minds, otherwise judicious, can be thrown by the perversity of selfishness.

"A farmer," says Say, "is a wheat manufacturer who, among other tools which serve him in modifying the material from which he makes the wheat, employs one large tool, which we call a field. If he is not the proprietor of the field, if he is only a tenant, he pays the proprietor for the productive service of this tool. The tenant is reimbursed by the purchaser, the latter by another, until the product reaches the consumer; who redeems the first payment, PLUS all the others, by means of which the product has at last come into his hands."

Let us lay aside the subsequent payments by which the product reaches the consumer, and, for the present, pay attention only to the first one of all,—the rent paid to the proprietor by the tenant. On what ground, we ask, is the proprietor entitled to this rent?

According to Ricardo, MacCulloch, and Mill, farm-rent, properly speaking, is simply the EXCESS OF THE PRODUCT OF THE MOST FERTILE LAND OVER THAT OF LANDS OF AN INFERIOR QUALITY; so that farm-rent is not demanded for the former until the increase of population renders necessary the cultivation of the latter.

It is difficult to see any sense in this. How can a right to the land be based upon a difference in the quality of the land? How can varieties of soil engender a principle of legislation and politics? This reasoning is either so subtle, or so stupid, that the more I think of it, the more bewildered I become. Suppose two pieces of land of equal area; the one, A, capable of supporting ten thousand inhabitants; the other, B, capable of supporting nine thousand only: when, owing to an increase in their number, the inhabitants of A shall be forced to cultivate B, the landed proprietors of A will exact from their tenants in A a rent proportional to the difference between ten and nine. So say, I think, Ricardo, MacCulloch, and Mill. But if A supports as many inhabitants as it can contain,—that is, if the inhabitants of A, by our hypothesis, have only just enough land to keep them alive,—how can they pay farm-rent?

If they had gone no farther than to say that the difference in land has OCCASIONED farm-rent, instead of CAUSED it, this observation would have taught us a valuable lesson; namely, that farm-rent grew out of a desire for equality. Indeed, if all men have an equal right to the possession of good land, no one can be forced to cultivate bad land without indemnification. Farm-rent—according to Ricardo, MacCulloch, and Mill—would then have been a compensation for loss and hardship. This system of practical equality is a bad one, no doubt; but it sprang from good intentions. What argument can Ricardo, MacCulloch, and Mill develop therefrom in favor of property? Their theory turns against themselves, and strangles them.

Malthus thinks that farm-rent has its source in the power possessed by land of producing more than is necessary to supply the wants of the men who cultivate it. I would ask Malthus why successful labor should entitle the idle to a portion of the products?

But the worthy Malthus is mistaken in regard to the fact. Yes; land has the power of producing more than is needed by those who cultivate it, if by CULTIVATORS is meant tenants only. The tailor also makes more clothes than he wears, and the cabinet-maker more furniture than he uses. But, since the various professions imply and sustain one another, not only the farmer, but the followers of all arts and trades—even to the doctor and the school-teacher—are, and ought to be, regarded as CULTIVATORS OF THE LAND. Malthus bases farm-rent upon the principle of commerce. Now, the fundamental law of commerce being equivalence of the products exchanged, any thing which destroys this equivalence violates the law. There is an error in the estimate which needs to be corrected.

Buchanan—a commentator on Smith—regarded farm-rent as the result of a monopoly, and maintained that labor alone is productive. Consequently, he thought that, without this monopoly, products would rise in price; and he found no basis for farm-rent save in the civil law. This opinion is a corollary of that which makes the civil law the basis of property. But why has the civil law—which ought to be the written expression of justice—authorized this monopoly? Whoever says monopoly, necessarily excludes justice. Now, to say that farm-rent is a monopoly sanctioned by the law, is to say that injustice is based on justice,—a contradiction in terms.

Say answers Buchanan, that the proprietor is not a monopolist, because a monopolist "is one who does not increase the utility of the merchandise which passes through his hands."

How much does the proprietor increase the utility of his tenant's products? Has he ploughed, sowed, reaped, mowed, winnowed, weeded? These are the processes by which the tenant and his employees increase the utility of the material which they consume for the purpose of reproduction.

"The landed proprietor increases the utility of products by means of his implement, the land. This implement receives in one state, and returns in another the materials of which wheat is composed. The action of the land is a chemical process, which so modifies the material that it multiplies it by destroying it. The soil is then a producer of utility; and when it [the soil?] asks its pay in the form of profit, or farm rent, for its proprietor, it at the same time gives something to the consumer in exchange for the amount which the consumer pays it. It gives him a produced utility; and it is the production of this utility which warrants us in calling land productive, as well as labor."

Let us clear up this matter.

The blacksmith who manufactures for the farmer implements of husbandry, the wheelwright who makes him a cart, the mason who builds his barn, the carpenter, the basket-maker, &c.,—all of whom contribute to agricultural production by the tools which they provide,—are producers of utility; consequently, they are entitled to a part of the products.

"Undoubtedly," says Say; "but the land also is an implement whose service must be paid for, then...."

I admit that the land is an implement; but who made it? Did the proprietor? Did he—by the efficacious virtue of the right of property, by this MORAL QUALITY infused into the soil—endow it with vigor and fertility? Exactly there lies the monopoly of the proprietor; in the fact that, though he did not make the implement, he asks pay for its use. When the Creator shall present himself and claim farm-rent, we will consider the matter with him; or even when the proprietor—his pretended representative—shall exhibit his power-of-attorney.

"The proprietor's service," adds Say, "is easy, I admit."

It is a frank confession.

"But we cannot disregard it. Without property, one farmer would contend with another for the possession of a field without a proprietor, and the field would remain uncultivated...."

Then the proprietor's business is to reconcile farmers by robbing them. O logic! O justice! O the marvellous wisdom of economists! The proprietor, if they are right, is like Perrin-Dandin who, when summoned by two travellers to settle a dispute about an oyster, opened it, gobbled it, and said to them:—

"The Court awards you each a shell."

Could any thing worse be said of property?

Will Say tell us why the same farmers, who, if there were no proprietors, would contend with each other for possession of the soil, do not contend to-day with the proprietors for this possession? Obviously, because they think them legitimate possessors, and because their respect for even an imaginary right exceeds their avarice. I proved, in Chapter II., that possession is sufficient, without property, to maintain social order. Would it be more difficult, then, to reconcile possessors without masters than tenants controlled by proprietors? Would laboring men, who respect—much to their own detriment—the pretended rights of the idler, violate the natural rights of the producer and the manufacturer? What! if the husbandman forfeited his right to the land as soon as he ceased to occupy it, would he become more covetous? And would the impossibility of demanding increase, of taxing another's labor, be a source of quarrels and law-suits? The economists use singular logic. But we are not yet through. Admit that the proprietor is the legitimate master of the land.

"The land is an instrument of production," they say. That is true. But when, changing the noun into an adjective, they alter the phrase, thus, "The land is a productive instrument," they make a wicked blunder.

According to Quesnay and the early economists, all production comes from the land. Smith, Ricardo, and de Tracy, on the contrary, say that labor is the sole agent of production. Say, and most of his successors, teach that BOTH land AND labor AND capital are productive. The latter constitute the eclectic school of political economy. The truth is, that NEITHER land NOR labor NOR capital is productive. Production results from the co-operation of these three equally necessary elements, which, taken separately, are equally sterile.

Political economy, indeed, treats of the production, distribution, and consumption of wealth or values. But of what values? Of the values that he may appropriate it to his own use, and not at all of Nature's spontaneous productions. Man's labor consists in a simple laying on of hands. When he has taken that trouble, he has produced a value. Until then, the salt of the sea, the water of the springs, the grass of the fields, and the trees of the forests are to him as if they were not. The sea, without the fisherman and his line, supplies no fish. The forest, without the wood-cutter and his axe, furnishes neither fuel nor timber. The meadow, without the mower, yields neither hay nor aftermath. Nature is a vast mass of material to be cultivated and converted into products; but Nature produces nothing for herself: in the economical sense, her products, in their relation to man, are not yet products.

Capital, tools, and machinery are likewise unproductive. The hammer and the anvil, without the blacksmith and the iron, do not forge. The mill, without the miller and the grain, does not grind, &c. Bring tools and raw material together; place a plough and some seed on fertile soil; enter a smithy, light the fire, and shut up the shop,—you will produce nothing. The following remark was made by an economist who possessed more good sense than most of his fellows: "Say credits capital with an active part unwarranted by its nature; left to itself, it is an idle tool." (J. Droz: Political Economy.)

Finally, labor and capital together, when unfortunately combined, produce nothing. Plough a sandy desert, beat the water of the rivers, pass type through a sieve,—you will get neither wheat, nor fish, nor books. Your trouble will be as fruitless as was the immense labor of the army of Xerxes; who, as Herodotus says, with his three million soldiers, scourged the Hellespont for twenty-four hours, as a punishment for having broken and scattered the pontoon bridge which the great king had thrown across it.

Tools and capital, land and labor, considered individually and abstractly, are not, literally speaking, productive. The proprietor who asks to be rewarded for the use of a tool, or the productive power of his land, takes for granted, then, that which is radically false; namely, that capital produces by its own effort,—and, in taking pay for this imaginary product, he literally receives something for nothing.

OBJECTION.—But if the blacksmith, the wheelwright, all manufacturers in short, have a right to the products in return for the implements which they furnish; and if land is an implement of production,—why does not this implement entitle its proprietor, be his claim real or imaginary, to a portion of the products; as in the case of the manufacturers of ploughs and wagons?

REPLY.—Here we touch the heart of the question, the mystery of property; which we must clear up, if we would understand any thing of the strange effects of the right of increase.

He who manufactures or repairs the farmer's tools receives the price ONCE, either at the time of delivery, or in several payments; and when this price is once paid to the manufacturer, the tools which he has delivered belong to him no more. Never does he claim double payment for the same tool, or the same job of repairs. If he annually shares in the products of the farmer, it is owing to the fact that he annually makes something for the farmer.

The proprietor, on the contrary, does not yield his implement; eternally he is paid for it, eternally he keeps it.

In fact, the rent received by the proprietor is not intended to defray the expense of maintaining and repairing the implement; this expense is charged to the borrower, and does not concern the proprietor except as he is interested in the preservation of the article. If he takes it upon himself to attend to the repairs, he takes care that the money which he expends for this purpose is repaid.

This rent does not represent the product of the implement, since of itself the implement produces nothing; we have just proved this, and we shall prove it more clearly still by its consequences.

Finally, this rent does not represent the participation of the proprietor in the production; since this participation could consist, like that of the blacksmith and the wheelwright, only in the surrender of the whole or a part of his implement, in which case he would cease to be its proprietor, which would involve a contradiction of the idea of property.

Then, between the proprietor and his tenant there is no exchange either of values or services; then, as our axiom says, farm-rent is real increase,—an extortion based solely upon fraud and violence on the one hand, and weakness and ignorance upon the other. PRODUCTS say the economists, ARE BOUGHT ONLY BY PRODUCTS. This maxim is property's condemnation. The proprietor, producing neither by his own labor nor by his implement, and receiving products in exchange for nothing, is either a parasite or a thief. Then, if property can exist only as a right, property is impossible.

COROLLARIES.—1. The republican constitution of 1793, which defined property as "the right to enjoy the fruit of one's labor," was grossly mistaken. It should have said, "Property is the right to enjoy and dispose at will of another's goods,—the fruit of another's industry and labor."

2. Every possessor of lands, houses, furniture, machinery, tools, money, &c., who lends a thing for a price exceeding the cost of repairs (the repairs being charged to the lender, and representing products which he exchanges for other products), is guilty of swindling and extortion. In short, all rent received (nominally as damages, but really as payment for a loan) is an act of property,—a robbery.

HISTORICAL COMMENT.—The tax which a victorious nation levies upon a conquered nation is genuine farm-rent. The seigniorial rights abolished by the Revolution of 1789,—tithes, mortmain, statute-labor, &c.,—were different forms of the rights of property; and they who under the titles of nobles, seigneurs, prebendaries, &c. enjoyed these rights, were neither more nor less than proprietors. To defend property to-day is to condemn the Revolution.

SECOND PROPOSITION.

Property is impossible because wherever it exists Production costs more than it is worth.

The preceding proposition was legislative in its nature; this one is economical. It serves to prove that property, which originates in violence, results in waste.

"Production," says Say, "is exchange on a large scale. To render the exchange productive the value of the whole amount of service must be balanced by the value of the product. If this condition is not complied with, the exchange is unequal; the producer gives more than he receives."

Now, value being necessarily based upon utility, it follows that every useless product is necessarily valueless,—that it cannot be exchanged; and, consequently, that it cannot be given in payment for productive services.

Then, though production may equal consumption, it never can exceed it; for there is no real production save where there is a production of utility, and there is no utility save where there is a possibility of consumption. Thus, so much of every product as is rendered by excessive abundance inconsumable, becomes useless, valueless, unexchangeable,—consequently, unfit to be given in payment for any thing whatever, and is no longer a product.

Consumption, on the other hand, to be legitimate,—to be true consumption,—must be reproductive of utility; for, if it is unproductive, the products which it destroys are cancelled values—things produced at a pure loss; a state of things which causes products to depreciate in value. Man has the power to destroy, but he consumes only that which he reproduces. Under a right system of economy, there is then an equation between production and consumption.

These points established, let us suppose a community of one thousand families, enclosed in a territory of a given circumference, and deprived of foreign intercourse. Let this community represent the human race, which, scattered over the face of the earth, is really isolated. In fact, the difference between a community and the human race being only a numerical one, the economical results will be absolutely the same in each case.

Suppose, then, that these thousand families, devoting themselves exclusively to wheat-culture, are obliged to pay to one hundred individuals, chosen from the mass, an annual revenue of ten per cent. on their product. It is clear that, in such a case, the right of increase is equivalent to a tax levied in advance upon social production. Of what use is this tax?

It cannot be levied to supply the community with provisions, for between that and farm-rent there is nothing in common; nor to pay for services and products,—for the proprietors, laboring like the others, have labored only for themselves. Finally, this tax is of no use to its recipients who, having harvested wheat enough for their own consumption, and not being able in a society without commerce and manufactures to procure any thing else in exchange for it, thereby lose the advantage of their income.

In such a society, one-tenth of the product being inconsumable, one-tenth of the labor goes unpaid—production costs more than it is worth.

Now, change three hundred of our wheat-producers into artisans of all kinds: one hundred gardeners and wine-growers, sixty shoemakers and tailors, fifty carpenters and blacksmiths, eighty of various professions, and, that nothing may be lacking, seven school-masters, one mayor, one judge, and one priest; each industry furnishes the whole community with its special product. Now, the total production being one thousand, each laborer's consumption is one; namely, wheat, meat, and grain, 0.7; wine and vegetables, 0.1; shoes and clothing, 0.06; iron-work and furniture, 0.05; sundries, 0.08; instruction, 0.007; administration, 0.002; mass, 0.001, Total 1.

But the community owes a revenue of ten per cent.; and it matters little whether the farmers alone pay it, or all the laborers are responsible for it,—the result is the same. The farmer raises the price of his products in proportion to his share of the debt; the other laborers follow his example. Then, after some fluctuations, equilibrium is established, and all pay nearly the same amount of the revenue. It would be a grave error to assume that in a nation none but farmers pay farm-rent—the whole nation pays it.

I say, then, that by this tax of ten per cent. each laborer's consumption is reduced as follows: wheat, 0.63; wine and vegetables, 0.09; clothing and shoes, 0.054; furniture and iron-work, 0.045; other products, 0.072; schooling, 0.0063; administration, 0.0018; mass, 0.0009. Total 0.9.

The laborer has produced 1; he consumes only 0.9. He loses, then, one-tenth of the price of his labor; his production still costs more than it is worth. On the other hand, the tenth received by the proprietors is no less a waste; for, being laborers themselves, they, like the others, possess in the nine-tenths of their product the wherewithal to live: they want for nothing. Why should they wish their proportion of bread, wine, meat, clothes, shelter, &c, to be doubled, if they can neither consume nor exchange them? Then farm-rent, with them as with the rest of the laborers, is a waste, and perishes in their hands. Extend the hypothesis, increase the number and variety of the products, you still have the same result.

Hitherto, we have considered the proprietor as taking part in the production, not only (as Say says) by the use of his instrument, but in an effective manner and by the labor of his hands. Now, it is easy to see that, under such circumstances, property will never exist. What happens?

The proprietor—an essentially libidinous animal, without virtue or shame—is not satisfied with an orderly and disciplined life. He loves property, because it enables him to do at leisure what he pleases and when he pleases. Having obtained the means of life, he gives himself up to trivialities and indolence; he enjoys, he fritters away his time, he goes in quest of curiosities and novel sensations. Property—to enjoy itself—has to abandon ordinary life, and busy itself in luxurious occupations and unclean enjoyments.

Instead of giving up a farm-rent, which is perishing in their hands, and thus lightening the labor of the community, our hundred proprietors prefer to rest. In consequence of this withdrawal,—the absolute production being diminished by one hundred, while the consumption remains the same,—production and consumption seem to balance. But, in the first place, since the proprietors no longer labor, their consumption is, according to economical principles, unproductive; consequently, the previous condition of the community—when the labor of one hundred was rewarded by no products—is superseded by one in which the products of one hundred are consumed without labor. The deficit is always the same, whichever the column of the account in which it is expressed. Either the maxims of political economy are false, or else property, which contradicts them, is impossible.

The economists—regarding all unproductive consumption as an evil, as a robbery of the human race—never fail to exhort proprietors to moderation, labor, and economy; they preach to them the necessity of making themselves useful, of remunerating production for that which they receive from it; they launch the most terrible curses against luxury and laziness. Very beautiful morality, surely; it is a pity that it lacks common sense. The proprietor who labors, or, as the economists say, WHO MAKES HIMSELF USEFUL, is paid for this labor and utility; is he, therefore, any the less idle as concerns the property which he does not use, and from which he receives an income? His condition, whatever he may do, is an unproductive and FELONIOUS one; he cannot cease to waste and destroy without ceasing to be a proprietor.

But this is only the least of the evils which property engenders.

Society has to maintain some idle people, whether or no. It will always have the blind, the maimed, the insane, and the idiotic. It can easily support a few sluggards. At this point, the impossibilities thicken and become complicated.

THIRD PROPOSITION.

Property is impossible, because, with a given capital, Production is proportional to labor, not to property.

To pay a farm-rent of one hundred at the rate of ten per cent. of the product, the product must be one thousand; that the product may be one thousand, a force of one thousand laborers is needed. It follows, that in granting a furlough, as we have just done, to our one hundred laborer-proprietors, all of whom had an equal right to lead the life of men of income,— we have placed ourselves in a position where we are unable to pay their revenues. In fact, the productive power, which at first was one thousand, being now but nine hundred, the production is also reduced to nine hundred, one-tenth of which is ninety. Either, then, ten proprietors out of the one hundred cannot be paid,—provided the remaining ninety are to get the whole amount of their farm-rent,—or else all must consent to a decrease of ten per cent. For it is not for the laborer, who has been wanting in no particular, who has produced as in the past, to suffer by the withdrawal of the proprietor. The latter must take the consequences of his own idleness. But, then, the proprietor becomes poorer for the very reason that he wishes to enjoy; by exercising his right, he loses it; so that property seems to decrease and vanish in proportion as we try to lay hold of it,—the more we pursue it, the more it eludes our grasp. What sort of a right is that which is governed by numerical relations, and which an arithmetical calculation can destroy?

The laborer-proprietor received, first, as laborer, 0.9 in wages; second, as proprietor, 1 in farm-rent. He said to himself, "My farm-rent is sufficient; I have enough and to spare without my labor." And thus it is that the income upon which he calculated gets diminished by one-tenth,—he at the same time not even suspecting the cause of this diminution. By taking part in the production, he was himself the creator of this tenth which has vanished; and while he thought to labor only for himself, he unwittingly suffered a loss in exchanging his products, by which he was made to pay to himself one-tenth of his own farm-rent. Like every one else, he produced 1, and received but 0.9

If, instead of nine hundred laborers, there had been but five hundred, the whole amount of farm-rent would have been reduced to fifty; if there had been but one hundred, it would have fallen to ten. We may posit, then, the following axiom as a law of proprietary economy: INCREASE MUST DIMINISH AS THE NUMBER OF IDLERS AUGMENTS.

This first result will lead us to another more surprising still. Its effect is to deliver us at one blow from all the evils of property, without abolishing it, without wronging proprietors, and by a highly conservative process.

We have just proved that, if the farm-rent in a community of one thousand laborers is one hundred, that of nine hundred would be ninety, that of eight hundred, eighty, that of one hundred, ten, &c. So that, in a community where there was but one laborer, the farm-rent would be but 0.1; no matter how great the extent and value of the land appropriated. Therefore, WITH A GIVEN LANDED CAPITAL, PRODUCTION IS PROPORTIONAL TO LABOR, NOT TO PROPERTY.

Guided by this principle, let us try to ascertain the maximum increase of all property whatever.

What is, essentially, a farm-lease? It is a contract by which the proprietor yields to a tenant possession of his land, in consideration of a portion of that which it yields him, the proprietor. If, in consequence of an increase in his household, the tenant becomes ten times as strong as the proprietor, he will produce ten times as much. Would the proprietor in such a case be justified in raising the farm-rent tenfold? His right is not, The more you produce, the more I demand. It is, The more I sacrifice, the more I demand. The increase in the tenant's household, the number of hands at his disposal, the resources of his industry,—all these serve to increase production, but bear no relation to the proprietor. His claims are to be measured by his own productive capacity, not that of others. Property is the right of increase, not a poll-tax. How could a man, hardly capable of cultivating even a few acres by himself, demand of a community, on the ground of its use of ten thousand acres of his property, ten thousand times as much as he is incapable of producing from one acre? Why should the price of a loan be governed by the skill and strength of the borrower, rather than by the utility sacrificed by the proprietor? We must recognize, then, this second economical law: INCREASE IS MEASURED BY A FRACTION OF THE PROPRIETORS PRODUCTION.

Now, this production, what is it? In other words, What can the lord and master of a piece of land justly claim to have sacrificed in lending it to a tenant?

The productive capacity of a proprietor, like that of any laborer, being one, the product which he sacrifices in surrendering his land is also one. If, then, the rate of increase is ten per cent., the maximum increase is 0.1.

But we have seen that, whenever a proprietor withdraws from production, the amount of products is lessened by 1. Then the increase which accrues to him, being equal to 0.1 while he remains among the laborers, will be equal after his withdrawal, by the law of the decrease of farm-rent, to 0.09. Thus we are led to this final formula: THE MAXIMUM INCOME OF A PROPRIETOR IS EQUAL TO THE SQUARE ROOT OF THE PRODUCT OF ONE LABORER (some number being agreed upon to express this product). THE DIMINUTION WHICH THIS INCOME SUFFERS, IF THE PROPRIETOR IS IDLE, IS EQUAL TO A FRACTION WHOSE NUMERATOR IS 1, AND WHOSE DENOMINATOR IS THE NUMBER WHICH EXPRESSES THE PRODUCT.

Thus the maximum income of an idle proprietor, or of one who labors in his own behalf outside of the community, figured at ten per cent. on an average production of one thousand francs per laborer, would be ninety francs. If, then, there are in France one million proprietors with an income of one thousand francs each, which they consume unproductively, instead of the one thousand millions which are paid them annually, they are entitled in strict justice, and by the most accurate calculation, to ninety millions only.

It is something of a reduction, to take nine hundred and ten millions from the burdens which weigh so heavily upon the laboring class! Nevertheless, the account is not finished, and the laborer is still ignorant of the full extent of his rights.

What is the right of increase when confined within just limits? A recognition of the right of occupancy. But since all have an equal right of occupancy, every man is by the same title a proprietor. Every man has a right to an income equal to a fraction of his product. If, then, the laborer is obliged by the right of property to pay a rent to the proprietor, the proprietor is obliged by the same right to pay the same amount of rent to the laborer; and, since their rights balance each other, the difference between them is zero.

Scholium.—If farm-rent is only a fraction of the supposed product of the proprietor, whatever the amount and value of the property, the same is true in the case of a large number of small and distinct proprietors. For, although one man may use the property of each separately, he cannot use the property of all at the same time.

To sum up. The right of increase, which can exist only within very narrow limits, defined by the laws of production, is annihilated by the right of occupancy. Now, without the right of increase, there is no property. Then property is impossible.

FOURTH PROPOSITION.

Property is impossible, because it is Homicide.

If the right of increase could be subjected to the laws of reason and justice, it would be reduced to an indemnity or reward whose MAXIMUM never could exceed, for a single laborer, a certain fraction of that which he is capable of producing. This we have just shown. But why should the right of increase—let us not fear to call it by its right name, the right of robbery—be governed by reason, with which it has nothing in common? The proprietor is not content with the increase allotted him by good sense and the nature of things: he demands ten times, a hundred times, a thousand times, a million times as much. By his own labor, his property would yield him a product equal only to one; and he demands of society, no longer a right proportional to his productive capacity, but a per capita tax. He taxes his fellows in proportion to their strength, their number, and their industry. A son is born to a farmer. "Good!" says the proprietor; "one more chance for increase!" By what process has farm-rent been thus changed into a poll-tax? Why have our jurists and our theologians failed, with all their shrewdness, to check the extension of the right of increase?

The proprietor, having estimated from his own productive capacity the number of laborers which his property will accommodate, divides it into as many portions, and says: "Each one shall yield me revenue." To increase his income, he has only to divide his property. Instead of reckoning the interest due him on his labor, he reckons it on his capital; and, by this substitution, the same property, which in the hands of its owner is capable of yielding only one, is worth to him ten, a hundred, a thousand, a million. Consequently, he has only to hold himself in readiness to register the names of the laborers who apply to him—his task consists in drafting leases and receipts.

Not satisfied with the lightness of his duties, the proprietor does not intend to bear even the deficit resulting from his idleness; he throws it upon the shoulders of the producer, of whom he always demands the same reward. When the farm-rent of a piece of land is once raised to its highest point, the proprietor never lowers it; high prices, the scarcity of labor, the disadvantages of the season, even pestilence itself, have no effect upon him—why should he suffer from hard times when he does not labor?

Here commences a new series of phenomena.

Say—who reasons with marvellous clearness whenever he assails taxation, but who is blind to the fact that the proprietor, as well as the tax-gatherer, steals from the tenant, and in the same manner—says in his second letter to Malthus:—

"If the collector of taxes and those who employ him consume one-sixth of the products, they thereby compel the producers to feed, clothe, and support themselves on five-sixths of what they produce. They admit this, but say at the same time that it is possible for each one to live on five-sixths of what he produces.

"I admit that, if they insist upon it; but I ask if they believe that the producer would live as well, in case they demanded of him, instead of one-sixth, two-sixths, or one-third, of their products? No; but he would still live. Then I ask whether he would still live, in case they should rob him of two-thirds,... then three-quarters? But I hear no reply."

If the master of the French economists had been less blinded by his proprietary prejudices, he would have seen that farm-rent has precisely the same effect.

Take a family of peasants composed of six persons,—father, mother, and four children,—living in the country, and cultivating a small piece of ground. Let us suppose that by hard labor they manage, as the saying is, to make both ends meet; that, having lodged, warmed, clothed, and fed themselves, they are clear of debt, but have laid up nothing. Taking the years together, they contrive to live. If the year is prosperous, the father drinks a little more wine, the daughters buy themselves a dress, the sons a hat; they eat a little cheese, and, occasionally, some meat. I say that these people are on the road to wreck and ruin.

For, by the third corollary of our axiom, they owe to themselves the interest on their own capital. Estimating this capital at only eight thousand francs at two and a half per cent., there is an annual interest of two hundred francs to be paid. If, then, these two hundred francs, instead of being subtracted from the gross product to be saved and capitalized, are consumed, there is an annual deficit of two hundred francs in the family assets; so that at the end of forty years these good people, without suspecting it, will have eaten up their property and become bankrupt!

This result seems ridiculous—it is a sad reality.

The conscription comes. What is the conscription? An act of property exercised over families by the government without warning—a robbery of men and money. The peasants do not like to part with their sons,—in that I do not think them wrong. It is hard for a young man of twenty to gain any thing by life in the barracks; unless he is depraved, he detests it. You can generally judge of a soldier's morality by his hatred of his uniform. Unfortunate wretches or worthless scamps,—such is the make-up of the French army. This ought not to be the case,—but so it is. Question a hundred thousand men, and not one will contradict my assertion.

Our peasant, in redeeming his two conscripted sons, expends four thousand francs, which he borrows for that purpose;

the interest on this, at five per cent., is two hundred francs;—a sum equal to that referred to above. If, up to this time, the production of the family, constantly balanced by its consumption, has been one thousand two hundred francs, or two hundred francs per persons—in order to pay this interest, either the six laborers must produce as much as seven, or must consume as little as five.

Curtail consumption they cannot—how can they curtail necessity? To produce more is impossible; they can work neither harder nor longer. Shall they take a middle course, and consume five and a half while producing six and a half? They would soon find that with the stomach there is no compromise—that beyond a certain degree of abstinence it is impossible to go—that strict necessity can be curtailed but little without injury to the health; and, as for increasing the product,—there comes a storm, a drought, an epizootic, and all the hopes of the farmer are dashed. In short, the rent will not be paid, the interest will accumulate, the farm will be seized, and the possessor ejected.

Thus a family, which lived in prosperity while it abstained from exercising the right of property, falls into misery as soon as the exercise of this right becomes a necessity. Property requires of the husbandman the double power of enlarging his land, and fertilizing it by a simple command. While a man is simply possessor of the land, he finds in it means of subsistence; as soon as he pretends to proprietorship, it suffices him no longer. Being able to produce only that which he consumes, the fruit of his labor is his recompense for his trouble—nothing is left for the instrument.

Required to pay what he cannot produce,—such is the condition of the tenant after the proprietor has retired from social production in order to speculate upon the labor of others by new methods.

Let us now return to our first hypothesis.

The nine hundred laborers, sure that their future production will equal that of the past, are quite surprised, after paying their farm-rent, to find themselves poorer by one-tenth than they were the previous year. In fact, this tenth—which was formerly produced and paid by the proprietor-laborer who then took part in the production, and paid part of the—public expenses—now has not been produced, and has been paid. It must then have been taken from the producer's consumption. To choke this inexplicable deficit, the laborer borrows, confident of his intention and ability to return,—a confidence which is shaken the following year by a new loan, PLUS the interest on the first. From whom does he borrow? From the proprietor. The proprietor lends his surplus to the laborer; and this surplus, which he ought to return, becomes—being lent at interest—a new source of profit to him. Then debts increase indefinitely; the proprietor makes advances to the producer who never returns them; and the latter, constantly robbed and constantly borrowing from the robbers, ends in bankruptcy, defrauded of all that he had.

Suppose that the proprietor—who needs his tenant to furnish him with an income—then releases him from his debts. He will thus do a very benevolent deed, which will procure for him a recommendation in the curate's prayers; while the poor tenant, overwhelmed by this unstinted charity, and taught by his catechism to pray for his benefactors, will promise to redouble his energy, and suffer new hardships that he may discharge his debt to so kind a master.

This time he takes precautionary measures; he raises the price of grains. The manufacturer does the same with his products. The reaction comes, and, after some fluctuation, the farm-rent—which the tenant thought to put upon the manufacturer's shoulders—becomes nearly balanced. So that, while he is congratulating himself upon his success, he finds himself again impoverished, but to an extent somewhat smaller than before. For the rise having been general, the proprietor suffers with the rest; so that the laborers, instead of being poorer by one-tenth, lose only nine-hundredths. But always it is a debt which necessitates a loan, the payment of interest, economy, and fasting. Fasting for the nine-hundredths which ought not to be paid, and are paid; fasting for the redemption of debts; fasting to pay the interest on them. Let the crop fail, and the fasting becomes starvation. They say, "IT IS NECESSARY TO WORK MORE." That means, obviously, that IT IS NECESSARY TO PRODUCE MORE. By what conditions is production effected? By the combined action of labor, capital, and land. As for the labor, the tenant undertakes to furnish it; but capital is formed only by economy. Now, if the tenant could accumulate any thing, he would pay his debts. But granting that he has plenty of capital, of what use would it be to him if the extent of the land which he cultivates always remained the same? He needs to enlarge his farm.

Will it be said, finally, that he must work harder and to better advantage? But, in our estimation of farm-rent, we have assumed the highest possible average of production. Were it not the highest, the proprietor would increase the farm-rent. Is not this the way in which the large landed proprietors have gradually raised their rents, as fast as they have ascertained by the increase in population and the development of industry how much society can produce from their property? The proprietor is a foreigner to society; but, like the vulture, his eyes fixed upon his prey, he holds himself ready to pounce upon and devour it.

The facts to which we have called attention, in a community of one thousand persons, are reproduced on a large scale in every nation and wherever human beings live, but with infinite variations and in innumerable forms, which it is no part of my intention to describe.

In fine, property—after having robbed the laborer by usury—murders him slowly by starvation. Now, without robbery and murder, property cannot exist; with robbery and murder, it soon dies for want of support. Therefore it is impossible.

FIFTH PROPOSITION.

Property is impossible, because, if it exists, Society devours itself.

When the ass is too heavily loaded, he lies down; man always moves on. Upon this indomitable courage, the proprietor—well knowing that it exists—bases his hopes of speculation. The free laborer produces ten; for me, thinks the proprietor, he will produce twelve.

Indeed,—before consenting to the confiscation of his fields, before bidding farewell to the paternal roof,—the peasant, whose story we have just told, makes a desperate effort; he leases new land; he will sow one-third more; and, taking half of this new product for himself, he will harvest an additional sixth, and thereby pay his rent. What an evil! To add one-sixth to his production, the farmer must add, not one-sixth, but two-sixths to his labor. At such a price, he pays a farm-rent which in God's eyes he does not owe.

The tenant's example is followed by the manufacturer. The former tills more land, and dispossesses his neighbors; the latter lowers the price of his merchandise, and endeavors to monopolize its manufacture and sale, and to crush out his competitors. To satisfy property, the laborer must first produce beyond his needs. Then, he must produce beyond his strength; for, by the withdrawal of laborers who become proprietors, the one always follows from the other. But to produce beyond his strength and needs, he must invade the production of another, and consequently diminish the number of producers. Thus the proprietor—after having lessened production by stepping outside—lessens it still further by encouraging the monopoly of labor. Let us calculate it.

The laborer's deficit, after paying his rent, being, as we have seen, one-tenth, he tries to increase his production by this amount. He sees no way of accomplishing this save by increasing his labor: this also he does. The discontent of the proprietors who have not received the full amount of their rent; the advantageous offers and promises made them by other farmers, whom they suppose more diligent, more industrious, and more reliable; the secret plots and intrigues,—all these give rise to a movement for the re-division of labor, and the elimination of a certain number of producers. Out of nine hundred, ninety will be ejected, that the production of the others may be increased one-tenth. But will the total product be increased? Not in the least: there will be eight hundred and ten laborers producing as nine hundred, while, to accomplish their purpose, they would have to produce as one thousand. Now, it having been proved that farm-rent is proportional to the landed capital instead of to labor, and that it never diminishes, the debts must continue as in the past, while the labor has increased. Here, then, we have a society which is continually decimating itself, and which would destroy itself, did not the periodical occurrence of failures, bankruptcies, and political and economical catastrophes re-establish equilibrium, and distract attention from the real causes of the universal distress.

The monopoly of land and capital is followed by economical processes which also result in throwing laborers out of employment. Interest being a constant burden upon the shoulders of the farmer and the manufacturer, they exclaim, each speaking for himself, "I should have the means wherewith to pay my rent and interest, had I not to pay so many hands." Then those admirable inventions, intended to assure the easy and speedy performance of labor, become so many infernal machines which kill laborers by thousands.

"A few years ago, the Countess of Strafford ejected fifteen thousand persons from her estate, who, as tenants, added to its value. This act of private administration was repeated in 1820, by another large Scotch proprietor, towards six hundred tenants and their families."—Tissot: on Suicide and Revolt.

The author whom I quote, and who has written eloquent words concerning the revolutionary spirit which prevails in modern society, does not say whether he would have disapproved of a revolt on the part of these exiles. For myself, I avow boldly that in my eyes it would have been the first of rights, and the holiest of duties; and all that I desire to-day is that my profession of faith be understood.

Society devours itself,—1. By the violent and periodical sacrifice of laborers: this we have just seen, and shall see again; 2. By the stoppage of the producer's consumption caused by property. These two modes of suicide are at first simultaneous; but soon the first is given additional force by the second, famine uniting with usury to render labor at once more necessary and more scarce.

By the principles of commerce and political economy, that an industrial enterprise may be successful, its product must furnish,—1. The interest on the capital employed; 2. Means for the preservation of this capital; 3. The wages of all the employees and contractors. Further, as large a profit as possible must be realized.

The financial shrewdness and rapacity of property is worthy of admiration. Each different name which increase takes affords the proprietor an opportunity to receive it,—1. In the form of interest; 2. In the form of profit. For, it says, a part of the income derived from manufactures consists of interest on the capital employed. If one hundred thousand francs have been invested in a manufacturing enterprise, and in a year's time five thousand francs have been received therefrom in addition to the expenses, there has been no profit, but only interest on the capital. Now, the proprietor is not a man to labor for nothing. Like the lion in the fable, he gets paid in each of his capacities; so that, after he has been served, nothing is left for his associates.

Ego primam tollo, nominor quia leo.
Secundam quia sum fortis tribuctis mihi.
Tum quia plus valeo, me sequetur tertia.
Malo adficietur, si quis quartam tetigerit.

I know nothing prettier than this fable.

"I am the contractor. I take the first share.
I am the laborer, I take the second.
I am the capitalist, I take the third.
I am the proprietor, I take the whole."

In four lines, Phaedrus has summed up all the forms of property.

I say that this interest, all the more then this profit, is impossible.

What are laborers in relation to each other? So many members of a large industrial society, to each of whom is assigned a certain portion of the general production, by the principle of the division of labor and functions. Suppose, first, that this society is composed of but three individuals,—a cattle-raiser, a tanner, and a shoemaker. The social industry, then, is that of shoemaking. If I should ask what ought to be each producer's share of the social product, the first schoolboy whom I should meet would answer, by a rule of commerce and association, that it should be one-third. But it is not our duty here to balance the rights of laborers conventionally associated: we have to prove that, whether associated or not, our three workers are obliged to act as if they were; that, whether they will or no, they are associated by the force of things, by mathematical necessity.

Three processes are required in the manufacture of shoes,—the rearing of cattle, the preparation of their hides, and the cutting and sewing. If the hide, on leaving the farmer's stable, is worth one, it is worth two on leaving the tanner's pit, and three on leaving the shoemaker's shop. Each laborer has produced a portion of the utility; so that, by adding all these portions together, we get the value of the article. To obtain any quantity whatever of this article, each producer must pay, then, first for his own labor, and second for the labor of the other producers. Thus, to obtain as many shoes as can be made from ten hides, the farmer will give thirty raw hides, and the tanner twenty tanned hides. For, the shoes that are made from ten hides are worth thirty raw hides, in consequence of the extra labor bestowed upon them; just as twenty tanned hides are worth thirty raw hides, on account of the tanner's labor. But if the shoemaker demands thirty-three in the farmer's product, or twenty-two in the tanner's, for ten in his own, there will be no exchange; for, if there were, the farmer and the tanner, after having paid the shoemaker ten for his labor, would have to pay eleven for that which they had themselves sold for ten, —which, of course, would be impossible. 18

Well, this is precisely what happens whenever an emolument of any kind is received; be it called revenue, farm-rent, interest, or profit. In the little community of which we are speaking, if the shoemaker—in order to procure tools, buy a stock of leather, and support himself until he receives something from his investment—borrows money at interest, it is clear that to pay this interest he will have to make a profit off the tanner and the farmer. But as this profit is impossible unless fraud is used, the interest will fall back upon the shoulders of the unfortunate shoemaker, and ruin him.

I have imagined a case of unnatural simplicity. There is no human society but sustains more than three vocations. The most uncivilized society supports numerous industries; to-day, the number of industrial functions (I mean by industrial functions all useful functions) exceeds, perhaps, a thousand. However numerous the occupations, the economic law remains the same,—THAT THE PRODUCER MAY LIVE, HIS WAGES MUST REPURCHASE HIS PRODUCT.

The economists cannot be ignorant of this rudimentary principle of their pretended science: why, then, do they so obstinately defend property, and inequality of wages, and the legitimacy of usury, and the honesty of profit,—all of which contradict the economic law, and make exchange impossible? A contractor pays one hundred thousand francs for raw material, fifty thousand francs in wages, and then expects to receive a product of two hundred thousand francs,—that is, expects to make a profit on the material and on the labor of his employees; but if the laborers and the purveyor of the material cannot, with their combined wages, repurchase that which they have produced for the contractor, how can they live? I will develop my question. Here details become necessary.

If the workingman receives for his labor an average of three francs per day, his employer (in order to gain any thing beyond his own salary, if only interest on his capital) must sell the day's labor of his employee, in the form of merchandise, for more than three francs. The workingman cannot, then, repurchase that which he has produced for his master. It is thus with all trades whatsoever. The tailor, the hatter, the cabinet-maker, the blacksmith, the tanner, the mason, the jeweller, the printer, the clerk, &c., even to the farmer and wine-grower, cannot repurchase their products; since, producing for a master who in one form or another makes a profit, they are obliged to pay more for their own labor than they get for it.

In France, twenty millions of laborers, engaged in all the branches of science, art, and industry, produce every thing which is useful to man. Their annual wages amount, it is estimated to twenty thousand millions; but, in consequence of the right of property, and the multifarious forms of increase, premiums, tithes, interests, fines, profits, farm-rents, house-rents, revenues, emoluments of every nature and description, their products are estimated by the proprietors and employers at twenty-five thousand millions. What does that signify? That the laborers, who are obliged to repurchase these products in order to live, must either pay five for that which they produced for four, or fast one day in five.

If there is an economist in France able to show that this calculation is false, I summon him to appear; and I promise to retract all that I have wrongfully and wickedly uttered in my attacks upon property.

Let us now look at the results of this profit.

If the wages of the workingmen were the same in all pursuits, the deficit caused by the proprietor's tax would be felt equally everywhere; but also the cause of the evil would be so apparent, that it would soon be discovered and suppressed. But, as there is the same inequality of wages (from that of the scavenger up to that of the minister of state) as of property, robbery continually rebounds from the stronger to the weaker; so that, since the laborer finds his hardships increase as he descends in the social scale, the lowest class of people are literally stripped naked and eaten alive by the others.

The laboring people can buy neither the cloth which they weave, nor the furniture which they manufacture, nor the metal which they forge, nor the jewels which they cut, nor the prints which they engrave. They can procure neither the wheat which they plant, nor the wine which they grow, nor the flesh of the animals which they raise. They are allowed neither to dwell in the houses which they build, nor to attend the plays which their labor supports, nor to enjoy the rest which their body requires. And why? Because the right of increase does not permit these things to be sold at the cost-price, which is all that laborers can afford to pay. On the signs of those magnificent warehouses which he in his poverty admires, the laborer reads in large letters: "This is thy work, and thou shalt not have it." *Sic vos non vobis*!

Every manufacturer who employs one thousand laborers, and gains from them daily one sou each, is slowly pushing them into a state of misery. Every man who makes a profit has entered into a conspiracy with famine. But the whole nation has not even this labor, by means of which property starves it. And why? Because the workers are forced by the insufficiency of their wages to monopolize labor; and because, before being destroyed by dearth, they destroy each other by competition. Let us pursue this truth no further.

If the laborer's wages will not purchase his product, it follows that the product is not made for the producer. For whom, then, is it intended? For the richer consumer; that is, for only a fraction of society. But when the whole society labors, it produces for the whole society. If, then, only a part of society consumes, sooner or later a part of society will be idle. Now, idleness is death, as well for the laborer as for the proprietor.

This conclusion is inevitable.

The most distressing spectacle imaginable is the sight of producers resisting and struggling against this mathematical necessity, this power of figures to which their prejudices blind them.

If one hundred thousand printers can furnish reading-matter enough for thirty-four millions of men, and if the price of books is so high that only one-third of that number can afford to buy them, it is clear that these one hundred thousand printers will produce three times as much as the booksellers can sell. That the products of the laborers may never exceed the demands of the consumers, the laborers must either rest two days out of three, or, separating into three groups, relieve each other three times a week, month, or quarter; that is, during two-thirds of their life they must not live. But industry, under the influence of property, does not proceed with such regularity. It endeavors to produce a great deal in a short time, because the greater the amount of products, and the shorter the time of production, the less each product costs. As soon as a demand begins to be felt, the factories fill up, and everybody goes to work. Then business is lively, and both governors and governed rejoice. But the more they work to-day, the more idle will they be hereafter; the more they laugh, the more they shall weep. Under the rule of property, the flowers of industry are woven into none but funeral wreaths. The laborer digs his own grave.

If the factory stops running, the manufacturer has to pay interest on his capital the same as before. He naturally tries, then, to continue production by lessening expenses. Then comes the lowering of wages; the introduction of machinery; the employment of women and children to do the work of men; bad workmen, and wretched work. They still produce, because the decreased cost creates a larger market; but they do not produce long, because, the cheapness being due to the quantity and rapidity of production, the productive power tends more than ever to outstrip consumption. It is when laborers, whose wages are scarcely sufficient to support them from one day to another, are thrown out of work, that the consequences of the principle of property become most frightful. They have not been able to economize, they have made no savings, they have accumulated no capital whatever to support them even one day more. Today the factory is closed. To-morrow the people starve in the streets. Day after tomorrow they will either die in the hospital, or eat in the jail.

And still new misfortunes come to complicate this terrible situation. In consequence of the cessation of business, and the extreme cheapness of merchandise, the manufacturer finds it impossible to pay the interest on his borrowed capital; whereupon his frightened creditors hasten to withdraw their funds. Production is suspended, and labor comes to a standstill. Then people are astonished to see capital desert commerce, and throw itself upon the Stock Exchange; and I once heard M. Blanqui bitterly lamenting the blind ignorance of capitalists. The cause of this movement of capital is very simple; but for that very reason an economist could not understand it, or rather must not explain it. The cause lies solely in COMPETITION.

I mean by competition, not only the rivalry between two parties engaged in the same business, but the general and simultaneous effort of all kinds of business to get ahead of each other. This effort is to-day so strong, that the price of merchandise scarcely covers the cost of production and distribution; so that, the wages of all laborers being lessened, nothing remains, not even interest for the capitalists.

The primary cause of commercial and industrial stagnations is, then, interest on capital,—that interest which the ancients with one accord branded with the name of usury, whenever it was paid for the use of money, but which they did not dare to condemn in the forms of house-rent, farm-rent, or profit: as if the nature of the thing lent could ever warrant a charge for the lending; that is, robbery.

In proportion to the increase received by the capitalist will be the frequency and intensity of commercial crises,—the first being given, we always can determine the two others; and vice versa. Do you wish to know the regulator of a society? Ascertain the amount of active capital; that is, the capital bearing interest, and the legal rate of this interest. The course of events will be a series of overturns, whose number and violence will be proportional to the activity of capital.

In 1839, the number of failures in Paris alone was one thousand and sixty-four. This proportion was kept up in the early months of 1840; and, as I write these lines, the crisis is not yet ended. It is said, further, that the number of houses which have wound up their business is greater than the number of declared failures. By this flood, we may judge of the waterspout's power of suction.

The decimation of society is now imperceptible and permanent, now periodical and violent; it depends upon the course which property takes. In a country where the property is pretty evenly distributed, and where little business is done,—the rights and claims of each being balanced by those of others,—the power of invasion is destroyed. There—it may be truly said—property does not exist, since the right of increase is scarcely exercised at all. The condition of the laborers—as regards security of life—is almost the same as if absolute equality prevailed among them. They are deprived of all the advantages of full and free association, but their existence is not endangered in the least. With the exception of a few isolated victims of the right of property—of this misfortune whose primary cause no one perceives—the society appears to rest calmly in the bosom of this sort of equality. But have a care; it is balanced on the edge of a sword: at the slightest shock, it will fall and meet with death!

Ordinarily, the whirlpool of property localizes itself. On the one hand, farm-rent stops at a certain point; on the other, in consequence of competition and over-production, the price of manufactured goods does not rise,—so that the condition of the peasant varies but little, and depends mainly on the seasons. The devouring action of property bears, then, principally upon business. We commonly say COMMERCIAL CRISES, not AGRICULTURAL CRISES; because, while the farmer is eaten up slowly by the right of increase, the manufacturer is swallowed at a single mouthful. This leads to the cessation of business, the destruction of fortunes, and the inactivity of the working people; who die one after another on the highways, and in the hospitals, prisons, and galleys.

To sum up this proposition:—

Property sells products to the laborer for more than it pays him for them; therefore it is impossible.

APPENDIX TO THE FIFTH PROPOSITION.

I. Certain reformers, and even the most of the publicists—who, though belonging to no particular school, busy themselves in devising means for the amelioration of the lot of the poorer and more numerous class—lay much stress now-a-days on a better organization of labor. The disciples of Fourier, especially, never stop shouting, "ON TO THE PHALANX!" declaiming in the same breath against the foolishness and absurdity of other sects.

They consist of half-a-dozen incomparable geniuses who have discovered that FIVE AND FOUR MAKE NINE; TAKE TWO AWAY, AND NINE REMAIN,—and who weep over the blindness of France, who refuses to believe in this astonishing arithmetic. [*]

> * Fourier, having to multiply a whole number by a fraction, never failed, they say, to obtain a product much greater than the multiplicand. He affirmed that under his system of harmony the mercury would solidify when the temperature was above zero. He might as well have said that the Harmonians would make burning ice. I once asked an intelligent phalansterian what he thought of such physics. "I do not know," he answered; "but I believe." And yet the same man disbelieved in the doctrine of the Real Presence.

In fact, the Fourierists proclaim themselves, on the one hand, defenders of property, of the right of increase, which they have thus formulated: TO EACH ACCORDING TO HIS CAPITAL, HIS LABOR, AND HIS SKILL. On the other hand, they wish the workingman to come into the enjoyment of all the wealth of society; that is,—abridging the expression,—into the undivided enjoyment of his own product. Is not this like saying to the workingman, "Labor, you shall have three francs per day; you shall live on fifty-five sous; you shall give the rest to the proprietor, and thus you will consume three francs"?

If the above speech is not an exact epitome of Charles Fourier's system, I will subscribe to the whole phalansterian folly with a pen dipped in my own blood.

Of what use is it to reform industry and agriculture,—of what use indeed, to labor at all,—if property is maintained, and labor can never meet its expenses? Without the abolition of property, the organization of labor is neither more nor less than a delusion. If production should be quadrupled,—a thing which does not seem to me at all impossible,—it would be labor lost: if the additional product was not consumed, it would be of no value, and the proprietor would decline to receive it as interest; if it was consumed, all the disadvantages of property would reappear. It must be confessed that the theory of passional attraction is gravely at fault in this particular, and that Fourier, when he tried to harmonize the PASSION for property,—a bad passion, whatever he may say to the contrary,—blocked his own chariot-wheels.

The absurdity of the phalansterian economy is so gross, that many people suspect Fourier, in spite of all the homage paid by him to proprietors, of having been a secret enemy of property. This opinion might be supported by plausible arguments; still it is not mine. Charlatanism was too important a part for such a man to play, and sincerity too insignificant a one. I would rather think Fourier ignorant (which is generally admitted) than disingenuous. As for his disciples, before they can formulate any opinion of their own, they must declare once for all, unequivocally and with no mental reservation, whether they mean to maintain property or not, and what they mean by their famous motto,—"To each according to his capital, his labor, and his skill."

II. But, some half-converted proprietor will observe, "Would it not be possible, by suppressing the bank, incomes, farm-rent, house-rent, usury of all kinds, and finally property itself, to proportion products to capacities? That was St. Simon's idea; it was also Fourier's; it is the desire of the human conscience; and no decent person would dare maintain that a minister of state should live no better than a peasant."

O Midas! your ears are long! What! will you never understand that disparity of wages and the right of increase are one and the same? Certainly, St. Simon, Fourier, and their respective flocks committed a serious blunder in attempting to unite, the one, inequality and communism; the other, inequality and property: but you, a man of figures, a man of economy,—you, who know by heart your LOGARITHMIC tables,—how can you make so stupid a mistake?

Does not political economy itself teach you that the product of a man, whatever be his individual capacity, is never worth more than his labor, and that a man's labor is worth no more than his consumption? You remind me of that great constitution-framer, poor Pinheiro-Ferreira, the Sieyes of the nineteenth century, who, dividing the citizens of a nation into twelve classes,—or, if you prefer, into twelve grades,—assigned to some a salary of one hundred thousand francs each; to others, eighty thousand; then twenty-five thousand, fifteen thousand, ten thousand, &c., down to one thousand five hundred, and one thousand francs, the minimum allowance of a citizen. Pinheiro loved distinctions, and could no more conceive of a State without great dignitaries than of an army without drum-majors; and as he also loved, or thought he loved, liberty, equality, and fraternity, he combined the good and the evil of our old society in an eclectic philosophy which he embodied in a constitution. Excellent Pinheiro! Liberty even to passive submission, fraternity even to identity of language, equality even in the jury-box and at the guillotine,—such was his ideal republic. Unappreciated genius, of whom the present century was unworthy, but whom the future will avenge!

Listen, proprietor. Inequality of talent exists in fact; in right it is not admissible, it goes for nothing, it is not thought of. One Newton in a century is equal to thirty millions of men; the psychologist admires the rarity of so fine a genius, the legislator sees only the rarity of the function. Now, rarity of function bestows no privilege upon the functionary; and that for several reasons, all equally forcible.

1. Rarity of genius was not, in the Creator's design, a motive to compel society to go down on its knees before the man of superior talents, but a providential means for the performance of all functions to the greatest advantage of all.

2. Talent is a creation of society rather than a gift of Nature; it is an accumulated capital, of which the receiver is only the guardian. Without society,—without the education and powerful assistance which it furnishes,—the finest nature would be inferior to the most ordinary capacities in the very respect in which it ought to shine. The more extensive a man's knowledge, the more luxuriant his imagination, the more versatile his talent,—the more costly has his education been, the more remarkable and numerous were his teachers and his models, and the greater is his debt. The farmer produces from the time that he leaves his cradle until he enters his grave: the fruits of art and science are late and scarce; frequently the tree dies before the fruit ripens. Society, in cultivating talent, makes a sacrifice to hope.

3. Capacities have no common standard of comparison: the conditions of development being equal, inequality of talent is simply speciality of talent.

4. Inequality of wages, like the right of increase, is economically impossible. Take the most favorable case,—that where each laborer has furnished his maximum production; that there may be an equitable distribution of products, the share of each must be equal to the quotient of the total production divided by the number of laborers. This done, what remains wherewith to pay the higher wages? Nothing whatever.

Will it be said that all laborers should be taxed? But, then, their consumption will not be equal to their production, their wages will not pay for their productive service, they will not be able to repurchase their product, and we shall once more be afflicted with all the calamities of property. I do not speak of the injustice done to the defrauded laborer, of rivalry, of excited ambition, and burning hatred,—these may all be important considerations, but they do not hit the point.

On the one hand, each laborer's task being short and easy, and the means for its successful accomplishment being equal in all cases, how could there be large and small producers? On the other hand, all functions being equal, either on account of the actual equivalence of talents and capacities, or on account of social co-operation, how could a functionary claim a salary proportional to the worth of his genius?

But, what do I say? In equality wages are always proportional to talents. What is the economical meaning of wages? The reproductive consumption of the laborer. The very act by which the laborer produces constitutes, then, this consumption, exactly equal to his production, of which we are speaking. When the astronomer produces observations, the poet verses, or the savant experiments, they consume instruments, books, travels, &c., &c.; now, if society supplies this consumption, what more can the astronomer, the savant, or the poet demand? We must conclude, then, that in equality, and only in equality, St. Simon's adage—TO EACH ACCORDING TO HIS CAPACITY TO EACH CAPACITY ACCORDING TO ITS RESULTS—finds its full and complete application.

III. The great evil—the horrible and ever-present evil—arising from property, is that, while property exists, population, however reduced, is, and always must be, over-abundant. Complaints have been made in all ages of the excess of population; in all ages property has been embarrassed by the presence of pauperism, not perceiving that it caused it. Further,—nothing is more curious than the diversity of the plans proposed for its extermination. Their atrocity is equalled only by their absurdity.

The ancients made a practice of abandoning their children. The wholesale and retail slaughter of slaves, civil and foreign wars, also lent their aid. In Rome (where property held full sway), these three means were employed so effectively, and for so long a time, that finally the empire found itself without inhabitants. When the barbarians arrived, nobody was to be found; the fields were no longer cultivated; grass grew in the streets of the Italian cities.

In China, from time immemorial, upon famine alone has devolved the task of sweeping away the poor. The people living almost exclusively upon rice, if an accident causes the crop to fail, in a few days hunger kills the inhabitants by myriads; and the Chinese historian records in the annals of the empire, that in such a year of such an emperor twenty, thirty, fifty, one hundred thousand inhabitants died of starvation. Then they bury the dead, and recommence the production of children until another famine leads to the same result. Such appears to have been, in all ages, the Confucian economy.

I borrow the following facts from a modern economist:—

"Since the fourteenth and fifteenth centuries, England has been preyed upon by pauperism. At that time beggars were punished by law." Nevertheless, she had not one-fourth as large a population as she has to-day.

"Edward prohibits alms-giving, on pain of imprisonment.... The laws of 1547 and 1656 prescribe a like punishment, in case of a second offence. Elizabeth orders that each parish shall support its own paupers. But what is a pauper? Charles II. decides that an UNDISPUTED residence of forty days constitutes a settlement in a parish; but, if disputed, the new-comer is forced to pack off. James II. modifies this decision, which is again modified by William. In the midst of trials, reports, and modifications, pauperism increases, and the workingman languishes and dies.

"The poor-tax in 1774 exceeded forty millions of francs; in 1783-4-5, it averaged fifty-three millions; 1813, more than a hundred and eighty-seven millions five hundred thousand francs; 1816, two hundred and fifty millions; in 1817, it is estimated at three hundred and seventeen millions.

"In 1821, the number of paupers enrolled upon the parish lists was estimated at four millions, nearly one-third of the population.

"FRANCE. In 1544, Francis I. establishes a compulsory tax in behalf of the poor. In 1566 and 1586, the same principle is applied to the whole kingdom.

"Under Louis XIV., forty thousand paupers infested the capital [as many in proportion as to-day]. Mendicity was punished severely. In 1740, the Parliament of Paris re-establishes within its own jurisdiction the compulsory assessment.

"The Constituent Assembly, frightened at the extent of the evil and the difficulty of curing it, ordains the *statu quo*.

"The Convention proclaims assistance of the poor to be a NATIONAL DEBT. Its law remains unexecuted.

"Napoleon also wishes to remedy the evil: his idea is imprisonment. 'In that way,' said he, 'I shall protect the rich from the importunity of beggars, and shall relieve them of the disgusting sight of abject poverty.'" O wonderful man!

From these facts, which I might multiply still farther, two things are to be inferred,—the one, that pauperism is independent of population; the other, that all attempts hitherto made at its extermination have proved abortive.

Catholicism founds hospitals and convents, and commands charity; that is, she encourages mendicity. That is the extent of her insight as voiced by her priests.

The secular power of Christian nations now orders taxes on the rich, now banishment and imprisonment for the poor; that is, on the one hand, violation of the right of property, and, on the other, civil death and murder.

The modern economists—thinking that pauperism is caused by the excess of population, exclusively—have devoted themselves to devising checks. Some wish to prohibit the poor from marrying; thus,—having denounced religious celibacy,—they propose compulsory celibacy, which will inevitably become licentious celibacy.

Others do not approve this method, which they deem too violent; and which, they say, deprives the poor man of THE ONLY PLEASURE WHICH HE KNOWS IN THIS WORLD. They would simply recommend him to be PRUDENT. This opinion is held by Malthus, Sismondi, Say, Droz, Duchatel, &c. But if the poor are to be PRUDENT, the rich must set the example. Why should the marriageable age of the latter be fixed at eighteen years, while that of the former is postponed until thirty?

Again, they would do well to explain clearly what they mean by this matrimonial prudence which they so urgently recommend to the laborer; for here equivocation is especially dangerous, and I suspect that the economists are not thoroughly understood. "Some half-enlightened ecclesiastics are alarmed when they hear prudence in marriage advised; they fear that the divine injunction—INCREASE AND MULTIPLY—is to be set aside. To be logical, they must anathematize bachelors." (J. Droz: Political Economy.)

M. Droz is too honest a man, and too little of a theologian, to see why these casuists are so alarmed; and this chaste ignorance is the very best evidence of the purity of his heart. Religion never has encouraged early marriages; and the kind of PRUDENCE which it condemns is that described in this Latin sentence from Sanchez,—*An licet ob metum liberorum semen extra vas ejicere*?

Destutt de Tracy seems to dislike prudence in either form. He says: "I confess that I no more share the desire of the moralists to diminish and restrain our pleasures, than that of the politicians to increase our procreative powers, and accelerate reproduction." He believes, then, that we should love and marry when and as we please. Widespread misery results from love and marriage, but this our philosopher does not heed. True to the dogma of the necessity of evil, to evil he looks for the solution of all problems. He adds: "The multiplication of men continuing in all classes of society, the surplus members of the upper classes are supported by the lower classes, and those of the latter are destroyed by poverty." This philosophy has few avowed partisans; but it has over every other the indisputable advantage of demonstration in practice. Not long since France heard it advocated in the Chamber of Deputies, in the course of the discussion on the electoral reform,—POVERTY WILL ALWAYS EXIST. That is the political aphorism with which the minister of state ground to powder the arguments of M. Arago. POVERTY WILL ALWAYS EXIST! Yes, so long as property does.

The Fourierists—INVENTORS of so many marvellous contrivances—could not, in this field, belie their character. They invented four methods of checking increase of population at will.

1. THE VIGOR OF WOMEN. On this point they are contradicted by experience; for, although vigorous women may be less likely to conceive, nevertheless they give birth to the healthiest children; so that the advantage of maternity is on their side.

2. INTEGRAL EXERCISE, or the equal development of all the physical powers. If this development is equal, how is the power of reproduction lessened?

3. THE GASTRONOMIC REGIME; or, in plain English, the philosophy of the belly. The Fourierists say, that abundance of rich food renders women sterile; just as too much sap—while enhancing the beauty of flowers—destroys their reproductive capacity. But the analogy is a false one. Flowers become sterile when the stamens—or male organs—are changed into petals, as may be seen by inspecting a rose; and when through excessive dampness the pollen loses its fertilizing power. Then,—in order that the gastronomic regime may produce the results claimed for it,—not only must the females be fattened, but the males must be rendered impotent.

4. PHANEROGAMIC MORALITY, or public concubinage. I know not why the phalansterians use Greek words to convey ideas which can be expressed so clearly in French. This method—like the preceding one—is copied from civilized customs. Fourier, himself, cites the example of prostitutes as a proof. Now we have no certain knowledge yet of the facts which he quotes. So states Parent Duchatelet in his work on "Prostitution."

From all the information which I have been able to gather, I find that all the remedies for pauperism and fecundity—sanctioned by universal practice, philosophy, political economy, and the latest reformers—may be summed up in the following list: masturbation, onanism, [19] sodomy, tribadie, polyandry, [20] prostitution, castration, continence, abortion, and infanticide. [21]

All these methods being proved inadequate, there remains proscription.

Unfortunately, proscription, while decreasing the number of the poor, increases their proportion. If the interest charged by the proprietor upon the product is equal only to one-twentieth of the product (by law it is equal to one-twentieth of the capital), it follows that twenty laborers produce for nineteen only; because there is one among them, called proprietor, who eats the share of two. Suppose that the twentieth laborer—the poor one—is killed: the production of the following year will be diminished one-twentieth; consequently the nineteenth will have to yield his portion, and perish. For, since it is not one-twentieth of the product of nineteen which must be paid to the proprietor, but one-twentieth of the product of twenty (see third proposition), each surviving laborer must sacrifice one-twentieth PLUS one four-hundredth of his product; in other words, one man out of nineteen must be killed. Therefore, while property exists, the more poor people we kill, the more there are born in proportion.

Malthus, who proved so clearly that population increases in geometrical progression, while production increases only in arithmetical progression, did not notice this PAUPERIZING power of property. Had he observed this, he would have understood that, before trying to check reproduction, the right of increase should be abolished; because, wherever that right is tolerated, there are always too many inhabitants, whatever the extent or fertility of the soil.

It will be asked, perhaps, how I would maintain a balance between population and production; for sooner or later this problem must be solved. The reader will pardon me, if I do not give my method here. For, in my opinion, it is useless to say a thing unless we prove it. Now, to explain my method fully would require no less than a formal treatise. It is a thing so simple and so vast, so common and so extraordinary, so true and so misunderstood, so sacred and so profane, that to name it without developing and proving it would serve only to excite contempt and incredulity. One thing at a time. Let us establish equality, and this remedy will soon appear; for truths follow each other, just as crimes and errors do.

SIXTH PROPOSITION.

Property is impossible, because it is the Mother of Tyranny.

What is government? Government is public economy, the supreme administrative power over public works and national possessions.

Now, the nation is like a vast society in which all the citizens are stockholders. Each one has a deliberative voice in the assembly; and, if the shares are equal, has one vote at his disposal. But, under the regime of property, there is great inequality between the shares of the stockholders; therefore, one may have several hundred votes, while another has only one. If, for example, I enjoy an income of one million; that is, if I am the proprietor of a fortune of thirty or forty millions well invested, and if this fortune constitutes 1/30000 of the national capital,—it is clear that the public administration of my property would form 1/30000 of the duties of the government; and, if the nation had a population of thirty-four millions, that I should have as many votes as one thousand one hundred and thirty-three simple stockholders.

Thus, when M. Arago demands the right of suffrage for all members of the National Guard, he is perfectly right; since every citizen is enrolled for at least one national share, which entitles him to one vote. But the illustrious orator ought at the same time to demand that each elector shall have as many votes as he has shares; as is the case in commercial associations. For to do otherwise is to pretend that the nation has a right to dispose of the property of individuals without consulting them; which is contrary to the right of property. In a country where property exists, equality of electoral rights is a violation of property.

Now, if each citizen's sovereignty must and ought to be proportional to his property, it follows that the small stock holders are at the mercy of the larger ones; who will, as soon as they choose, make slaves of the former, marry them at pleasure, take from them their wives, castrate their sons, prostitute their daughters, throw the aged to the sharks,—and finally will be forced to serve themselves in the same way, unless they prefer to tax themselves for the support of their servants. In such a condition is Great Britain to-day. John Bull—caring little for liberty, equality, or dignity—prefers to serve and beg. But you, bonhomme Jacques?

Property is incompatible with political and civil equality; then property is impossible.

HISTORICAL COMMENTS.—1. When the vote of the third estate was doubled by the States-General of 1789, property was grossly violated. The nobility and the clergy possessed three-fourths of the soil of France; they should have controlled three-fourths of the votes in the national representation. To double the vote of the third estate was just, it is said, since the people paid nearly all the taxes. This argument would be sound, if there were nothing to be voted upon but taxes. But it was a question at that time of reforming the government and the constitution; consequently, the doubling of the vote of the third estate was a usurpation, and an attack on property.

2. If the present representatives of the radical opposition should come into power, they would work a reform by which every National Guard should be an elector, and every elector eligible for office,—an attack on property.

They would lower the rate of interest on public funds,—an attack on property.

They would, in the interest of the public, pass laws to regulate the exportation of cattle and wheat,—an attack on property.

They would alter the assessment of taxes,—an attack on property.

They would educate the people gratuitously,—a conspiracy against property.

They would organize labor; that is, they would guarantee labor to the workingman, and give him a share in the profits,—the abolition of property.

Now, these same radicals are zealous defenders of property,—a radical proof that they know not what they do, nor what they wish.

3. Since property is the grand cause of privilege and despotism, the form of the republican oath should be changed. Instead of, "I swear hatred to royalty," henceforth the new member of a secret society should say, "I swear hatred to property."

SEVENTH PROPOSITION.

Property is impossible, because, in consuming its Receipts, it loses them; in hoarding them, it nullifies them; and in using them as Capital, it turns them against Production.

I. If, with the economists, we consider the laborer as a living machine, we must regard the wages paid to him as the amount necessary to support this machine, and keep it in repair. The head of a manufacturing establishment—who employs laborers at three, five, ten, and fifteen francs per day, and who charges twenty francs for his superintendence—does not regard his disbursements as losses, because he knows they will return to him in the form of products. Consequently, LABOR and REPRODUCTIVE CONSUMPTION are identical.

What is the proprietor? He is a machine which does not work; or, which working for its own pleasure, and only when it sees fit, produces nothing.

What is it to consume as a proprietor? It is to consume without working, to consume without reproducing. For, once more, that which the proprietor consumes as a laborer comes back to him; he does not give his labor in exchange for his property, since, if he did, he would thereby cease to be a proprietor. In consuming as a laborer, the proprietor gains, or at least does not lose, since he recovers that which he consumes; in consuming as a proprietor, he impoverishes himself. To enjoy property, then, it is necessary to destroy it; to be a real proprietor, one must cease to be a proprietor.

The laborer who consumes his wages is a machine which destroys and reproduces; the proprietor who consumes his income is a bottomless gulf,—sand which we water, a stone which we sow. So true is this, that the proprietor—neither wishing nor knowing how to produce, and perceiving that as fast as he uses his property he destroys it for ever—has taken the precaution to make some one produce in his place. That is what political economy, speaking in the name of eternal justice, calls PRODUCING BY HIS CAPITAL,—PRODUCING BY HIS TOOLS. And that is what ought to be called PRODUCING BY A SLAVE—PRODUCING AS A THIEF AND AS A TYRANT. He, the proprietor, produce!... The robber might say, as well: "I produce."

The consumption of the proprietor has been styled luxury, in opposition to USEFUL consumption. From what has just been said, we see that great luxury can prevail in a nation which is not rich,—that poverty even increases with luxury, and vice versa. The economists (so much credit must be given them, at least) have caused such a horror of luxury, that to-day a very large number of proprietors—not to say almost all—ashamed of their idleness—labor, economize, and capitalize. They have jumped from the frying-pan into the fire.

I cannot repeat it too often: the proprietor who thinks to deserve his income by working, and who receives wages for his labor, is a functionary who gets paid twice; that is the only difference between an idle proprietor and a laboring proprietor. By his labor, the proprietor produces his wages only—not his income. And since his condition enables him to engage in the most lucrative pursuits, it may be said that the proprietor's labor harms society more than it helps it. Whatever the proprietor does, the consumption of his income is an actual loss, which his salaried functions neither repair nor justify; and which would annihilate property, were it not continually replenished by outside production.

II. Then, the proprietor who consumes annihilates the product: he does much worse if he lays it up. The things which he lays by pass into another world; nothing more is seen of them, not even the *caput mortuum*,—the smoke. If we had some means of transportation by which to travel to the moon, and if the proprietors should be seized with a sudden fancy to carry their savings thither, at the end of a certain time our terraqueous planet would be transported by them to its satellite!

The proprietor who lays up products will neither allow others to enjoy them, nor enjoy them himself; for him there is neither possession nor property. Like the miser, he broods over his treasures: he does not use them. He may feast his eyes upon them; he may lie down with them; he may sleep with them in his arms: all very fine, but coins do not breed coins. No real property without enjoyment; no enjoyment without consumption; no consumption without loss of property,—such is the inflexible necessity to which God's judgment compels the proprietor to bend. A curse upon property!

III. The proprietor who, instead of consuming his income, uses it as capital, turns it against production, and thereby makes it impossible for him to exercise his right. For the more he increases the amount of interest to be paid upon it, the more he is compelled to diminish wages. Now, the more he diminishes wages,—that is, the less he devotes to the maintenance and repair of the machines,—the more he diminishes the quantity of labor; and with the quantity of labor the quantity of product, and with the quantity of product the very source of his income. This is clearly shown by the following example:—

Take an estate consisting of arable land, meadows, and vineyards, containing the dwellings of the owner and the tenant; and worth, together with the farming implements, one hundred thousand francs, the rate of increase being three per cent. If, instead of consuming his revenue, the proprietor uses it, not in enlarging but in beautifying his estate, can he annually demand of his tenant an additional ninety francs on account of the three thousand francs which he has thus added to his capital? Certainly not; for on such conditions the tenant, though producing no more than before, would soon be obliged to labor for nothing,—what do I say? to actually suffer loss in order to hold his lease.

In fact, revenue can increase only as productive soil increases: it is useless to build walls of marble, and work with plows of gold. But, since it is impossible to go on acquiring for ever, to add estate to estate, to CONTINUE ONE'S POSSESSIONS, as the Latins said; and since, moreover, the proprietor always has means wherewith to capitalize,—it follows that the exercise of his right finally becomes impossible.

Well, in spite of this impossibility, property capitalizes, and in capitalizing increases its revenue; and, without stopping to look at the particular cases which occur in commerce, manufacturing operations, and banking, I will cite a graver fact,—one which directly affects all citizens. I mean the indefinite increase of the budget.

The taxes increase every year. It would be difficult to tell in which department of the government the expenses increase; for who can boast of any knowledge as to the budget? On this point, the ablest financiers continually disagree. What is to be thought, I ask, of the science of government, when its professors cannot understand one another's figures? Whatever be the immediate causes of this growth of the budget, it is certain that taxation increases at a rate which causes everybody to despair. Everybody sees it, everybody acknowledges it; but nobody seems to understand the primary cause.[*] Now, I say that it cannot be otherwise,—that it is necessary and inevitable.

> * "The financial situation of the English government was shown up in the House of Lords during the session of January 23. It is not an encouraging one. For several years the expenses have exceeded the receipts, and the Minister has been able to re-establish the balance only by loans renewed annually. The combined deficits of the years 1838 and 1839 amount to forty-seven million five hundred thousand francs. In

> 1840, the excess of expenses over receipts is expected to be twenty-two million five hundred thousand francs. Attention was called to these figures by Lord Ripon. Lord Melbourne replied: 'The noble earl unhappily was right in declaring that the public expenses continually increase, and with him I must say that there is no room for hope that they can be diminished or met in any way.'"—National: January 26, 1840.

A nation is the tenant of a rich proprietor called the GOVERNMENT, to whom it pays, for the use of the soil, a farm-rent called a tax. Whenever the government makes war, loses or gains a battle, changes the outfit of its army, erects a monument, digs a canal, opens a road, or builds a railway, it borrows money, on which the tax-payers pay interest; that is, the government, without adding to its productive capacity, increases its active capital,—in a word, capitalizes after the manner of the proprietor of whom I have just spoken.

Now, when a governmental loan is once contracted, and the interest is once stipulated, the budget cannot be reduced. For, to accomplish that, either the capitalists must relinquish their interest, which would involve an abandonment of property; or the government must go into bankruptcy, which would be a fraudulent denial of the political principle; or it must pay the debt, which would require another loan; or it must reduce expenses, which is impossible, since the loan was contracted for the sole reason that the ordinary receipts were insufficient; or the money expended by the government must be reproductive, which requires an increase of productive capacity,—a condition excluded by our hypothesis; or, finally, the tax-payers must submit to a new tax in order to pay the debt,—an impossible thing. For, if this new tax were levied upon all citizens alike, half, or even more, of the citizens would be unable to pay it; if the rich had to bear the whole, it would be a forced contribution,—an invasion of property. Long financial experience has shown that the method of loans, though exceedingly dangerous, is much surer, more convenient, and less costly than any other method; consequently the government borrows,—that is, goes on capitalizing,—and increases the budget.

Then, a budget, instead of ever diminishing, must necessarily and continually increase. It is astonishing that the economists, with all their learning, have failed to perceive a fact so simple and so evident. If they have perceived it, why have they neglected to condemn it?

HISTORICAL COMMENT.—Much interest is felt at present in a financial operation which is expected to result in a reduction of the budget. It is proposed to change the present rate of increase, five per cent. Laying aside the politico-legal question to deal only with the financial question,—is it not true that, when five per cent. is changed to four per cent., it will then be necessary, for the same reasons, to change four to three; then three to two, then two to one, and finally to sweep away increase altogether? But that would be the advent of equality of conditions and the abolition of property. Now it seems to me, that an intelligent nation should voluntarily meet an inevitable revolution half way, instead of suffering itself to be dragged after the car of inflexible necessity.

EIGHTH PROPOSITION.

Property is impossible, because its power of Accumulation is infinite, and is exercised only over finite quantities.

If men, living in equality, should grant to one of their number the exclusive right of property; and this sole proprietor should lend one hundred francs to the human race at compound interest, payable to his descendants twenty-four generations hence,—at the end of six hundred years this sum of one hundred francs, at five per cent., would amount to 107,854,010,777,600 francs; two thousand six hundred and ninety-six and one-third times the capital of France (supposing her capital to be 40,000,000,000), or more than twenty times the value of the terrestrial globe!

Suppose that a man, in the reign of St. Louis, had borrowed one hundred francs, and had refused,—he and his heirs after him,—to return it. Even though it were known that the said heirs were not the rightful possessors, and that prescription had been interrupted always at the right moment,—nevertheless, by our laws, the last heir would be obliged to return the one hundred francs with interest, and interest on the interest; which in all would amount, as we have seen, to nearly one hundred and eight thousand billions.

Every day, fortunes are growing in our midst much more rapidly than this. The preceding example supposed the interest equal to one-twentieth of the capital,—it often equals one-tenth, one-fifth, one-half of the capital; and sometimes the capital itself.

The Fourierists—irreconcilable enemies of equality, whose partisans they regard as SHARKS—intend, by quadrupling production, to satisfy all the demands of capital, labor, and skill. But, should production be multiplied by four, ten, or even one hundred, property would soon absorb, by its power of accumulation and the effects of its capitalization, both products and capital, and the land, and even the laborers. Is the phalanstery to be prohibited from capitalizing and lending at interest? Let it explain, then, what it means by property.

I will carry these calculations no farther. They are capable of infinite variation, upon which it would be puerile for me to insist. I only ask by what standard judges, called upon to decide a suit for possession, fix the interest? And, developing the question, I ask,—

Did the legislator, in introducing into the Republic the principle of property, weigh all the consequences? Did he know the law of the possible? If he knew it, why is it not in the Code? Why is so much latitude allowed to the proprietor in accumulating property and charging interest,—to the judge in recognizing and fixing the domain of property,—to the State in its power to levy new taxes continually? At what point is the nation justified in repudiating the budget, the tenant his farm-rent, and the manufacturer the interest on his capital? How far may the idler take advantage of the laborer? Where does the right of spoliation begin, and where does it end? When may the producer say to the proprietor, "I owe you nothing more"? When is property satisfied? When must it cease to steal?

If the legislator did know the law of the possible, and disregarded it, what must be thought of his justice? If he did not know it, what must be thought of his wisdom? Either wicked or foolish, how can we recognize his authority?

If our charters and our codes are based upon an absurd hypothesis, what is taught in the law-schools? What does a judgment of the Court of Appeal amount to? About what do our Chambers deliberate? What is POLITICS? What is our definition of a STATESMAN? What is the meaning of JURISPRUDENCE? Should we not rather say JURISIGNORANCE?

If all our institutions are based upon an error in calculation, does it not follow that these institutions are so many shams? And if the entire social structure is built upon this absolute impossibility of property, is it not true that the government under which we live is a chimera, and our present society a utopia?

NINTH PROPOSITION.

Property is impossible, because it is powerless against Property.

I. By the third corollary of our axiom, interest tells against the proprietor as well as the stranger. This economical principle is universally admitted. Nothing simpler at first blush; yet, nothing more absurd, more contradictory in terms, or more absolutely impossible.

The manufacturer, it is said, pays himself the rent on his house and capital. HE PAYS HIMSELF; that is, he gets paid by the public who buy his products. For, suppose the manufacturer, who seems to make this profit on his property, wishes also to make it on his merchandise, can he then pay himself one franc for that which cost him ninety centimes, and make money by the operation? No: such a transaction would transfer the merchant's money from his right hand to his left, but without any profit whatever.

Now, that which is true of a single individual trading with himself is true also of the whole business world. Form a chain of ten, fifteen, twenty producers; as many as you wish. If the producer A makes a profit out of the producer B. B's loss must, according to economical principles, be made up by C, C's by D; and so on through to Z.

But by whom will Z be paid for the loss caused him by the profit charged by A in the beginning? BY THE CONSUMER, replies Say. Contemptible equivocation! Is this consumer any other, then, than A, B. C, D, &c., or Z? By whom will Z be paid? If he is paid by A, no one makes a profit; consequently, there is no property. If, on the contrary, Z bears the burden himself, he ceases to be a member of society; since it refuses him the right of property and profit, which it grants to the other associates.

Since, then, a nation, like universal humanity, is a vast industrial association which cannot act outside of itself, it is clear that no man can enrich himself without impoverishing another. For, in order that the right of property, the right of increase, may be respected in the case of A, it must be denied to Z; thus we see how equality of rights, separated from equality of conditions, may be a truth. The iniquity of political economy in this respect is flagrant. "When I, a manufacturer, purchase the labor of a workingman, I do not include his wages in the net product of my business; on the contrary, I deduct them. But the workingman includes them in his net product...." (Say: Political Economy.)

That means that all which the workingman gains is NET PRODUCT; but that only that part of the manufacturer's gains is NET PRODUCT, which remains after deducting his wages. But why is the right of profit confined to the manufacturer? Why is this right, which is at bottom the right of property itself, denied to the workingman? In the terms of economical science, the workingman is capital. Now, all capital, beyond the cost of its maintenance and repair, must bear interest. This the proprietor takes care to get, both for his capital and for himself. Why is the workingman prohibited from charging a like interest for his capital, which is himself?

Property, then, is inequality of rights; for, if it were not inequality of rights, it would be equality of goods,—in other words, it would not exist. Now, the charter guarantees to all equality of rights. Then, by the charter, property is impossible.

II. Is A, the proprietor of an estate, entitled by the fact of his proprietorship to take possession of the field belonging to B. his neighbor? "No," reply the proprietors; "but what has that to do with the right of property?" That I shall show you by a series of similar propositions.

Has C, a hatter, the right to force D, his neighbor and also a hatter, to close his shop, and cease his business? Not the least in the world.

But C wishes to make a profit of one franc on every hat, while D is content with fifty centimes. It is evident that D's moderation is injurious to C's extravagant claims. Has the latter a right to prevent D from selling? Certainly not.

Since D is at liberty to sell his hats fifty centimes cheaper than C if he chooses, C in his turn is free to reduce his price one franc. Now, D is poor, while C is rich; so that at the end of two or three years D is ruined by this intolerable competition, and C has complete control of the market. Can the proprietor D get any redress from the proprietor C? Can he bring a suit against him to recover his business and property? No; for D could have done the same thing, had he been the richer of the two.

On the same ground, the large proprietor A may say to the small proprietor B: "Sell me your field, otherwise you shall not sell your wheat,"—and that without doing him the least wrong, or giving him ground for complaint. So that A can devour B if he likes, for the very reason that A is stronger than B. Consequently, it is not the right of property which enables A and C to rob B and D, but the right of might. By the right of property, neither the two neighbors A and B, nor the two merchants C and D, could harm each other. They could neither dispossess nor destroy one another, nor gain at one another's expense. The power of invasion lies in superior strength.

But it is superior strength also which enables the manufacturer to reduce the wages of his employees, and the rich merchant and well-stocked proprietor to sell their products for what they please. The manufacturer says to the laborer, "You are as free to go elsewhere with your services as I am to receive them. I offer you so much." The merchant says to the customer, "Take it or leave it; you are master of your money, as I am of my goods. I want so much." Who will yield? The weaker.

Therefore, without force, property is powerless against property, since without force it has no power to increase; therefore, without force, property is null and void.

HISTORICAL COMMENT.—The struggle between colonial and native sugars furnishes us a striking example of this impossibility of property. Leave these two industries to themselves, and the native manufacturer will be ruined by the colonist. To maintain the beet-root, the cane must be taxed: to protect the property of the one, it is necessary to injure the property of the other. The most remarkable feature of this business is precisely that to which the least attention is paid; namely, that, in one way or another, property has to be violated. Impose on each industry a proportional tax, so as to preserve a balance in the market, and you create a MAXIMUM PRICE,—you attack property in two ways. On the one hand, your tax interferes with the liberty of trade; on the other, it does not recognize equality of proprietors. Indemnify the beet-root, you violate the property of the tax-payer. Cultivate the two varieties of sugar at the nation's expense, just as different varieties of tobacco are cultivated,—you abolish one species of property. This last course would be the simpler and better one; but, to induce the nations to adopt it, requires such a co-operation of able minds and generous hearts as is at present out of the question.

Competition, sometimes called liberty of trade,—in a word, property in exchange,—will be for a long time the basis of our commercial legislation; which, from the economical point of view, embraces all civil laws and all government. Now, what is competition? A duel in a closed field, where arms are the test of right.

"Who is the liar,—the accused or the accuser?" said our barbarous ancestors. "Let them fight it out," replied the still more barbarous judge; "the stronger is right."

Which of us two shall sell spices to our neighbor? "Let each offer them for sale," cries the economist; "the sharper, or the more cunning, is the more honest man, and the better merchant."

Such is the exact spirit of the Code Napoleon.

TENTH PROPOSITION.

Property is impossible, because it is the Negation of equality.

The development of this proposition will be the resume of the preceding ones.

1. It is a principle of economical justice, that PRODUCTS ARE BOUGHT ONLY BY PRODUCTS. Property, being capable of defence only on the ground that it produces utility, is, since it produces nothing, for ever condemned.

2. It is an economical law, that LABOR MUST BE BALANCED BY PRODUCT. It is a fact that, with property, production costs more than it is worth.

3. Another economical law: THE CAPITAL BEING GIVEN, PRODUCTION IS MEASURED, NOT BY THE AMOUNT OF CAPITAL, BUT BY PRODUCTIVE CAPACITY. Property, requiring income to be always proportional to capital without regard to labor, does not recognize this relation of equality between effect and cause.

4 and 5. Like the insect which spins its silk, the laborer never produces for himself alone. Property, demanding a double product and unable to obtain it, robs the laborer, and kills him.

6. Nature has given to every man but one mind, one heart, one will. Property, granting to one individual a plurality of votes, supposes him to have a plurality of minds.

7. All consumption which is not reproductive of utility is destruction. Property, whether it consumes or hoards or capitalizes, is productive of INUTILITY,—the cause of sterility and death.

8. The satisfaction of a natural right always gives rise to an equation; in other words, the right to a thing is necessarily balanced by the possession of the thing. Thus, between the right to liberty and the condition of a free man there is a balance, an equation; between the right to be a father and paternity, an equation; between the right to security and the social guarantee, an equation. But between the right of increase and the receipt of this increase there is never an equation; for every new increase carries with it the right to another, the latter to a third, and so on for ever. Property, never being able to accomplish its object, is a right against Nature and against reason.

9. Finally, property is not self-existent. An extraneous cause—either FORCE or FRAUD—is necessary to its life and action. In other words, property is not equal to property: it is a negation—a delusion—NOTHING.

CHAPTER V. PSYCHOLOGICAL EXPOSITION OF THE IDEA OF JUSTICE

PSYCHOLOGICAL EXPOSITION OF THE IDEA OF JUSTICE AND INJUSTICE, AND A DETERMINATION OF THE PRINCIPLE OF GOVERNMENT AND OF RIGHT.

Property is impossible; equality does not exist. We hate the former, and yet wish to possess it; the latter rules all our thoughts, yet we know not how to reach it. Who will explain this profound antagonism between our conscience and our will? Who will point out the causes of this pernicious error, which has become the most sacred principle of justice and society?

I am bold enough to undertake the task, and I hope to succeed.

But before explaining why man has violated justice, it is necessary to determine what justice is.

PART FIRST.

% 1.—Of the Moral Sense in Man and the Animals.

The philosophers have endeavored often to locate the line which separates man's intelligence from that of the brutes; and, according to their general custom, they gave utterance to much foolishness before resolving upon the only course possible for them to take,—observation. It was reserved for an unpretending savant—who perhaps did not pride himself on his philosophy—to put an end to the interminable controversy by a simple distinction; but one of those luminous distinctions which are worth more than systems. Frederic Cuvier separated INSTINCT from INTELLIGENCE.

But, as yet, no one has proposed this question:—

IS THE DIFFERENCE BETWEEN MAN'S MORAL SENSE AND THAT OF THE BRUTE A DIFFERENCE IN KIND OR ONLY IN DEGREE?

If, hitherto, any one had dared to maintain the latter alternative, his arguments would have seemed scandalous, blasphemous, and offensive to morality and religion. The ecclesiastical and secular tribunals would have condemned him with one voice. And, mark the style in which they would have branded the immoral paradox! "Conscience,"—they would have cried,—"conscience, man's chief glory, was given to him exclusively; the notion of justice and injustice, of merit and demerit, is his noble privilege; to man, alone,—the lord of creation,—belongs the sublime power to resist his worldly propensities, to choose between good and evil, and to bring himself more and more into the resemblance of God through liberty and justice.... No; the holy image of virtue was never graven save on the heart of man." Words full of feeling, but void of sense.

Man is a rational and social animal—{GREEK ' c g}—said Aristotle. This definition is worth more than all which have been given since. I do not except even M. de Bonald's celebrated definition,—MAN IS AN INTELLECT SERVED BY ORGANS—a definition which has the double fault of explaining the known by the unknown; that is, the living being by the intellect; and of neglecting man's essential quality,—animality.

Man, then, is an animal living in society. Society means the sum total of relationships; in short, system. Now, all systems exist only on certain conditions. What, then, are the conditions, the LAWS, of human society?

What are the RIGHTS of men with respect to each other; what is JUSTICE?

It amounts to nothing to say,—with the philosophers of various schools,—"It is a divine instinct, an immortal and heavenly voice, a guide given us by Nature, a light revealed unto every man on coming into the world, a law engraved upon our hearts; it is the voice of conscience, the dictum of reason, the inspiration of sentiment, the penchant of feeling; it is the love of self in others; it is enlightened self-interest; or else it is an innate idea, the imperative command of applied reason, which has its source in the concepts of pure reason; it is a passional attraction," &c., &c. This may be as true as it seems beautiful; but it is utterly meaningless. Though we should prolong this litany through ten pages (it has been filtered through a thousand volumes), we should be no nearer to the solution of the question.

"Justice is public utility," says Aristotle. That is true, but it is a tautology. "The principle that the public welfare ought to be the object of the legislator"—says M. Ch. Comte in his "Treatise on Legislation"—"cannot be overthrown. But legislation is advanced no farther by its announcement and demonstration, than is medicine when it is said that it is the business of physicians to cure the sick."

Let us take another course. RUGHT is the sum total of the principles which govern society. Justice, in man, is the respect and observation of those principles. To practise justice is to obey the social instinct; to do an act of justice is to do a social act. If, then, we watch the conduct of men towards each other under different circumstances, it will be easy for us to distinguish between the presence and absence of society; from the result we may inductively infer the law.

Let us commence with the simplest and least doubtful cases.

The mother, who protects her son at the peril of her life, and sacrifices every thing to his support, is in society with him—she is a good mother. She, on the contrary, who abandons her child, is unfaithful to the social instinct,—maternal love being one of its many features; she is an unnatural mother.

If I plunge into the water to rescue a drowning man, I am his brother, his associate; if, instead of aiding him, I sink him, I am his enemy, his murderer.

Whoever bestows alms treats the poor man as his associate; not thoroughly, it is true, but only in respect to the amount which he shares with him. Whoever takes by force or stratagem that which is not the product of his labor, destroys his social character—he is a brigand.

The Samaritan who relieves the traveller lying by the wayside, dresses his wounds, comforts him, and supplies him with money, thereby declares himself his associate—his neighbor; the priest, who passes by on the other side, remains unassociated, and is his enemy.

In all these cases, man is moved by an internal attraction towards his fellow, by a secret sympathy which causes him to love, congratulate, and condole; so that, to resist this attraction, his will must struggle against his nature.

But in these respects there is no decided difference between man and the animals. With them, as long as the weakness of their young endears them to their mothers,—in a word, associates them with their mothers,—the latter protect the former, at the peril of their lives, with a courage which reminds us of our heroes dying for their country. Certain species unite for hunting purposes, seek each other, call each other (a poet would say invite each other), to share their prey; in danger they aid, protect, and warn each other. The elephant knows how to help his companion out of the ditch into which the latter has fallen. Cows form a circle, with their horns outward and their calves in the centre, in order to repel the attacks of wolves. Horses and pigs, on hearing a cry of distress from one of their number, rush to the spot whence it comes. What descriptions I might give of their marriages, the tenderness of the males towards the females, and the fidelity of their loves! Let us add, however,—to be entirely just—that these touching demonstrations of society, fraternity, and love of neighbor, do not prevent the animals from quarrelling, fighting, and outrageously abusing one another while gaining their livelihood and showing their gallantry; the resemblance between them and ourselves is perfect.

The social instinct, in man and beast, exists to a greater or less degree—its nature is the same. Man has the greater need of association, and employs it more; the animal seems better able to endure isolation. In man, social needs are more imperative and complex; in the beast, they seem less intense, less diversified, less regretted. Society, in a word, aims, in the case of man, at the preservation of the race and the individual; with the animals, its object is more exclusively the preservation of the race.

As yet, we have met with no claim which man can make for himself alone. The social instinct and the moral sense he shares with the brutes; and when he thinks to become god-like by a few acts of charity, justice, and devotion, he does not perceive that in so acting he simply obeys an instinct wholly animal in its nature. As we are good, loving, tender, just, so we are passionate, greedy, lewd, and vindictive; that is, we are like the beasts. Our highest virtues appear, in the last analysis, as blind, impulsive instincts. What subjects for canonization and apotheosis!

There is, however, a difference between us two-handed bipeds and other living creatures—what is it?

A student of philosophy would hasten to reply: "This difference lies in the fact that we are conscious of our social faculty, while the animals are unconscious of theirs—in the fact that while we reflect and reason upon the operation of our social instinct, the animals do nothing of the kind."

I will go farther. It is by our reflective and reasoning powers, with which we seem to be exclusively endowed, that we know that it is injurious, first to others and then to ourselves, to resist the social instinct which governs us, and which we call JUSTICE. It is our reason which teaches us that the selfish man, the robber, the murderer—in a word, the traitor to society—sins against Nature, and is guilty with respect to others and himself, when he does wrong wilfully. Finally, it is our social sentiment on the one hand, and our reason on the other, which cause us to think that beings such as we should take the responsibility of their acts. Such is the principle of remorse, revenge, and penal justice.

But this proves only an intellectual diversity between the animals and man, not at all an affectional one; for, although we reason upon our relations with our fellows, we likewise reason upon our most trivial actions,—such as drinking, eating, choosing a wife, or selecting a dwelling-place. We reason upon things earthly and things heavenly; there is nothing to which our reasoning powers are not applicable. Now, just as the knowledge of external phenomena, which we acquire, has no influence upon their causes and laws, so reflection, by illuminating our instinct, enlightens us as to our sentient nature, but does not alter its character; it tells us what our morality is, but neither changes nor modifies it. Our dissatisfaction with ourselves after doing wrong, the indignation which we feel at the sight of injustice, the idea of deserved punishment and due remuneration, are effects of reflection, and not immediate effects of instinct and emotion. Our appreciation (I do not say exclusive appreciation, for the animals also realize that they have done wrong, and are indignant when one of their number is attacked, but), our infinitely superior appreciation of our social duties, our knowledge of good and evil, does not establish, as regards morality, any vital difference between man and the beasts.

% 2.—Of the first and second degrees of Sociability.

I insist upon the fact, which I have just pointed out, as one of the most important facts of anthropology.

The sympathetic attraction, which causes us to associate, is, by reason of its blind, unruly nature, always governed by temporary impulse, without regard to higher rights, and without distinction of merit or priority. The bastard dog follows indifferently all who call it; the suckling child regards every man as its father and every woman as its nurse; every living creature, when deprived of the society of animals of its species, seeks companionship in its solitude. This fundamental characteristic of the social instinct renders intolerable and even hateful the friendship of frivolous persons, liable to be infatuated with every new face, accommodating to all whether good or bad, and ready to sacrifice, for a passing liaison, the oldest and most honorable affections. The fault of such beings is not in the heart—it is in the judgment. Sociability, in this degree, is a sort of magnetism awakened in us by the contemplation of a being similar to ourselves, but which never goes beyond the person who feels it; it may be reciprocated, but not communicated. Love, benevolence, pity, sympathy, call it what you will, there is nothing in it which deserves esteem,—nothing which lifts man above the beast.

The second degree of sociability is justice, which may be defined as the RECOGNITION OF THE EQUALITY BETWEEN ANOTHER'S PERSONALITY AND OUR OWN. The sentiment of justice we share with the animals; we alone can form an exact idea of it; but our idea, as has been said already, does not change its nature. We shall soon see how man rises to a third degree of sociability which the animals are incapable of reaching. But I must first prove by metaphysics that SOCIETY, JUSTICE, and EQUALITY, are three equivalent terms,—three expressions meaning the same thing,—whose mutual conversion is always allowable.

If, amid the confusion of a shipwreck, having escaped in a boat with some provisions, I see a man struggling with the waves, am I bound to go to his assistance? Yes, I am bound under penalty of being adjudged guilty of murder and treason against society.

But am I also bound to share with him my provisions?

To settle this question, we must change the phraseology. If society is binding on the boat, is it also binding on the provisions? Undoubtedly. The duty of an associate is absolute. Man's occupancy succeeds his social nature, and is subordinate to it; possession can become exclusive only when permission to occupy is granted to all alike. That which in this instance obscures our duty is our power of foresight, which, causing us to fear an eventual danger, impels us to usurpation, and makes us robbers and murderers. Animals do not calculate the duty of instinct any more than the disadvantages resulting to those who exercise it; it would be strange if the intellect of man—the most sociable of animals—should lead him to disobey the law.

He betrays society who attempts to use it only for his own advantage; better that God should deprive us of prudence, if it is to serve as the tool of our selfishness.

"What!" you will say, "must I share my bread, the bread which I have earned and which belongs to me, with the stranger whom I do not know; whom I may never see again, and who, perhaps, will reward me with ingratitude? If we had earned this bread together, if this man had done something to obtain it, he might demand his share, since his co-operation would entitle him to it; but as it is, what claim has he on me? We have not produced together—we shall not eat together."

The fallacy in this argument lies in the false supposition, that each producer is not necessarily associated with every other producer.

When two or more individuals have regularly organized a society,—when the contracts have been agreed upon, drafted, and signed,—there is no difficulty about the future. Everybody knows that when two men associate—for instance—in order to fish, if one of them catches no fish, he is none the less entitled to those caught by his associate. If two merchants form a partnership, while the partnership lasts, the profits and losses are divided between them; since each produces, not for himself, but for the society: when the time of distribution arrives, it is not the producer who is considered, but the associate. That is why the slave, to whom the planter gives straw and rice; and the civilized laborer, to whom the capitalist pays a salary which is always too small,—not being associated with their employers, although producing with them,—are disregarded when the product is divided. Thus, the horse who draws our coaches, and the ox who draws our carts produce with us, but are not associated with us; we take their product, but do not share it with them. The animals and laborers whom we employ hold the same relation to us. Whatever we do for them, we do, not from a sense of justice, but out of pure benevolence. [22]

But is it possible that we are not all associated? Let us call to mind what was said in the last two chapters, That even though we do not want to be associated, the force of things, the necessity of consumption, the laws of production, and the mathematical principle of exchange combine to associate us. There is but a single exception to this rule,—that of the proprietor, who, producing by his right of increase, is not associated with any one, and consequently is not obliged to share his product with any one; just as no one else is bound to share with him. With the exception of the proprietor, we labor for each other; we can do nothing by ourselves unaided by others, and we continually exchange products and services with each other. If these are not social acts, what are they?

Now, neither a commercial, nor an industrial, nor an agricultural association can be conceived of in the absence of equality; equality is its sine qua non. So that, in all matters which concern this association, to violate society is to violate justice and equality. Apply this principle to humanity at large.

After what has been said, I assume that the reader has sufficient insight to enable him to dispense with any aid of mine.

By this principle, the man who takes possession of a field, and says, "This field is mine," will not be unjust so long as every one else has an equal right of possession; nor will he be unjust, if, wishing to change his location, he exchanges this field for an equivalent. But if, putting another in his place, he says to him, "Work for me while I rest," he then becomes unjust, unassociated, UNEQUAL. He is a proprietor.

Reciprocally, the sluggard, or the rake, who, without performing any social task, enjoys like others—and often more than others—the products of society, should be proceeded against as a thief and a parasite. We owe it to ourselves to give him nothing; but, since he must live, to put him under supervision, and compel him to labor.

Sociability is the attraction felt by sentient beings for each other. Justice is this same attraction, accompanied by thought and knowledge. But under what general concept, in what category of the understanding, is justice placed? In the category of equal quantities. Hence, the ancient definition of justice—*Justum aequale est, injustum inaequale*. What is it, then, to practise justice? It is to give equal wealth to each, on condition of equal labor. It is to act socially. Our selfishness may complain; there is no escape from evidence and necessity.

What is the right of occupancy? It is a natural method of dividing the earth, by reducing each laborer's share as fast as new laborers present themselves. This right disappears if the public interest requires it; which, being the social interest, is also that of the occupant.

What is the right of labor? It is the right to obtain one's share of wealth by fulfilling the required conditions. It is the right of society, the right of equality.

Justice, which is the product of the combination of an idea and an instinct, manifests itself in man as soon as he is capable of feeling, and of forming ideas. Consequently, it has been regarded as an innate and original sentiment; but this opinion is logically and chronologically false. But justice, by its composition hybrid—if I may use the term,—justice, born of emotion and intellect combined, seems to me one of the strongest proofs of the unity and simplicity of the ego; the organism being no more capable of producing such a mixture by itself, than are the combined senses of hearing and sight of forming a binary sense, half auditory and half visual.

This double nature of justice gives us the definitive basis of all the demonstrations in Chapters II., III., and IV. On the one hand, the idea of JUSTICE being identical with that of society, and society necessarily implying equality, equality must underlie all the sophisms invented in defence of property; for, since property can be defended only as a just and social institution, and property being inequality, in order to prove that property is in harmony with society, it must be shown that injustice is justice, and that inequality is equality,—a contradiction in terms. On the other hand, since the idea of equality—the second element of justice—has its source in the mathematical proportions of things; and since property, or the unequal distribution of wealth among laborers, destroys the necessary balance between labor, production, and consumption,—property must be impossible.

All men, then, are associated; all are entitled to the same justice; all are equal. Does it follow that the preferences of love and friendship are unjust?

This requires explanation. I have already supposed the case of a man in peril, I being in a position to help him. Now, I suppose myself appealed to at the same time by two men exposed to danger.

Am I not allowed—am I not commanded even—to rush first to the aid of him who is endeared to me by ties of blood, friendship, acquaintance, or esteem, at the risk of leaving the other to perish? Yes. And why? Because within universal society there exist for each of us as many special societies as there are individuals; and we are bound, by the principle of sociability itself, to fulfil the obligations which these impose upon us, according to the intimacy of our relations with them.

Therefore we must give our father, mother, children, friends, relatives, &c., the preference over all others. But in what consists this preference?

A judge has a case to decide, in which one of the parties is his friend, and the other his enemy. Should he, in this instance, prefer his INTIMATE ASSOCIATE to his DISTANT ASSOCIATE; and decide the case in favor of his friend, in spite of evidence to the contrary? No: for, if he should favor his friend's injustice, he would become his accomplice in his violation of the social compact; he would form with him a sort of conspiracy against the social body. Preference should be shown only in personal matters, such as love, esteem, confidence, or intimacy, when all cannot be considered at once. Thus, in case of fire, a father would save his own child before thinking of his neighbor's; but the recognition of a right not being an optional matter with a judge, he is not at liberty to favor one person to the detriment of another.

The theory of these special societies—which are formed concentrically, so to speak, by each of us inside of the main body—gives the key to all the problems which arise from the opposition and conflict of the different varieties of social duty,—problems upon which the ancient tragedies are based.

The justice practised among animals is, in a certain degree, negative. With the exception of protecting their young, hunting and plundering in troops, uniting for common defence and sometimes for individual assistance, it consists more in prevention than in action. A sick animal who cannot arise from the ground, or an imprudent one who has fallen over a precipice, receives neither medicine nor nourishment. If he cannot cure himself, nor relieve himself of his trouble, his life is in danger: he will neither be cared for in bed, nor fed in a prison.

Their neglect of their fellows arises as much from the weakness of their intellect as from their lack of resources. Still, the degrees of intimacy common among men are not unknown to the animals. They have friendships of habit and of choice; friendships neighborly, and friendships parental. In comparison with us, they have feeble memories, sluggish feelings, and are almost destitute of intelligence; but the identity of these faculties is preserved to some extent, and our superiority in this respect arises entirely from our understanding.

It is our strength of memory and penetration of judgment which enable us to multiply and combine the acts which our social instinct impels us to perform, and which teaches us how to render them more effective, and how to distribute them justly. The beasts who live in society practise justice, but are ignorant of its nature, and do not reason upon it; they obey their instinct without thought or philosophy. They know not how to unite the social sentiment with the idea of equality, which they do not possess; this idea being an abstract one. We, on the contrary, starting with the principle that society implies equality, can, by our reasoning faculty, understand and agree with each other in settling our rights; we have even used our judgment to a great extent. But in all this our conscience plays a small part, as is proved by the fact that the idea of RIGHT—of which we catch a glimpse in certain animals who approach nearer than any others to our standard of intelligence—seems to grow, from the low level at which it stands in savages, to the lofty height which it reaches in a Plato or a Franklin. If we trace the development of the moral sense in individuals, and the progress of laws in nations, we shall be convinced that the ideas of justice and legislative perfection are always proportional to intelligence. The notion of justice—which has been regarded by some philosophers as simple—is then, in reality, complex. It springs from the social instinct on the one hand, and the idea of equality on the other; just as the notion of guilt arises from the feeling that justice has been violated, and from the idea of free-will.

In conclusion, instinct is not modified by acquaintance with its nature; and the facts of society, which we have thus far observed, occur among beasts as well as men. We know the meaning of justice; in other words, of sociability viewed from the standpoint of equality. We have met with nothing which separates us from the animals.

% 3.—Of the third degree of Sociability.

The reader, perhaps, has not forgotten what was said in the third chapter concerning the division of labor and the speciality of talents. The sum total of the talents and capacities of the race is always the same, and their nature is always similar. We are all born poets, mathematicians, philosophers, artists, artisans, or farmers, but we are not born equally endowed; and between one man and another in society, or between one faculty and another in the same individual, there is an infinite difference. This difference of degree in the same faculties, this predominance of talent in certain directions, is, we have said, the very foundation of our society. Intelligence and natural genius have been distributed by Nature so economically, and yet so liberally, that in society there is no danger of either a surplus or a scarcity of special talents; and that each laborer, by devoting himself to his function, may always attain to the degree of proficiency necessary to enable him to benefit by the labors and discoveries of his fellows. Owing to this simple and wise precaution of Nature, the laborer is not isolated by his task. He communicates with his fellows through the mind, before he is united with them in heart; so that with him love is born of intelligence.

It is not so with societies of animals. In every species, the aptitudes of all the individuals—though very limited—are equal in number and (when they are not the result of instinct) in intensity. Each one does as well as all the others what all the others do; provides his food, avoids the enemy, burrows in the earth, builds a nest, &c. No animal, when free and healthy, expects or requires the aid of his neighbor; who, in his turn, is equally independent.

Associated animals live side by side without any intellectual intercourse or intimate communication,—all doing the same things, having nothing to learn or to remember; they see, feel, and come in contact with each other, but never penetrate each other. Man continually exchanges with man ideas and feelings, products and services. Every discovery and act in society is necessary to him. But of this immense quantity of products and ideas, that which each one has to produce and acquire for himself is but an atom in the sun. Man would not be man were it not for society, and society is supported by the balance and harmony of the powers which compose it.

Society, among the animals, is SIMPLE; with man it is COMPLEX. Man is associated with man by the same instinct which associates animal with animal; but man is associated differently from the animal, and it is this difference in association which constitutes the difference in morality.

I have proved,—at too great length, perhaps,—both by the spirit of the laws which regard property as the basis of society, and by political economy, that inequality of conditions is justified neither by priority of occupation nor superiority of talent, service, industry, and capacity. But, although equality of conditions is a necessary consequence of natural right, of liberty, of the laws of production, of the capacity of physical nature, and of the principle of society itself,—it does not prevent the social sentiment from stepping over the boundaries of DEBT and CREDIT. The fields of benevolence and love extend far beyond; and when economy has adjusted its balance, the mind begins to benefit by its own justice, and the heart expands in the boundlessness of its affection.

The social sentiment then takes on a new character, which varies with different persons. In the strong, it becomes the pleasure of generosity; among equals, frank and cordial friendship; in the weak, the pleasure of admiration and gratitude.

The man who is superior in strength, skill, or courage, knows that he owes all that he is to society, without which he could not exist. He knows that, in treating him precisely as it does the lowest of its members, society discharges its whole duty towards him. But he does not underrate his faculties; he is no less conscious of his power and greatness; and it is this voluntary reverence which he pays to humanity, this avowal that he is but an instrument of Nature,—who is alone worthy of glory and worship,—it is, I say, this simultaneous confession of the heart and the mind, this genuine adoration of the Great Being, that distinguishes and elevates man, and lifts him to a degree of social morality to which the beast is powerless to attain. Hercules destroying the monsters and punishing brigands for the safety of Greece, Orpheus teaching the rough and wild Pelasgians,—neither of them putting a price upon their services,—there we see the noblest creations of poetry, the loftiest expression of justice and virtue.

The joys of self-sacrifice are ineffable.

If I were to compare human society to the old Greek tragedies, I should say that the phalanx of noble minds and lofty souls dances the strophe, and the humble multitude the antistrophe. Burdened with painful and disagreeable tasks, but rendered omnipotent by their number and the harmonic arrangement of their functions, the latter execute what the others plan. Guided by them, they owe them nothing; they honor them, however, and lavish upon them praise and approbation.

Gratitude fills people with adoration and enthusiasm.

But equality delights my heart. Benevolence degenerates into tyranny, and admiration into servility. Friendship is the daughter of equality. O my friends! may I live in your midst without emulation, and without glory; let equality bring us together, and fate assign us our places. May I die without knowing to whom among you I owe the most esteem!

Friendship is precious to the hearts of the children of men.

Generosity, gratitude (I mean here only that gratitude which is born of admiration of a superior power), and friendship are three distinct shades of a single sentiment which I will call equite, or SOCIAL PROPORTIONALITY. [23] Equite does not change justice: but, always taking equite for the base, it superadds esteem, and thereby forms in man a third degree of sociability. Equite makes it at once our duty and our pleasure to aid the weak who have need of us, and to make them our equals; to pay to the strong a just tribute of gratitude and honor, without enslaving ourselves to them; to cherish our neighbors, friends, and equals, for that which we receive from them, even by right of exchange. Equite is sociability raised to its ideal by reason and justice; its commonest manifestation is URBANITY or POLITENESS, which, among certain nations, sums up in a single word nearly all the social duties.

It is the just distribution of social sympathy and universal love.

Now, this feeling is unknown among the beasts, who love and cling to each other, and show their preferences, but who cannot conceive of esteem, and who are incapable of generosity, admiration, or politeness.

This feeling does not spring from intelligence, which calculates, computes, and balances, but does not love; which sees, but does not feel. As justice is the product of social instinct and reflection combined, so equite is a product of justice and taste combined—that is, of our powers of judging and of idealizing.

This product—the third and last degree of human sociability—is determined by our complex mode of association; in which inequality, or rather the divergence of faculties, and the speciality of functions—tending of themselves to isolate laborers—demand a more active sociability.

That is why the force which oppresses while protecting is execrable; why the silly ignorance which views with the same eye the marvels of art, and the products of the rudest industry, excites unutterable contempt; why proud mediocrity, which glories in saying, "I have paid you—I owe you nothing," is especially odious.

SOCIABILITY, JUSTICE, EQUITE—such, in its triplicity, is the exact definition of the instinctive faculty which leads us into communication with our fellows, and whose physical manifestation is expressed by the formula: EQUALITY IN NATURAL WEALTH, AND THE PRODUCTS OF LABOR.

These three degrees of sociability support and imply each other.

Equite cannot exist without justice; society without justice is a solecism. If, in order to reward talent, I take from one to give to another, in unjustly stripping the first, I do not esteem his talent as I ought; if, in society, I award more to myself than to my associate, we are not really associated. Justice is sociability as manifested in the division of material things, susceptible of weight and measure; equite is justice accompanied by admiration and esteem,—things which cannot be measured.

From this several inferences may be drawn.

1. Though we are free to grant our esteem to one more than to another, and in all possible degrees, yet we should give no one more than his proportion of the common wealth; because the duty of justice, being imposed upon us before that of equite, must always take precedence of it. The woman honored by the ancients, who, when forced by a tyrant to choose between the death of her brother and that of her husband, sacrificed the latter on the ground that she could find another husband but not another brother,—that woman, I say, in obeying her sense of equite, failed in point of justice, and did a bad deed, because conjugal association is a closer relation than fraternal association, and because the life of our neighbor is not our property.

By the same principle, inequality of wages cannot be admitted by law on the ground of inequality of talents; because the just distribution of wealth is the function of economy,—not of enthusiasm.

Finally, as regards donations, wills, and inheritance, society, careful both of the personal affections and its own rights, must never permit love and partiality to destroy justice. And, though it is pleasant to think that the son, who has been long associated with his father in business, is more capable than any one else of carrying it on; and that the citizen, who is surprised in the midst of his task by death, is best fitted, in consequence of his natural taste for his occupation, to designate his successor; and though the heir should be allowed the right of choice in case of more than one inheritance,—nevertheless, society can tolerate no concentration of capital and industry for the benefit of a single man, no monopoly of labor, no encroachment. 24

"Suppose that some spoils, taken from the enemy, and equal to twelve, are to be divided between Achilles and Ajax. If the two persons were equal, their respective shares would be arithmetically equal: Achilles would have six, Ajax six. And if we should carry out this arithmetical equality, Thersites would be entitled to as much as Achilles, which would be unjust in the extreme. To avoid this injustice, the worth of the persons should be estimated, and the spoils divided accordingly. Suppose that the worth of Achilles is double that of Ajax: the former's share is eight, the latter four. There is no arithmetical equality, but a proportional equality. It is this comparison of merits, rationum, that Aristotle calls distributive justice. It is a geometrical proportion."—Toullier: French Law according to the Code.

Are Achilles and Ajax associated, or are they not? Settle that, and you settle the whole question. If Achilles and Ajax, instead of being associated, are themselves in the service of Agamemnon who pays them, there is no objection to Aristotle's method. The slave-owner, who controls his slaves, may give a double allowance of brandy to him who does double work. That is the law of despotism; the right of slavery.

But if Achilles and Ajax are associated, they are equals. What matters it that Achilles has a strength of four, while that of Ajax is only two? The latter may always answer that he is free; that if Achilles has a strength of four, five could kill him; finally, that in doing personal service he incurs as great a risk as Achilles. The same argument applies to Thersites. If he is unable to fight, let him be cook, purveyor, or butler. If he is good for nothing, put him in the hospital. In no case wrong him, or impose upon him laws.

Man must live in one of two states: either in society, or out of it. In society, conditions are necessarily equal, except in the degree of esteem and consideration which each one may receive. Out of society, man is so much raw material, a capitalized tool, and often an incommodious and useless piece of furniture.

2. Equite, justice, and society, can exist only between individuals of the same species. They form no part of the relations of different races to each other,—for instance, of the wolf to the goat, of the goat to man, of man to God, much less of God to man. The attribution of justice, equity, and love to the Supreme Being is pure anthropomorphism; and the adjectives just, merciful, pitiful, and the like, should be stricken from our litanies. God can be regarded as just, equitable, and good, only to another God. Now, God has no associate; consequently, he cannot experience social affections,—such as goodness, equite, and justice. Is the shepherd said to be just to his sheep and his dogs? No: and if he saw fit to shear as much wool from a lamb six months old, as from a ram of two years; or, if he required as much work from a young dog as from an old one,—they would say, not that he was unjust, but that he was foolish. Between man and beast there is no society, though there may be affection. Man loves the animals as THINGS,—as SENTIENT THINGS, if you will,—but not as PERSONS. Philosophy, after having eliminated from the idea of God the passions ascribed to him by superstition, will then be obliged to eliminate also the virtues which our liberal piety awards to him. 25

The rights of woman and her relations with man are yet to be determined Matrimonial legislation, like civil legislation, is a matter for the future to settle.

If God should come down to earth, and dwell among us, we could not love him unless he became like us; nor give him any thing unless he produced something; nor listen to him unless he proved us mistaken; nor worship him unless he manifested his power. All the laws of our nature, affectional, economical, and intellectual, would prevent us from treating him as we treat our fellow-men,—that is, according to reason, justice, and equite.

I infer from this that, if God should wish ever to put himself into immediate communication with man, he would have to become a man.

Now, if kings are images of God, and executors of his will, they cannot receive love, wealth, obedience, and glory from us, unless they consent to labor and associate with us—produce as much as they consume, reason with their subjects, and do wonderful things. Still more; if, as some pretend, kings are public functionaries, the love which is due them is measured by their personal amiability; our obligation to obey them, by the wisdom of their commands; and their civil list, by the total social production divided by the number of citizens.

Thus, jurisprudence, political economy, and psychology agree in admitting the law of equality. Right and duty—the due reward of talent and labor—the outbursts of love and enthusiasm,—all are regulated in advance by an invariable standard; all depend upon number and balance. Equality of conditions is the law of society, and universal solidarity is the ratification of this law.

Equality of conditions has never been realized, thanks to our passions and our ignorance; but our opposition to this law has made it all the more a necessity. To that fact history bears perpetual testimony, and the course of events reveals it to us. Society advances from equation to equation. To the eyes of the economist, the revolutions of empires seem now like the reduction of algebraical quantities, which are inter-deducible; now like the discovery of unknown quantities, induced by the inevitable influence of time. Figures are the providence of history. Undoubtedly there are other elements in human progress; but in the multitude of hidden causes which agitate nations, there is none more powerful or constant, none less obscure, than the periodical explosions of the proletariat against property. Property, acting by exclusion and encroachment, while population was increasing, has been the life-principle and definitive cause of all revolutions. Religious wars, and wars of conquest, when they have stopped short of the extermination of races, have been only accidental disturbances, soon repaired by the mathematical progression of the life of nations. The downfall and death of societies are due to the power of accumulation possessed by property.

In the middle ages, take Florence,—a republic of merchants and brokers, always rent by its well-known factions, the Guelphs and Ghibellines, who were, after all, only the people and the proprietors fighting against each other,—Florence, ruled by bankers, and borne down at last by the weight of her debts;[26] in ancient times, take Rome, preyed upon from its birth by usury, flourishing, nevertheless, as long as the known world furnished its terrible proletaires with LABOR stained with blood by civil war at every interval of rest, and dying of exhaustion when the people lost, together with their former energy, their last spark of moral sense; Carthage, a commercial and financial city, continually divided by internal competition; Tyre, Sidon, Jerusalem, Nineveh, Babylon, ruined, in turn, by commercial rivalry and, as we now express it, by panics in the market,—do not these famous examples show clearly enough the fate which awaits modern nations, unless the people, unless France, with a sudden burst of her powerful voice, proclaims in thunder-tones the abolition of the regime of property?

Here my task should end. I have proved the right of the poor; I have shown the usurpation of the rich. I demand justice; it is not my business to execute the sentence. If it should be argued—in order to prolong for a few years an illegitimate privilege—that it is not enough to demonstrate equality, that it is necessary also to organize it, and above all to establish it peacefully, I might reply: The welfare of the oppressed is of more importance than official composure. Equality of conditions is a natural law upon which public economy and jurisprudence are based. The right to labor, and the principle of equal distribution of wealth, cannot give way to the anxieties of power. It is not for the proletaire to reconcile the contradictions of the codes, still less to suffer for the errors of the government. On the contrary, it is the duty of the civil and administrative power to reconstruct itself on the basis of political equality. An evil, when known, should be condemned and destroyed. The legislator cannot plead ignorance as an excuse for upholding a glaring iniquity. Restitution should not be delayed. Justice, justice! recognition of right! reinstatement of the proletaire!—when these results are accomplished, then, judges and consuls, you may attend to your police, and provide a government for the Republic!

For the rest, I do not think that a single one of my readers accuses me of knowing how to destroy, but of not knowing how to construct. In demonstrating the principle of equality, I have laid the foundation of the social structure I have done more. I have given an example of the true method of solving political and legislative problems. Of the science itself, I confess that I know nothing more than its principle; and I know of no one at present who can boast of having penetrated deeper. Many people cry, "Come to me, and I will teach you the truth!" These people mistake for the truth their cherished opinion and ardent conviction, which is usually any thing but the truth. The science of society—like all human sciences—will be for ever incomplete. The depth and variety of the questions which it embraces are infinite. We hardly know the A B C of this science, as is proved by the fact that we have not yet emerged from the period of systems, and have not ceased to put the authority of the majority in the place of facts. A certain philological society decided linguistic questions by a plurality of votes. Our parliamentary debates—were their results less pernicious—would be even more ridiculous. The task of the true publicist, in the age in which we live, is to close the mouths of quacks and charlatans, and to teach the public to demand demonstrations, instead of being contented with symbols and programmes. Before talking of the science itself, it is necessary to ascertain its object, and discover its method and principle. The ground must be cleared of the prejudices which encumber it. Such is the mission of the nineteenth century.

For my part, I have sworn fidelity to my work of demolition, and I will not cease to pursue the truth through the ruins and rubbish. I hate to see a thing half done; and it will be believed without any assurance of mine, that, having dared to raise my hand against the Holy Ark, I shall not rest contented with the removal of the cover. The mysteries of the sanctuary of iniquity must be unveiled, the tables of the old alliance broken, and all the objects of the ancient faith thrown in a heap to the swine. A charter has been given to us,—a resume of political science, the monument of twenty legislatures. A code has been written,—the pride of a conqueror, and the summary of ancient wisdom. Well! of this charter and this code not one article shall be left standing upon another! The time has come for the wise to choose their course, and prepare for reconstruction.

But, since a destroyed error necessarily implies a counter-truth, I will not finish this treatise without solving the first problem of political science,—that which receives the attention of all minds.

WHEN PROPERTY IS ABOLISHED, WHAT WILL BE THE FORM OF SOCIETY! WILL IT BE COMMUNISM?

PART SECOND.

% 1.—Of the Causes of our Mistakes. The Origin of Property.

The true form of human society cannot be determined until the following question has been solved:—

Property not being our natural condition, how did it gain a foothold? Why has the social instinct, so trustworthy among the animals, erred in the case of man? Why is man, who was born for society, not yet associated?

I have said that human society is COMPLEX in its nature. Though this expression is inaccurate, the fact to which it refers is none the less true; namely, the classification of talents and capacities. But who does not see that these talents and capacities, owing to their infinite variety, give rise to an infinite variety of wills, and that the character, the inclinations, and —if I may venture to use the expression—the form of the ego, are necessarily changed; so that in the order of liberty, as in the order of intelligence, there are as many types as individuals, as many characters as heads, whose tastes, fancies, and propensities, being modified by dissimilar ideas, must necessarily conflict? Man, by his nature and his instinct, is predestined to society; but his personality, ever varying, is adverse to it.

In societies of animals, all the members do exactly the same things. The same genius directs them; the same will animates them. A society of beasts is a collection of atoms, round, hooked, cubical, or triangular, but always perfectly identical. These personalities do not vary, and we might say that a single ego governs them all. The labors which animals perform, whether alone or in society, are exact reproductions of their character. Just as the swarm of bees is composed of individual bees, alike in nature and equal in value, so the honeycomb is formed of individual cells, constantly and invariably repeated.

But man's intelligence, fitted for his social destiny and his personal needs, is of a very different composition, and therefore gives rise to a wonderful variety of human wills. In the bee, the will is constant and uniform, because the instinct which guides it is invariable, and constitutes the animal's whole life and nature. In man, talent varies, and the mind wavers; consequently, his will is multiform and vague. He seeks society, but dislikes constraint and monotony; he is an imitator, but fond of his own ideas, and passionately in love with his works.

If, like the bees, every man were born possessed of talent, perfect knowledge of certain kinds, and, in a word, an innate acquaintance with the functions he has to perform, but destitute of reflective and reasoning faculties, society would organize itself. We should see one man plowing a field, another building houses; this one forging metals, that one cutting clothes; and still others storing the products, and superintending their distribution. Each one, without inquiring as to the object of his labor, and without troubling himself about the extent of his task, would obey orders, bring his product, receive his salary, and would then rest for a time; keeping meanwhile no accounts, envious of nobody, and satisfied with the distributor, who never would be unjust to any one. Kings would govern, but would not reign; for to reign is to be a *proprietor a l'engrais*, as Bonaparte said: and having no commands to give, since all would be at their posts, they would serve rather as rallying centres than as authorities or counsellors. It would be a state of ordered communism, but not a society entered into deliberately and freely.

But man acquires skill only by observation and experiment. He reflects, then, since to observe and experiment is to reflect; he reasons, since he cannot help reasoning. In reflecting, he becomes deluded; in reasoning, he makes mistakes, and, thinking himself right, persists in them. He is wedded to his opinions; he esteems himself, and despises others. Consequently, he isolates himself; for he could not submit to the majority without renouncing his will and his reason,—that is, without disowning himself, which is impossible. And this isolation, this intellectual egotism, this individuality of opinion, lasts until the truth is demonstrated to him by observation and experience. A final illustration will make these facts still clearer.

If to the blind but convergent and harmonious instincts of a swarm of bees should be suddenly added reflection and judgment, the little society could not long exist. In the first place, the bees would not fail to try some new industrial process; for instance, that of making their cells round or square. All sorts of systems and inventions would be tried, until long experience, aided by geometry, should show them that the hexagonal shape is the best. Then insurrections would occur. The drones would be told to provide for themselves, and the queens to labor; jealousy would spread among the laborers; discords would burst forth; soon each one would want to produce on his own account; and finally the hive would be abandoned, and the bees would perish. Evil would be introduced into the honey-producing republic by the power of reflection,—the very faculty which ought to constitute its glory.

Thus, moral evil, or, in this case, disorder in society, is naturally explained by our power of reflection. The mother of poverty, crime, insurrection, and war was inequality of conditions; which was the daughter of property, which was born of selfishness, which was engendered by private opinion, which descended in a direct line from the autocracy of reason. Man, in his infancy, is neither criminal nor barbarous, but ignorant and inexperienced. Endowed with imperious instincts which are under the control of his reasoning faculty, at first he reflects but little, and reasons inaccurately; then, benefiting by his mistakes, he rectifies his ideas, and perfects his reason. In the first place, it is the savage sacrificing all his possessions for a trinket, and then repenting and weeping; it is Esau selling his birthright for a mess of pottage, and afterwards wishing to cancel the bargain; it is the civilized workman laboring in insecurity, and continually demanding that his wages be increased, neither he nor his employer understanding that, in the absence of equality, any salary, however large, is always insufficient. Then it is Naboth dying to defend his inheritance; Cato tearing out his entrails that he might not be enslaved; Socrates drinking the fatal cup in defence of liberty of thought; it is the third estate of '89 reclaiming its liberty: soon it will be the people demanding equality of wages and an equal division of the means of production.

Man is born a social being,—that is, he seeks equality and justice in all his relations, but he loves independence and praise. The difficulty of satisfying these various desires at the same time is the primary cause of the despotism of the will, and the appropriation which results from it. On the other hand, man always needs a market for his products; unable to compare values of different kinds, he is satisfied to judge approximately, according to his passion and caprice; and he engages in dishonest commerce, which always results in wealth and poverty. Thus, the greatest evils which man suffers arise from the misuse of his social nature, of this same justice of which he is so proud, and which he applies with such deplorable ignorance.

The practice of justice is a science which, when once discovered and diffused, will sooner or later put an end to social disorder, by teaching us our rights and duties.

This progressive and painful education of our instinct, this slow and imperceptible transformation of our spontaneous perceptions into deliberate knowledge, does not take place among the animals, whose instincts remain fixed, and never become enlightened.

"According to Frederic Cuvier, who has so clearly distinguished between instinct and intelligence in animals, 'instinct is a natural and inherent faculty, like feeling, irritability, or intelligence. The wolf and the fox who recognize the traps in which they have been caught, and who avoid them; the dog and the horse, who understand the meaning of several of our words, and who obey us,—thereby show *intelligence*. The dog who hides the remains of his dinner, the bee who constructs his cell, the bird who builds his nest, act only from *instinct*. Even man has instincts: it is a special instinct which leads the new-born child to suck. But, in man, almost every thing is accomplished by intelligence; and intelligence supplements instinct. The opposite is true of animals: their instinct is given them as a supplement to their intelligence.'"—Flourens: Analytical Summary of the Observations of F. Cuvier.

"We can form a clear idea of instinct only by admitting that animals have in their *sensorium*, images or innate and constant sensations, which influence their actions in the same manner that ordinary and accidental sensations commonly do. It is a sort of dream, or vision, which always follows them and in all which relates to instinct they may be regarded as somnambulists."—F. Cuvier: Introduction to the Animal Kingdom.

Intelligence and instinct being common, then, though in different degrees, to animals and man, what is the distinguishing characteristic of the latter? According to F. Cuvier, it is REFLECTION OR THE POWER OF INTELLECTUALLY CONSIDERING OUR OWN MODIFICATIONS BY A SURVEY OF OURSELVES. This lacks clearness, and requires an explanation.

If we grant intelligence to animals, we must also grant them, in some degree, reflection; for, the first cannot exist without the second, as F. Cuvier himself has proved by numerous examples. But notice that the learned observer defines the kind of reflection which distinguishes us from the animals as the POWER OF CONSIDERING OUR OWN MODIFICATIONS. This I shall endeavour to interpret, by developing to the best of my ability the laconism of the philosophical naturalist.

The intelligence acquired by animals never modifies the operations which they perform by instinct: it is given them only as a provision against unexpected accidents which might disturb these operations. In man, on the contrary, instinctive action is constantly changing into deliberate action. Thus, man is social by instinct, and is every day becoming social by reflection and choice. At first, he formed his words by instinct; [*] he was a poet by inspiration: to-day, he makes grammar a science, and poetry an art. His conception of God and a future life is spontaneous and instinctive, and his expressions of this conception have been, by turns, monstrous, eccentric, beautiful, comforting, and terrible. All these different creeds, at which the frivolous irreligion of the eighteenth century mocked, are modes of expression of the religious sentiment. Some day, man will explain to himself the character of the God whom he believes in, and the nature of that other world to which his soul aspires.

```
       * "The problem of the origin of language is solved by the distinctio
made by Frederic Cuvier between instinct and intelligence. Language
is not a premeditated, arbitrary, or conventional device; nor is it
communicated or revealed to us by God. Language is an instinctive and
unpremeditated creation of man, as the hive is of the bee. In this
sense, it may be said that language is not the work of man, since it is
not the work of his mind. Further, the mechanism of language seems
more wonderful and ingenious when it is not regarded as the result of
reflection. This fact is one of the most curious and indisputable which
philology has observed. See, among other works, a Latin essay by F. G.
Bergmann (Strasbourg, 1839), in which the learned author explains how
the phonetic germ is born of sensation; how language passes through
three successive stages of development; why man, endowed at birth with
the instinctive faculty of creating a language, loses this faculty
as fast as his mind develops; and that the study of languages is real
natural history,—in fact, a science. France possesses to-day several
philologists of the first rank, endowed with rare talents and deep
philosophic insight,—modest savants developing a science almost without
the knowledge of the public; devoting themselves to studies which are
scornfully looked down upon, and seeming to shun applause as much as
others seek it."
```

All that he does from instinct man despises; or, if he admires it, it is as Nature's work, not as his own. This explains the obscurity which surrounds the names of early inventors; it explains also our indifference to religious matters, and the ridicule heaped upon religious customs. Man esteems only the products of reflection and of reason. The most wonderful works of instinct are, in his eyes, only lucky GOD-SENDS; he reserves the name DISCOVERY—I had almost said creation —for the works of intelligence. Instinct is the source of passion and enthusiasm; it is intelligence which causes crime and virtue.

In developing his intelligence, man makes use of not only his own observations, but also those of others. He keeps an account of his experience, and preserves the record; so that the race, as well as the individual, becomes more and more intelligent. The animals do not transmit their knowledge; that which each individual accumulates dies with him.

It is not enough, then, to say that we are distinguished from the animals by reflection, unless we mean thereby the CONSTANT TENDENCY OF OUR INSTINCT TO BECOME INTELLIGENCE. While man is governed by instinct, he is unconscious of his acts. He never would deceive himself, and never would be troubled by errors, evils, and disorder, if, like the animals, instinct were his only guide. But the Creator has endowed us with reflection, to the end that our instinct might become intelligence; and since this reflection and resulting knowledge pass through various stages, it happens that in the beginning our instinct is opposed, rather than guided, by reflection; consequently, that our power of thought leads us to act in opposition to our nature and our end; that, deceiving ourselves, we do and suffer evil, until instinct which points us towards good, and reflection which makes us stumble into evil, are replaced by the science of good and evil, which invariably causes us to seek the one and avoid the other.

Thus, evil—or error and its consequences—is the firstborn son of the union of two opposing faculties, instinct and reflection; good, or truth, must inevitably be the second child. Or, to again employ the figure, evil is the product of incest between adverse powers; good will sooner or later be the legitimate child of their holy and mysterious union.

Property, born of the reasoning faculty, intrenches itself behind comparisons. But, just as reflection and reason are subsequent to spontaneity, observation to sensation, and experience to instinct, so property is subsequent to communism. Communism—or association in a simple form—is the necessary object and original aspiration of the social nature, the spontaneous movement by which it manifests and establishes itself. It is the first phase of human civilization. In this state of society,—which the jurists have called NEGATIVE COMMUNISM—man draws near to man, and shares with him the fruits of the field and the milk and flesh of animals. Little by little this communism—negative as long as man does not produce—tends to become positive and organic through the development of labor and industry. But it is then that the sovereignty of thought, and the terrible faculty of reasoning logically or illogically, teach man that, if equality is the sine qua non of society, communism is the first species of slavery. To express this idea by an Hegelian formula, I will say:

Communism—the first expression of the social nature—is the first term of social development,—the THESIS; property, the reverse of communism, is the second term,—the ANTITHESIS. When we have discovered the third term, the SYNTHESIS, we shall have the required solution. Now, this synthesis necessarily results from the correction of the thesis by the antithesis. Therefore it is necessary, by a final examination of their characteristics, to eliminate those features which are hostile to sociability. The union of the two remainders will give us the true form of human association.

% 2.—Characteristics of Communism and of Property.

I. I ought not to conceal the fact that property and communism have been considered always the only possible forms of society. This deplorable error has been the life of property. The disadvantages of communism are so obvious that its critics never have needed to employ much eloquence to thoroughly disgust men with it. The irreparability of the injustice which it causes, the violence which it does to attractions and repulsions, the yoke of iron which it fastens upon the will, the moral torture to which it subjects the conscience, the debilitating effect which it has upon society; and, to sum it all up, the pious and stupid uniformity which it enforces upon the free, active, reasoning, unsubmissive personality of man, have shocked common sense, and condemned communism by an irrevocable decree.

The authorities and examples cited in its favor disprove it. The communistic republic of Plato involved slavery; that of Lycurgus employed Helots, whose duty it was to produce for their masters, thus enabling the latter to devote themselves exclusively to athletic sports and to war. Even J. J. Rousseau—confounding communism and equality—has said somewhere that, without slavery, he did not think equality of conditions possible. The communities of the early Church did not last the first century out, and soon degenerated into monasteries. In those of the Jesuits of Paraguay, the condition of the blacks is said by all travellers to be as miserable as that of slaves; and it is a fact that the good Fathers were obliged to surround themselves with ditches and walls to prevent their new converts from escaping. The followers of Baboeuf—guided by a lofty horror of property rather than by any definite belief—were ruined by exaggeration of their principles; the St. Simonians, lumping communism and inequality, passed away like a masquerade. The greatest danger to which society is exposed to-day is that of another shipwreck on this rock.

Singularly enough, systematic communism—the deliberate negation of property—is conceived under the direct influence of the proprietary prejudice; and property is the basis of all communistic theories.

The members of a community, it is true, have no private property; but the community is proprietor, and proprietor not only of the goods, but of the persons and wills. In consequence of this principle of absolute property, labor, which should be only a condition imposed upon man by Nature, becomes in all communities a human commandment, and therefore odious. Passive obedience, irreconcilable with a reflecting will, is strictly enforced. Fidelity to regulations, which are always defective, however wise they may be thought, allows of no complaint. Life, talent, and all the human faculties are the property of the State, which has the right to use them as it pleases for the common good. Private associations are sternly prohibited, in spite of the likes and dislikes of different natures, because to tolerate them would be to introduce small communities within the large one, and consequently private property; the strong work for the weak, although this ought to be left to benevolence, and not enforced, advised, or enjoined; the industrious work for the lazy, although this is unjust; the clever work for the foolish, although this is absurd; and, finally, man—casting aside his personality, his spontaneity, his genius, and his affections—humbly annihilates himself at the feet of the majestic and inflexible Commune!

Communism is inequality, but not as property is. Property is the exploitation of the weak by the strong. Communism is the exploitation of the strong by the weak. In property, inequality of conditions is the result of force, under whatever name it be disguised: physical and mental force; force of events, chance, FORTUNE; force of accumulated property, &c. In communism, inequality springs from placing mediocrity on a level with excellence. This damaging equation is repellent to the conscience, and causes merit to complain; for, although it may be the duty of the strong to aid the weak, they prefer to do it out of generosity,—they never will endure a comparison. Give them equal opportunities of labor, and equal wages, but never allow their jealousy to be awakened by mutual suspicion of unfaithfulness in the performance of the common task.

Communism is oppression and slavery. Man is very willing to obey the law of duty, serve his country, and oblige his friends; but he wishes to labor when he pleases, where he pleases, and as much as he pleases. He wishes to dispose of his own time, to be governed only by necessity, to choose his friendships, his recreation, and his discipline; to act from judgment, not by command; to sacrifice himself through selfishness, not through servile obligation. Communism is essentially opposed to the free exercise of our faculties, to our noblest desires, to our deepest feelings. Any plan which could be devised for reconciling it with the demands of the individual reason and will would end only in changing the thing while preserving the name. Now, if we are honest truth-seekers, we shall avoid disputes about words.

Thus, communism violates the sovereignty of the conscience, and equality: the first, by restricting spontaneity of mind and heart, and freedom of thought and action; the second, by placing labor and laziness, skill and stupidity, and even vice and virtue on an equality in point of comfort. For the rest, if property is impossible on account of the desire to accumulate, communism would soon become so through the desire to shirk.

II. Property, in its turn, violates equality by the rights of exclusion and increase, and freedom by despotism. The former effect of property having been sufficiently developed in the last three chapters, I will content myself here with establishing by a final comparison, its perfect identity with robbery.

The Latin words for robber are *fur* and *latro;* the former taken from the Greek {GREEK m }, from {GREEK m }, Latin *fero*, I carry away; the latter from {GREEK 'i }, I play the part of a brigand, which is derived from {GREEK i }, Latin *lateo*, I conceal myself. The Greeks have also {GREEK ncg }, from {GREEK ncg }, I filch, whose radical consonants are the same as those of {GREEK ' cg }, I cover, I conceal. Thus, in these languages, the idea of a robber is that of a man who conceals, carries away, or diverts, in any manner whatever, a thing which does not belong to him.

The Hebrews expressed the same idea by the word *gannab*,—robber,—from the verb *ganab*, which means to put away, to turn aside: *lo thi-gnob (Decalogue: Eighth Commandment)*, thou shalt not steal,—that is, thou shalt not hold back, thou shalt not put away any thing for thyself. That is the act of a man who, on entering into a society into which he agrees to bring all that he has, secretly reserves a portion, as did the celebrated disciple Ananias.

The etymology of the French verb *voler* is still more significant. *Voler*, or *faire la vole* (from the Latin *vola*, palm of the hand), means to take all the tricks in a game of ombre; so that *le voleur*, the robber, is the capitalist who takes all, who gets the lion's share. Probably this verb *voler* had its origin in the professional slang of thieves, whence it has passed into common use, and, consequently into the phraseology of the law.

Robbery is committed in a variety of ways, which have been very cleverly distinguished and classified by legislators according to their heinousness or merit, to the end that some robbers may be honored, while others are punished.

We rob,—1. By murder on the highway; 2. Alone, or in a band; 3. By breaking into buildings, or scaling walls; 4. By abstraction; 5. By fraudulent bankruptcy; 6. By forgery of the handwriting of public officials or private individuals; 7. By manufacture of counterfeit money.

```
    This species includes all robbers who practise their profession with no
other aid than force and open fraud. Bandits, brigands, pirates, rovers
by land and sea,—these names were gloried in by the ancient heroes, who
thought their profession as noble as it was lucrative. Nimrod, Theseus,
Jason and his Argonauts; Jephthah, David, Cacus, Romulus, Clovis and
all his Merovingian descendants; Robert Guiscard, Tancred de Hauteville,
Bohemond, and most of the Norman heroes,—were brigands and robbers. The
heroic character of the robber is expressed in this line from Horace, in
reference to Achilles,—

     "Jura neget sibi nata, nihil non arroget armis," 27
and by this sentence from the dying words of Jacob (Gen. xlviii.), which
the Jews apply to David, and the Christians to their Christ: Manus ejus
contra omnes. In our day, the robber—the warrior of the ancients—is
pursued with the utmost vigor. His profession, in the language of the
code, entails ignominious and corporal penalties, from imprisonment to
the scaffold. A sad change in opinions here below!
```

We rob,—8. By cheating; 9. By swindling; 10. By abuse of trust; 11. By games and lotteries.

This second species was encouraged by the laws of Lycurgus, in order to sharpen the wits of the young. It is the kind practised by Ulysses, Solon, and Sinon; by the ancient and modern Jews, from Jacob down to Deutz; and by the Bohemians, the Arabs, and all savage tribes. Under Louis XIII. and Louis XIV., it was not considered dishonorable to cheat at play. To do so was a part of the game; and many worthy people did not scruple to correct the caprice of Fortune by dexterous jugglery. To-day even, and in all countries, it is thought a mark of merit among peasants, merchants, and shopkeepers to KNOW HOW TO MAKE A BARGAIN,—that is, to deceive one's man. This is so universally accepted, that the cheated party takes no offence. It is known with what reluctance our government resolved upon the abolition of lotteries. It felt that it was dealing a stab thereby at property. The pickpocket, the blackleg, and the charlatan make especial use of their dexterity of hand, their subtlety of mind, the magic power of their eloquence, and their great fertility of invention. Sometimes they offer bait to cupidity. Therefore the penal code—which much prefers intelligence to muscular vigor—has made, of the four varieties mentioned above, a second category, liable only to correctional, not to Ignominious, punishments.

Let them now accuse the law of being materialistic and atheistic.

We rob,—12. By usury.

This species of robbery, so odious and so severely punished since the publication of the Gospel, is the connecting link between forbidden and authorized robbery. Owing to its ambiguous nature, it has given rise to a multitude of contradictions in the laws and in morals,—contradictions which have been very cleverly turned to account by lawyers, financiers, and merchants. Thus the usurer, who lends on mortgage at ten, twelve, and fifteen per cent., is heavily fined when detected; while the banker, who receives the same interest (not, it is true, upon a loan, but in the way of exchange or discount,—that is, of sale), is protected by royal privilege. But the distinction between the banker and the usurer is a purely nominal one. Like the usurer, who lends on property, real or personal, the banker lends on business paper; like the usurer, he takes his interest in advance; like the usurer, he can recover from the borrower if the property is destroyed (that is, if the note is not redeemed),—a circumstance which makes him a money-lender, not a money-seller. But the banker lends for a short time only, while the usurer's loan may be for one, two, three, or more years. Now, a difference in the duration of the loan, or the form of the act, does not alter the nature of the transaction. As for the capitalists who invest their money, either with the State or in commercial operations, at three, four, and five per cent.,—that is, who lend on usury at a little lower rate than the bankers and usurers,—they are the flower of society, the cream of honesty! Moderation in robbery is the height of virtue! [28]

But what, then, is usury? Nothing is more amusing than to see these INSTRUCTORS OF NATIONS hesitate between the authority of the Gospel, which, they say, NEVER CAN HAVE SPOKEN IN VAIN, and the authority of economical demonstrations. Nothing, to my mind, is more creditable to the Gospel than this old infidelity of its pretended teachers. Salmasius, having assimilated interest to rent, was REFUTED by Grotius, Pufendorf, Burlamaqui, Wolf, and Heineccius; and, what is more curious still, Salmasius ADMITTED HIS ERROR. Instead of inferring from this doctrine of Salmasius that all increase is illegitimate, and proceeding straight on to the demonstration of Gospel equality, they arrived at just the opposite conclusion; namely, that since everybody acknowledges that rent is permissible, if we allow that interest does not differ from rent, there is nothing left which can be called usury, and, consequently, that the commandment of Jesus Christ is an ILLUSION, and amounts to NOTHING, which is an impious conclusion.

If this memoir had appeared in the time of Bossuet, that great theologian would have PROVED by scripture, the fathers, traditions, councils, and popes, that property exists by Divine right, while usury is an invention of the devil; and the heretical work would have been burned, and the author imprisoned.

We rob,—13. By farm-rent, house-rent, and leases of all kinds.

The author of the "Provincial Letters" entertained the honest Christians of the seventeenth century at the expense of Escobar, the Jesuit, and the contract Mohatra. "The contract Mohatra," said Escobar, "is a contract by which goods are bought, at a high price and on credit, to be again sold at the same moment to the same person, cash down, and at a lower price." Escobar found a way to justify this kind of usury. Pascal and all the Jansenists laughed at him. But what would the satirical Pascal, the learned Nicole, and the invincible Arnaud have said, if Father Antoine Escobar de Valladolid had answered them thus: "A lease is a contract by which real estate is bought, at a high price and on credit, to be again sold, at the expiration of a certain time, to the same person, at a lower price; only, to simplify the transaction, the buyer is content to pay the difference between the first sale and the second. Either deny the identity of the lease and the contract Mohatra, and then I will annihilate you in a moment; or, if you admit the similarity, admit also the soundness of my doctrine: otherwise you proscribe both interest and rent at one blow"?

In reply to this overwhelming argument of the Jesuit, the sire of Montalte would have sounded the tocsin, and would have shouted that society was in peril,—that the Jesuits were sapping its very foundations.

We rob,—14. By commerce, when the profit of the merchant exceeds his legitimate salary.

Everybody knows the definition of commerce—THE ART OF BUYING FOR THREE FRANCS THAT WHICH IS WORTH SIX, AND OF SELLING FOR SIX THAT WHICH IS WORTH THREE. Between commerce thus defined and *vol a l'americaine*, the only difference is in the relative proportion of the values exchanged,—in short, in the amount of the profit.

We rob,—15. By making profit on our product, by accepting sinecures, and by exacting exorbitant wages.

The farmer, who sells a certain amount of corn to the consumer, and who during the measurement thrusts his hand into the bushel and takes out a handful of grains, robs; the professor, whose lectures are paid for by the State, and who through the intervention of a bookseller sells them to the public a second time, robs; the sinecurist, who receives an enormous product in exchange for his vanity, robs; the functionary, the laborer, whatever he may be, who produces only one and gets paid four, one hundred, or one thousand, robs; the publisher of this book, and I, its author,—we rob, by charging for it twice as much as it is worth.

In recapitulation:—

Justice, after passing through the state of negative communism, called by the ancient poets the AGE OF GOLD, commences as the right of the strongest. In a society which is trying to organize itself, inequality of faculties calls up the idea of merit; equite suggests the plan of proportioning not only esteem, but also material comforts, to personal merit; and since the highest and almost the only merit then recognized is physical strength, the strongest, {GREEK ' eg }, and consequently the best, {GREEK ' eg }, is entitled to the largest share; and if it is refused him, he very naturally takes it by force. From this to the assumption of the right of property in all things, it is but one step.

Such was justice in the heroic age, preserved, at least by tradition, among the Greeks and Romans down to the last days of their republics. Plato, in the "Gorgias," introduces a character named Callicles, who spiritedly defends the right of the strongest, which Socrates, the advocate of equality, {GREEK g e }, seriously refutes. It is related of the great Pompey, that he blushed easily, and, nevertheless, these words once escaped his lips: "Why should I respect the laws, when I have arms in my hand?" This shows him to have been a man in whom the moral sense and ambition were struggling for the mastery, and who sought to justify his violence by the motto of the hero and the brigand.

From the right of the strongest springs the exploitation of man by man, or bondage; usury, or the tribute levied upon the conquered by the conqueror; and the whole numerous family of taxes, duties, monarchical prerogatives, house-rents, farm-rents, &c.; in one word,—property.

Force was followed by artifice, the second manifestation of justice, which was detested by the ancient heroes, who, not excelling in that direction, were heavy losers by it. Force was still employed, but mental force instead of physical. Skill in deceiving an enemy by treacherous propositions seemed deserving of reward; nevertheless, the strong always prided themselves upon their honesty. In those days, oaths were observed and promises kept according to the letter rather than the spirit: *Uti lingua nuncupassit, ita jus esto*,—"As the tongue has spoken, so must the right be," says the law of the Twelve Tables. Artifice, or rather perfidy, was the main element in the politics of ancient Rome. Among other examples, Vico cites the following, also quoted by Montesquieu: The Romans had guaranteed to the Carthaginians the preservation of their goods and their CITY,—intentionally using the word civitas, that is, the society, the State; the Carthaginians, on the contrary, understood them to mean the material city, urbs, and accordingly began to rebuild their walls. They were immediately attacked on account of their violation of the treaty, by the Romans, who, acting upon the old heroic idea of right, did not imagine that, in taking advantage of an equivocation to surprise their enemies, they were waging unjust war.

From artifice sprang the profits of manufactures, commerce, and banking, mercantile frauds, and pretensions which are honored with the beautiful names of TALENT and GENIUS, but which ought to be regarded as the last degree of knavery and deception; and, finally, all sorts of social inequalities.

In those forms of robbery which are prohibited by law, force and artifice are employed alone and undisguised; in the authorized forms, they conceal themselves within a useful product, which they use as a tool to plunder their victim.

The direct use of violence and stratagem was early and universally condemned; but no nation has yet got rid of that kind of robbery which acts through talent, labor, and possession, and which is the source of all the dilemmas of casuistry and the innumerable contradictions of jurisprudence.

The right of force and the right of artifice—glorified by the rhapsodists in the poems of the "Iliad" and the "Odyssey"—inspired the legislation of the Greeks and Romans, from which they passed into our morals and codes. Christianity has not changed at all. The Gospel should not be blamed, because the priests, as stupid as the legists, have been unable either to expound or to understand it. The ignorance of councils and popes upon all questions of morality is equal to that of the market-place and the money-changers; and it is this utter ignorance of right, justice, and society, which is killing the Church, and discrediting its teachings for ever. The infidelity of the Roman church and other Christian churches is flagrant; all have disregarded the precept of Jesus; all have erred in moral and doctrinal points; all are guilty of teaching false and absurd dogmas, which lead straight to wickedness and murder. Let it ask pardon of God and men,—this church which called itself infallible, and which has grown so corrupt in morals; let its reformed sisters humble themselves,... and the people, undeceived, but still religious and merciful, will begin to think. 29

One of the main causes of Ireland's poverty to-day is the immense revenues of the English clergy. So heretics and orthodox—Protestants and Papists—cannot reproach each other. All have strayed from the path of justice; all have disobeyed the eighth commandment of the Decalogue: "Thou shalt not steal."

The development of right has followed the same order, in its various expressions, that property has in its forms. Every where we see justice driving robbery before it and confining it within narrower and narrower limits. Hitherto the victories of justice over injustice, and of equality over inequality, have been won by instinct and the simple force of things; but the final triumph of our social nature will be due to our reason, or else we shall fall back into feudal chaos. Either this glorious height is reserved for our intelligence, or this miserable depth for our baseness.

The second effect of property is despotism. Now, since despotism is inseparably connected with the idea of legitimate authority, in explaining the natural causes of the first, the principle of the second will appear.

What is to be the form of government in the future? hear some of my younger readers reply: "Why, how can you ask such a question?

"You are a republican." "A republican! Yes; but that word specifies nothing. *Res publica;* that is, the public thing. Now, whoever is interested in public affairs—no matter under what form of government—may call himself a republican. Even kings are republicans."—

"Well! you are a democrat?"—"No."—"What! you would have a monarchy."—"No."—"A constitutionalist?"—"God forbid!"—"You are then an aristocrat?"—"Not at all."—"You want a mixed government?"—"Still less."—"What are you, then?"—"I am an anarchist."

"Oh! I understand you; you speak satirically. This is a hit at the government."—"By no means. I have just given you my serious and well-considered profession of faith. Although a firm friend of order, I am (in the full force of the term) an anarchist. Listen to me."

In all species of sociable animals, "the weakness of the young is the principle of their obedience to the old," who are strong; and from habit, which is a kind of conscience with them, the power remains with the oldest, although he finally becomes the weakest.

Whenever the society is under the control of a chief, this chief is almost always the oldest of the troop. I say almost always, because the established order may be disturbed by violent outbreaks. Then the authority passes to another; and, having been re-established by force, it is again maintained by habit. Wild horses go in herds: they have a chief who marches at their head, whom they confidently follow, and who gives the signal for flight or battle.

"The sheep which we have raised follows us, but it follows in company with the flock in the midst of which it was born. It regards man AS THE CHIEF OF ITS FLOCK.... Man is regarded by domestic animals as a member of their society. All that he has to do is to get himself accepted by them as an associate: he soon becomes their chief, in consequence of his superior intelligence. He does not, then, change the NATURAL CONDITION of these animals, as Buffon has said. On the contrary, he uses this natural condition to his own advantage; in other words, he finds SOCIABLE animals, and renders them DOMESTIC by becoming their associate and chief. Thus, the DOMESTICITY of animals is only a special condition, a simple modification, a definitive consequence of their SOCIABILITY. All domestic animals are by nature sociable animals."...—Flourens: Summary of the Observations of F. Cuvier.

Sociable animals follow their chief by INSTINCT; but take notice of the fact (which F. Cuvier omitted to state), that the function of the chief is altogether one of INTELLIGENCE. The chief does not teach the others to associate, to unite under his lead, to reproduce their kind, to take to flight, or to defend themselves. Concerning each of these particulars, his subordinates are as well informed as he. But it is the chief who, by his accumulated experience, provides against accidents; he it is whose private intelligence supplements, in difficult situations, the general instinct; he it is who deliberates, decides, and leads; he it is, in short, whose enlightened prudence regulates the public routine for the greatest good of all.

Man (naturally a sociable being) naturally follows a chief. Originally, the chief is the father, the patriarch, the elder; in other words, the good and wise man, whose functions, consequently, are exclusively of a reflective and intellectual nature.

The human race—like all other races of sociable animals—has its instincts, its innate faculties, its general ideas, and its categories of sentiment and reason. Its chiefs, legislators, or kings have devised nothing, supposed nothing, imagined nothing. They have only guided society by their accumulated experience, always however in conformity with opinions and beliefs.

Those philosophers who (carrying into morals and into history their gloomy and factious whims) affirm that the human race had originally neither chiefs nor kings, know nothing of the nature of man. Royalty, and absolute royalty, is—as truly and more truly than democracy—a primitive form of government. Perceiving that, in the remotest ages, crowns and kingships were worn by heroes, brigands, and knight-errants, they confound the two things,—royalty and despotism. But royalty dates from the creation of man; it existed in the age of negative communism. Ancient heroism (and the despotism which it engendered) commenced only with the first manifestation of the idea of justice; that is, with the reign of force. As soon as the strongest, in the comparison of merits, was decided to be the best, the oldest had to abandon his position, and royalty became despotic.

The spontaneous, instinctive, and—so to speak—physiological origin of royalty gives it, in the beginning, a superhuman character. The nations connected it with the gods, from whom they said the first kings descended. This notion was the origin of the divine genealogies of royal families, the incarnations of gods, and the messianic fables. From it sprang the doctrine of divine right, which is still championed by a few singular characters.

Royalty was at first elective, because—at a time when man produced but little and possessed nothing—property was too weak to establish the principle of heredity, and secure to the son the throne of his father; but as soon as fields were cleared, and cities built, each function was, like every thing else, appropriated, and hereditary kingships and priesthoods were the result. The principle of heredity was carried into even the most ordinary professions,—a circumstance which led to class distinctions, pride of station, and abjection of the common people, and which confirms my assertion, concerning the principle of patrimonial succession, that it is a method suggested by Nature of filling vacancies in business, and completing unfinished tasks.

From time to time, ambition caused usurpers, or SUPPLANTERS of kings, to start up; and, in consequence, some were called kings by right, or legitimate kings, and others TYRANTS. But we must not let these names deceive us. There have been execrable kings, and very tolerable tyrants. Royalty may always be good, when it is the only possible form of government; legitimate it is never. Neither heredity, nor election, nor universal suffrage, nor the excellence of the sovereign, nor the consecration of religion and of time, can make royalty legitimate. Whatever form it takes,—monarchic, oligarchic, or democratic,—royalty, or the government of man by man, is illegitimate and absurd.

Man, in order to procure as speedily as possible the most thorough satisfaction of his wants, seeks RULE. In the beginning, this rule is to him living, visible, and tangible. It is his father, his master, his king. The more ignorant man is, the more obedient he is, and the more absolute is his confidence in his guide. But, it being a law of man's nature to conform to rule,—that is, to discover it by his powers of reflection and reason,—man reasons upon the commands of his chiefs. Now, such reasoning as that is a protest against authority,—a beginning of disobedience. At the moment that man inquires into the motives which govern the will of his sovereign,—at that moment man revolts. If he obeys no longer because the king commands, but because the king demonstrates the wisdom of his commands, it may be said that henceforth he will recognize no authority, and that he has become his own king. Unhappy he who shall dare to command him, and shall offer, as his authority, only the vote of the majority; for, sooner or later, the minority will become the majority, and this imprudent despot will be overthrown, and all his laws annihilated.

In proportion as society becomes enlightened, royal authority diminishes. That is a fact to which all history bears witness. At the birth of nations, men reflect and reason in vain. Without methods, without principles, not knowing how to use their reason, they cannot judge of the justice of their conclusions. Then the authority of kings is immense, no knowledge having been acquired with which to contradict it. But, little by little, experience produces habits, which develop into customs; then the customs are formulated in maxims, laid down as principles,—in short, transformed into laws, to which the king, the living law, has to bow. There comes a time when customs and laws are so numerous that the will of the prince is, so to speak, entwined by the public will; and that, on taking the crown, he is obliged to swear that he will govern in conformity with established customs and usages; and that he is but the executive power of a society whose laws are made independently of him.

Up to this point, all is done instinctively, and, as it were, unconsciously; but see where this movement must end.

By means of self-instruction and the acquisition of ideas, man finally acquires the idea of SCIENCE,—that is, of a system of knowledge in harmony with the reality of things, and inferred from observation. He searches for the science, or the system, of inanimate bodies,—the system of organic bodies, the system of the human mind, and the system of the universe: why should he not also search for the system of society? But, having reached this height, he comprehends that political truth, or the science of politics, exists quite independently of the will of sovereigns, the opinion of majorities, and popular beliefs,—that kings, ministers, magistrates, and nations, as wills, have no connection with the science, and are worthy of no consideration. He comprehends, at the same time, that, if man is born a sociable being, the authority of his father over him ceases on the day when, his mind being formed and his education finished, he becomes the associate of his father; that his true chief and his king is the demonstrated truth; that politics is a science, not a stratagem; and that the function of the legislator is reduced, in the last analysis, to the methodical search for truth.

Thus, in a given society, the authority of man over man is inversely proportional to the stage of intellectual development which that society has reached; and the probable duration of that authority can be calculated from the more or less general desire for a true government,—that is, for a scientific government. And just as the right of force and the right of artifice retreat before the steady advance of justice, and must finally be extinguished in equality, so the sovereignty of the will yields to the sovereignty of the reason, and must at last be lost in scientific socialism. Property and royalty have been crumbling to pieces ever since the world began. As man seeks justice in equality, so society seeks order in anarchy.

ANARCHY,—the absence of a master, of a sovereign, 30—such is the form of government to which we are every day approximating, and which our accustomed habit of taking man for our rule, and his will for law, leads us to regard as the height of disorder and the expression of chaos. The story is told, that a citizen of Paris in the seventeenth century having heard it said that in Venice there was no king, the good man could not recover from his astonishment, and nearly died from laughter at the mere mention of so ridiculous a thing. So strong is our prejudice. As long as we live, we want a chief or chiefs; and at this very moment I hold in my hand a brochure, whose author—a zealous communist—dreams, like a second Marat, of the dictatorship. The most advanced among us are those who wish the greatest possible number of sovereigns,—their most ardent wish is for the royalty of the National Guard. Soon, undoubtedly, some one, jealous of the citizen militia, will say, "Everybody is king." But, when he has spoken, I will say, in my turn, "Nobody is king; we are, whether we will or no, associated." Every question of domestic politics must be decided by departmental statistics; every question of foreign politics is an affair of international statistics. The science of government rightly belongs to one of the sections of the Academy of Sciences, whose permanent secretary is necessarily prime minister; and, since every citizen may address a memoir to the Academy, every citizen is a legislator. But, as the opinion of no one is of any value until its truth has been proven, no one can substitute his will for reason,—nobody is king.

All questions of legislation and politics are matters of science, not of opinion. The legislative power belongs only to the reason, methodically recognized and demonstrated. To attribute to any power whatever the right of veto or of sanction, is the last degree of tyranny. Justice and legality are two things as independent of our approval as is mathematical truth. To compel, they need only to be known; to be known, they need only to be considered and studied. What, then, is the nation, if it is not the sovereign,—if it is not the source of the legislative power?

The nation is the guardian of the law—the nation is the EXECUTIVE POWER. Every citizen may assert: "This is true; that is just;" but his opinion controls no one but himself. That the truth which he proclaims may become a law, it must be recognized. Now, what is it to recognize a law? It is to verify a mathematical or a metaphysical calculation; it is to repeat an experiment, to observe a phenomenon, to establish a fact. Only the nation has the right to say, "Be it known and decreed."

I confess that this is an overturning of received ideas, and that I seem to be attempting to revolutionize our political system; but I beg the reader to consider that, having begun with a paradox, I must, if I reason correctly, meet with paradoxes at every step, and must end with paradoxes. For the rest, I do not see how the liberty of citizens would be endangered by entrusting to their hands, instead of the pen of the legislator, the sword of the law. The executive power, belonging properly to the will, cannot be confided to too many proxies. That is the true sovereignty of the nation. 31

The proprietor, the robber, the hero, the sovereign—for all these titles are synonymous—imposes his will as law, and suffers neither contradiction nor control; that is, he pretends to be the legislative and the executive power at once. Accordingly, the substitution of the scientific and true law for the royal will is accomplished only by a terrible struggle; and this constant substitution is, after property, the most potent element in history, the most prolific source of political disturbances. Examples are too numerous and too striking to require enumeration.

Now, property necessarily engenders despotism,—the government of caprice, the reign of libidinous pleasure. That is so clearly the essence of property that, to be convinced of it, one need but remember what it is, and observe what happens around him. Property is the right to USE and ABUSE. If, then, government is economy,—if its object is production and consumption, and the distribution of labor and products,—how is government possible while property exists? And if goods are property, why should not the proprietors be kings, and despotic kings—kings in proportion to their *facultes bonitaires*? And if each proprietor is sovereign lord within the sphere of his property, absolute king throughout his own domain, how could a government of proprietors be any thing but chaos and confusion?

% 3.—Determination of the third form of Society. Conclusion.

Then, no government, no public economy, no administration, is possible, which is based upon property.

Communism seeks EQUALITY and LAW. Property, born of the sovereignty of the reason, and the sense of personal merit, wishes above all things INDEPENDENCE and PROPORTIONALITY.

But communism, mistaking uniformity for law, and levelism for equality, becomes tyrannical and unjust. Property, by its despotism and encroachments, soon proves itself oppressive and anti-social.

The objects of communism and property are good—their results are bad. And why? Because both are exclusive, and each disregards two elements of society. Communism rejects independence and proportionality; property does not satisfy equality and law.

Now, if we imagine a society based upon these four principles,—equality, law, independence, and proportionality,—we find:—

1. That EQUALITY, consisting only in EQUALITY OF CONDITIONS, that is, OF MEANS, and not in EQUALITY OF COMFORT,—which it is the business of the laborers to achieve for themselves, when provided with equal means,—in no way violates justice and equite.

2. That LAW, resulting from the knowledge of facts, and consequently based upon necessity itself, never clashes with independence.

3. That individual INDEPENDENCE, or the autonomy of the private reason, originating in the difference in talents and capacities, can exist without danger within the limits of the law.

4. That PROPORTIONALITY, being admitted only in the sphere of intelligence and sentiment, and not as regards material objects, may be observed without violating justice or social equality.

This third form of society, the synthesis of communism and property, we will call LIBERTY. 32

In determining the nature of liberty, we do not unite communism and property indiscriminately; such a process would be absurd eclecticism. We search by analysis for those elements in each which are true, and in harmony with the laws of Nature and society, disregarding the rest altogether; and the result gives us an adequate expression of the natural form of human society,—in one word, liberty.

Liberty is equality, because liberty exists only in society; and in the absence of equality there is no society.

Liberty is anarchy, because it does not admit the government of the will, but only the authority of the law; that is, of necessity.

Liberty is infinite variety, because it respects all wills within the limits of the law.

Liberty is proportionality, because it allows the utmost latitude to the ambition for merit, and the emulation of glory.

We can now say, in the words of M. Cousin: "Our principle is true; it is good, it is social; let us not fear to push it to its ultimate."

Man's social nature becoming JUSTICE through reflection, EQUITE through the classification of capacities, and having LIBERTY for its formula, is the true basis of morality,—the principle and regulator of all our actions. This is the universal motor, which philosophy is searching for, which religion strengthens, which egotism supplants, and whose place pure reason never can fill. DUTY and RIGHT are born of NEED, which, when considered in connection with others, is a RIGHT, and when considered in connection with ourselves, a DUTY.

We need to eat and sleep. It is our right to procure those things which are necessary to rest and nourishment. It is our duty to use them when Nature requires it.

We need to labor in order to live. To do so is both our right and our duty.

We need to love our wives and children. It is our duty to protect and support them. It is our right to be loved in preference to all others. Conjugal fidelity is justice. Adultery is high treason against society.

We need to exchange our products for other products. It is our right that this exchange should be one of equivalents; and since we consume before we produce, it would be our duty, if we could control the matter, to see to it that our last product shall follow our last consumption. Suicide is fraudulent bankruptcy.

We need to live our lives according to the dictates of our reason. It is our right to maintain our freedom. It is our duty to respect that of others.

We need to be appreciated by our fellows. It is our duty to deserve their praise. It is our right to be judged by our works.

Liberty is not opposed to the rights of succession and bequest. It contents itself with preventing violations of equality. "Choose," it tells us, "between two legacies, but do not take them both." All our legislation concerning transmissions, entailments, adoptions, and, if I may venture to use such a word, COADJUTORERIES, requires remodelling.

Liberty favors emulation, instead of destroying it. In social equality, emulation consists in accomplishing under like conditions; it is its own reward. No one suffers by the victory.

Liberty applauds self-sacrifice, and honors it with its votes, but it can dispense with it. Justice alone suffices to maintain the social equilibrium. Self-sacrifice is an act of supererogation. Happy, however, the man who can say, "I sacrifice myself." 33

Liberty is essentially an organizing force. To insure equality between men and peace among nations, agriculture and industry, and the centres of education, business, and storage, must be distributed according to the climate and the geographical position of the country, the nature of the products, the character and natural talents of the inhabitants, &c., in proportions so just, so wise, so harmonious, that in no place shall there ever be either an excess or a lack of population, consumption, and products. There commences the science of public and private right, the true political economy. It is for the writers on jurisprudence, henceforth unembarrassed by the false principle of property, to describe the new laws, and bring peace upon earth. Knowledge and genius they do not lack; the foundation is now laid for them. 34

I have accomplished my task; property is conquered, never again to arise. Wherever this work is read and discussed, there will be deposited the germ of death to property; there, sooner or later, privilege and servitude will disappear, and the despotism of will will give place to the reign of reason. What sophisms, indeed, what prejudices (however obstinate) can stand before the simplicity of the following propositions:—

I. Individual POSSESSION 35 is the condition of social life; five thousand years of property demonstrate it. PROPERTY is the suicide of society. Possession is a right; property is against right. Suppress property while maintaining possession, and, by this simple modification of the principle, you will revolutionize law, government, economy, and institutions; you will drive evil from the face of the earth.

II. All having an equal right of occupancy, possession varies with the number of possessors; property cannot establish itself.

III. The effect of labor being the same for all, property is lost in the common prosperity.

IV. All human labor being the result of collective force, all property becomes, in consequence, collective and unitary. To speak more exactly, labor destroys property.

V. Every capacity for labor being, like every instrument of labor, an accumulated capital, and a collective property, inequality of wages and fortunes (on the ground of inequality of capacities) is, therefore, injustice and robbery.

VI. The necessary conditions of commerce are the liberty of the contracting parties and the equivalence of the products exchanged. Now, value being expressed by the amount of time and outlay which each product costs, and liberty being inviolable, the wages of laborers (like their rights and duties) should be equal.

VII. Products are bought only by products. Now, the condition of all exchange being equivalence of products, profit is impossible and unjust. Observe this elementary principle of economy, and pauperism, luxury, oppression, vice, crime, and hunger will disappear from our midst.

VIII. Men are associated by the physical and mathematical law of production, before they are voluntarily associated by choice. Therefore, equality of conditions is demanded by justice; that is, by strict social law: esteem, friendship, gratitude, admiration, all fall within the domain of EQUITABLE or PROPORTIONAL law only.

IX. Free association, liberty—whose sole function is to maintain equality in the means of production and equivalence in exchanges—is the only possible, the only just, the only true form of society.

X. Politics is the science of liberty. The government of man by man (under whatever name it be disguised) is oppression. Society finds its highest perfection in the union of order with anarchy.

The old civilization has run its race; a new sun is rising, and will soon renew the face of the earth. Let the present generation perish, let the old prevaricators die in the desert! the holy earth shall not cover their bones. Young man, exasperated by the corruption of the age, and absorbed in your zeal for justice!—if your country is dear to you, and if you have the interests of humanity at heart, have the courage to espouse the cause of liberty! Cast off your old selfishness, and plunge into the rising flood of popular equality! There your regenerate soul will acquire new life and vigor; your enervated genius will recover unconquerable energy; and your heart, perhaps already withered, will be rejuvenated! Every thing will wear a different look to your illuminated vision; new sentiments will engender new ideas within you; religion, morality, poetry, art, language will appear before you in nobler and fairer forms; and thenceforth, sure of your faith, and thoughtfully enthusiastic, you will hail the dawn of universal regeneration!

And you, sad victims of an odious law!—you, whom a jesting world despoils and outrages!—you, whose labor has always been fruitless, and whose rest has been without hope,—take courage! your tears are numbered! The fathers have sown in affliction, the children shall reap in rejoicings!

O God of liberty! God of equality! Thou who didst place in my heart the sentiment of justice, before my reason could comprehend it, hear my ardent prayer! Thou hast dictated all that I have written; Thou hast shaped my thought; Thou hast directed my studies; Thou hast weaned my mind from curiosity and my heart from attachment, that I might publish Thy truth to the master and the slave. I have spoken with what force and talent Thou hast given me: it is Thine to finish the work. Thou knowest whether I seek my welfare or Thy glory, O God of liberty! Ah! perish my memory, and let humanity be free! Let me see from my obscurity the people at last instructed; let noble teachers enlighten them; let generous spirits guide them! Abridge, if possible, the time of our trial; stifle pride and avarice in equality; annihilate this love of glory which enslaves us; teach these poor children that in the bosom of liberty there are neither heroes nor great men! Inspire the powerful man, the rich man, him whose name my lips shall never pronounce in Thy presence, with a horror of his crimes; let him be the first to apply for admission to the redeemed society; let the promptness of his repentance be the ground of his forgiveness! Then, great and small, wise and foolish, rich and poor, will unite in an ineffable fraternity; and, singing in unison a new hymn, will rebuild Thy altar, O God of liberty and equality!

END OF FIRST MEMOIR.

WHAT IS PROPERTY? SECOND MEMOIR

A LETTER TO M. BLANQUI.

SECOND MEMOIR.

PARIS, April 1, 1841.

MONSIEUR,—

Before resuming my "Inquiries into Government and Property," it is fitting, for the satisfaction of some worthy people, and also in the interest of order, that I should make to you a plain, straightforward explanation. In a much-governed State, no one would be allowed to attack the external form of the society, and the groundwork of its institutions, until he had established his right to do so,—first, by his morality; second, by his capacity; and, third, by the purity of his intentions. Any one who, wishing to publish a treatise upon the constitution of the country, could not satisfy this threefold condition, would be obliged to procure the endorsement of a responsible patron possessing the requisite qualifications.

But we Frenchmen have the liberty of the press. This grand right—the sword of thought, which elevates the virtuous citizen to the rank of legislator, and makes the malicious citizen an agent of discord—frees us from all preliminary responsibility to the law; but it does not release us from our internal obligation to render a public account of our sentiments and thoughts. I have used, in all its fulness, and concerning an important question, the right which the charter grants us. I come to-day, sir, to submit my conscience to your judgment, and my feeble insight to your discriminating reason. You have criticised in a kindly spirit—I had almost said with partiality for the writer—a work which teaches a doctrine that you thought it your duty to condemn. "The Academy of Moral and Political Sciences," said you in your report, "can accept the conclusions of the author only as far as it likes." I venture to hope, sir, that, after you have read this letter, if your prudence still restrains you, your fairness will induce you to do me justice.

MEN, EQUAL IN THE DIGNITY OF THEIR PERSONS AND EQUAL BEFORE THE LAW, SHOULD BE

EQUAL IN THEIR CONDITIONS,—such is the thesis which I maintained and developed in a memoir bearing the title, "What is Property? or, An Inquiry into the Principle of Right and of Government."

The idea of social equality, even in individual fortunes, has in all ages besieged, like a vague presentiment, the human imagination. Poets have sung of it in their hymns; philosophers have dreamed of it in their Utopias; priests teach it, but only for the spiritual world. The people, governed by it, never have had faith in it; and the civil power is never more disturbed than by the fables of the age of gold and the reign of Astrea. A year ago, however, this idea received a scientific demonstration, which has not yet been satisfactorily answered, and, permit me to add, never will be. This demonstration, owing to its slightly impassioned style, its method of reasoning,—which was so at variance with that employed by the generally recognized authorities,—and the importance and novelty of its conclusions, was of a nature to cause some alarm; and might have been dangerous, had it not been—as you, sir, so well said—a sealed letter, so far as the general public was concerned, addressed only to men of intelligence. I was glad to see that through its metaphysical dress you recognized the wise foresight of the author; and I thank you for it. May God grant that my intentions, which are wholly peaceful, may never be charged upon me as treasonable!

Like a stone thrown into a mass of serpents, the First Memoir on Property excited intense animosity, and aroused the passions of many. But, while some wished the author and his work to be publicly denounced, others found in them simply the solution of the fundamental problems of society; a few even basing evil speculations upon the new light which they had obtained. It was not to be expected that a system of inductions abstractly gathered together, and still more abstractly expressed, would be understood with equal accuracy in its ensemble and in each of its parts.

To find the law of equality, no longer in charity and self-sacrifice (which are not binding in their nature), but in justice; to base equality of functions upon equality of persons; to determine the absolute principle of exchange; to neutralize the inequality of individual faculties by collective force; to establish an equation between property and robbery; to change the law of succession without destroying the principle; to maintain the human personality in a system of absolute association, and to save liberty from the chains of communism; to synthetize the monarchical and democratic forms of government; to reverse the division of powers; to give the executive power to the nation, and to make legislation a positive, fixed, and absolute science,—what a series of paradoxes! what a string of delusions! if I may not say, what a chain of truths! But it is not my purpose here to pass upon the theory of the right of possession. I discuss no dogmas. My only object is to justify my views, and to show that, in writing as I did, I not only exercised a right, but performed a duty.

Yes, I have attacked property, and shall attack it again; but, sir, before demanding that I shall make the amende honorable for having obeyed my conscience and spoken the exact truth, condescend, I beg of you, to cast a glance at the events which are happening around us; look at our deputies, our magistrates, our philosophers, our ministers, our professors, and our publicists; examine their methods of dealing with the matter of property; count up with me the restrictions placed upon it every day in the name of the public welfare; measure the breaches already made; estimate those which society thinks of making hereafter; add the ideas concerning property held by all theories in common; interrogate history, and then tell me what will be left, half a century hence, of this old right of property; and, thus perceiving that I have so many accomplices, you will immediately declare me innocent.

What is the law of expropriation on the ground of public utility, which everybody favors, and which is even thought too lenient? [36]

A flagrant violation of the right of property. Society indemnifies, it is said, the dispossessed proprietor; but does it return to him the traditional associations, the poetic charm, and the family pride which accompany property? Naboth, and the miller of Sans-Souci, would have protested against French law, as they protested against the caprice of their kings. "It is the field of our fathers," they would have cried, "and we will not sell it!" Among the ancients, the refusal of the individual limited the powers of the State. The Roman law bowed to the will of the citizen, and an emperor—Commodus, if I remember rightly—abandoned the project of enlarging the forum out of respect for the rights of the occupants who refused to abdicate. Property is a real right, *jus in re,*—a right inherent in the thing, and whose principle lies in the external manifestation of man's will. Man leaves his imprint, stamps his character, upon the objects of his handiwork. This plastic force of man, as the modern jurists say, is the seal which, set upon matter, makes it holy. Whoever lays hands upon it, against the proprietor's will, does violence to the latter's personality. And yet, when an administrative committee saw fit to declare that public utility required it, property had to give way to the general will. Soon, in the name of public utility, methods of cultivation and conditions of enjoyment will be prescribed; inspectors of agriculture and manufactures will be appointed; property will be taken away from unskilful hands, and entrusted to laborers who are more deserving of it; and a general superintendence of production will be established. It is not two years since I saw a proprietor destroy a forest more than five hundred acres in extent. If public utility had interfered, that forest—the only one for miles around—would still be standing.

But, it is said, expropriation on the ground of public utility is only an exception which confirms the principle, and bears testimony in favor of the right. Very well; but from this exception we will pass to another, from that to a third, and so on from exceptions to exceptions, until we have reduced the rule to a pure abstraction.

How many supporters do you think, sir, can be claimed for the project of the conversion of the public funds? I venture to say that everybody favors it, except the fund-holders. Now, this so-called conversion is an extensive expropriation, and in this case with no indemnity whatever. The public funds are so much real estate, the income from which the proprietor counts upon with perfect safety, and which owes its value to the tacit promise of the government to pay interest upon it at the established rate, until the fund-holder applies for redemption. For, if the income is liable to diminution, it is less profitable than house-rent or farm-rent, whose rates may rise or fall according to the fluctuations in the market; and in that case, what inducement has the capitalist to invest his money in the State? When, then, you force the fund-holder to submit to a diminution of interest, you make him bankrupt to the extent of the diminution; and since, in consequence of the conversion, an equally profitable investment becomes impossible, you depreciate his property.

That such a measure may be justly executed, it must be generalized; that is, the law which provides for it must decree also that interest on sums lent on deposit or on mortgage throughout the realm, as well as house and farm-rents, shall be reduced to three per cent. This simultaneous reduction of all kinds of income would be not a whit more difficult to accomplish than the proposed conversion; and, further, it would offer the advantage of forestalling at one blow all objections to it, at the same time that it would insure a just assessment of the land-tax. See! If at the moment of conversion a piece of real estate yields an income of one thousand francs, after the new law takes effect it will yield only six hundred francs. Now, allowing the tax to be an aliquot part—one-fourth for example—of the income derived from each piece of property, it is clear on the one hand that the proprietor would not, in order to lighten his share of the tax, underestimate the value of his property; since, house and farm-rents being fixed by the value of the capital, and the latter being measured by the tax, to depreciate his real estate would be to reduce his revenue. On the other hand, it is equally evident that the same proprietors could not overestimate the value of their property, in order to increase their incomes beyond the limits of the law, since the tenants and farmers, with their old leases in their hands, would enter a protest.

Such, sir, must be the result sooner or later of the conversion which has been so long demanded; otherwise, the financial operation of which we are speaking would be a crying injustice, unless intended as a stepping-stone. This last motive seems the most plausible one; for in spite of the clamors of interested parties, and the flagrant violation of certain rights, the public conscience is bound to fulfil its desire, and is no more affected when charged with attacking property, than when listening to the complaints of the bondholders. In this case, instinctive justice belies legal justice.

Who has not heard of the inextricable confusion into which the Chamber of Deputies was thrown last year, while discussing the question of colonial and native sugars? Did they leave these two industries to themselves? The native manufacturer was ruined by the colonist. To maintain the beet-root, the cane had to be taxed. To protect the property of the one, it became necessary to violate the property of the other. The most remarkable feature of this business was precisely that to which the least attention was paid; namely, that, in one way or another, property had to be violated. Did they impose on each industry a proportional tax, so as to preserve a balance in the market? They created a maximum PRICE for each variety of sugar; and, as this maximum PRICE was not the same, they attacked property in two ways,—on the one hand, interfering with the liberty of trade; on the other, disregarding the equality of proprietors. Did they suppress the beet-root by granting an indemnity to the manufacturer? They sacrificed the property of the tax-payer. Finally, did they prefer to cultivate the two varieties of sugar at the nation's expense, just as different varieties of tobacco are cultivated? They abolished, so far as the sugar industry was concerned, the right of property. This last course, being the most social, would have been certainly the best; but, if property is the necessary basis of civilization, how is this deep-seated antagonism to be explained? [37]

Not satisfied with the power of dispossessing a citizen on the ground of public utility, they want also to dispossess him on the ground of PRIVATE UTILITY. For a long time, a revision of the law concerning mortgages was clamored for; a process was demanded, in behalf of all kinds of credit and in the interest of even the debtors themselves, which would render the expropriation of real estate as prompt, as easy, and as effective as that which follows a commercial protest. The Chamber of Deputies, in the early part of this year, 1841, discussed this project, and the law was passed almost unanimously. There is nothing more just, nothing more reasonable, nothing more philosophical apparently, than the motives which gave rise to this reform.

I. Formerly, the small proprietor whose obligation had arrived at maturity, and who found himself unable to meet it, had to employ all that he had left, after being released from his debt, in defraying the legal costs. Henceforth, the promptness of expropriation will save him from total ruin. 2. The difficulties in the way of payment arrested credit, and prevented the employment of capital in agricultural enterprises. This cause of distrust no longer existing, capitalists will find new markets, agriculture will rapidly develop, and farmers will be the first to enjoy the benefit of the new law. 3. Finally, it was iniquitous and absurd, that, on account of a protested note, a poor manufacturer should see in twenty-four hours his business arrested, his labor suspended, his merchandise seized, his machinery sold at auction, and finally himself led off to prison, while two years were sometimes necessary to expropriate the most miserable piece of real estate.

These arguments, and others besides, you clearly stated, sir, in your first lectures of this academic year.

But, when stating these excellent arguments, did you ask yourself, sir, whither would tend such a transformation of our system of mortgages?... To monetize, if I may say so, landed property; to accumulate it within portfolios; to separate the laborer from the soil, man from Nature; to make him a wanderer over the face of the earth; to eradicate from his heart every trace of family feeling, national pride, and love of country; to isolate him more and more; to render him indifferent to all around him; to concentrate his love upon one object,—money; and, finally, by the dishonest practices of usury, to monopolize the land to the profit of a financial aristocracy,—a worthy auxiliary of that industrial feudality whose pernicious influence we begin to feel so bitterly. Thus, little by little, the subordination of the laborer to the idler, the restoration of abolished castes, and the distinction between patrician and plebeian, would be effected; thus, thanks to the new privileges granted to the property of the capitalists, that of the small and intermediate proprietors would gradually disappear, and with it the whole class of free and honest laborers. This certainly is not my plan for the abolition of property. Far from mobilizing the soil, I would, if possible, immobilize even the functions of pure intelligence, so that society might be the fulfilment of the intentions of Nature, who gave us our first possession, the land. For, if the instrument or capital of production is the mark of the laborer, it is also his pedestal, his support, his country, and, as the Psalmist says, THE PLACE OF HIS ACTIVITY AND HIS REST. [38]

Let us examine more closely still the inevitable and approaching result of the last law concerning judicial sales and mortgages. Under the system of competition which is killing us, and whose necessary expression is a plundering and tyrannical government, the farmer will need always capital in order to repair his losses, and will be forced to contract loans. Always depending upon the future for the payment of his debts, he will be deceived in his hope, and surprised by maturity. For what is there more prompt, more unexpected, more abbreviatory of space and time, than the maturity of an obligation? I address this question to all whom this pitiless Nemesis pursues, and even troubles in their dreams. Now, under the new law, the expropriation of a debtor will be effected a hundred times more rapidly; then, also, spoliation will be a hundred times surer, and the free laborer will pass a hundred times sooner from his present condition to that of a serf attached to the soil. Formerly, the length of time required to effect the seizure curbed the usurer's avidity, gave the borrower an opportunity to recover himself, and gave rise to a transaction between him and his creditor which might result finally in a complete release. Now, the debtor's sentence is irrevocable: he has but a few days of grace.

And what advantages are promised by this law as an offset to this sword of Damocles, suspended by a single hair over the head of the unfortunate husbandman? The expenses of seizure will be much less, it is said; but will the interest on the borrowed capital be less exorbitant? For, after all, it is interest which impoverishes the peasant and leads to his expropriation. That the law may be in harmony with its principle, that it may be truly inspired by that spirit of justice for which it is commended, it must—while facilitating expropriation—lower the legal price of money. Otherwise, the reform concerning mortgages is but a trap set for small proprietors,—a legislative trick.

Lower interest on money! But, as we have just seen, that is to limit property. Here, sir, you shall make your own defence. More than once, in your learned lectures, I have heard you deplore the precipitancy of the Chambers, who, without previous study and without profound knowledge of the subject, voted almost unanimously to maintain the statutes and privileges of the Bank. Now these privileges, these statutes, this vote of the Chambers, mean simply this,—that the market price of specie, at five or six per cent., is not too high, and that the conditions of exchange, discount, and circulation, which generally double this interest, are none too severe. So the government thinks. M. Blanqui—a professor of political economy, paid by the State—maintains the contrary, and pretends to demonstrate, by decisive arguments, the necessity of a reform. Who, then, best understands the interests of property,—the State, or M. Blanqui?

If specie could be borrowed at half the present rate, the revenues from all sorts of property would soon be reduced one-half also. For example: when it costs less to build a house than to hire one, when it is cheaper to clear a field than to procure one already cleared, competition inevitably leads to a reduction of house and farm-rents, since the surest way to depreciate active capital is to increase its amount. But it is a law of political economy that an increase of production augments the mass of available capital, consequently tends to raise wages, and finally to annihilate interest. Then, proprietors are interested in maintaining the statutes and privileges of the Bank; then, a reform in this matter would compromise the right of increase; then, the peers and deputies are better informed than Professor Blanqui.

But these same deputies,—so jealous of their privileges whenever the equalizing effects of a reform are within their intellectual horizon,—what did they do a few days before they passed the law concerning judicial sales? They formed a conspiracy against property! Their law to regulate the labor of children in factories will, without doubt, prevent the manufacturer from compelling a child to labor more than so many hours a day; but it will not force him to increase the pay of the child, nor that of its father. To-day, in the interest of health, we diminish the subsistence of the poor; to-morrow it will be necessary to protect them by fixing their MINIMUM wages. But to fix their minimum wages is to compel the proprietor, is to force the master to accept his workman as an associate, which interferes with freedom and makes mutual insurance obligatory. Once entered upon this path, we never shall stop. Little by little the government will become manufacturer, commission-merchant, and retail dealer.

It will be the sole proprietor. Why, at all epochs, have the ministers of State been so reluctant to meddle with the question of wages? Why have they always refused to interfere between the master and the workman? Because they knew the touchy and jealous nature of property, and, regarding it as the principle of all civilization, felt that to meddle with it would be to unsettle the very foundations of society. Sad condition of the proprietary regime,—one of inability to exercise charity without violating justice! [39]

And, sir, this fatal consequence which necessity forces upon the State is no mere imagination. Even now the legislative power is asked, no longer simply to regulate the government of factories, but to create factories itself. Listen to the millions of voices shouting on all hands for THE ORGANISATION OF LABOR, THE CREATION OF NATIONAL WORKSHOPS! The whole laboring class is agitated: it has its journals, organs, and representatives. To guarantee labor to the workingman, to balance production with sale, to harmonize industrial proprietors, it advocates to-day—as a sovereign remedy—one sole head, one national wardenship, one huge manufacturing company. For, sir, all this is included in the idea of national workshops. On this subject I wish to quote, as proof, the views of an illustrious economist, a brilliant mind, a progressive intellect, an enthusiastic soul, a true patriot, and yet an official defender of the right of property. [40]

The honorable professor of the Conservatory proposes then,—

1. TO CHECK THE CONTINUAL EMIGRATION OF LABORERS FROM THE COUNTRY INTO THE CITIES.

But, to keep the peasant in his village, his residence there must be made endurable: to be just to all, the proletaire of the country must be treated as well as the proletaire of the city. Reform is needed, then, on farms as well as in factories; and, when the government enters the workshop, the government must seize the plough! What becomes, during this progressive invasion, of independent cultivation, exclusive domain, property?

2. TO FIX FOR EACH PROFESSION A MODERATE SALARY, VARYING WITH TIME AND PLACE AND BASED UPON CERTAIN DATA.

The object of this measure would be to secure to laborers their subsistence, and to proprietors their profits, while obliging the latter to sacrifice from motives of prudence, if for no other reason, a portion of their income. Now, I say, that this portion, in the long run, would swell until at last there would be an equality of enjoyment between the proletaire and the proprietor. For, as we have had occasion to remark several times already, the interest of the capitalist—in other words the increase of the idler—tends, on account of the power of labor, the multiplication of products and exchanges, to continually diminish, and, by constant reduction, to disappear. So that, in the society proposed by M. Blanqui, equality would not be realized at first, but would exist potentially; since property, though outwardly seeming to be industrial feudality, being no longer a principle of exclusion and encroachment, but only a privilege of division, would not be slow, thanks to the intellectual and political emancipation of the proletariat, in passing into absolute equality,—as absolute at least as any thing can be on this earth.

I omit, for the sake of brevity, the numerous considerations which the professor adduces in support of what he calls, too modestly in my opinion, his Utopia. They would serve only to prove beyond all question that, of all the charlatans of radicalism who fatigue the public ear, no one approaches, for depth and clearness of thought, the audacious M. Blanqui.

3. NATIONAL WORKSHOPS SHOULD BE IN OPERATION ONLY DURING PERIODS OF STAGNATION IN ORDINARY INDUSTRIES; AT SUCH TIMES THEY SHOULD BE OPENED AS VAST OUTLETS TO THE FLOOD OF THE LABORING POPULATION.

But, sir, the stoppage of private industry is the result of over-production, and insufficient markets. If, then, production continues in the national workshops, how will the crisis be terminated? Undoubtedly, by the general depreciation of merchandise, and, in the last analysis, by the conversion of private workshops into national workshops. On the other hand, the government will need capital with which to pay its workmen; now, how will this capital be obtained? By taxation. And upon what will the tax be levied? Upon property. Then you will have proprietary industry sustaining against itself, and at its own expense, another industry with which it cannot compete. What, think you, will become, in this fatal circle, of the possibility of profit,—in a word, of property?

Thank Heaven! equality of conditions is taught in the public schools; let us fear revolutions no longer. The most implacable enemy of property could not, if he wished to destroy it, go to work in a wiser and more effective way. Courage, then, ministers, deputies, economists! make haste to seize this glorious initiative; let the watchwords of equality, uttered from the heights of science and power, be repeated in the midst of the people; let them thrill the breasts of the proletaires, and carry dismay into the ranks of the last representatives of privilege!

The tendency of society in favor of compelling proprietors to support national workshops and public manufactories is so strong that for several years, under the name of ELECTORAL REFORM, it has been exclusively the question of the day. What is, after all, this electoral reform which the people grasp at, as if it were a bait, and which so many ambitious persons either call for or denounce? It is the acknowledgment of the right of the masses to a voice in the assessment of taxes, and the making of the laws; which laws, aiming always at the protection of material interests, affect, in a greater or less degree, all questions of taxation or wages. Now the people, instructed long since by their journals, their dramas, [41] and their songs, [42] know to-day that taxation, to be equitably divided, must be graduated, and must be borne mainly by the rich,—that it must be levied upon luxuries, &c. And be sure that the people, once in the majority in the Chamber, will not fail to apply these lessons. Already we have a minister of public works. National workshops will follow; and soon, as a consequence, the excess of the proprietor's revenue over the workingman's wages will be swallowed up in the coffers of the laborers of the State. Do you not see that in this way property is gradually reduced, as nobility was formerly, to a nominal title, to a distinction purely honorary in its nature?

Either the electoral reform will fail to accomplish that which is hoped from it, and will disappoint its innumerable partisans, or else it will inevitably result in a transformation of the absolute right under which we live into a right of possession; that is, that while, at present, property makes the elector, after this reform is accomplished, the citizen, the producer will be the possessor. [43] Consequently, the radicals are right in saying that the electoral reform is in their eyes only a means; but, when they are silent as to the end, they show either profound ignorance, or useless dissimulation. There should be no secrets or reservations from peoples and powers. He disgraces himself and fails in respect for his fellows, who, in publishing his opinions, employs evasion and cunning. Before the people act, they need to know the whole truth. Unhappy he who shall dare to trifle with them! For the people are credulous, but they are strong. Let us tell them, then, that this reform which is proposed is only a means,—a means often tried, and hitherto without effect,—but that the logical object of the electoral reform is equality of fortunes; and that this equality itself is only a new means having in view the superior and definitive object of the salvation of society, the restoration of morals and religion, and the revival of poetry and art.

This assertion of M. Rossi is not borne out by history. Property is the cause of the electoral right, not as a PRESUMPTION OF CAPACITY,—an idea which never prevailed until lately, and which is extremely absurd,—but as a GUARANTEE OF DEVOTION TO THE ESTABLISHED ORDER. The electoral body is a league of those interested in the maintenance of property, against those not interested. There are thousands of documents, even official documents, to prove this, if necessary. For the rest, the present system is only a continuation of the municipal system, which, in the middle ages, sprang up in connection with feudalism,—an oppressive, mischief-making system, full of petty passions and base intrigues.

It would be an abuse of the reader's patience to insist further upon the tendency of our time towards equality. There are, moreover, so many people who denounce the present age, that nothing is gained by exposing to their view the popular, scientific, and representative tendencies of the nation.

Prompt to recognize the accuracy of the inferences drawn from observation, they confine themselves to a general censure of the facts, and an absolute denial of their legitimacy. "What wonder," they say, "that this atmosphere of equality intoxicates us, considering all that has been said and done during the past ten years!... Do you not see that society is dissolving, that a spirit of infatuation is carrying us away? All these hopes of regeneration are but forebodings of death; your songs of triumph are like the prayers of the departing, your trumpet peals announce the baptism of a dying man. Civilization is falling in ruin: *Imus, imus, praecipites!*"

Such people deny God. I might content myself with the reply that the spirit of 1830 was the result of the maintenance of the violated charter; that this charter arose from the Revolution of '89; that '89 implies the States-General's right of remonstrance, and the enfranchisement of the communes; that the communes suppose feudalism, which in its turn supposes invasion, Roman law, Christianity, &c.

But it is necessary to look further. We must penetrate to the very heart of ancient institutions, plunge into the social depths, and uncover this indestructible leaven of equality which the God of justice breathed into our souls, and which manifests itself in all our works.

Labor is man's contemporary; it is a duty, since it is a condition of existence: "In the sweat of thy face shalt thou eat bread." It is more than a duty, it is a mission: "God put the man into the garden to dress it." I add that labor is the cause and means of equality.

Cast away upon a desert island two men: one large, strong, and active; the other weak, timid, and domestic. The latter will die of hunger; while the other, a skilful hunter, an expert fisherman, and an indefatigable husbandman, will overstock himself with provisions. What greater inequality, in this state of Nature so dear to the heart of Jean Jacques, could be imagined! But let these two men meet and associate themselves: the second immediately attends to the cooking, takes charge of the household affairs, and sees to the provisions, beds, and clothes; provided the stronger does not abuse his superiority by enslaving and ill-treating his companion, their social condition will be perfectly equal. Thus, through exchange of services, the inequalities of Nature neutralize each other, talents associate, and forces balance. Violence and inertia are found only among the poor and the aristocratic. And in that lies the philosophy of political economy, the mystery of human brotherhood. *Hic est sapientia.* Let us pass from the hypothetical state of pure Nature into civilization.

The proprietor of the soil, who produces, I will suppose with the economists, by lending his instrument, receives at the foundation of a society so many bushels of grain for each acre of arable land. As long as labor is weak, and the variety of its products small, the proprietor is powerful in comparison with the laborers; he has ten times, one hundred times, the portion of an honest man. But let labor, by multiplying its inventions, multiply its enjoyments and wants, and the proprietor, if he wishes to enjoy the new products, will be obliged to reduce his income every day; and since the first products tend rather to depreciate than to rise in value,—in consequence of the continual addition of the new ones, which may be regarded as supplements of the first ones,—it follows that the idle proprietor grows poor as fast as public prosperity increases. "Incomes" (I like to quote you, sir, because it is impossible to give too good an authority for these elementary principles of economy, and because I cannot express them better myself), "incomes," you have said, "tend to disappear as capital increases. He who possesses to-day an income of twenty thousand pounds is not nearly as rich as he who possessed the same amount fifty years ago. The time is coming when all property will be a burden to the idle, and will necessarily pass into the hands of the able and industrious. 44..."

In order to live as a proprietor, or to consume without producing, it is necessary, then, to live upon the labor of another; in other words, it is necessary to kill the laborer. It is upon this principle that proprietors of those varieties of capital which are of primary necessity increase their farm-rents as fast as industry develops, much more careful of their privileges in that respect, than those economists who, in order to strengthen property, advocate a reduction of interest. But the crime is unavailing: labor and production increase; soon the proprietor will be forced to labor, and then property is lost.

The proprietor is a man who, having absolute control of an instrument of production, claims the right to enjoy the product of the instrument without using it himself. To this end he lends it; and we have just seen that from this loan the laborer derives a power of exchange, which sooner or later will destroy the right of increase. In the first place, the proprietor is obliged to allow the laborer a portion of the product, for without it the laborer could not live. Soon the latter, through the development of his industry, finds a means of regaining the greater portion of that which he gives to the proprietor; so that at last, the objects of enjoyment increasing continually, while the income of the idler remains the same, the proprietor, having exhausted his resources, begins to think of going to work himself. Then the victory of the producer is certain. Labor commences to tip the balance towards its own side, and commerce leads to equilibrium.

Man's instinct cannot err; as, in liberty, exchange of functions leads inevitably to equality among men, so commerce—or exchange of products, which is identical with exchange of functions—is a new cause of equality. As long as the proprietor does not labor, however small his income, he enjoys a privilege; the laborer's welfare may be equal to his, but equality of conditions does not exist. But as soon as the proprietor becomes a producer,—since he can exchange his special product only with his tenant or his *commandite*,—sooner or later this tenant, this *exploited* man, if violence is not done him, will make a profit out of the proprietor, and will oblige him to restore—in the exchange of their respective products—the interest on his capital. So that, balancing one injustice by another, the contracting parties will be equal. Labor and exchange, when liberty prevails, lead, then, to equality of fortunes; mutuality of services neutralizes privilege. That is why despots in all ages and countries have assumed control of commerce; they wished to prevent the labor of their subjects from becoming an obstacle to the rapacity of tyrants.

Up to this point, all takes place in the natural order; there is no premeditation, no artifice. The whole proceeding is governed by the laws of necessity alone. Proprietors and laborers act only in obedience to their wants. Thus, the exercise of the right of increase, the art of robbing the producer, depends—during this first period of civilization—upon physical violence, murder, and war.

But at this point a gigantic and complicated conspiracy is hatched against the capitalists. The weapon of the EXPLOITERS is met by the EXPLOITED with the instrument of commerce,—a marvellous invention, denounced at its origin by the moralists who favored property, but inspired without doubt by the genius of labor, by the Minerva of the proletaires.

The principal cause of the evil lay in the accumulation and immobility of capital of all sorts,—an immobility which prevented labor, enslaved and subalternized by haughty idleness, from ever acquiring it. The necessity was felt of dividing and mobilizing wealth, of rendering it portable, of making it pass from the hands of the possessor into those of the worker. Labor invented MONEY. Afterwards, this invention was revived and developed by the BILL OF EXCHANGE and the BANK. For all these things are substantially the same, and proceed from the same mind. The first man who conceived the idea of representing a value by a shell, a precious stone, or a certain weight of metal, was the real inventor of the Bank. What is a piece of money, in fact? It is a bill of exchange written upon solid and durable material, and carrying with it its own redemption. By this means, oppressed equality was enabled to laugh at the efforts of the proprietors, and the balance of justice was adjusted for the first time in the tradesman's shop. The trap was cunningly set, and accomplished its purpose so thoroughly that in idle hands money became only dissolving wealth, a false symbol, a shadow of riches. An excellent economist and profound philosopher was that miser who took as his motto, "WHEN A GUINEA IS EXCHANGED, IT EVAPORATES." So it may be said, "When real estate is converted into money, it is lost." This explains the constant fact of history, that the nobles—the unproductive proprietors of the soil—have every where been dispossessed by industrial and commercial plebeians. Such was especially the case in the formation of the Italian republics, born, during the middle ages, of the impoverishment of the seigniors. I will not pursue the interesting considerations which this matter suggests; I could only repeat the testimony of historians, and present economical demonstrations in an altered form.

The greatest enemy of the landed and industrial aristocracy to-day, the incessant promoter of equality of fortunes, is the BANKER. Through him immense plains are divided, mountains change their positions, forests are grown upon the public squares, one hemisphere produces for another, and every corner of the globe has its usufructuaries. By means of the Bank new wealth is continually created, the use of which (soon becoming indispensable to selfishness) wrests the dormant capital from the hands of the jealous proprietor. The banker is at once the most potent creator of wealth, and the main distributor of the products of art and Nature. And yet, by the strangest antinomy, this same banker is the most relentless collector of profits, increase, and usury ever inspired by the demon of property. The importance of the services which he renders leads us to endure, though not without complaint, the taxes which he imposes. Nevertheless, since nothing can avoid its providential mission, since nothing which exists can escape the end for which it exists the banker (the modern Croesus) must some day become the restorer of equality. And following in your footsteps, sir, I have already given the reason; namely, that profit decreases as capital multiplies, since an increase of capital—calling for more laborers, without whom it remains unproductive—always causes an increase of wages. Whence it follows that the Bank, to-day the suction-pump of wealth, is destined to become the steward of the human race.

The phrase EQUALITY OF FORTUNES chafes people, as if it referred to a condition of the other world, unknown here below. There are some persons, radicals as well as moderates, whom the very mention of this idea fills with indignation. Let, then, these silly aristocrats abolish mercantile societies and insurance companies, which are founded by prudence for mutual assistance. For all these social facts, so spontaneous and free from all levelling intentions, are the legitimate fruits of the instinct of equality.

When the legislator makes a law, properly speaking he does not MAKE it,—he does not CREATE it: he DESCRIBES it. In legislating upon the moral, civil, and political relations of citizens, he does not express an arbitrary notion: he states the general idea,—the higher principle which governs the matter which he is considering; in a word, he is the proclaimer, not the inventor, of the law. So, when two or more men form among themselves, by synallagmatic contract, an industrial or an insurance association, they recognize that their interests, formerly isolated by a false spirit of selfishness and independence, are firmly connected by their inner natures, and by the mutuality of their relations. They do not really bind themselves by an act of their private will: they swear to conform henceforth to a previously existing social law hitherto disregarded by them. And this is proved by the fact that these same men, could they avoid association, would not associate. Before they can be induced to unite their interests, they must acquire full knowledge of the dangers of competition and isolation; hence the experience of evil is the only thing which leads them into society.

Now I say that, to establish equality among men, it is only necessary to generalize the principle upon which insurance, agricultural, and commercial associations are based. I say that competition, isolation of interests, monopoly, privilege, accumulation of capital, exclusive enjoyment, subordination of functions, individual production, the right of profit or increase, the exploitation of man by man, and, to sum up all these species under one head, that PROPERTY is the principal cause of misery and crime. And, for having arrived at this offensive and anti-proprietary conclusion, I am an abhorred monster; radicals and conservatives alike point me out as a fit subject for prosecution; the academies shower their censures upon me; the most worthy people regard me as mad; and those are excessively tolerant who content themselves with the assertion that I am a fool. Oh, unhappy the writer who publishes the truth otherwise than as a performance of a duty! If he has counted upon the applause of the crowd; if he has supposed that avarice and self-interest would forget themselves in admiration of him; if he has neglected to encase himself within three thicknesses of brass,—he will fail, as he ought, in his selfish undertaking. The unjust criticisms, the sad disappointments, the despair of his mistaken ambition, will kill him.

But, if I am no longer permitted to express my own personal opinion concerning this interesting question of social equilibrium, let me, at least, make known the thought of my masters, and develop the doctrines advocated in the name of the government.

It never has been my intention, sir, in spite of the vigorous censure which you, in behalf of your academy, have pronounced upon the doctrine of equality of fortunes, to contradict and cope with you. In listening to you, I have felt my inferiority too keenly to permit me to enter upon such a discussion. And then,—if it must be said,—however different your language is from mine, we believe in the same principles; you share all my opinions. I do not mean to insinuate thereby, sir, that you have (to use the phraseology of the schools) an ESOTERIC and an EXOTERIC doctrine,—that, secretly believing in equality, you defend property only from motives of prudence and by command. I am not rash enough to regard you as my colleague in my revolutionary projects; and I esteem you too highly, moreover, to suspect you of dissimulation. I only mean that the truths which methodical investigation and laborious metaphysical speculation have painfully demonstrated to me, a profound acquaintance with political economy and a long experience reveal to you. While I have reached my belief in equality by long reflection, and almost in spite of my desires, you hold yours, sir, with all the zeal of faith,—with all the spontaneity of genius. That is why your course of lectures at the Conservatory is a perpetual war upon property and inequality of fortunes; that is why your most learned investigations, your most ingenious analyses, and your innumerable observations always conclude in a formula of progress and equality; that is why, finally, you are never more admired and applauded than at those moments of inspiration when, borne upon the wings of science, you ascend to those lofty truths which cause plebeian hearts to beat with enthusiasm, and which chill with horror men whose intentions are evil. How many times, from the place where I eagerly drank in your eloquent words, have I inwardly thanked Heaven for exempting you from the judgment passed by St. Paul upon the philosophers of his time,—"They have known the truth, and have not made it known"! How many times have I rejoiced at finding my own justification in each of your discourses! No, no; I neither wish nor ask for any thing which you do not teach yourself. I appeal to your numerous audience; let it belie me if, in commenting upon you, I pervert your meaning.

A disciple of Say, what in your eyes is more anti-social than the custom-houses; or, as you correctly call them, the barriers erected by monopoly between nations? What is more annoying, more unjust, or more absurd, than this prohibitory system which compels us to pay forty sous in France for that which in England or Belgium would bring us but fifteen? It is the custom-house, you once said, 45 which arrests the development of civilization by preventing the specialization of industries; it is the custom-house which enriches a hundred monopolists by impoverishing millions of citizens; it is the custom-house which produces famine in the midst of abundance, which makes labor sterile by prohibiting exchange, and which stifles production in a mortal embrace. It is the custom-house which renders nations jealous of, and hostile to, each other; four-fifths of the wars of all ages were caused originally by the custom-house. And then, at the highest pitch of your enthusiasm, you shouted: "Yes, if to put an end to this hateful system, it should become necessary for me to shed the last drop of my blood, I would joyfully spring into the gap, asking only time enough to give thanks to God for having judged me worthy of martyrdom!"

And, at that solemn moment, I said to myself: "Place in every department of France such a professor as that, and the revolution is avoided."

But, sir, by this magnificent theory of liberty of commerce you render military glory impossible,—you leave nothing for diplomacy to do; you even take away the desire for conquest, while abolishing profit altogether. What matters it, indeed, who restores Constantinople, Alexandria, and Saint Jean d'Acre, if the Syrians, Egyptians, and Turks are free to choose their masters; free to exchange their products with whom they please? Why should Europe get into such a turmoil over this petty Sultan and his old Pasha, if it is only a question whether we or the English shall civilize the Orient,—shall instruct Egypt and Syria in the European arts, and shall teach them to construct machines, dig canals, and build railroads? For, if to national independence free trade is added, the foreign influence of these two countries is thereafter exerted only through a voluntary relationship of producer to producer, or apprentice to journeyman.

Alone among European powers, France cheerfully accepted the task of civilizing the Orient, and began an invasion which was quite apostolic in its character,—so joyful and high-minded do noble thoughts render our nation! But diplomatic rivalry, national selfishness, English avarice, and Russian ambition stood in her way. To consummate a long-meditated usurpation, it was necessary to crush a too generous ally: the robbers of the Holy Alliance formed a league against dauntless and blameless France. Consequently, at the news of this famous treaty, there arose among us a chorus of curses upon the principle of property, which at that time was acting under the hypocritical formulas of the old political system. The last hour of property seemed to have struck by the side of Syria; from the Alps to the ocean, from the Rhine to the Pyrenees, the popular conscience was aroused. All France sang songs of war, and the coalition turned pale at the sound of these shuddering cries: "War upon the autocrat, who wishes to be proprietor of the old world! War upon the English perjurer, the devourer of India, the poisoner of China, the tyrant of Ireland, and the eternal enemy of France! War upon the allies who have conspired against liberty and equality! War! war! war upon property!"

By the counsel of Providence the emancipation of the nations is postponed. France is to conquer, not by arms, but by example. Universal reason does not yet understand this grand equation, which, commencing with the abolition of slavery, and advancing over the ruins of aristocracies and thrones, must end in equality of rights and fortunes; but the day is not far off when the knowledge of this truth will be as common as that of equality of origin. Already it seems to be understood that the Oriental question is only a question of custom-houses. Is it, then, so difficult for public opinion to generalize this idea, and to comprehend, finally, that if the suppression of custom-houses involves the abolition of national property, it involves also, as a consequence, the abolition of individual property?

In fact, if we suppress the custom-houses, the alliance of the nations is declared by that very act; their solidarity is recognized, and their equality proclaimed. If we suppress the custom-houses, the principle of association will not be slow in reaching from the State to the province, from the province to the city, and from the city to the workshop. But, then, what becomes of the privileges of authors and artists? Of what use are the patents for invention, imagination, amelioration, and improvement? When our deputies write a law of literary property by the side of a law which opens a large breach in the custom-house they contradict themselves, indeed, and pull down with one hand what they build up with the other. Without the custom-house, literary property does not exist, and the hopes of our starving authors are frustrated. For, certainly you do not expect, with the good man Fourier, that literary property will exercise itself in China to the profit of a French writer; and that an ode of Lamartine, sold by privilege all over the world, will bring in millions to its author! The poet's work is peculiar to the climate in which he lives; every where else the reproduction of his works, having no market value, should be frank and free. But what! will it be necessary for nations to put themselves under mutual surveillance for the sake of verses, statues, and elixirs? We shall always have, then, an excise, a city-toll, rights of entrance and transit, custom-houses finally; and then, as a reaction against privilege, smuggling.

Smuggling! That word reminds me of one of the most horrible forms of property. "Smuggling," you have said, sir, 46 "is an offence of political creation; it is the exercise of natural liberty, defined as a crime in certain cases by the will of the sovereign. The smuggler is a gallant man,—a man of spirit, who gaily busies himself in procuring for his neighbor, at a very low price, a jewel, a shawl, or any other object of necessity or luxury, which domestic monopoly renders excessively dear." Then, to a very poetical monograph of the smuggler, you add this dismal conclusion,—that the smuggler belongs to the family of Mandrin, and that the galleys should be his home!

But, sir, you have not called attention to the horrible exploitation which is carried on in this way in the name of property.

It is said,—and I give this report only as an hypothesis and an illustration, for I do not believe it,—it is said that the present minister of finances owes his fortune to smuggling. M. Humann, of Strasbourg, sent out of France, it is said, enormous quantities of sugar, for which he received the bounty on exportation promised by the State; then, smuggling this sugar back again, he exported it anew, receiving the bounty on exportation a second time, and so on. Notice, sir, that I do not state this as a fact; I give it only as it is told, not endorsing or even believing it. My sole design is to fix the idea in the mind by an example. If I believed that a minister had committed such a crime, that is, if I had personal and authentic knowledge that he had, I would denounce M. Humann, the minister of finances, to the Chamber of Deputies, and would loudly demand his expulsion from the ministry.

But that which is undoubtedly false of M. Humann is true of many others, as rich and no less honorable than he. Smuggling, organized on a large scale by the eaters of human flesh, is carried on to the profit of a few pashas at the risk and peril of their imprudent victims. The inactive proprietor offers his merchandise for sale; the actual smuggler risks his liberty, his honor, and his life. If success crowns the enterprise, the courageous servant gets paid for his journey; the profit goes to the coward. If fortune or treachery delivers the instrument of this execrable traffic into the hands of the custom-house officer, the master-smuggler suffers a loss which a more fortunate voyage will soon repair. The agent, pronounced a scoundrel, is thrown into prison in company with robbers; while his glorious patron, a juror, elector, deputy, or minister, makes laws concerning expropriation, monopoly, and custom-houses!

I promised, at the beginning of this letter, that no attack on property should escape my pen, my only object being to justify myself before the public by a general recrimination. But I could not refrain from branding so odious a mode of exploitation, and I trust that this short digression will be pardoned. Property does not avenge, I hope, the injuries which smuggling suffers.

The conspiracy against property is general; it is flagrant; it takes possession of all minds, and inspires all our laws; it lies at the bottom of all theories. Here the proletaire pursues property in the street, there the legislator lays an interdict upon it; now, a professor of political economy or of industrial legislation,[47] paid to defend it, undermines it with redoubled blows; at another—time, an academy calls it in question,[48] or inquires as to the progress of its demolition.[49] To-day there is not an idea, not an opinion, not a sect, which does not dream of muzzling property. None confess it, because none are yet conscious of it; there are too few minds capable of grasping spontaneously this ensemble of causes and effects, of principles and consequences, by which I try to demonstrate the approaching disappearance of property; on the other hand, the ideas that are generally formed of this right are too divergent and too loosely determined to allow an admission, so soon, of the contrary theory. Thus, in the middle and lower ranks of literature and philosophy, no less than among the common people, it is thought that, when property is abolished, no one will be able to enjoy the fruit of his labor; that no one will have any thing peculiar to himself, and that tyrannical communism will be established on the ruins of family and liberty!—chimeras, which are to support for a little while longer the cause of privilege.

But, before determining precisely the idea of property, before seeking amid the contradictions of systems for the common element which must form the basis of the new right, let us cast a rapid glance at the changes which, at the various periods of history, property has undergone. The political forms of nations are the expression of their beliefs. The mobility of these forms, their modification and their destruction, are solemn experiences which show us the value of ideas, and gradually eliminate from the infinite variety of customs the absolute, eternal, and immutable truth. Now, we shall see that every political institution tends, necessarily, and on pain of death, to equalize conditions; that everywhere and always equality of fortunes (like equality of rights) has been the social aim, whether the plebeian classes have endeavored to rise to political power by means of property, or whether—rulers already—they have used political power to overthrow property. We shall see, in short, by the progress of society, that the consummation of justice lies in the extinction of individual domain.

For the sake of brevity, I will disregard the testimony of ecclesiastical history and Christian theology: this subject deserves a separate treatise, and I propose hereafter to return to it. Moses and Jesus Christ proscribed, under the names of usury and inequality,[50] all sorts of profit and increase. The church itself, in its purest teachings, has always condemned property; and when I attacked, not only the authority of the church, but also its infidelity to justice, I did it to the glory of religion. I wanted to provoke a peremptory reply, and to pave the way for Christianity's triumph, in spite of the innumerable attacks of which it is at present the object. I hoped that an apologist would arise forthwith, and, taking his stand upon the Scriptures, the Fathers, the canons, and the councils and constitutions of the Popes, would demonstrate that the church always has maintained the doctrine of equality, and would attribute to temporary necessity the contradictions of its discipline. Such a labor would serve the cause of religion as well as that of equality. We must know, sooner or later, whether Christianity is to be regenerated in the church or out of it, and whether this church accepts the reproaches cast upon it of hatred to liberty and antipathy to progress. Until then we will suspend judgment, and content ourselves with placing before the clergy the teachings of history.

When Lycurgus undertook to make laws for Sparta, in what condition did he find this republic? On this point all historians agree. The people and the nobles were at war. The city was in a confused state, and divided by two parties,—the party of the poor, and the party of the rich. Hardly escaped from the barbarism of the heroic ages, society was rapidly declining. The proletariat made war upon property, which, in its turn, oppressed the proletariat. What did Lycurgus do? His first measure was one of general security, at the very idea of which our legislators would tremble. He abolished all debts; then, employing by turns persuasion and force, he induced the nobles to renounce their privileges, and re-established equality.

Lycurgus, in a word, hunted property out of Lacedaemon, seeing no other way to harmonize liberty, equality, and law. I certainly should not wish France to follow the example of Sparta; but it is remarkable that the most ancient of Greek legislators, thoroughly acquainted with the nature and needs of the people, more capable than any one else of appreciating the legitimacy of the obligations which he, in the exercise of his absolute authority, cancelled; who had compared the legislative systems of his time, and whose wisdom an oracle had proclaimed,—it is remarkable, I say, that Lycurgus should have judged the right of property incompatible with free institutions, and should have thought it his duty to preface his legislation by a coup d'etat which destroyed all distinctions of fortune.

Lycurgus understood perfectly that the luxury, the love of enjoyments, and the inequality of fortunes, which property engenders, are the bane of society; unfortunately the means which he employed to preserve his republic were suggested to him by false notions of political economy, and by a superficial knowledge of the human heart. Accordingly, property, which this legislator wrongly confounded with wealth, reentered the city together with the swarm of evils which he was endeavoring to banish; and this time Sparta was hopelessly corrupted.

"The introduction of wealth," says M. Pastoret, "was one of the principal causes of the misfortunes which they experienced. Against these, however, the laws had taken extraordinary precautions, the best among which was the inculcation of morals which tended to suppress desire."

The best of all precautions would have been the anticipation of desire by satisfaction. Possession is the sovereign remedy for cupidity, a remedy which would have been the less perilous to Sparta because fortunes there were almost equal, and conditions were nearly alike. As a general thing, fasting and abstinence are bad teachers of moderation.

"There was a law," says M. Pastoret again, "to prohibit the rich from wearing better clothing than the poor, from eating more delicate food, and from owning elegant furniture, vases, carpets, fine houses," &c. Lycurgus hoped, then, to maintain equality by rendering wealth useless. How much wiser he would have been if, in accordance with his military discipline, he had organized industry and taught the people to procure by their own labor the things which he tried in vain to deprive them of. In that case, enjoying happy thoughts and pleasant feelings, the citizen would have known no other desire than that with which the legislator endeavored to inspire him,—love of honor and glory, the triumphs of talent and virtue.

"Gold and all kinds of ornaments were forbidden the women." Absurd. After the death of Lycurgus, his institutions became corrupted; and four centuries before the Christian era not a vestige remained of the former simplicity. Luxury and the thirst for gold were early developed among the Spartans in a degree as intense as might have been expected from their enforced poverty and their inexperience in the arts. Historians have accused Pausanias, Lysander, Agesilaus, and others of having corrupted the morals of their country by the introduction of wealth obtained in war. It is a slander. The morals of the Spartans necessarily grew corrupt as soon as the Lacedaemonian poverty came in contact with Persian luxury and Athenian elegance. Lycurgus, then, made a fatal mistake in attempting to inspire generosity and modesty by enforcing vain and proud simplicity.

"Lycurgus was not frightened at idleness! A Lacedemonian, happening to be in Athens (where idleness was forbidden) during the punishment of a citizen who had been found guilty, asked to see the Athenian thus condemned for having exercised the rights of a free man.... It was one of the principles of Lycurguss, acted upon for several centuries, that free men should not follow lucrative professions.... The women disdained domestic labor; they did not spin their wool themselves, as did the other Greeks [they did not, then, read Homer!]; they left their slaves to make their clothing for them."—Pastoret: History of Legislation.

Could any thing be more contradictory? Lycurgus proscribed property among the citizens, and founded the means of subsistence on the worst form of property,—on property obtained by force. What wonder, after that, that a lazy city, where no industry was carried on, became a den of avarice? The Spartans succumbed the more easily to the allurements of luxury and Asiatic voluptuousness, being placed entirely at their mercy by their own coarseness. The same thing happened to the Romans, when military success took them out of Italy,—a thing which the author of the prosopopoeia of Fabricius could not explain. It is not the cultivation of the arts which corrupts morals, but their degradation, induced by inactive and luxurious opulence. The instinct of property is to make the industry of Daedalus, as well as the talent of Phidias, subservient to its own fantastic whims and disgraceful pleasures. Property, not wealth, ruined the Spartans.

When Solon appeared, the anarchy caused by property was at its height in the Athenian republic. "The inhabitants of Attica were divided among themselves as to the form of government. Those who lived on the mountains (the poor) preferred the popular form; those of the plain (the middle class), the oligarchs; those by the sea coast, a mixture of oligarchy and democracy. Other dissensions were arising from the inequality of fortunes. The mutual antagonism of the rich and poor had become so violent, that the one-man power seemed the only safe-guard against the revolution with which the republic was threatened." (Pastoret: History of Legislation.)

Quarrels between the rich and the poor, which seldom occur in monarchies, because a well established power suppresses dissensions, seem to be the life of popular governments. Aristotle had noticed this. The oppression of wealth submitted to agrarian laws, or to excessive taxation; the hatred of the lower classes for the upper class, which is exposed always to libellous charges made in hopes of confiscation,—these were the features of the Athenian government which were especially revolting to Aristotle, and which caused him to favor a limited monarchy. Aristotle, if he had lived in our day, would have supported the constitutional government. But, with all deference to the Stagirite, a government which sacrifices the life of the proletaire to that of the proprietor is quite as irrational as one which supports the former by robbing the latter; neither of them deserve the support of a free man, much less of a philosopher.

Solon followed the example of Lycurgus. He celebrated his legislative inauguration by the abolition of debts,—that is, by bankruptcy. In other words, Solon wound up the governmental machine for a longer or shorter time depending upon the rate of interest. Consequently, when the spring relaxed and the chain became unwound, the republic had either to perish, or to recover itself by a second bankruptcy. This singular policy was pursued by all the ancients. After the captivity of Babylon, Nehemiah, the chief of the Jewish nation, abolished debts; Lycurgus abolished debts; Solon abolished debts; the Roman people, after the expulsion of the kings until the accession of the Caesars, struggled with the Senate for the abolition of debts. Afterwards, towards the end of the republic, and long after the establishment of the empire, agriculture being abandoned, and the provinces becoming depopulated in consequence of the excessive rates of interest, the emperors freely granted the lands to whoever would cultivate them,—that is, they abolished debts. No one, except Lycurgus, who went to the other extreme, ever perceived that the great point was, not to release debtors by a coup d'etat, but to prevent the contraction of debts in future.

On the contrary, the most democratic governments were always exclusively based upon individual property; so that the social element of all these republics was war between the citizens.

Solon decreed that a census should be taken of all fortunes, regulated political rights by the result, granted to the larger proprietors more influence, established the balance of powers,—in a word, inserted in the constitution the most active leaven of discord; as if, instead of a legislator chosen by the people, he had been their greatest enemy. Is it not, indeed, the height of imprudence to grant equality of political rights to men of unequal conditions? If a manufacturer, uniting all his workmen in a joint-stock company, should give to each of them a consultative and deliberative voice,—that is, should make all of them masters,—would this equality of mastership secure continued inequality of wages? That is the whole political system of Solon, reduced to its simplest expression.

"In giving property a just preponderance," says M. Pastoret, "Solon repaired, as far as he was able, his first official act, —the abolition of debts.... He thought he owed it to public peace to make this great sacrifice of acquired rights and natural equity. But the violation of individual property and written contracts is a bad preface to a public code."

In fact, such violations are always cruelly punished. In '89 and '93, the possessions of the nobility and the clergy were confiscated, the clever proletaires were enriched; and to-day the latter, having become aristocrats, are making us pay dearly for our fathers' robbery. What, therefore, is to be done now? It is not for us to violate right, but to restore it. Now, it would be a violation of justice to dispossess some and endow others, and then stop there. We must gradually lower the rate of interest, organize industry, associate laborers and their functions, and take a census of the large fortunes, not for the purpose of granting privileges, but that we may effect their redemption by settling a life-annuity upon their proprietors. We must apply on a large scale the principle of collective production, give the State eminent domain over all capital! make each producer responsible, abolish the custom-house, and transform every profession and trade into a public function. Thereby large fortunes will vanish without confiscation or violence; individual possession will establish itself, without communism, under the inspection of the republic; and equality of conditions will no longer depend simply on the will of citizens.

Of the authors who have written upon the Romans, Bossuet and Montesquieu occupy prominent positions in the first rank; the first being generally regarded as the father of the philosophy of history, and the second as the most profound writer upon law and politics. Nevertheless, it could be shown that these two great writers, each of them imbued with the prejudices of their century and their cloth, have left the question of the causes of the rise and fall of the Romans precisely where they found it.

Bossuet is admirable as long as he confines himself to description: witness, among other passages, the picture which he has given us of Greece before the Persian War, and which seems to have inspired "Telemachus;" the parallel between Athens and Sparta, drawn twenty times since Bossuet; the description of the character and morals of the ancient Romans; and, finally, the sublime peroration which ends the "Discourse on Universal History." But when the famous historian deals with causes, his philosophy is at fault.

"The tribunes always favored the division of captured lands, or the proceeds of their sale, among the citizens. The Senate steadfastly opposed those laws which were damaging to the State, and wanted the price of lands to be awarded to the public treasury."

Thus, according to Bossuet, the first and greatest wrong of civil wars was inflicted upon the people, who, dying of hunger, demanded that the lands, which they had shed their blood to conquer, should be given to them for cultivation. The patricians, who bought them to deliver to their slaves, had more regard for justice and the public interests. How little affects the opinions of men! If the roles of Cicero and the Gracchi had been inverted, Bossuet, whose sympathies were aroused by the eloquence of the great orator more than by the clamors of the tribunes, would have viewed the agrarian laws in quite a different light. He then would have when the captured lands were put up at auction, the patricians hastened to buy them, in order to profit by the revenues from them,—certain, moreover, that the price paid would come back to them sooner or later, in exchange either for supplies furnished by them to the republic, or for the subsistence of the multitude, who could buy only of them, and whose services at one time, and poverty at another, were rewarded by the State. For a State does not hoard; on the contrary, the public funds always return to the people. If, then, a certain number of men are the sole dealers in articles of primary necessity, it follows that the public treasury, in passing and repassing through their hands, deposits and accumulates real property there.

When Menenius related to the people his fable of the limbs and the stomach, if any one had remarked to this story-teller that the stomach freely gives to the limbs the nourishment which it freely receives, but that the patricians gave to the plebeians only for cash, and lent to them only at usury, he undoubtedly would have silenced the wily senator, and saved the people from a great imposition. The Conscript Fathers were fathers only of their own line. As for the common people, they were regarded as an impure race, exploitable, taxable, and workable at the discretion and mercy of their masters.

As a general thing, Bossuet shows little regard for the people. His monarchical and theological instincts know nothing but authority, obedience, and alms-giving, under the name of charity.

This unfortunate disposition constantly leads him to mistake symptoms for causes; and his depth, which is so much admired, is borrowed from his authors, and amounts to very little, after all.

When he says, for instance, that "the dissensions in the republic, and finally its fall, were caused by the jealousies of its citizens, and their love of liberty carried to an extreme and intolerable extent," are we not tempted to ask him what caused those JEALOUSIES?—what inspired the people with that LOVE OF LIBERTY, EXTREME AND INTOLERABLE? It would be useless to reply, The corruption of morals; the disregard for the ancient poverty; the debaucheries, luxury, and class jealousies; the seditious character of the Gracchi, &c. Why did the morals become corrupt, and whence arose those eternal dissensions between the patricians and the plebeians?

In Rome, as in all other places, the dissension between the rich and the poor was not caused directly by the desire for wealth (people, as a general thing, do not covet that which they deem it illegitimate to acquire), but by a natural instinct of the plebeians, which led them to seek the cause of their adversity in the constitution of the republic. So we are doing to-day; instead of altering our public economy, we demand an electoral reform. The Roman people wished to return to the social compact; they asked for reforms, and demanded a revision of the laws, and a creation of new magistracies. The patricians, who had nothing to complain of, opposed every innovation. Wealth always has been conservative. Nevertheless, the people overcame the resistance of the Senate; the electoral right was greatly extended; the privileges of the plebeians were increased,—they had their representatives, their tribunes, and their consuls; but, notwithstanding these reforms, the republic could not be saved. When all political expedients had been exhausted, when civil war had depleted the population, when the Caesars had thrown their bloody mantle over the cancer which was consuming the empire,—inasmuch as accumulated property always was respected, and since the fire never stopped, the nation had to perish in the flames. The imperial power was a compromise which protected the property of the rich, and nourished the proletaires with wheat from Africa and Sicily: a double error, which destroyed the aristocrats by plethora and the commoners by famine. At last there was but one real proprietor left,—the emperor,—whose dependent, flatterer, parasite, or slave, each citizen became; and when this proprietor was ruined, those who gathered the crumbs from under his table, and laughed when he cracked his jokes, perished also.

Montesquieu succeeded no better than Bossuet in fathoming the causes of the Roman decline; indeed, it may be said that the president has only developed the ideas of the bishop. If the Romans had been more moderate in their conquests, more just to their allies, more humane to the vanquished; if the nobles had been less covetous, the emperors less lawless, the people less violent, and all classes less corrupt; if... &c.,—perhaps the dignity of the empire might have been preserved, and Rome might have retained the sceptre of the world! That is all that can be gathered from the teachings of Montesquieu. But the truth of history does not lie there; the destinies of the world are not dependent upon such trivial causes. The passions of men, like the contingencies of time and the varieties of climate, serve to maintain the forces which move humanity and produce all historical changes; but they do not explain them. The grain of sand of which Pascal speaks would have caused the death of one man only, had not prior action ordered the events of which this death was the precursor.

Montesquieu has read extensively; he knows Roman history thoroughly, is perfectly well acquainted with the people of whom he speaks, and sees very clearly why they were able to conquer their rivals and govern the world. While reading him we admire the Romans, but we do not like them; we witness their triumphs without pleasure, and we watch their fall without sorrow. Montesquieu's work, like the works of all French writers, is skilfully composed,—spirited, witty, and filled with wise observations. He pleases, interests, instructs, but leads to little reflection; he does not conquer by depth of thought; he does not exalt the mind by elevated reason or earnest feeling. In vain should we search his writings for knowledge of antiquity, the character of primitive society, or a description of the heroic ages, whose morals and prejudices lived until the last days of the republic. Vico, painting the Romans with their horrible traits, represents them as excusable, because he shows that all their conduct was governed by preexisting ideas and customs, and that they were informed, so to speak, by a superior genius of which they were unconscious; in Montesquieu, the Roman atrocity revolts, but is not explained. Therefore, as a writer, Montesquieu brings greater credit upon French literature; as a philosopher, Vico bears away the palm.

Originally, property in Rome was national, not private. Numa was the first to establish individual property by distributing the lands captured by Romulus. What was the dividend of this distribution effected by Numa? What conditions were imposed upon individuals, what powers reserved to the State? None whatever. Inequality of fortunes, absolute abdication by the republic of its right of eminent domain over the property of citizens,—such were the first results of the division of Numa, who justly may be regarded as the originator of Roman revolutions. He it was who instituted the worship of the god Terminus,—the guardian of private possession, and one of the most ancient gods of Italy. It was Numa who placed property under the protection of Jupiter; who, in imitation of the Etrurians, wished to make priests of the land-surveyors; who invented a liturgy for cadastral operations, and ceremonies of consecration for the marking of boundaries,—who, in short, made a religion of property. [51] All these fancies would have been more beneficial than dangerous, if the holy king had not forgotten one essential thing; namely, to fix the amount that each citizen could possess, and on what conditions he could possess it. For, since it is the essence of property to continually increase by accession and profit, and since the lender will take advantage of every opportunity to apply this principle inherent in property, it follows that properties tend, by means of their natural energy and the religious respect which protects them, to absorb each other, and fortunes to increase or diminish to an indefinite extent,—a process which necessarily results in the ruin of the people, and the fall of the republic. Roman history is but the development of this law.

Scarcely had the Tarquins been banished from Rome and the monarchy abolished, when quarrels commenced between the orders. In the year 494 B.C., the secession of the commonalty to the Mons Sacer led to the establishment of the tribunate. Of what did the plebeians complain? That they were poor, exhausted by the interest which they paid to the proprietors,—*foeneratoribus;* that the republic, administered for the benefit of the nobles, did nothing for the people; that, delivered over to the mercy of their creditors, who could sell them and their children, and having neither hearth nor home, they were refused the means of subsistence, while the rate of interest was kept at its highest point, &c. For five centuries, the sole policy of the Senate was to evade these just complaints; and, notwithstanding the energy of the tribunes, notwithstanding the eloquence of the Gracchi, the violence of Marius, and the triumph of Caesar, this execrable policy succeeded only too well. The Senate always temporized; the measures proposed by the tribunes might be good, but they were inopportune. It admitted that something should be done; but first it was necessary that the people should resume the performance of their duties, because the Senate could not yield to violence, and force must be employed only by the law. If the people—out of respect for legality—took this beautiful advice, the Senate conjured up a difficulty; the reform was postponed, and that was the end of it. On the contrary, if the demands of the proletaires became too pressing, it declared a foreign war, and neighboring nations were deprived of their liberty, to maintain the Roman aristocracy.

But the toils of war were only a halt for the plebeians in their onward march towards pauperism. The lands confiscated from the conquered nations were immediately added to the domain of the State, to the ager publicus; and, as such, cultivated for the benefit of the treasury; or, as was more often the case, they were sold at auction. None of them were granted to the proletaires, who, unlike the patricians and knights, were not supplied by the victory with the means of buying them. War never enriched the soldier; the extensive plundering has been done always by the generals. The vans of Augereau, and of twenty others, are famous in our armies; but no one ever heard of a private getting rich. Nothing was more common in Rome than charges of peculation, extortion, embezzlement, and brigandage, carried on in the provinces at the head of armies, and in other public capacities. All these charges were quieted by intrigue, bribery of the judges, or desistance of the accuser. The culprit was allowed always in the end to enjoy his spoils in peace; his son was only the more respected on account of his father's crimes. And, in fact, it could not be otherwise. What would become of us, if every deputy, peer, or public functionary should be called upon to show his title to his fortune!

"The patricians arrogated the exclusive enjoyment of the ager publicus; and, like the feudal seigniors, granted some portions of their lands to their dependants,—a wholly precarious concession, revocable at the will of the grantor. The plebeians, on the contrary, were entitled to the enjoyment of only a little pasture-land left to them in common: an utterly unjust state of things, since, in consequence of it, taxation—*census*—weighed more heavily upon the poor than upon the rich. The patrician, in fact, always exempted himself from the tithe which he owed as the price and as the acknowledgment of the concession of domain; and, on the other hand, paid no taxes on his POSSESSIONS, if, as there is good reason to believe, only citizens' property was taxed."—Laboulaye: History of Property.

In order thoroughly to understand the preceding quotation, we must know that the estates of CITIZENS—that is, estates independent of the public domain, whether they were obtained in the division of Numa, or had since been sold by the questors—were alone regarded as PROPERTY; upon these a tax, or *cense*, was imposed. On the contrary, the estates obtained by concessions of the public domain, of the ager publicus (for which a light rent was paid), were called POSSESSIONS. Thus, among the Romans, there was a RIGHT OF PROPERTY and a RIGHT OF POSSESSION regulating the administration of all estates. Now, what did the proletaires wish? That the jus possessionis—the simple right of possession—should be extended to them at the expense, as is evident, not of private property, but of the public domain, —agri publici. The proletaires, in short, demanded that they should be tenants of the land which they had conquered. This demand, the patricians in their avarice never would accede to. Buying as much of this land as they could, they afterwards found means of obtaining the rest as POSSESSIONS. Upon this land they employed their slaves. The people, who could not buy, on account of the competition of the rich, nor hire, because—cultivating with their own hands—they could not promise a rent equal to the revenue which the land would yield when cultivated by slaves, were always deprived of possession and property.

Civil wars relieved, to some extent, the sufferings of the multitude. "The people enrolled themselves under the banners of the ambitious, in order to obtain by force that which the law refused them,—property. A colony was the reward of a victorious legion. But it was no longer the ager publicus only; it was all Italy that lay at the mercy of the legions. The ager publicus disappeared almost entirely,... but the cause of the evil—accumulated property—became more potent than ever." (Laboulaye: History of Property.)

The author whom I quote does not tell us why this division of territory which followed civil wars did not arrest the encroachments of accumulated property; the omission is easily supplied. Land is not the only requisite for cultivation; a working-stock is also necessary,—animals, tools, harnesses, a house, an advance, &c. Where did the colonists, discharged by the dictator who rewarded them, obtain these things? From the purse of the usurers; that is, of the patricians, to whom all these lands finally returned, in consequence of the rapid increase of usury, and the seizure of estates. Sallust, in his account of the conspiracy of Catiline, tells us of this fact. The conspirators were old soldiers of Sylla, who, as a reward for their services, had received from him lands in Cisalpine Gaul, Tuscany, and other parts of the peninsula Less than twenty years had elapsed since these colonists, free of debt, had left the service and commenced farming; and already they were crippled by usury, and almost ruined. The poverty caused by the exactions of creditors was the life of this conspiracy which well-nigh inflamed all Italy, and which, with a worthier chief and fairer means, possibly would have succeeded. In Rome, the mass of the people were favorable to the conspirators—*cuncta plebes Catilinae incepta probabat;* the allies were weary of the patricians' robberies; deputies from the Allobroges (the Savoyards) had come to Rome to appeal to the Senate in behalf of their fellow-citizens involved in debt; in short, the complaint against the large proprietors was universal. "We call men and gods to witness," said the soldiers of Catiline, who were Roman citizens with not a slave among them, "that we have taken arms neither against the country, nor to attack any one, but in defence of our lives and liberties. Wretched, poor, most of us deprived of country, all of us of fame and fortune, by the violence and cruelty of usurers, we have no rights, no property, no liberty." [52]

The bad reputation of Catiline, and his atrocious designs, the imprudence of his accomplices, the treason of several, the strategy of Cicero, the angry outbursts of Cato, and the terror of the Senate, baffled this enterprise, which, in furnishing a precedent for expeditions against the rich, would perhaps have saved the republic, and given peace to the world. But Rome could not evade her destiny; the end of her expiations had not come. A nation never was known to anticipate its punishment by a sudden and unexpected conversion. Now, the long-continued crimes of the Eternal City could not be atoned for by the massacre of a few hundred patricians. Catiline came to stay divine vengeance; therefore his conspiracy failed.

The encroachment of large proprietors upon small proprietors, by the aid of usury, farm-rent, and profits of all sorts, was common throughout the empire. The most honest citizens invested their money at high rates of interest. [53] Cato, Cicero, Brutus, all the stoics so noted for their frugality, *viri frugi,*—Seneca, the teacher of virtue,—levied enormous taxes in the provinces, under the name of usury; and it is something remarkable, that the last defenders of the republic, the proud Pompeys, were all usurious aristocrats, and oppressors of the poor. But the battle of Pharsalus, having killed men only, without touching institutions, the encroachments of the large domains became every day more active. Ever since the birth of Christianity, the Fathers have opposed this invasion with all their might. Their writings are filled with burning curses upon this crime of usury, of which Christians are not always innocent.

St. Cyprian complains of certain bishops of his time, who, absorbed in disgraceful stock-jobbing operations, abandoned their churches, and went about the provinces appropriating lands by artifice and fraud, while lending money and piling up interests upon interests. 54 Why, in the midst of this passion for accumulation, did not the possession of the public land, like private property, become concentrated in a few hands?

By law, the domain of the State was inalienable, and consequently possession was always revocable; but the edict of the praetor continued it indefinitely, so that finally the possessions of the patricians were transformed into absolute property, though the name, possessions, was still applied to them. This conversion, instigated by senatorial avarice, owed its accomplishment to the most deplorable and indiscreet policy. If, in the time of Tiberius Gracchus, who wished to limit each citizen's possession of the ager publicus to five hundred acres, the amount of this possession had been fixed at as much as one family could cultivate, and granted on the express condition that the possessor should cultivate it himself, and should lease it to no one, the empire never would have been desolated by large estates; and possession, instead of increasing property, would have absorbed it. On what, then, depended the establishment and maintenance of equality in conditions and fortunes? On a more equitable division of the ager publicus, a wiser distribution of the right of possession.

I insist upon this point, which is of the utmost importance, because it gives us an opportunity to examine the history of this individual possession, of which I said so much in my first memoir, and which so few of my readers seem to have understood. The Roman republic—having, as it did, the power to dispose absolutely of its territory, and to impose conditions upon possessors—was nearer to liberty and equality than any nation has been since. If the Senate had been intelligent and just,—if, at the time of the retreat to the Mons Sacer, instead of the ridiculous farce enacted by Menenius Agrippa, a solemn renunciation of the right to acquire had been made by each citizen on attaining his share of possessions, —the republic, based upon equality of possessions and the duty of labor, would not, in attaining its wealth, have degenerated in morals; Fabricius would have enjoyed the arts without controlling artists; and the conquests of the ancient Romans would have been the means of spreading civilization, instead of the series of murders and robberies that they were.

But property, having unlimited power to amass and to lease, was daily increased by the addition of new possessions. From the time of Nero, six individuals were the sole proprietors of one-half of Roman Africa. In the fifth century, the wealthy families had incomes of no less than two millions: some possessed as many as twenty thousand slaves. All the authors who have written upon the causes of the fall of the Roman republic concur.

M. Giraud of Aix 55 quotes the testimony of Cicero, Seneca, Plutarch, Olympiodorus, and Photius. Under Vespasian and Titus, Pliny, the naturalist, exclaimed: "Large estates have ruined Italy, and are ruining the provinces."

But it never has been understood that the extension of property was effected then, as it is to-day, under the aegis of the law, and by virtue of the constitution. When the Senate sold captured lands at auction, it was in the interest of the treasury and of public welfare. When the patricians bought up possessions and property, they realized the purpose of the Senate's decrees; when they lent at high rates of interest, they took advantage of a legal privilege. "Property," said the lender, "is the right to enjoy even to the extent of abuse, *jus utendi et abutendi*; that is, the right to lend at interest,—to lease, to acquire, and then to lease and lend again." But property is also the right to exchange, to transfer, and to sell. If, then, the social condition is such that the proprietor, ruined by usury, may be compelled to sell his possession, the means of his subsistence, he will sell it; and, thanks to the law, accumulated property—devouring and anthropophagous property—will be established. 56

The immediate and secondary cause of the decline of the Romans was, then, the internal dissensions between the two orders of the republic,—the patricians and the plebeians,—dissensions which gave rise to civil wars, proscriptions, and loss of liberty, and finally led to the empire; but the primary and mediate cause of their decline was the establishment by Numa of the institution of property.

I end with an extract from a work which I have quoted several times already, and which has recently received a prize from the Academy of Moral and Political Sciences:—

"The concentration of property," says M. Laboulaye, "while causing extreme poverty, forced the emperors to feed and amuse the people, that they might forget their misery. *Panem et circenses:* that was the Roman law in regard to the poor; a dire and perhaps a necessary evil wherever a landed aristocracy exists.

"To feed these hungry mouths, grain was brought from Africa and the provinces, and distributed gratuitously among the needy. In the time of Caesar, three hundred and twenty thousand people were thus fed. Augustus saw that such a measure led directly to the destruction of husbandry; but to abolish these distributions was to put a weapon within the reach of the first aspirant for power.

"The emperor shrank at the thought.

"While grain was gratuitous, agriculture was impossible. Tillage gave way to pasturage, another cause of depopulation, even among slaves.

"Finally, luxury, carried further and further every day, covered the soil of Italy with elegant villas, which occupied whole cantons. Gardens and groves replaced the fields, and the free population fled to the towns. Husbandry disappeared almost entirely, and with husbandry the husbandman. Africa furnished the wheat, and Greece the wine. Tiberius complained bitterly of this evil, which placed the lives of the Roman people at the mercy of the winds and waves: that was his anxiety. One day later, and three hundred thousand starving men walked the streets of Rome: that was a revolution.

"This decline of Italy and the provinces did not stop. After the reign of Nero, depopulation commenced in towns as noted as Antium and Tarentum. Under the reign of Pertinax, there was so much desert land that the emperor abandoned it, even that which belonged to the treasury, to whoever would cultivate it, besides exempting the farmers from taxation for a period of ten years. Senators were compelled to invest one-third of their fortunes in real estate in Italy; but this measure served only to increase the evil which they wished to cure. To force the rich to possess in Italy was to increase the large estates which had ruined the country. And must I say, finally, that Aurelian wished to send the captives into the desert lands of Etruria, and that Valentinian was forced to settle the Alamanni on the fertile banks of the Po?"

If the reader, in running through this book, should complain of meeting with nothing but quotations from other works, extracts from journals and public lectures, comments upon laws, and interpretations of them, I would remind him that the very object of this memoir is to establish the conformity of my opinion concerning property with that universally held; that, far from aiming at a paradox, it has been my main study to follow the advice of the world; and, finally, that my sole pretension is to clearly formulate the general belief. I cannot repeat it too often,—and I confess it with pride,—I teach absolutely nothing that is new; and I should regard the doctrine which I advocate as radically erroneous, if a single witness should testify against it.

Let us now trace the revolutions in property among the Barbarians.

As long as the German tribes dwelt in their forests, it did not occur to them to divide and appropriate the soil. The land was held in common: each individual could plow, sow, and reap. But, when the empire was once invaded, they bethought themselves of sharing the land, just as they shared spoils after a victory. "Hence," says M. Laboulaye, "the expressions *sortes Burgundiorum Gothorum* and {GREEK, ' k }; hence the German words *allod*, allodium, and *loos*, lot, which are used in all modern languages to designate the gifts of chance."

Allodial property, at least with the mass of coparceners, was originally held, then, in equal shares; for all of the prizes were equal, or, at least, equivalent. This property, like that of the Romans, was wholly individual, independent, exclusive, transferable, and consequently susceptible of accumulation and invasion. But, instead of its being, as was the case among the Romans, the large estate which, through increase and usury, subordinated and absorbed the small one, among the Barbarians —fonder of war than of wealth, more eager to dispose of persons than to appropriate things—it was the warrior who, through superiority of arms, enslaved his adversary. The Roman wanted matter; the Barbarian wanted man. Consequently, in the feudal ages, rents were almost nothing,—simply a hare, a partridge, a pie, a few pints of wine brought by a little girl, or a Maypole set up within the suzerain's reach. In return, the vassal or incumbent had to follow the seignior to battle (a thing which happened almost every day), and equip and feed himself at his own expense. "This spirit of the German tribes—this spirit of companionship and association—governed the territory as it governed individuals. The lands, like the men, were secured to a chief or seignior by a bond of mutual protection and fidelity. This subjection was the labor of the German epoch which gave birth to feudalism. By fair means or foul, every proprietor who could not be a chief was forced to be a vassal." (Laboulaye: History of Property.)

By fair means or foul, every mechanic who cannot be a master has to be a journeyman; every proprietor who is not an invader will be invaded; every producer who cannot, by the exploitation of other men, furnish products at less than their proper value, will lose his labor. Corporations and masterships, which are hated so bitterly, but which will reappear if we are not careful, are the necessary results of the principle of competition which is inherent in property; their organization was patterned formerly after that of the feudal hierarchy, which was the result of the subordination of men and possessions.

The times which paved the way for the advent of feudalism and the reappearance of large proprietors were times of carnage and the most frightful anarchy. Never before had murder and violence made such havoc with the human race. The tenth century, among others, if my memory serves me rightly, was called the CENTURY OF IRON. His property, his life, and the honor of his wife and children always in danger the small proprietor made haste to do homage to his seignior, and to bestow something on the church of his freehold, that he might receive protection and security.

"Both facts and laws bear witness that from the sixth to the tenth century the proprietors of small freeholds were gradually plundered, or reduced by the encroachments of large proprietors and counts to the condition of either vassals or tributaries. The Capitularies are full of repressive provisions; but the incessant reiteration of these threats only shows the perseverance of the evil and the impotency of the government. Oppression, moreover, varies but little in its methods. The complaints of the free proprietors, and the groans of the plebeians at the time of the Gracchi, were one and the same. It is said that, whenever a poor man refused to give his estate to the bishop, the curate, the count, the judge, or the centurion, these immediately sought an opportunity to ruin him. They made him serve in the army until, completely ruined, he was induced, by fair means or foul, to give up his freehold."—Laboulaye: History of Property.

How many small proprietors and manufacturers have not been ruined by large ones through chicanery, law-suits, and competition? Strategy, violence, and usury,—such are the proprietor's methods of plundering the laborer.

Thus we see property, at all ages and in all its forms, oscillating by virtue of its principle between two opposite terms, —extreme division and extreme accumulation.

Property, at its first term, is almost null. Reduced to personal exploitation, it is property only potentially. At its second term, it exists in its perfection; then it is truly property.

When property is widely distributed, society thrives, progresses, grows, and rises quickly to the zenith of its power. Thus, the Jews, after leaving Babylon with Esdras and Nehemiah, soon became richer and more powerful than they had been under their kings. Sparta was in a strong and prosperous condition during the two or three centuries which followed the death of Lycurgus. The best days of Athens were those of the Persian war; Rome, whose inhabitants were divided from the beginning into two classes,—the exploiters and the exploited,—knew no such thing as peace.

When property is concentrated, society, abusing itself, polluted, so to speak, grows corrupt, wears itself out—how shall I express this horrible idea?—plunges into long-continued and fatal luxury.

When feudalism was established, society had to die of the same disease which killed it under the Caesars,—I mean accumulated property. But humanity, created for an immortal destiny, is deathless; the revolutions which disturb it are purifying crises, invariably followed by more vigorous health. In the fifth century, the invasion of the Barbarians partially restored the world to a state of natural equality. In the twelfth century, a new spirit pervading all society gave the slave his rights, and through justice breathed new life into the heart of nations. It has been said, and often repeated, that Christianity regenerated the world. That is true; but it seems to me that there is a mistake in the date. Christianity had no influence upon Roman society; when the Barbarians came, that society had disappeared. For such is God's curse upon property; every political organization based upon the exploitation of man, shall perish: slave-labor is death to the race of tyrants. The patrician families became extinct, as the feudal families did, and as all aristocracies must.

It was in the middle ages, when a reactionary movement was beginning to secretly undermine accumulated property, that the influence of Christianity was first exercised to its full extent.

The destruction of feudalism, the conversion of the serf into the commoner, the emancipation of the communes, and the admission of the Third Estate to political power, were deeds accomplished by Christianity exclusively. I say Christianity, not ecclesiasticism; for the priests and bishops were themselves large proprietors, and as such often persecuted the villeins. Without the Christianity of the middle ages, the existence of modern society could not be explained, and would not be possible.

The truth of this assertion is shown by the very facts which M. Laboulaye quotes, although this author inclines to the opposite opinion. 57

Now, we did not commence to love God and to think of our salvation until after the promulgation of the Gospel.

1. Slavery among the Romans.—"The Roman slave was, in the eyes of the law, only a thing,—no more than an ox or a horse. He had neither property, family, nor personality; he was defenceless against his master's cruelty, folly, or cupidity. 'Sell your oxen that are past use,' said Cato, 'sell your calves, your lambs, your wool, your hides, your old ploughs, your old iron, your old slave, and your sick slave, and all that is of no use to you.' When no market could be found for the slaves that were worn out by sickness or old age, they were abandoned to starvation. Claudius was the first defender of this shameful practice."

"Discharge your old workman," says the economist of the proprietary school; "turn off that sick domestic, that toothless and worn-out servant. Put away the unserviceable beauty; to the hospital with the useless mouths!"

"The condition of these wretched beings improved but little under the emperors; and the best that can be said of the goodness of Antoninus is that he prohibited intolerable cruelty, as an ABUSE OF PROPERTY. *Expedit enim reipublicae ne quis re re sua male utatur*, says Gaius.

"As soon as the Church met in council, it launched an anathema against the masters who had exercised over their slaves this terrible right of life and death. Were not the slaves, thanks to the right of sanctuary and to their poverty, the dearest proteges of religion? Constantine, who embodied in the laws the grand ideas of Christianity, valued the life of a slave as highly as that of a freeman, and declared the master, who had intentionally brought death upon his slave, guilty of murder. Between this law and that of Antoninus there is a complete revolution in moral ideas: the slave was a thing; religion has made him a man."

Note the last words: "Between the law of the Gospel and that of Antoninus there is a complete revolution in moral ideas: the slave was a thing; religion has made him a man." The moral revolution which transformed the slave into a citizen was effected, then, by Christianity before the Barbarians set foot upon the soil of the empire. We have only to trace the progress of this MORAL revolution in the PERSONNEL of society. "But," M. Laboulaye rightly says, "it did not change the condition of men in a moment, any more than that of things; between slavery and liberty there was an abyss which could not be filled in a day; the transitional step was servitude."

Now, what was servitude? In what did it differ from Roman slavery, and whence came this difference? Let the same author answer.

2. Of servitude.—"I see, in the lord's manor, slaves charged with domestic duties. Some are employed in the personal service of the master; others are charged with household cares. The women spin the wool; the men grind the grain, make the bread, or practise, in the interest of the seignior, what little they know of the industrial arts. The master punishes them when he chooses, kills them with impunity, and sells them and theirs like so many cattle. The slave has no personality, and consequently no *wehrgeld* 58 peculiar to himself: he is a thing. The *wehrgeld* belongs to the master as a compensation for the loss of his property. Whether the slave is killed or stolen, the indemnity does not change, for the injury is the same; but the indemnity increases or diminishes according to the value of the serf. In all these particulars Germanic slavery and Roman servitude are alike."

This similarity is worthy of notice. Slavery is always the same, whether in a Roman villa or on a Barbarian farm. The man, like the ox and the ass, is a part of the live-stock; a price is set upon his head; he is a tool without a conscience, a chattel without personality, an impeccable, irresponsible being, who has neither rights nor duties.

Why did his condition improve?

"In good season..." [when?] "the serf began to be regarded as a man; and, as such, the law of the Visigoths, under the influence of Christian ideas, punished with fine or banishment any one who maimed or killed him."

Always Christianity, always religion, though we should like to speak of the laws only. Did the philanthropy of the Visigoths make its first appearance before or after the preaching of the Gospel? This point must be cleared up.

"After the conquest, the serfs were scattered over the large estates of the Barbarians, each having his house, his lot, and his peculium, in return for which he paid rent and performed service. They were rarely separated from their homes when their land was sold; they and all that they had became the property of the purchaser. The law favored this realization of the serf, in not allowing him to be sold out of the country."

What inspired this law, destructive not only of slavery, but of property itself? For, if the master cannot drive from his domain the slave whom he has once established there, it follows that the slave is proprietor, as well as the master.

"The Barbarians," again says M. Laboulaye, "were the first to recognize the slave's rights of family and property,—two rights which are incompatible with slavery."

But was this recognition the necessary result of the mode of servitude in vogue among the Germanic nations previous to their conversion to Christianity, or was it the immediate effect of that spirit of justice infused with religion, by which the seignior was forced to respect in the serf a soul equal to his own, a brother in Jesus Christ, purified by the same baptism, and redeemed by the same sacrifice of the Son of God in the form of man? For we must not close our eyes to the fact that, though the Barbarian morals and the ignorance and carelessness of the seigniors, who busied themselves mainly with wars and battles, paying little or no attention to agriculture, may have been great aids in the emancipation of the serfs, still the vital principle of this emancipation was essentially Christian. Suppose that the Barbarians had remained Pagans in the midst of a Pagan world. As they did not change the Gospel, so they would not have changed the polytheistic customs; slavery would have remained what it was; they would have continued to kill the slaves who were desirous of liberty, family, and property; whole nations would have been reduced to the condition of Helots; nothing would have changed upon the terrestrial stage, except the actors. The Barbarians were less selfish, less imperious, less dissolute, and less cruel than the Romans. Such was the nature upon which, after the fall of the empire and the renovation of society, Christianity was to act. But this nature, grounded as in former times upon slavery and war, would, by its own energy, have produced nothing but war and slavery.

"GRADUALLY the serfs obtained the privilege of being judged by the same standard as their masters...."

When, how, and by what title did they obtain this privilege?

"GRADUALLY their duties were regulated."

Whence came the regulations? Who had the authority to introduce them?

"The master took a part of the labor of the serf,—three days, for instance,—and left the rest to him. As for Sunday, that belonged to God."

And what established Sunday, if not religion? Whence I infer, that the same power which took it upon itself to suspend hostilities and to lighten the duties of the serf was also that which regulated the judiciary and created a sort of law for the slave.

But this law itself, on what did it bear?—what was its principle?—what was the philosophy of the councils and popes with reference to this matter? The reply to all these questions, coming from me alone, would be distrusted. The authority of M. Laboulaye shall give credence to my words. This holy philosophy, to which the slaves were indebted for every thing, this invocation of the Gospel, was an anathema against property.

The proprietors of small freeholds, that is, the freemen of the middle class, had fallen, in consequence of the tyranny of the nobles, into a worse condition than that of the tenants and serfs. "The expenses of war weighed less heavily upon the serf than upon the freeman; and, as for legal protection, the seigniorial court, where the serf was judged by his peers, was far preferable to the cantonal assembly. It was better to have a noble for a seignior than for a judge."

So it is better to-day to have a man of large capital for an associate than for a rival. The honest tenant—the laborer who earns weekly a moderate but constant salary—is more to be envied than the independent but small farmer, or the poor licensed mechanic.

At that time, all were either seigniors or serfs, oppressors or oppressed. "Then, under the protection of convents, or of the seigniorial turret, new societies were formed, which silently spread over the soil made fertile by their hands, and which derived their power from the annihilation of the free classes whom they enlisted in their behalf. As tenants, these men acquired, from generation to generation, sacred rights over the soil which they cultivated in the interest of lazy and pillaging masters. As fast as the social tempest abated, it became necessary to respect the union and heritage of these villeins, who by their labor had truly prescribed the soil for their own profit."

I ask how prescription could take effect where a contrary title and possession already existed? M. Laboulaye is a lawyer. Where, then, did he ever see the labor of the slave and the cultivation by the tenant prescribe the soil for their own profit, to the detriment of a recognized master daily acting as a proprietor? Let us not disguise matters. As fast as the tenants and the serfs grew rich, they wished to be independent and free; they commenced to associate, unfurl their municipal banners, raise belfries, fortify their towns, and refuse to pay their seigniorial dues. In doing these things they were perfectly right; for, in fact, their condition was intolerable. But in law—I mean in Roman and Napoleonic law—their refusal to obey and pay tribute to their masters was illegitimate.

Now, this imperceptible usurpation of property by the commonalty was inspired by religion.

The seignior had attached the serf to the soil; religion granted the serf rights over the soil. The seignior imposed duties upon the serf; religion fixed their limits. The seignior could kill the serf with impunity, could deprive him of his wife, violate his daughter, pillage his house, and rob him of his savings; religion checked his invasions: it excommunicated the seignior. Religion was the real cause of the ruin of feudal property. Why should it not be bold enough to-day to resolutely condemn capitalistic property? Since the middle ages, there has been no change in social economy except in its forms; its relations remain unaltered.

The only result of the emancipation of the serfs was that property changed hands; or, rather, that new proprietors were created. Sooner or later the extension of privilege, far from curing the evil, was to operate to the disadvantage of the plebeians. Nevertheless, the new social organization did not meet with the same end in all places. In Lombardy, for example, where the people rapidly growing rich through commerce and industry soon conquered the authorities, even to the exclusion of the nobles,—first, the nobility became poor and degraded, and were forced, in order to live and maintain their credit, to gain admission to the guilds; then, the ordinary subalternization of property leading to inequality of fortunes, to wealth and poverty, to jealousies and hatreds, the cities passed rapidly from the rankest democracy under the yoke of a few ambitious leaders. Such was the fate of most of the Lombardic cities,—Genoa, Florence, Bologna, Milan, Pisa, &c,.—which afterwards changed rulers frequently, but which have never since risen in favor of liberty. The people can easily escape from the tyranny of despots, but they do not know how to throw off the effects of their own despotism; just as we avoid the assassin's steel, while we succumb to a constitutional malady. As soon as a nation becomes proprietor, either it must perish, or a foreign invasion must force it again to begin its evolutionary round. 59

"The communes once organized, the kings treated them as superior vassals. Now, just as the under vassal had no communication with the king except through the direct vassal, so also the commoners could enter no complaints except through the commune."

"Like causes produce like effects. Each commune became a small and separate State, governed by a few citizens, who sought to extend their authority over the others; who, in their turn, revenged themselves upon the unfortunate inhabitants who had not the right of citizenship. Feudalism in unemancipated countries, and oligarchy in the communes, made nearly the same ravages. There were sub-associations, fraternities, tradesmen's associations in the communes, and colleges in the universities. The oppression was so great, that it was no rare thing to see the inhabitants of a commune demanding its suppression...."—Meyer: Judicial Institutions of Europe.

In France, the Revolution was much more gradual. The communes, in taking refuge under the protection of the kings, had found them masters rather than protectors. Their liberty had long since been lost, or, rather, their emancipation had been suspended, when feudalism received its death-blow at the hand of Richelieu. Then liberty halted; the prince of the feudatories held sole and undivided sway. The nobles, the clergy, the commoners, the parliaments, every thing in short except a few seeming privileges, were controlled by the king; who, like his early predecessors, consumed regularly, and nearly always in advance, the revenues of his domain,—and that domain was France.

Finally, '89 arrived; liberty resumed its march; a century and a half had been required to wear out the last form of feudal property,—monarchy.

The French Revolution may be defined as *the substitution of real right for personal right;* that is to say, in the days of feudalism, the value of property depended upon the standing of the proprietor, while, after the Revolution, the regard for the man was proportional to his property. Now, we have seen from what has been said in the preceding pages, that this recognition of the right of laborers had been the constant aim of the serfs and communes, the secret motive of their efforts. The movement of '89 was only the last stage of that long insurrection. But it seems to me that we have not paid sufficient attention to the fact that the Revolution of 1789, instigated by the same causes, animated by the same spirit, triumphing by the same struggles, was consummated in Italy four centuries ago. Italy was the first to sound the signal of war against feudalism; France has followed; Spain and England are beginning to move; the rest still sleep. If a grand example should be given to the world, the day of trial would be much abridged.

Note the following summary of the revolutions of property, from the days of the Roman Empire down to the present time:—

1. Fifth century.—Barbarian invasions; division of the lands of the empire into independent portions or freeholds.

2. From the fifth to the eighth century.—Gradual concentration of freeholds, or transformation of the small freeholds into fiefs, feuds, tenures, &c. Large properties, small possessions. Charlemagne (771-814) decrees that all freeholds are dependent upon the king of France.

3. From the eighth to the tenth century.—The relation between the crown and the superior dependents is broken; the latter becoming freeholders, while the smaller dependents cease to recognize the king, and adhere to the nearest suzerain. Feudal system.

4. Twelfth century.—Movement of the serfs towards liberty; emancipation of the communes.

5. Thirteenth century.—Abolition of personal right, and of the feudal system in Italy. Italian Republics.

6. Seventeenth century.—Abolition of feudalism in France during Richelieu's ministry. Despotism.

7. 1789.—Abolition of all privileges of birth, caste, provinces, and corporations; equality of persons and of rights. French democracy.

8. 1830.—The principle of concentration inherent in individual property is REMARKED. Development of the idea of association.

The more we reflect upon this series of transformations and changes, the more clearly we see that they were necessary in their principle, in their manifestations, and in their result.

It was necessary that inexperienced conquerors, eager for liberty, should divide the Roman Empire into a multitude of estates, as free and independent as themselves.

It was necessary that these men, who liked war even better than liberty, should submit to their leaders; and, as the freehold represented the man, that property should violate property.

It was necessary that, under the rule of a nobility always idle when not fighting, there should grow up a body of laborers, who, by the power of production, and by the division and circulation of wealth, would gradually gain control over commerce, industry, and a portion of the land, and who, having become rich, would aspire to power and authority also.

It was necessary, finally, that liberty and equality of rights having been achieved, and individual property still existing, attended by robbery, poverty, social inequality, and oppression, there should be an inquiry into the cause of this evil, and an idea of universal association formed, whereby, on condition of labor, all interests should be protected and consolidated.

"Evil, when carried too far," says a learned jurist, "cures itself; and the political innovation which aims to increase the power of the State, finally succumbs to the effects of its own work. The Germans, to secure their independence, chose chiefs; and soon they were oppressed by their kings and noblemen. The monarchs surrounded themselves with volunteers, in order to control the freemen; and they found themselves dependent upon their proud vassals. The *missi dominici* were sent into the provinces to maintain the power of the emperors, and to protect the people from the oppressions of the noblemen; and not only did they usurp the imperial power to a great extent, but they dealt more severely with the inhabitants. The freemen became vassals, in order to get rid of military service and court duty; and they were immediately involved in all the personal quarrels of their seigniors, and compelled to do jury duty in their courts.... The kings protected the cities and the communes, in the hope of freeing them from the yoke of the grand vassals, and of rendering their own power more absolute; and those same communes have, in several European countries, procured the establishment of a constitutional power, are now holding royalty in check, and are giving rise to a universal desire for political reform."—Meyer: Judicial Institutions of Europe.

In recapitulation.

What was feudalism? A confederation of the grand seigniors against the villeins, and against the king. [60] What is constitutional government? A confederation of the bourgeoisie against the laborers, and against the king. [61]

How did feudalism end? In the union of the communes and the royal authority. How will the bourgeoisie aristocracy end? In the union of the proletariat and the sovereign power.

What was the immediate result of the struggle of the communes and the king against the seigniors? The monarchical unity of Louis XIV. What will be the result of the struggle of the proletariat and the sovereign power combined against the bourgeoisie? The absolute unity of the nation and the government.

It remains to be seen whether the nation, one and supreme, will be represented in its executive and central power by ONE, by FIVE, by ONE HUNDRED, or ONE THOUSAND; that is, it remains to be seen, whether the royalty of the barricades intends to maintain itself by the people, or without the people, and whether Louis Philippe wishes his reign to be the most famous in all history.

I have made this statement as brief, but at the same time as accurate as I could, neglecting facts and details, that I might give the more attention to the economical relations of society. For the study of history is like the study of the human organism; just as the latter has its system, its organs, and its functions, which can be treated separately, so the former has its ensemble, its instruments, and its causes. Of course I do not pretend that the principle of property is a complete resume of all the social forces; but, as in that wonderful machine which we call our body, the harmony of the whole allows us to draw a general conclusion from the consideration of a single function or organ, so, in discussing historical causes, I have been able to reason with absolute accuracy from a single order of facts, certain as I was of the perfect correlation which exists between this special order and universal history. As is the property of a nation, so is its family, its marriage, its religion, its civil and military organization, and its legislative and judicial institutions. History, viewed from this standpoint, is a grand and sublime psychological study.

Well, sir, in writing against property, have I done more than quote the language of history? I have said to modern society,—the daughter and heiress of all preceding societies,—*Age quod agis:* complete the task which for six thousand years you have been executing under the inspiration and by the command of God; hasten to finish your journey; turn neither to the right nor the left, but follow the road which lies before you. You seek reason, law, unity, and discipline; but hereafter you can find them only by stripping off the veils of your infancy, and ceasing to follow instinct as a guide. Awaken your sleeping conscience; open your eyes to the pure light of reflection and science; behold the phantom which troubled your dreams, and so long kept you in a state of unutterable anguish. Know thyself, O long-deluded society, know thy enemy!... And I have denounced property.

We often hear the defenders of the right of domain quote in defence of their views the testimony of nations and ages. We can judge, from what has just been said, how far this historical argument conforms to the real facts and the conclusions of science.

To complete this apology, I must examine the various theories.

Neither politics, nor legislation, nor history, can be explained and understood, without a positive theory which defines their elements, and discovers their laws; in short, without a philosophy. Now, the two principal schools, which to this day divide the attention of the world, do not satisfy this condition.

The first, essentially PRACTICAL in its character, confined to a statement of facts, and buried in learning, cares very little by what laws humanity develops itself. To it these laws are the secret of the Almighty, which no one can fathom without a commission from on high. In applying the facts of history to government, this school does not reason; it does not anticipate; it makes no comparison of the past with the present, in order to predict the future. In its opinion, the lessons of experience teach us only to repeat old errors, and its whole philosophy consists in perpetually retracing the tracks of antiquity, instead of going straight ahead forever in the direction in which they point.

The second school may be called either FATALISTIC or PANTHEISTIC. To it the movements of empires and the revolutions of humanity are the manifestations, the incarnations, of the Almighty. The human race, identified with the divine essence, wheels in a circle of appearances, informations, and destructions, which necessarily excludes the idea of absolute truth, and destroys providence and liberty.

Corresponding to these two schools of history, there are two schools of jurisprudence, similarly opposed, and possessed of the same peculiarities.

1. The practical and conventional school, to which the law is always a creation of the legislator, an expression of his will, a privilege which he condescends to grant,—in short, a gratuitous affirmation to be regarded as judicious and legitimate, no matter what it declares.

2. The fatalistic and pantheistic school, sometimes called the historical school, which opposes the despotism of the first, and maintains that law, like literature and religion, is always the expression of society,—its manifestation, its form, the external realization of its mobile spirit and its ever-changing inspirations.

Each of these schools, denying the absolute, rejects thereby all positive and a priori philosophy.

Now, it is evident that the theories of these two schools, whatever view we take of them, are utterly unsatisfactory: for, opposed, they form no dilemma,—that is, if one is false, it does not follow that the other is true; and, united, they do not constitute the truth, since they disregard the absolute, without which there is no truth. They are respectively a THESIS and an ANTITHESIS. There remains to be found, then, a SYNTHESIS, which, predicating the absolute, justifies the will of the legislator, explains the variations of the law, annihilates the theory of the circular movement of humanity, and demonstrates its progress.

The legists, by the very nature of their studies and in spite of their obstinate prejudices, have been led irresistibly to suspect that the absolute in the science of law is not as chimerical as is commonly supposed; and this suspicion arose from their comparison of the various relations which legislators have been called upon to regulate.

M. Laboulaye, the laureate of the Institute, begins his "History of Property" with these words:—

"While the law of contract, which regulates only the mutual interests of men, has not varied for centuries (except in certain forms which relate more to the proof than to the character of the obligation), the civil law of property, which regulates the mutual relations of citizens, has undergone several radical changes, and has kept pace in its variations with all the vicissitudes of society. The law of contract, which holds essentially to those principles of eternal justice which are engraven upon the depths of the human heart, is the immutable element of jurisprudence, and, in a certain sense, its philosophy. Property, on the contrary, is the variable element of jurisprudence, its history, its policy."

Marvellous! There is in law, and consequently in politics, something variable and something invariable. The invariable element is obligation, the bond of justice, duty; the variable element is property,—that is, the external form of law, the subject-matter of the contract. Whence it follows that the law can modify, change, reform, and judge property. Reconcile that, if you can, with the idea of an eternal, absolute, permanent, and indefectible right.

However, M. Laboulaye is in perfect accord with himself when he adds, "Possession of the soil rests solely upon force until society takes it in hand, and espouses the cause of the possessor;" [62] and, a little farther, "The right of property is not natural, but social. The laws not only protect property: they give it birth," &c. Now, that which the law has made the law can unmake; especially since, according to M. Laboulaye,—an avowed partisan of the historical or pantheistic school,—the law is not absolute, is not an idea, but a form.

But why is it that property is variable, and, unlike obligation, incapable of definition and settlement? Before affirming, somewhat boldly without doubt, that in right there are no absolute principles (the most dangerous, most immoral, most tyrannical—in a word, most anti-social—assertion imaginable), it was proper that the right of property should be subjected to a thorough examination, in order to put in evidence its variable, arbitrary, and contingent elements, and those which are eternal, legitimate, and absolute; then, this operation performed, it became easy to account for the laws, and to correct all the codes.

Now, this examination of property I claim to have made, and in the fullest detail; but, either from the public's lack of interest in an unrecommended and unattractive pamphlet, or—which is more probable—from the weakness of exposition and want of genius which characterize the work, the First Memoir on Property passed unnoticed; scarcely would a few communists, having turned its leaves, deign to brand it with their disapprobation. You alone, sir, in spite of the disfavor which I showed for your economical predecessors in too severe a criticism of them,—you alone have judged me justly; and although I cannot accept, at least literally, your first judgment, yet it is to you alone that I appeal from a decision too equivocal to be regarded as final.

It not being my intention to enter at present into a discussion of principles, I shall content myself with estimating, from the point of view of this simple and intelligible absolute, the theories of property which our generation has produced.

The most exact idea of property is given us by the Roman law, faithfully followed in this particular by the ancient legists. It is the absolute, exclusive, autocratic domain of a man over a thing,—a domain which begins by USUCAPTION, is maintained by POSSESSION, and finally, by the aid of PRESCRIPTION, finds its sanction in the civil law; a domain which so identifies the man with the thing, that the proprietor can say, "He who uses my field, virtually compels me to labor for him; therefore he owes me compensation."

I pass in silence the secondary modes by which property can be acquired,—*tradition, sale, exchange, inheritance*, &c.,—which have nothing in common with the origin of property.

Accordingly, Pothier said THE DOMAIN OF PROPERTY, and not simply PROPERTY. And the most learned writers on jurisprudence—in imitation of the Roman praetor who recognized a RIGHT OF PROPERTY and a RIGHT OF POSSESSION—have carefully distinguished between the DOMAIN and the right of USUFRUCT, USE, and HABITATION, which, reduced to its natural limits, is the very expression of justice; and which is, in my opinion, to supplant domanial property, and finally form the basis of all jurisprudence.

But, sir, admire the clumsiness of systems, or rather the fatality of logic! While the Roman law and all the savants inspired by it teach that property in its origin is the right of first occupancy sanctioned by law, the modern legists, dissatisfied with this brutal definition, claim that property is based upon LABOR. Immediately they infer that he who no longer labors, but makes another labor in his stead, loses his right to the earnings of the latter. It is by virtue of this principle that the serfs of the middle ages claimed a legal right to property, and consequently to the enjoyment of political rights; that the clergy were despoiled in '89 of their immense estates, and were granted a pension in exchange; that at the restoration the liberal deputies opposed the indemnity of one billion francs. "The nation," said they, "has acquired by twenty-five years of labor and possession the property which the emigrants forfeited by abandonment and long idleness: why should the nobles be treated with more favor than the priests?" [63]

This position is quite in harmony with my principles, and I heartily applaud the indignation of M. Lerminier; but I do not know that a proprietor was ever deprived of his property because UNWORTHY; and as reasonable, social, and even useful as the thing may seem, it is quite contrary to the uses and customs of property.

All usurpations, not born of war, have been caused and supported by labor. All modern history proves this, from the end of the Roman empire down to the present day. And as if to give a sort of legal sanction to these usurpations, the doctrine of labor, subversive of property, is professed at great length in the Roman law under the name of PRESCRIPTION.

The man who cultivates, it has been said, makes the land his own; consequently, no more property. This was clearly seen by the old jurists, who have not failed to denounce this novelty; while on the other hand the young school hoots at the absurdity of the first-occupant theory. Others have presented themselves, pretending to reconcile the two opinions by uniting them. They have failed, like all the *juste-milieux* of the world, and are laughed at for their eclecticism. At present, the alarm is in the camp of the old doctrine; from all sides pour IN DEFENCES OF PROPERTY, STUDIES REGARDING PROPERTY, THEORIES OF PROPERTY, each one of which, giving the lie to the rest, inflicts a fresh wound upon property.

Consider, indeed, the inextricable embarrassments, the contradictions, the absurdities, the incredible nonsense, in which the bold defenders of property so lightly involve themselves. I choose the eclectics, because, those killed, the others cannot survive.

M. Troplong, jurist, passes for a philosopher in the eyes of the editors of "Le Droit." I tell the gentlemen of "Le Droit" that, in the judgment of philosophers, M. Troplong is only an advocate; and I prove my assertion.

M. Troplong is a defender of progress. "The words of the code," says he, "are fruitful sap with which the classic works of the eighteenth century overflow. To wish to suppress them... is to violate the law of progress, and to forget that a science which moves is a science which grows." [64]

Now, the only mutable and progressive portion of law, as we have already seen, is that which concerns property. If, then, you ask what reforms are to be introduced into the right of property? M. Troplong makes no reply; what progress is to be hoped for? no reply; what is to be the destiny of property in case of universal association? no reply; what is the absolute and what the contingent, what the true and what the false, in property? no reply. M. Troplong favors quiescence and *in statu quo* in regard to property. What could be more unphilosophical in a progressive philosopher?

Nevertheless, M. Troplong has thought about these things. "There are," he says, "many weak points and antiquated ideas in the doctrines of modern authors concerning property: witness the works of MM. Toullier and Duranton." The doctrine of M. Troplong promises, then, strong points, advanced and progressive ideas. Let us see; let us examine:—

"Man, placed in the presence of matter, is conscious of a power over it, which has been given to him to satisfy the needs of his being. King of inanimate or unintelligent nature, he feels that he has a right to modify it, govern it, and fit it for his use. There it is, the subject of property, which is legitimate only when exercised over things, never when over persons."

M. Troplong is so little of a philosopher, that he does not even know the import of the philosophical terms which he makes a show of using. He says of matter that it is the SUBJECT of property; he should have said the OBJECT. M. Troplong uses the language of the anatomists, who apply the term SUBJECT to the human matter used in their experiments.

This error of our author is repeated farther on: "Liberty, which overcomes matter, the subject of property, &c." The SUBJECT of property is man; its OBJECT is matter. But even this is but a slight mortification; directly we shall have some crucifixions.

Thus, according to the passage just quoted, it is in the conscience and personality of man that the principle of property must be sought. Is there any thing new in this doctrine? Apparently it never has occurred to those who, since the days of Cicero and Aristotle, and earlier, have maintained that THINGS BELONG TO THE FIRST OCCUPANT, that occupation may be exercised by beings devoid of conscience and personality. The human personality, though it may be the principle or the subject of property, as matter is the object, is not the CONDITION. Now, it is this condition which we most need to know. So far, M. Troplong tells us no more than his masters, and the figures with which he adorns his style add nothing to the old idea.

Property, then, implies three terms: The subject, the object, and the condition. There is no difficulty in regard to the first two terms. As to the third, the condition of property down to this day, for the Greek as for the Barbarian, has been that of first occupancy. What now would you have it, progressive doctor?

"When man lays hands for the first time upon an object without a master, he performs an act which, among individuals, is of the greatest importance. The thing thus seized and occupied participates, so to speak, in the personality of him who holds it. It becomes sacred, like himself. It is impossible to take it without doing violence to his liberty, or to remove it without rashly invading his person. Diogenes did but express this truth of intuition, when he said: 'Stand out of my light!'"

Very good! but would the prince of cynics, the very personal and very haughty Diogenes, have had the right to charge another cynic, as rent for this same place in the sunshine, a bone for twenty-four hours of possession? It is that which constitutes the proprietor; it is that which you fail to justify. In reasoning from the human personality and individuality to the right of property, you unconsciously construct a syllogism in which the conclusion includes more than the premises, contrary to the rules laid down by Aristotle. The individuality of the human person proves INDIVIDUAL POSSESSION, originally called *proprietas*, in opposition to collective possession, *communio*.

It gives birth to the distinction between THINE and MINE, true signs of equality, not, by any means, of subordination. "From equivocation to equivocation," says M. Michelet, [65] "property would crawl to the end of the world; man could not limit it, were not he himself its limit. Where they clash, there will be its frontier." In short, individuality of being destroys the hypothesis of communism, but it does not for that reason give birth to domain,—that domain by virtue of which the holder of a thing exercises over the person who takes his place a right of prestation and suzerainty, that has always been identified with property itself.

Further, that he whose legitimately acquired possession injures nobody cannot be nonsuited without flagrant injustice, is a truth, not of INTUITION, as M. Troplong says, but of INWARD SENSATION, [66] which has nothing to do with property.

M. Troplong admits, then, occupancy as a condition of property. In that, he is in accord with the Roman law, in accord with MM. Toullier and Duranton; but in his opinion this condition is not the only one, and it is in this particular that his doctrine goes beyond theirs.

"But, however exclusive the right arising from sole occupancy, does it not become still more so, when man has moulded matter by his labor; when he has deposited in it a portion of himself, re-creating it by his industry, and setting upon it the seal of his intelligence and activity? Of all conquests, that is the most legitimate, for it is the price of labor.

"He who should deprive a man of the thing thus remodelled, thus humanized, would invade the man himself, and would inflict the deepest wounds upon his liberty."

I pass over the very beautiful explanations in which M. Troplong, discussing labor and industry, displays the whole wealth of his eloquence. M. Troplong is not only a philosopher, he is an orator, an artist. HE ABOUNDS WITH APPEALS TO THE CONSCIENCE AND THE PASSIONS. I might make sad work of his rhetoric, should I undertake to dissect it; but I confine myself for the present to his philosophy.

If M. Troplong had only known how to think and reflect, before abandoning the original fact of occupancy and plunging into the theory of labor, he would have asked himself: "What is it to occupy?" And he would have discovered that

OCCUPANCY is only a generic term by which all modes of possession are expressed,—seizure, station, immanence, habitation, cultivation, use, consumption, &c.; that labor, consequently, is but one of a thousand forms of occupancy. He would have understood, finally, that the right of possession which is born of labor is governed by the same general laws as that which results from the simple seizure of things. What kind of a legist is he who declaims when he ought to reason, who continually mistakes his metaphors for legal axioms, and who does not so much as know how to obtain a universal by induction, and form a category?

If labor is identical with occupancy, the only benefit which it secures to the laborer is the right of individual possession of the object of his labor; if it differs from occupancy, it gives birth to a right equal only to itself,—that is, a right which begins, continues, and ends, with the labor of the occupant. It is for this reason, in the words of the law, that one cannot acquire a just title to a thing by labor alone. He must also hold it for a year and a day, in order to be regarded as its possessor; and possess it twenty or thirty years, in order to become its proprietor.

These preliminaries established, M. Troplong's whole structure falls of its own weight, and the inferences, which he attempts to draw, vanish.

"Property once acquired by occupation and labor, it naturally preserves itself, not only by the same means, but also by the refusal of the holder to abdicate; for from the very fact that it has risen to the height of a right, it is its nature to perpetuate itself and to last for an indefinite period.... Rights, considered from an ideal point of view, are imperishable and eternal; and time, which affects only the contingent, can no more disturb them than it can injure God himself." It is astonishing that our author, in speaking of the IDEAL, TIME, and ETERNITY, did not work into his sentence the DIVINE WINGS of Plato,—so fashionable to-day in philosophical works.

With the exception of falsehood, I hate nonsense more than any thing else in the world. PROPERTY ONCE ACQUIRED! Good, if it is acquired; but, as it is not acquired, it cannot be preserved. RIGHTS ARE ETERNAL! Yes, in the sight of God, like the archetypal ideas of the Platonists. But, on the earth, rights exist only in the presence of a subject, an object, and a condition. Take away one of these three things, and rights no longer exist. Thus, individual possession ceases at the death of the subject, upon the destruction of the object, or in case of exchange or abandonment.

Let us admit, however, with M. Troplong, that property is an absolute and eternal right, which cannot be destroyed save by the deed and at the will of the proprietor. What are the consequences which immediately follow from this position?

To show the justice and utility of prescription, M. Troplong supposes the case of a bona fide possessor whom a proprietor, long since forgotten or even unknown, is attempting to eject from his possession. "At the start, the error of the possessor was excusable but not irreparable. Pursuing its course and growing old by degrees, it has so completely clothed itself in the colors of truth, it has spoken so loudly the language of right, it has involved so many confiding interests, that it fairly may be asked whether it would not cause greater confusion to go back to the reality than to sanction the fictions which it (an error, without doubt) has sown on its way? Well, yes; it must be confessed, without hesitation, that the remedy would prove worse than the disease, and that its application would lead to the most outrageous injustice."

How long since utility became a principle of law? When the Athenians, by the advice of Aristides, rejected a proposition eminently advantageous to their republic, but also utterly unjust, they showed finer moral perception and greater clearness of intellect than M. Troplong. Property is an eternal right, independent of time, indestructible except by the act and at the will of the proprietor; and here this right is taken from the proprietor, and on what ground? Good God! on the ground of ABSENCE! Is it not true that legists are governed by caprice in giving and taking away rights? When it pleases these gentlemen, idleness, unworthiness, or absence can invalidate a right which, under quite similar circumstances, labor, residence, and virtue are inadequate to obtain. Do not be astonished that legists reject the absolute. Their good pleasure is law, and their disordered imaginations are the real cause of the EVOLUTIONS in jurisprudence.

"If the nominal proprietor should plead ignorance, his claim would be none the more valid. Indeed, his ignorance might arise from inexcusable carelessness, etc."

What! in order to legitimate dispossession through prescription, you suppose faults in the proprietor! You blame his absence,—which may have been involuntary; his neglect,—not knowing what caused it; his carelessness,—a gratuitous supposition of your own! It is absurd. One very simple observation suffices to annihilate this theory. Society, which, they tell us, makes an exception in the interest of order in favor of the possessor as against the old proprietor, owes the latter an indemnity; since the privilege of prescription is nothing but expropriation for the sake of public utility.

But here is something stronger:—

"In society a place cannot remain vacant with impunity. A new man arises in place of the old one who disappears or goes away; he brings here his existence, becomes entirely absorbed, and devotes himself to this post which he finds abandoned. Shall the deserter, then, dispute the honor of the victory with the soldier who fights with the sweat standing on his brow, and bears the burden of the day, in behalf of a cause which he deems just?"

When the tongue of an advocate once gets in motion, who can tell where it will stop? M. Troplong admits and justifies usurpation in case of the ABSENCE of the proprietor, and on a mere presumption of his CARELESSNESS. But when the neglect is authenticated; when the abandonment is solemnly and voluntarily set forth in a contract in the presence of a magistrate; when the proprietor dares to say, "I cease to labor, but I still claim a share of the product,"—then the absentee's right of property is protected; the usurpation of the possessor would be criminal; farm-rent is the reward of idleness. Where is, I do not say the consistency, but, the honesty of this law?

Prescription is a result of the civil law, a creation of the legislator. Why has not the legislator fixed the conditions differently?—why, instead of twenty and thirty years, is not a single year sufficient to prescribe?—why are not voluntary absence and confessed idleness as good grounds for dispossession as involuntary absence, ignorance, or apathy?

But in vain should we ask M. Troplong, the philosopher, to tell us the ground of prescription. Concerning the code, M. Troplong does not reason. "The interpreter," he says, "must take things as they are, society as it exists, laws as they are made: that is the only sensible starting-point." Well, then, write no more books; cease to reproach your predecessors—who, like you, have aimed only at interpretation of the law—for having remained in the rear; talk no more of philosophy and progress, for the lie sticks in your throat.

M. Troplong denies the reality of the right of possession; he denies that possession has ever existed as a principle of society; and he quotes M. de Savigny, who holds precisely the opposite position, and whom he is content to leave unanswered. At one time, M. Troplong asserts that possession and property are CONTEMPORANEOUS, and that they exist AT THE SAME TIME, which implies that the RIGHT of property is based on the FACT of possession,—a conclusion which is evidently absurd; at another, he denies that possession HAD ANY HISTORICAL EXISTENCE PRIOR TO PROPERTY,—an assertion which is contradicted by the customs of many nations which cultivate the land without appropriating it; by the Roman law, which distinguished so clearly between POSSESSION and PROPERTY; and by our code itself, which makes possession for twenty or thirty years the condition of property. Finally, M. Troplong goes so far as to maintain that the Roman maxim, *Nihil comune habet proprietas cum possessione*—which contains so striking an allusion to the possession of the *ager publicus*, and which, sooner or later, will be again accepted without qualification—expresses in French law only a judicial axiom, a simple rule forbidding the union of an *action possessoire* with an *action petitoire*,—an opinion as retrogressive as it is unphilosophical.

In treating of *actions possessoires*, M. Troplong is so unfortunate or awkward that he mutilates economy through failure to grasp its meaning "Just as property," he writes, "gave rise to the action for revendication, so possession—the *jus possessionis*—was the cause of possessory interdicts.... There were two kinds of interdicts,—the interdict *recuperandae possessionis*, and the interdict *retinendae possessionis*,—which correspond to our *complainte en cas de saisine et nouvelete*. There is also a third,—*adipiscendae possessionis*,—of which the Roman law-books speak in connection with the two others. But, in reality, this interdict is not possessory: for he who wishes to acquire possession by this means does not possess, and has not possessed; and yet acquired possession is the condition of possessory interdicts." Why is not an action to acquire possession equally conceivable with an action to be reinstated in possession? When the Roman plebeians demanded a division of the conquered territory; when the proletaires of Lyons took for their motto, *Vivre en travaillant, ou mourir en combattant* (to live working, or die fighting); when the most enlightened of the modern economists claim for every man the right to labor and to live,—they only propose this interdict, *adipiscendae possessionis*, which embarrasses M. Troplong so seriously. And what is my object in pleading against property, if not to obtain possession? How is it that M. Troplong—the legist, the orator, the philosopher—does not see that logically this interdict must be admitted, since it is the necessary complement of the two others, and the three united form an indivisible trinity,—to RECOVER, to MAINTAIN, to ACQUIRE? To break this series is to create a blank, destroy the natural synthesis of things, and follow the example of the geometrician who tried to conceive of a solid with only two dimensions. But it is not astonishing that M. Troplong rejects the third class of *actions possessoires*, when we consider that he rejects possession itself. He is so completely controlled by his prejudices in this respect, that he is unconsciously led, not to unite (that would be horrible in his eyes), but to identify the *action possessoire* with the *action petitoire*. This could be easily proved, were it not too tedious to plunge into these metaphysical obscurities.

As an interpreter of the law, M. Troplong is no more successful than as a philosopher. One specimen of his skill in this direction, and I am done with him:—

Code of Civil Procedure, Art. 23: "*Actions possessoires* are only when commenced within the year of trouble by those who have held possession for at least a year by an irrevocable title."

M. Troplong's comments:—

"Ought we to maintain—as Duparc, Poullain, and Lanjuinais would have us—the rule *spoliatus ante omnia restituendus*, when an individual, who is neither proprietor nor annual possessor, is expelled by a third party, who has no right to the estate? I think not. Art. 23 of the Code is general: it absolutely requires that the plaintiff in *actions possessoires* shall have been in peaceable possession for a year at least. That is the invariable principle: it can in no case be modified. And why should it be set aside? The plaintiff had no seisin; he had no privileged possession; he had only a temporary occupancy, insufficient to warrant in his favor the presumption of property, which renders the annual possession so valuable. Well! this *ae facto* occupancy he has lost; another is invested with it: possession is in the hands of this new-comer. Now, is not this a case for the application of the principle, *In pari causa possesser potior habetur*? Should not the actual possessor be preferred to the evicted possessor? Can he not meet the complaint of his adversary by saying to him: 'Prove that you were an annual possessor before me, for you are the plaintiff. As far as I am concerned, it is not for me to tell you how I possess, nor how long I have possessed. *Possideo quia possideo*. I have no other reply, no other defence. When you have shown that your action is admissible, then we will see whether you are entitled to lift the veil which hides the origin of my possession.'"

And this is what is honored with the name of jurisprudence and philosophy,—the restoration of force. What! when I have "moulded matter by my labor" [I quote M. Troplong]; when I have "deposited in it a portion of myself" [M. Troplong]; when I have "re-created it by my industry, and set upon it the seal of my intelligence" [M. Troplong],—on the ground that I have not possessed it for a year, a stranger may dispossess me, and the law offers me no protection! And if M. Troplong is my judge, M. Troplong will condemn me! And if I resist my adversary,—if, for this bit of mud which I may call MY FIELD, and of which they wish to rob me, a war breaks out between the two competitors,—the legislator will gravely wait until the stronger, having killed the other, has had possession for a year! No, no, Monsieur Troplong! you do not understand the words of the law; for I prefer to call in question your intelligence rather than the justice of the legislator. You are mistaken in your application of the principle, *In pari causa possessor potior habetur*: the actuality of possession here refers to him who possessed at the time when the difficulty arose, not to him who possesses at the time of the complaint. And when the code prohibits the reception of *actions possessoires*, in cases where the possession is not of a year's duration, it simply means that if, before a year has elapsed, the holder relinquishes possession, and ceases actually to occupy *in propria persona*, he cannot avail himself of an *action possessoire* against his successor. In a word, the code treats possession of less than a year as it ought to treat all possession, however long it has existed,—that is, the condition of property ought to be, not merely seisin for a year, but perpetual seisin.

I will not pursue this analysis farther. When an author bases two volumes of quibbles on foundations so uncertain, it may be boldly declared that his work, whatever the amount of learning displayed in it, is a mess of nonsense unworthy a critic's attention.

At this point, sir, I seem to hear you reproaching me for this conceited dogmatism, this lawless arrogance, which respects nothing, claims a monopoly of justice and good sense, and assumes to put in the pillory anyone who dares to maintain an opinion contrary to its own. This fault, they tell me, more odious than any other in an author, was too prominent a characteristic of my First Memoir, and I should do well to correct it.

It is important to the success of my defence, that I should vindicate myself from this reproach; and since, while perceiving in myself other faults of a different character, I still adhere in this particular to my disputatious style, it is right that I should give my reasons for my conduct. I act, not from inclination, but from necessity.

I say, then, that I treat my authors as I do for two reasons: a REASON OF RIGHT, and a REASON OF INTENTION; both peremptory.

1. Reason of right. When I preach equality of fortunes, I do not advance an opinion more or less probable, a utopia more or less ingenious, an idea conceived within my brain by means of imagination only. I lay down an absolute truth, concerning which hesitation is impossible, modesty superfluous, and doubt ridiculous.

But, do you ask, what assures me that that which I utter is true?

What assures me, sir? The logical and metaphysical processes which I use, the correctness of which I have demonstrated by a priori reasoning; the fact that I possess an infallible method of investigation and verification with which my authors are unacquainted; and finally, the fact that for all matters relating to property and justice I have found a formula which explains all legislative variations, and furnishes a key for all problems. Now, is there so much as a shadow of method in M. Toullier, M. Troplong, and this swarm of insipid commentators, almost as devoid of reason and moral sense as the code itself? Do you give the name of method to analphabetical, chronological, analogical, or merely nominal classification of subjects? Do you give the name of method to these lists of paragraphs gathered under an arbitrary head, these sophistical vagaries, this mass of contradictory quotations and opinions, this nauseous style, this spasmodic rhetoric, models of which are so common at the bar, though seldom found elsewhere? Do you take for philosophy this twaddle, this intolerable pettifoggery adorned with a few scholastic trimmings? No, no! a writer who respects himself, never will consent to enter the balance with these manipulators of law, misnamed JURISTS; and for my part I object to a comparison.

2. Reason of intention. As far as I am permitted to divulge this secret, I am a conspirator in an immense revolution, terrible to charlatans and despots, to all exploiters of the poor and credulous, to all salaried idlers, dealers in political panaceas and parables, tyrants in a word of thought and of opinion. I labor to stir up the reason of individuals to insurrection against the reason of authorities.

According to the laws of the society of which I am a member, all the evils which afflict humanity arise from faith in external teachings and submission to authority. And not to go outside of our own century, is it not true, for instance, that France is plundered, scoffed at, and tyrannized over, because she speaks in masses, and not by heads? The French people are penned up in three or four flocks, receiving their signal from a chief, responding to the voice of a leader, and thinking just as he says. A certain journal, it is said, has fifty thousand subscribers; assuming six readers to every subscriber, we have three hundred thousand sheep browsing and bleating at the same cratch. Apply this calculation to the whole periodical press, and you find that, in our free and intelligent France, there are two millions of creatures receiving every morning from the journals spiritual pasturage. Two millions! In other words, the entire nation allows a score of little fellows to lead it by the nose.

By no means, sir, do I deny to journalists talent, science, love of truth, patriotism, and what you please. They are very worthy and intelligent people, whom I undoubtedly should wish to resemble, had I the honor to know them. That of which I complain, and that which has made me a conspirator, is that, instead of enlightening us, these gentlemen command us, impose upon us articles of faith, and that without demonstration or verification. When, for example, I ask why these fortifications of Paris, which, in former times, under the influence of certain prejudices, and by means of a concurrence of extraordinary circumstances supposed for the sake of the argument to have existed, may perhaps have served to protect us, but which it is doubtful whether our descendants will ever use,—when I ask, I say, on what grounds they assimilate the future to a hypothetical past, they reply that M. Thiers, who has a great mind, has written upon this subject a report of admirable elegance and marvellous clearness. At this I become angry, and reply that M. Thiers does not know what he is talking about. Why, having wanted no detached forts seven years ago, do we want them to-day?

"Oh! damn it," they say, "the difference is great; the first forts were too near to us; with these we cannot be bombarded." You cannot be bombarded; but you can be blockaded, and will be, if you stir. What! to obtain blockade forts from the Parisians, it has sufficed to prejudice them against bombardment forts! And they thought to outwit the government! Oh, the sovereignty of the people!...

"Damn it! M. Thiers, who is wiser than you, says that it would be absurd to suppose a government making war upon citizens, and maintaining itself by force and in spite of the will of the people. That would be absurd!" Perhaps so: such a thing has happened more than once, and may happen again. Besides, when despotism is strong, it appears almost legitimate. However that may be, they lied in 1833, and they lie again in 1841,—those who threaten us with the bomb-shell. And then, if M. Thiers is so well assured of the intentions of the government, why does he not wish the forts to be built before the circuit is extended? Why this air of suspicion of the government, unless an intrigue has been planned between the government and M. Thiers?

"Damn it! we do not wish to be again invaded. If Paris had been fortified in 1815, Napoleon would not have been conquered!" But I tell you that Napoleon was not conquered, but sold; and that if, in 1815, Paris had had fortifications, it would have been with them as with the thirty thousand men of Grouchy, who were misled during the battle. It is still easier to surrender forts than to lead soldiers. Would the selfish and the cowardly ever lack reasons for yielding to the enemy?

"But do you not see that the absolutist courts are provoked at our fortifications?—a proof that they do not think as you do." You believe that; and, for my part, I believe that in reality they are quite at ease about the matter; and, if they appear to tease our ministers, they do so only to give the latter an opportunity to decline. The absolutist courts are always on better terms with our constitutional monarchy, than our monarchy with us. Does not M. Guizot say that France needs to be defended within as well as without? Within! against whom? Against France. O Parisians! it is but six months since you demanded war, and now you want only barricades. Why should the allies fear your doctrines, when you cannot even control yourselves?... How could you sustain a siege, when you weep over the absence of an actress?

"But, finally, do you not understand that, by the rules of modern warfare, the capital of a country is always the objective point of its assailants? Suppose our army defeated on the Rhine, France invaded, and defenceless Paris falling into the hands of the enemy. It would be the death of the administrative power; without a head it could not live. The capital taken, the nation must submit. What do you say to that?"

The reply is very simple. Why is society constituted in such a way that the destiny of the country depends upon the safety of the capital? Why, in case our territory be invaded and Paris besieged, cannot the legislative, executive, and military powers act outside of Paris? Why this localization of all the vital forces of France?... Do not cry out upon decentralization. This hackneyed reproach would discredit only your own intelligence and sincerity. It is not a question of decentralization; it is your political fetichism which I attack. Why should the national unity be attached to a certain place, to certain functionaries, to certain bayonets? Why should the Place Maubert and the Palace of the Tuileries be the palladium of France?

Now let me make an hypothesis.

Suppose it were written in the charter, "In case the country be again invaded, and Paris forced to surrender, the government being annihilated and the national assembly dissolved, the electoral colleges shall reassemble spontaneously and without other official notice, for the purpose of appointing new deputies, who shall organize a provisional government at Orleans.

"If Orleans succumbs, the government shall reconstruct itself in the same way at Lyons; then at Bordeaux, then at Bayonne, until all France be captured or the enemy driven from the land. For the government may perish, but the nation never dies. The king, the peers, and the deputies massacred, VIVE LA FRANCE!"

Do you not think that such an addition to the charter would be a better safeguard for the liberty and integrity of the country than walls and bastions around Paris? Well, then! do henceforth for administration, industry, science, literature, and art that which the charter ought to prescribe for the central government and common defence. Instead of endeavoring to render Paris impregnable, try rather to render the loss of Paris an insignificant matter. Instead of accumulating about one point academies, faculties, schools, and political, administrative, and judicial centres; instead of arresting intellectual development and weakening public spirit in the provinces by this fatal agglomeration,—can you not, without destroying unity, distribute social functions among places as well as among persons? Such a system—in allowing each province to participate in political power and action, and in balancing industry, intelligence, and strength in all parts of the country—would equally secure, against enemies at home and enemies abroad, the liberty of the people and the stability of the government.

Discriminate, then, between the centralization of functions and the concentration of organs; between political unity and its material symbol.

"Oh! that is plausible; but it is impossible!"—which means that the city of Paris does not intend to surrender its privileges, and that there is still a question of property.

Idle talk! The country, in a state of panic which has been cleverly worked upon, has asked for fortifications. I dare to affirm that it has abdicated its sovereignty. All parties are to blame for this suicide,—the conservatives, by their acquiescence in the plans of the government; the friends of the dynasty, because they wish no opposition to that which pleases them, and because a popular revolution would annihilate them; the democrats, because they hope to rule in their turn. 67 That which all rejoice at having obtained is a means of future repression. As for the defence of the country, they are not troubled about that. The idea of tyranny dwells in the minds of all, and brings together into one conspiracy all forms of selfishness. We wish the regeneration of society, but we subordinate this desire to our ideas and convenience. That our approaching marriage may take place, that our business may succeed, that our opinions may triumph, we postpone reform. Intolerance and selfishness lead us to put fetters upon liberty; and, because we cannot wish all that God wishes, we would, if it rested with us, stay the course of destiny rather than sacrifice our own interests and self-love. Is not this an instance where the words of Solomon apply,—"*L'iniquite a menti a elle-meme*"?

It is said that on this question of the fortification of Paris the staff of "Le National" are not agreed. This would prove, if proof were needed, that a journal may blunder and falsify, without entitling any one to accuse its editors. A journal is a metaphysical being, for which no one is really responsible, and which owes its existence solely to mutual concessions. This idea ought to frighten those worthy citizens who, because they borrow their opinions from a journal, imagine that they belong to a political party, and who have not the faintest suspicion that they are really without a head.

For this reason, sir, I have enlisted in a desperate war against every form of authority over the multitude. Advance sentinel of the proletariat, I cross bayonets with the celebrities of the day, as well as with spies and charlatans. Well, when I am fighting with an illustrious adversary, must I stop at the end of every phrase, like an orator in the tribune, to say "the learned author," "the eloquent writer," "the profound publicist," and a hundred other platitudes with which it is fashionable to mock people? These civilities seem to me no less insulting to the man attacked than dishonorable to the aggressor. But when, rebuking an author, I say to him, "Citizen, your doctrine is absurd, and, if to prove my assertion is an offence against you, I am guilty of it," immediately the listener opens his ears; he is all attention; and, if I do not succeed in convincing him, at least I give his thought an impulse, and set him the wholesome example of doubt and free examination.

Then do not think, sir, that, in tripping up the philosophy of your very learned and very estimable confrere, M.

Troplong, I fail to appreciate his talent as a writer (in my opinion, he has too much for a jurist); nor his knowledge, though it is too closely confined to the letter of the law, and the reading of old books. In these particulars, M. Troplong offends on the side of excess rather than deficiency. Further, do not believe that I am actuated by any personal animosity towards him, or that I have the slightest desire to wound his self-love. I know M. Troplong only by his "Treatise on Prescription," which I wish he had not written; and as for my critics, neither M. Troplong, nor any of those whose opinion I value, will ever read me. Once more, my only object is to prove, as far as I am able, to this unhappy French nation, that those who make the laws, as well as those who interpret them, are not infallible organs of general, impersonal, and absolute reason.

I had resolved to submit to a systematic criticism the semi-official defence of the right of property recently put forth by M. Wolowski, your colleague at the Conservatory. With this view, I had commenced to collect the documents necessary for each of his lectures, but, soon perceiving that the ideas of the professor were incoherent, that his arguments contradicted each other, that one affirmation was sure to be overthrown by another, and that in M. Wolowski's lucubrations the good was always mingled with the bad, and being by nature a little suspicious, it suddenly occurred to me that M. Wolowski was an advocate of equality in disguise, thrown in spite of himself into the position in which the patriarch Jacob pictures one of his sons,—*inter duas clitellas*, between two stools, as the proverb says. In more parliamentary language, I saw clearly that M. Wolowski was placed between his profound convictions on the one hand and his official duties on the other, and that, in order to maintain his position, he had to assume a certain slant. Then I experienced great pain at seeing the reserve, the circumlocution, the figures, and the irony to which a professor of legislation, whose duty it is to teach dogmas with clearness and precision, was forced to resort; and I fell to cursing the society in which an honest man is not allowed to say frankly what he thinks. Never, sir, have you conceived of such torture: I seemed to be witnessing the martyrdom of a mind. I am going to give you an idea of these astonishing meetings, or rather of these scenes of sorrow.

Monday, Nov. 20, 1840.—The professor declares, in brief,—1. That the right of property is not founded upon occupation, but upon the impress of man; 2. That every man has a natural and inalienable right to the use of matter.

Now, if matter can be appropriated, and if, notwithstanding, all men retain an inalienable right to the use of this matter, what is property?—and if matter can be appropriated only by labor, how long is this appropriation to continue?—questions that will confuse and confound all jurists whatsoever.

Then M. Wolowski cites his authorities. Great God! what witnesses he brings forward! First, M. Troplong, the great metaphysician, whom we have discussed; then, M. Louis Blanc, editor of the "Revue du Progres," who came near being tried by jury for publishing his "Organization of Labor," and who escaped from the clutches of the public prosecutor only by a juggler's trick; [68] Corinne,—I mean Madame de Stael,—who, in an ode, making a poetical comparison of the land with the waves, of the furrow of a plough with the wake of a vessel, says "that property exists only where man has left his trace," which makes property dependent upon the solidity of the elements; Rousseau, the apostle of liberty and equality, but who, according to M. Wolowski, attacked property only AS A JOKE, and in order to point a paradox; Robespierre, who prohibited a division of the land, because he regarded such a measure as a rejuvenescence of property, and who, while awaiting the definitive organization of the republic, placed all property in the care?? of the people,—that is, transferred the right of eminent domain from the individual to society; Babeuf, who wanted property for the nation, and communism for the citizens; M. Considerant, who favors a division of landed property into shares,—that is, who wishes to render property nominal and fictitious: the whole being intermingled with jokes and witticisms (intended undoubtedly to lead people away from the HORNETS' NESTS) at the expense of the adversaries of the right of property!

November 26.—M. Wolowski supposes this objection: Land, like water, air, and light, is necessary to life, therefore it cannot be appropriated; and he replies: The importance of landed property diminishes as the power of industry increases.

Good! this importance DIMINISHES, but it does not DISAPPEAR; and this, of itself, shows landed property to be illegitimate. Here M. Wolowski pretends to think that the opponents of property refer only to property in land, while they merely take it as a term of comparison; and, in showing with wonderful clearness the absurdity of the position in which he places them, he finds a way of drawing the attention of his hearers to another subject without being false to the truth which it is his office to contradict.

"Property," says M. Wolowski, "is that which distinguishes man from the animals." That may be; but are we to regard this as a compliment or a satire?

"Mahomet," says M. Wolowski, "decreed property." And so did Genghis Khan, and Tamerlane, and all the ravagers of nations. What sort of legislators were they?

"Property has been in existence ever since the origin of the human race." Yes, and so has slavery, and despotism also; and likewise polygamy and idolatry. But what does this antiquity show?

The members of the Council of the State—M. Portalis at their head—did not raise, in their discussion of the Code, the question of the legitimacy of property. "Their silence," says M. Wolowski, "is a precedent in favor of this right." I may regard this reply as personally addressed to me, since the observation belongs to me. I reply, "As long as an opinion is universally admitted, the universality of belief serves of itself as argument and proof. When this same opinion is attacked, the former faith proves nothing; we must resort to reason. Ignorance, however old and pardonable it may be, never outweighs reason."

Property has its abuses, M. Wolowski confesses. "But," he says, "these abuses gradually disappear. To-day their cause is known. They all arise from a false theory of property. In principle, property is inviolable, but it can and must be checked and disciplined." Such are the conclusions of the professor.

When one thus remains in the clouds, he need not fear to equivocate. Nevertheless, I would like him to define these ABUSES of property, to show their cause, to explain this true theory from which no abuse is to spring; in short, to tell me how, without destroying property, it can be governed for the greatest good of all. "Our civil code," says M. Wolowski, in speaking of this subject, "leaves much to be desired." I think it leaves every thing undone.

Finally, M. Wolowski opposes, on the one hand, the concentration of capital, and the absorption which results therefrom; and, on the other, he objects to the extreme division of the land. Now I think that I have demonstrated in my

First Memoir, that large accumulation and minute division are the first two terms of an economical trinity,—a THESIS and an ANTITHESIS. But, while M. Wolowski says nothing of the third term, the SYNTHESIS, and thus leaves the inference in suspense, I have shown that this third term is ASSOCIATION, which is the annihilation of property.

November 30.—LITERARY PROPERTY. M. Wolowski grants that it is just to recognize the rights of talent (which is not in the least hostile to equality); but he seriously objects to perpetual and absolute property in the works of genius, to the profit of the authors' heirs. His main argument is, that society has a right of collective production over every creation of the mind. Now, it is precisely this principle of collective power that I developed in my "Inquiries into Property and Government," and on which I have established the complete edifice of a new social organization. M. Wolowski is, as far as I know, the first jurist who has made a legislative application of this economical law. Only, while I have extended the principle of collective power to every sort of product, M. Wolowski, more prudent than it is my nature to be, confines it to neutral ground. So, that that which I am bold enough to say of the whole, he is contented to affirm of a part, leaving the intelligent hearer to fill up the void for himself. However, his arguments are keen and close. One feels that the professor, finding himself more at ease with one aspect of property, has given the rein to his intellect, and is rushing on towards liberty.

1. Absolute literary property would hinder the activity of other men, and obstruct the development of humanity. It would be the death of progress; it would be suicide. What would have happened if the first inventions,—the plough, the level, the saw, &c.,—had been appropriated?

Such is the first proposition of M. Wolowski.

I reply: Absolute property in land and tools hinders human activity, and obstructs progress and the free development of man.

What happened in Rome, and in all the ancient nations? What occurred in the middle ages? What do we see to-day in England, in consequence of absolute property in the sources of production?

The suicide of humanity.

2. Real and personal property is in harmony with the social interest. In consequence of literary property, social and individual interests are perpetually in conflict.

The statement of this proposition contains a rhetorical figure, common with those who do not enjoy full and complete liberty of speech. This figure is the *anti-phrasis* or *contre-verite*. It consists, according to Dumarsais and the best humanists, in saying one thing while meaning another. M. Wolowski's proposition, naturally expressed, would read as follows: "Just as real and personal property is essentially hostile to society, so, in consequence of literary property, social and individual interests are perpetually in conflict."

3. M. de Montalembert, in the Chamber of Peers, vehemently protested against the assimilation of authors to inventors of machinery; an assimilation which he claimed to be injurious to the former. M. Wolowski replies, that the rights of authors, without machinery, would be nil; that, without paper-mills, type foundries, and printing-offices, there could be no sale of verse and prose; that many a mechanical invention,—the compass, for instance, the telescope, or the steam-engine,—is quite as valuable as a book.

Prior to M. Montalembert, M. Charles Comte had laughed at the inference in favor of mechanical inventions, which logical minds never fail to draw from the privileges granted to authors. "He," says M. Comte, "who first conceived and executed the idea of transforming a piece of wood into a pair of sabots, or an animal's hide into a pair of sandals, would thereby have acquired an exclusive right to make shoes for the human race!" Undoubtedly, under the system of property. For, in fact, this pair of sabots, over which you make so merry, is the creation of the shoemaker, the work of his genius, the expression of his thought; to him it is his poem, quite as much as "Le Roi s'amuse," is M. Victor Hugo's drama. Justice for all alike. If you refuse a patent to a perfecter of boots, refuse also a privilege to a maker of rhymes.

4. That which gives importance to a book is a fact external to the author and his work. Without the intelligence of society, without its development, and a certain community of ideas, passions, and interests between it and the authors, the works of the latter would be worth nothing. The exchangeable value of a book is due even more to the SOCIAL CONDITION than to the talent displayed in it.

Indeed, it seems as if I were copying my own words. This proposition of M. Wolowski contains a special expression of a general and absolute idea, one of the strongest and most conclusive against the right of property. Why do artists, like mechanics, find the means to live? Because society has made the fine arts, like the rudest industries, objects of consumption and exchange, governed consequently by all the laws of commerce and political economy. Now, the first of these laws is the equipoise of functions; that is, the equality of associates.

5. M. Wolowski indulges in sarcasm against the petitioners for literary property. "There are authors," he says, "who crave the privileges of authors, and who for that purpose point out the power of the melodrama. They speak of the niece of Corneille, begging at the door of a theatre which the works of her uncle had enriched…. To satisfy the avarice of literary people, it would be necessary to create literary majorats, and make a whole code of exceptions."

I like this virtuous irony. But M. Wolowski has by no means exhausted the difficulties which the question involves. And first, is it just that MM. Cousin, Guizot, Villemain, Damiron, and company, paid by the State for delivering lectures, should be paid a second time through the booksellers?—that I, who have the right to report their lectures, should not have the right to print them? Is it just that MM. Noel and Chapsal, overseers of the University, should use their influence in selling their selections from literature to the youth whose studies they are instructed to superintend in consideration of a salary? And, if that is not just, is it not proper to refuse literary property to every author holding public offices, and receiving pensions or sinecures?

Again, shall the privilege of the author extend to irreligious and immoral works, calculated only to corrupt the heart, and obscure the understanding? To grant this privilege is to sanction immorality by law; to refuse it is to censure the author. And since it is impossible, in the present imperfect state of society, to prevent all violations of the moral law, it will be necessary to open a license-office for books as well as morals. But, then, three-fourths of our literary people will be obliged to register; and, recognized thenceforth on their own declaration as PROSTITUTES, they will necessarily belong to the public. We pay toll to the prostitute; we do not endow her.

Finally, shall plagiarism be classed with forgery? If you reply "Yes," you appropriate in advance all the subjects of which books treat; if you say "No," you leave the whole matter to the decision of the judge. Except in the case of a clandestine reprint, how will he distinguish forgery from quotation, imitation, plagiarism, or even coincidence? A savant spends two years in calculating a table of logarithms to nine or ten decimals. He prints it. A fortnight after his book is selling at half-price; it is impossible to tell whether this result is due to forgery or competition. What shall the court do? In case of doubt, shall it award the property to the first occupant? As well decide the question by lot.

These, however, are trifling considerations; but do we see that, in granting a perpetual privilege to authors and their heirs, we really strike a fatal blow at their interests? We think to make booksellers dependent upon authors,—a delusion. The booksellers will unite against works, and their proprietors. Against works, by refusing to push their sale, by replacing them with poor imitations, by reproducing them in a hundred indirect ways; and no one knows how far the science of plagiarism, and skilful imitation may be carried. Against proprietors. Are we ignorant of the fact, that a demand for a dozen copies enables a bookseller to sell a thousand; that with an edition of five hundred he can supply a kingdom for thirty years? What will the poor authors do in the presence of this omnipotent union of booksellers? I will tell them what they will do. They will enter the employ of those whom they now treat as pirates; and, to secure an advantage, they will become wage laborers. A fit reward for ignoble avarice, and insatiable pride. [69]

Contradictions of contradictions! "Genius is the great leveller of the world," cries M. de Lamartine; "then genius should be a proprietor. Literary property is the fortune of democracy." This unfortunate poet thinks himself profound when he is only puffed up. His eloquence consists solely in coupling ideas which clash with each other: ROUND SQUARE, DARK SUN, FALLEN ANGEL, PRIEST and LOVE, THOUGHT and POETRY, GUNIUS {???}, and FORTUNE, LEVELING and PROPERTY. Let us tell him, in reply, that his mind is a dark luminary; that each of his discourses is a disordered harmony; and that all his successes, whether in verse or prose, are due to the use of the extraordinary in the treatment of the most ordinary subjects.

"Le National," in reply to the report of M. Lamartine, endeavors to prove that literary property is of quite a different nature from landed property; as if the nature of the right of property depended on the object to which it is applied, and not on the mode of its exercise and the condition of its existence. But the main object of "Le National" is to please a class of proprietors whom an extension of the right of property vexes: that is why "Le National" opposes literary property. Will it tell us, once for all, whether it is for equality or against it?

6. OBJECTION.—Property in occupied land passes to the heirs of the occupant. "Why," say the authors, "should not the work of genius pass in like manner to the heirs of the man of genius?" M. Wolowski's reply: "Because the labor of the first occupant is continued by his heirs, while the heirs of an author neither change nor add to his works. In landed property, the continuance of labor explains the continuance of the right."

Yes, when the labor is continued; but if the labor is not continued, the right ceases. Thus is the right of possession, founded on personal labor, recognized by M. Wolowski.

M. Wolowski decides in favor of granting to authors property in their works for a certain number of years, dating from the day of their first publication.

The succeeding lectures on patents on inventions were no less instructive, although intermingled with shocking contradictions inserted with a view to make the useful truths more palatable. The necessity for brevity compels me to terminate this examination here, not without regret.

Thus, of two eclectic jurists, who attempt a defence of property, one is entangled in a set of dogmas without principle or method, and is constantly talking nonsense; and the other designedly abandons the cause of property, in order to present under the same name the theory of individual possession. Was I wrong in claiming that confusion reigned among legists, and ought I to be legally prosecuted for having said that their science henceforth stood convicted of falsehood, its glory eclipsed?

The ordinary resources of the law no longer sufficing, philosophy, political economy, and the framers of systems have been consulted. All the oracles appealed to have been discouraging.

The philosophers are no clearer to-day than at the time of the eclectic efflorescence; nevertheless, through their mystical apothegms, we can distinguish the words PROGRESS, UNITY, ASSOCIATION, SOLIDARITY, FRATERNITY, which are certainly not reassuring to proprietors. One of these philosophers, M. Pierre Leroux, has written two large books, in which he claims to show by all religious, legislative, and philosophical systems that, since men are responsible to each other, equality of conditions is the final law of society. It is true that this philosopher admits a kind of property; but as he leaves us to imagine what property would become in presence of equality, we may boldly class him with the opponents of the right of increase.

I must here declare freely—in order that I may not be suspected of secret connivance, which is foreign to my nature—that M. Leroux has my full sympathy. Not that I am a believer in his quasi-Pythagorean philosophy (upon this subject I should have more than one observation to submit to him, provided a veteran covered with stripes would not despise the remarks of a conscript); not that I feel bound to this author by any special consideration for his opposition to property. In my opinion, M. Leroux could, and even ought to, state his position more explicitly and logically. But I like, I admire, in M. Leroux, the antagonist of our philosophical demigods, the demolisher of usurped reputations, the pitiless critic of every thing that is respected because of its antiquity. Such is the reason for my high esteem of M. Leroux; such would be the principle of the only literary association which, in this century of coteries, I should care to form. We need men who, like M. Leroux, call in question social principles,—not to diffuse doubt concerning them, but to make them doubly sure; men who excite the mind by bold negations, and make the conscience tremble by doctrines of annihilation. Where is the man who does not shudder on hearing M. Leroux exclaim, "There is neither a paradise nor a hell; the wicked will not be punished, nor the good rewarded. Mortals! cease to hope and fear; you revolve in a circle of appearances; humanity is an immortal tree, whose branches, withering one after another, feed with their debris the root which is always young!" Where is the man who, on hearing this desolate confession of faith, does not demand with terror, "Is it then true that I am only an aggregate of elements organized by an unknown force, an idea realized for a few moments, a form which passes and disappears? Is it true that my mind is only a harmony, and my soul a vortex? What is the ego? what is God? what is the sanction of society?"

In former times, M. Leroux would have been regarded as a great culprit, worthy only (like Vanini) of death and universal execration. To-day, M. Leroux is fulfilling a mission of salvation, for which, whatever he may say, he will be rewarded. Like those gloomy invalids who are always talking of their approaching death, and who faint when the doctor's opinion confirms their pretence, our materialistic society is agitated and loses countenance while listening to this startling decree of the philosopher, "Thou shalt die!" Honor then to M. Leroux, who has revealed to us the cowardice of the Epicureans; to M. Leroux, who renders new philosophical solutions necessary! Honor to the anti-eclectic, to the apostle of equality!

In his work on "Humanity," M. Leroux commences by positing the necessity of property: "You wish to abolish property; but do you not see that thereby you would annihilate man and even the name of man?... You wish to abolish property; but could you live without a body? I will not tell you that it is necessary to support this body;... I will tell you that this body is itself a species of property."

In order clearly to understand the doctrine of M. Leroux, it must be borne in mind that there are three necessary and primitive forms of society,—communism, property, and that which to-day we properly call association. M. Leroux rejects in the first place communism, and combats it with all his might. Man is a personal and free being, and therefore needs a sphere of independence and individual activity. M. Leroux emphasizes this in adding: "You wish neither family, nor country, nor property; therefore no more fathers, no more sons, no more brothers. Here you are, related to no being in time, and therefore without a name; here you are, alone in the midst of a billion of men who to-day inhabit the earth. How do you expect me to distinguish you in space in the midst of this multitude?"

If man is indistinguishable, he is nothing. Now, he can be distinguished, individualized, only through a devotion of certain things to his use,—such as his body, his faculties, and the tools which he uses. "Hence," says M. Leroux, "the necessity of appropriation;" in short, property.

But property on what condition? Here M. Leroux, after having condemned communism, denounces in its turn the right of domain. His whole doctrine can be summed up in this single proposition,—*Man may be made by property a slave or a despot by turns.*

That posited, if we ask M. Leroux to tell us under what system of property man will be neither a slave nor a despot, but free, just, and a citizen, M. Leroux replies in the third volume of his work on "Humanity:"—

"There are three ways of destroying man's communion with his fellows and with the universe:... 1. By separating man in time; 2. by separating him in space; 3. by dividing the land, or, in general terms, the instruments of production; by attaching men to things, by subordinating man to property, by making man a proprietor."

This language, it must be confessed, savors a little too strongly of the metaphysical heights which the author frequents, and of the school of M. Cousin. Nevertheless, it can be seen, clearly enough it seems to me, that M. Leroux opposes the exclusive appropriation of the instruments of production; only he calls this non-appropriation of the instruments of production a NEW METHOD of establishing property, while I, in accordance with all precedent, call it a destruction of property. In fact, without the appropriation of instruments, property is nothing.

"Hitherto, we have confined ourselves to pointing out and combating the despotic features of property, by considering property alone. We have failed to see that the despotism of property is a correlative of the division of the human race;... that property, instead of being organized in such a way as to facilitate the unlimited communion of man with his fellows and with the universe, has been, on the contrary, turned against this communion."

Let us translate this into commercial phraseology. In order to destroy despotism and the inequality of conditions, men must cease from competition and must associate their interests. Let employer and employed (now enemies and rivals) become associates.

Now, ask any manufacturer, merchant, or capitalist, whether he would consider himself a proprietor if he were to share his revenue and profits with this mass of wage-laborers whom it is proposed to make his associates.

"Family, property, and country are finite things, which ought to be organized with a view to the infinite. For man is a finite being, who aspires to the infinite. To him, absolute finiteness is evil. The infinite is his aim, the indefinite his right."

Few of my readers would understand these hierophantic words, were I to leave them unexplained. M. Leroux means, by this magnificent formula, that humanity is a single immense society, which, in its collective unity, represents the infinite; that every nation, every tribe, every commune, and every citizen are, in different degrees, fragments or finite members of the infinite society, the evil in which results solely from individualism and privilege,—in other words, from the subordination of the infinite to the finite; finally, that, to attain humanity's end and aim, each part has a right to an indefinitely progressive development.

"All the evils which afflict the human race arise from caste. The family is a blessing; the family caste (the nobility) is an evil. Country is a blessing; the country caste (supreme, domineering, conquering) is an evil; property (individual possession) is a blessing; the property caste (the domain of property of Pothier, Toullier, Troplong, &c.) is an evil."

Thus, according to M. Leroux, there is property and property,—the one good, the other bad. Now, as it is proper to call different things by different names, if we keep the name "property" for the former, we must call the latter robbery, rapine, brigandage. If, on the contrary, we reserve the name "property" for the latter, we must designate the former by the term POSSESSION, or some other equivalent; otherwise we should be troubled with an unpleasant synonymy.

What a blessing it would be if philosophers, daring for once to say all that they think, would speak the language of ordinary mortals! Nations and rulers would derive much greater profit from their lectures, and, applying the same names to the same ideas, would come, perhaps, to understand each other. I boldly declare that, in regard to property, I hold no other opinion than that of M. Leroux; but, if I should adopt the style of the philosopher, and repeat after him, "Property is a blessing, but the property caste—the *statu quo* of property—is an evil," I should be extolled as a genius by all the bachelors who write for the reviews. [70] If, on the contrary, I prefer the classic language of Rome and the civil code, and say accordingly, "Possession is a blessing, but property is robbery," immediately the aforesaid bachelors raise a hue and cry against the monster, and the judge threatens me. Oh, the power of language!

"Le National," on the other hand, has laughed at M. Leroux and his ideas on property, charging him with TAUTOLOGY and CHILDISHNESS. "Le National" does not wish to understand. Is it necessary to remind this journal that it has no right to deride a dogmatic philosopher, because it is without a doctrine itself? From its foundation, "Le National" has been a nursery of intriguers and renegades. From time to time it takes care to warn its readers. Instead of lamenting over all its defections, the democratic sheet would do better to lay the blame on itself, and confess the shallowness of its theories. When will this organ of popular interests and the electoral reform cease to hire sceptics and spread doubt? I will wager, without going further, that M. Leon Durocher, the critic of M. Leroux, is an anonymous or pseudonymous editor of some bourgeois, or even aristocratic, journal.

The economists, questioned in their turn, propose to associate capital and labor. You know, sir, what that means. If we follow out the doctrine, we soon find that it ends in an absorption of property, not by the community, but by a general and indissoluble commandite, so that the condition of the proprietor would differ from that of the workingman only in receiving larger wages. This system, with some peculiar additions and embellishments, is the idea of the phalanstery. But it is clear that, if inequality of conditions is one of the attributes of property, it is not the whole of property. That which makes property a DELIGHTFUL THING, as some philosopher (I know not who) has said, is the power to dispose at will, not only of one's own goods, but of their specific nature; to use them at pleasure; to confine and enclose them; to excommunicate mankind, as M. Pierre Leroux says; in short, to make such use of them as passion, interest, or even caprice, may suggest. What is the possession of money, a share in an agricultural or industrial enterprise, or a government-bond coupon, in comparison with the infinite charm of being master of one's house and grounds, under one's vine and fig-tree? "*Beati possidentes!*" says an author quoted by M. Troplong. Seriously, can that be applied to a man of income, who has no other possession under the sun than the market, and in his pocket his money? As well maintain that a trough is a coward. A nice method of reform! They never cease to condemn the thirst for gold, and the growing individualism of the century; and yet, most inconceivable of contradictions, they prepare to turn all kinds of property into one,—property in coin.

I must say something further of a theory of property lately put forth with some ado: I mean the theory of M. Considerant.

The Fourierists are not men who examine a doctrine in order to ascertain whether it conflicts with their system. On the contrary, it is their custom to exult and sing songs of triumph whenever an adversary passes without perceiving or noticing them.

These gentlemen want direct refutations, in order that, if they are beaten, they may have, at least, the selfish consolation of having been spoken of. Well, let their wish be gratified.

M. Considerant makes the most lofty pretensions to logic. His method of procedure is always that of MAJOR, MINOR, AND CONCLUSION. He would willingly write upon his hat, "*Argumentator in barbara.*" But M. Considerant is too intelligent and quick-witted to be a good logician, as is proved by the fact that he appears to have taken the syllogism for logic.

The syllogism, as everybody knows who is interested in philosophical curiosities, is the first and perpetual sophism of the human mind,—the favorite tool of falsehood, the stumbling-block of science, the advocate of crime. The syllogism has produced all the evils which the fabulist so eloquently condemned, and has done nothing good or useful: it is as devoid of truth as of justice. We might apply to it these words of Scripture: "*Celui qui met en lui sa confiance, perira.*" Consequently, the best philosophers long since condemned it; so that now none but the enemies of reason wish to make the syllogism its weapon.

M. Considerant, then, has built his theory of property upon a syllogism. Would he be disposed to stake the system of Fourier upon his arguments, as I am ready to risk the whole doctrine of equality upon my refutation of that system? Such a duel would be quite in keeping with the warlike and chivalric tastes of M. Considerant, and the public would profit by it; for, one of the two adversaries falling, no more would be said about him, and there would be one grumbler less in the world.

The theory of M. Considerant has this remarkable feature, that, in attempting to satisfy at the same time the claims of both laborers and proprietors, it infringes alike upon the rights of the former and the privileges of the latter. In the first place, the author lays it down as a principle: "1. That the use of the land belongs to each member of the race; that it is a natural and imprescriptible right, similar in all respects to the right to the air and the sunshine. 2. That the right to labor is equally fundamental, natural, and imprescriptible." I have shown that the recognition of this double right would be the death of property. I denounce M. Considerant to the proprietors!

But M. Considerant maintains that the right to labor creates the right of property, and this is the way he reasons:—

Major Premise.—"Every man legitimately possesses the thing which his labor, his skill,—or, in more general terms, his action,—has created."

To which M. Considerant adds, by way of comment: "Indeed, the land not having been created by man, it follows from the fundamental principle of property, that the land, being given to the race in common, can in no wise be the exclusive and legitimate property of such and such individuals, who were not the creators of this value."

If I am not mistaken, there is no one to whom this proposition, at first sight and in its entirety, does not seem utterly irrefutable. Reader, distrust the syllogism.

First, I observe that the words LEGITIMATELY POSSESSES signify to the author's mind is *LEGITIMATE PROPRIETOR;* otherwise the argument, being intended to prove the legitimacy of property, would have no meaning. I might here raise the question of the difference between property and possession, and call upon M. Considerant, before going further, to define the one and the other; but I pass on.

This first proposition is doubly false. 1. In that it asserts the act of CREATION to be the only basis of property. 2. In that it regards this act as sufficient in all cases to authorize the right of property.

And, in the first place, if man may be proprietor of the game which he does not create, but which he KILLS; of the fruits which he does not create, but which he GATHERS; of the vegetables which he does not create, but which he PLANTS; of the animals which he does not create, but which he REARS,—it is conceivable that men may in like manner become proprietors of the land which they do not create, but which they clear and fertilize. The act of creation, then, is not NECESSARY to the acquisition of the right of property. I say further, that this act alone is not always sufficient, and I prove it by the second premise of M. Considerant:—

Minor Premise.—"Suppose that on an isolated island, on the soil of a nation, or over the whole face of the earth (the extent of the scene of action does not affect our judgment of the facts), a generation of human beings devotes itself for the first time to industry, agriculture, manufactures, &c. This generation, by its labor, intelligence, and activity, creates products, develops values which did not exist on the uncultivated land. Is it not perfectly clear that the property of this industrious generation will stand on a basis of right, if the value or according to each one's assistance in the creation of the general wealth? That is unquestionable."

ACTIVITY OF ALL, is by the very fact of its creation COLLECTIVE wealth, the use of which, like that of the land, may be divided, but which as property remains UNDIVIDED. And why this undivided ownership? Because the society which creates is itself indivisible,—a permanent unit, incapable of reduction to fractions. And it is this unity of society which makes the land common property, and which, as M. Considerant says, renders its use imprescriptible in the case of every individual. Suppose, indeed, that at a given time the soil should be equally divided; the very next moment this division, if it allowed the right of property, would become illegitimate. Should there be the slightest irregularity in the method of transfer, men, members of society, imprescriptible possessors of the land, might be deprived at one blow of property, possession, and the means of production. In short, property in capital is indivisible, and consequently inalienable, not necessarily when the capital is UNCREATED, but when it is COMMON or COLLECTIVE.

I confirm this theory against M. Considerant, by the third term of his syllogism:—

Conclusion.—"The results of the labor performed by this generation are

divisible into two classes, between which it is important clearly to distinguish. The first class includes the products of the soil which belong to this first generation in its usufructuary capacity, augmented, improved and refined by its labor and industry. These products consist either of objects of consumption or instruments of labor. It is clear that these products are the legitimate property of those who have created them by their activity.... Second class.—Not only has this generation created the products just mentioned (objects of consumption and instruments of labor), but it has also added to the original value of the soil by cultivation, by the erection of buildings, by all the labor producing permanent results, which it has performed. This additional value evidently constitutes a product—a value created by the activity of the first generation; and if, BY ANY MEANS WHATEVER, the ownership of this value be distributed among the members of society equitably,—that is, in proportion to the labor which each has performed,—each will legitimately possess the portion which he receives. He may then dispose of this legitimate and private property as he sees fit,—exchange it, give it away, or transfer it; and no other individual, or collection of other individuals,—that is, society,—can lay any claim to these values."

Thus, by the distribution of collective capital, to the use of which each associate, either in his own right or in right of his authors, has an imprescriptible and undivided title, there will be in the phalanstery, as in the France of 1841, the poor and the rich; some men who, to live in luxury, have only, as Figaro says, to take the trouble to be born, and others for whom the fortune of life is but an opportunity for long-continued poverty; idlers with large incomes, and workers whose fortune is always in the future; some privileged by birth and caste, and others pariahs whose sole civil and political rights are THE RIGHT TO LABOR, AND THE RIGHT TO LAND. For we must not be deceived; in the phalanstery every thing will be as it is to-day, an object of property,—machines, inventions, thought, books, the products of art, of agriculture, and of industry; animals, houses, fences, vineyards, pastures, forests, fields,—every thing, in short, except the UNCULTIVATED LAND. Now, would you like to know what uncultivated land is worth, according to the advocates of property? "A square league hardly suffices for the support of a savage," says M. Charles Comte. Estimating the wretched subsistence of this savage at three hundred francs per year, we find that the square league necessary to his life is, relatively to him, faithfully represented by a rent of fifteen francs. In France there are twenty-eight thousand square leagues, the total rent of which, by this estimate, would be four hundred and twenty thousand francs, which, when divided among nearly thirty-four millions of people, would give each an INCOME OF A CENTIME AND A QUARTER. That is the new right which the great genius of Fourier has invented IN BEHALF OF THE FRENCH PEOPLE, and with which his first disciple hopes to reform the world. I denounce M. Considerant to the proletariat!

If the theory of M. Considerant would at least really guarantee this property which he cherishes so jealously, I might pardon him the flaws in his syllogism, certainly the best one he ever made in his life. But, no: that which M. Considerant takes for property is only a privilege of extra pay. In Fourier's system, neither the created capital nor the increased value of the soil are divided and appropriated in any effective manner: the instruments of labor, whether created or not, remain in the hands of the phalanx; the pretended proprietor can touch only the income. He is permitted neither to realize his share of the stock, nor to possess it exclusively, nor to administer it, whatever it be. The cashier throws him his dividend; and then, proprietor, eat the whole if you can!

The system of Fourier would not suit the proprietors, since it takes away the most delightful feature of property,—the free disposition of one's goods. It would please the communists no better, since it involves unequal conditions. It is repugnant to the friends of free association and equality, in consequence of its tendency to wipe out human character and individuality by suppressing possession, family, and country,—the threefold expression of the human personality.

Of all our active publicists, none seem to me more fertile in resources, richer in imagination, more luxuriant and varied in style, than M. Considerant. Nevertheless, I doubt if he will undertake to reestablish his theory of property. If he has this courage, this is what I would say to him: "Before writing your reply, consider well your plan of action; do not scour the country; have recourse to none of your ordinary expedients; no complaints of civilization; no sarcasms upon equality; no glorification of the phalanstery. Leave Fourier and the departed in peace, and endeavor only to re-adjust the pieces of your syllogism. To this end, you ought, first, to analyze closely each proposition of your adversary; second, to show the error, either by a direct refutation, or by proving the converse; third, to oppose argument to argument, so that, objection and reply meeting face to face, the stronger may break down the weaker, and shiver it to atoms. By that method only can you boast of having conquered, and compel me to regard you as an honest reasoner, and a good artillery-man."

I should have no excuse for tarrying longer with these phalansterian crotchets, if the obligation which I have imposed upon myself of making a clean sweep, and the necessity of vindicating my dignity as a writer, did not prevent me from passing in silence the reproach uttered against me by a correspondent of "La Phalange." "We have seen but lately," says this journalist, [71] "that M. Proudhon, enthusiast as he has been for the science created by Fourier, is, or will be, an enthusiast for any thing else whatsoever."

If ever sectarians had the right to reproach another for changes in his beliefs, this right certainly does not belong to the disciples of Fourier, who are always so eager to administer the phalansterian baptism to the deserters of all parties. But why regard it as a crime, if they are sincere? Of what consequence is the constancy or inconstancy of an individual to the truth which is always the same? It is better to enlighten men's minds than to teach them to be obstinate in their prejudices. Do we not know that man is frail and fickle, that his heart is full of delusions, and that his lips are a distillery of falsehood? *Omnis homo meudax.* Whether we will or no, we all serve for a time as instruments of this truth, whose kingdom comes every day.

God alone is immutable, because he is eternal.

That is the reply which, as a general rule, an honest man is entitled always to make, and which I ought perhaps to be content to offer as an excuse; for I am no better than my fathers. But, in a century of doubt and apostasy like ours, when it is of importance to set the small and the weak an example of strength and honesty of utterance, I must not suffer my character as a public assailant of property to be dishonored. I must render an account of my old opinions.

Examining myself, therefore, upon this charge of Fourierism, and endeavoring to refresh my memory, I find that, having been connected with the Fourierists in my studies and my friendships, it is possible that, without knowing it, I have been one of Fourier's partisans. Jerome Lalande placed Napoleon and Jesus Christ in his catalogue of atheists. The Fourierists resemble this astronomer: if a man happens to find fault with the existing civilization, and to admit the truth of a few of their criticisms, they straightway enlist him, willy-nilly, in their school. Nevertheless, I do not deny that I have been a Fourierist; for, since they say it, of course it may be so. But, sir, that of which my ex-associates are ignorant, and which doubtless will astonish you, is that I have been many other things,—in religion, by turns a Protestant, a Papist, an Arian and Semi-Arian, a Manichean, a Gnostic, an Adamite even and a Pre-Adamite, a Sceptic, a Pelagian, a Socinian, an Anti-Trinitarian, and a Neo-Christian; [72] in philosophy and politics, an Idealist, a Pantheist, a Platonist, a Cartesian, an Eclectic (that is, a sort of *juste-milieu*), a Monarchist, an Aristocrat, a Constitutionalist, a follower of Babeuf, and a Communist. I have wandered through a whole encyclopaedia of systems. Do you think it surprising, sir, that, among them all, I was for a short time a Fourierist?

For my part, I am not at all surprised, although at present I have no recollection of it. One thing is sure,—that my superstition and credulity reached their height at the very period of my life which my critics reproachfully assign as the date of my Fourieristic beliefs. Now I hold quite other views. My mind no longer admits that which is demonstrated by syllogisms, analogies, or metaphors, which are the methods of the phalanstery, but demands a process of generalization and induction which excludes error. Of my past OPINIONSS I retain absolutely none. I have acquired some KNOWLEDGE. I no longer BELIEVE. I either KNOW, or am IGNORANT. In a word, in seeking for the reason of things, I saw that I was a RATIONALIST.

Undoubtedly, it would have been simpler to begin where I have ended. But then, if such is the law of the human mind; if all society, for six thousand years, has done nothing but fall into error; if all mankind are still buried in the darkness of faith, deceived by their prejudices and passions, guided only by the instinct of their leaders; if my accusers, themselves, are not free from sectarianism (for they call themselves FOURIERISTS),—am I alone inexcusable for having, in my inner self, at the secret tribunal of my conscience, begun anew the journey of our poor humanity?

I would by no means, then, deny my errors; but, sir, that which distinguishes me from those who rush into print is the fact that, though my thoughts have varied much, my writings do not vary. To-day, even, and on a multitude of questions, I am beset by a thousand extravagant and contradictory opinions; but my opinions I do not print, for the public has nothing to do with them. Before addressing my fellow-men, I wait until light breaks in upon the chaos of my ideas, in order that what I may say may be, not the whole truth (no man can know that), but nothing but the truth.

This singular disposition of my mind to first identify itself with a system in order to better understand it, and then to reflect upon it in order to test its legitimacy, is the very thing which disgusted me with Fourier, and ruined in my esteem the societary school. To be a faithful Fourierist, in fact, one must abandon his reason and accept every thing from a master,—

doctrine, interpretation, and application. M. Considerant, whose excessive intolerance anathematizes all who do not abide by his sovereign decisions, has no other conception of Fourierism. Has he not been appointed Fourier's vicar on earth and pope of a Church which, unfortunately for its apostles, will never be of this world? Passive belief is the theological virtue of all sectarians, especially of the Fourierists.

Now, this is what happened to me. While trying to demonstrate by argument the religion of which I had become a follower in studying Fourier, I suddenly perceived that by reasoning I was becoming incredulous; that on each article of the creed my reason and my faith were at variance, and that my six weeks' labor was wholly lost. I saw that the Fourierists—in spite of their inexhaustible gabble, and their extravagant pretension to decide in all things—were neither savants, nor logicians, nor even believers; that they were SCIENTIFIC QUACKS, who were led more by their self-love than their conscience to labor for the triumph of their sect, and to whom all means were good that would reach that end. I then understood why to the Epicureans they promised women, wine, music, and a sea of luxury; to the rigorists, maintenance of marriage, purity of morals, and temperance; to laborers, high wages; to proprietors, large incomes; to philosophers, solutions the secret of which Fourier alone possessed; to priests, a costly religion and magnificent festivals; to savants, knowledge of an unimaginable nature; to each, indeed, that which he most desired. In the beginning, this seemed to me droll; in the end, I regarded it as the height of impudence. No, sir; no one yet knows of the foolishness and infamy which the phalansterian system contains. That is a subject which I mean to treat as soon as I have balanced my accounts with property. 73

It is rumored that the Fourierists think of leaving France and going to the new world to found a phalanstery. When a house threatens to fall, the rats scamper away; that is because they are rats. Men do better; they rebuild it. Not long since, the St. Simonians, despairing of their country which paid no heed to them, proudly shook the dust from their feet, and started for the Orient to fight the battle of free woman. Pride, wilfulness, mad selfishness! True charity, like true faith, does not worry, never despairs; it seeks neither its own glory, nor its interest, nor empire; it does every thing for all, speaks with indulgence to the reason and the will, and desires to conquer only by persuasion and sacrifice. Remain in France, Fourierists, if the progress of humanity is the only thing which you have at heart! There is more to do here than in the new world. Otherwise, go! you are nothing but liars and hypocrites!

The foregoing statement by no means embraces all the political elements, all the opinions and tendencies, which threaten the future of property; but it ought to satisfy any one who knows how to classify facts, and to deduce their law or the idea which governs them. Existing society seems abandoned to the demon of falsehood and discord; and it is this sad sight which grieves so deeply many distinguished minds who lived too long in a former age to be able to understand ours. Now, while the short-sighted spectator begins to despair of humanity, and, distracted and cursing that of which he is ignorant, plunges into scepticism and fatalism, the true observer, certain of the spirit which governs the world, seeks to comprehend and fathom Providence. The memoir on "Property," published last year by the pensioner of the Academy of Besancon, is simply a study of this nature.

The time has come for me to relate the history of this unlucky treatise, which has already caused me so much chagrin, and made me so unpopular; but which was on my part so involuntary and unpremeditated, that I would dare to affirm that there is not an economist, not a philosopher, not a jurist, who is not a hundred times guiltier than I. There is something so singular in the way in which I was led to attack property, that if, on hearing my sad story, you persist, sir, in your blame, I hope at least you will be forced to pity me.

I never have pretended to be a great politician; far from that, I always have felt for controversies of a political nature the greatest aversion; and if, in my "Essay on Property," I have sometimes ridiculed our politicians, believe, sir, that I was governed much less by my pride in the little that I know, than by my vivid consciousness of their ignorance and excessive vanity. Relying more on Providence than on men; not suspecting at first that politics, like every other science, contained an absolute truth; agreeing equally well with Bossuet and Jean Jacques,—I accepted with resignation my share of human misery, and contented myself with praying to God for good deputies, upright ministers, and an honest king. By taste as well as by discretion and lack of confidence in my powers, I was slowly pursuing some commonplace studies in philology, mingled with a little metaphysics, when I suddenly fell upon the greatest problem that ever has occupied philosophical minds: I mean the criterion of certainty.

Those of my readers who are unacquainted with the philosophical terminology will be glad to be told in a few words what this criterion is, which plays so great a part in my work.

The criterion of certainty, according to the philosophers, will be, when discovered, an infallible method of establishing the truth of an opinion, a judgment, a theory, or a system, in nearly the same way as gold is recognized by the touchstone, as iron approaches the magnet, or, better still, as we verify a mathematical operation by applying the PROOF. TIME has hitherto served as a sort of criterion for society. Thus, the primitive men—having observed that they were not all equal in strength, beauty, and labor—judged, and rightly, that certain ones among them were called by nature to the performance of simple and common functions; but they concluded, and this is where their error lay, that these same individuals of duller intellect, more restricted genius, and weaker personality, were predestined to SERVE the others; that is, to labor while the latter rested, and to have no other will than theirs: and from this idea of a natural subordination among men sprang domesticity, which, voluntarily accepted at first, was imperceptibly converted into horrible slavery. Time, making this error more palpable, has brought about justice. Nations have learned at their own cost that the subjection of man to man is a false idea, an erroneous theory, pernicious alike to master and to slave. And yet such a social system has stood several thousand years, and has been defended by celebrated philosophers; even to-day, under somewhat mitigated forms, sophists of every description uphold and extol it. But experience is bringing it to an end.

Time, then, is the criterion of societies; thus looked at, history is the demonstration of the errors of humanity by the argument *reductio ad absurdum*.

Now, the criterion sought for by metaphysicians would have the advantage of discriminating at once between the true and the false in every opinion; so that in politics, religion, and morals, for example, the true and the useful being immediately recognized, we should no longer need to await the sorrowful experience of time. Evidently such a secret would be death to the sophists,—that cursed brood, who, under different names, excite the curiosity of nations, and, owing to the difficulty of separating the truth from the error in their artistically woven theories, lead them into fatal ventures, disturb their peace, and fill them with such extraordinary prejudice.

Up to this day, the criterion of certainty remains a mystery; this is owing to the multitude of criteria that have been successively proposed. Some have taken for an absolute and definite criterion the testimony of the senses; others intuition; these evidence; those argument. M. Lamennais affirms that there is no other criterion than universal reason. Before him, M. de Bonald thought he had discovered it in language. Quite recently, M. Buchez has proposed morality; and, to harmonize them all, the eclectics have said that it was absurd to seek for an absolute criterion, since there were as many criteria as special orders of knowledge.

Of all these hypotheses it may be observed, That the testimony of the senses is not a criterion, because the senses, relating us only to phenomena, furnish us with no ideas; that intuition needs external confirmation or objective certainty; that evidence requires proof, and argument verification; that universal reason has been wrong many a time; that language serves equally well to express the true or the false; that morality, like all the rest, needs demonstration and rule; and finally, that the eclectic idea is the least reasonable of all, since it is of no use to say that there are several criteria if we cannot point out one. I very much fear that it will be with the criterion as with the philosopher's stone; that it will finally be abandoned, not only as insolvable, but as chimerical. Consequently, I entertain no hopes of having found it; nevertheless, I am not sure that some one more skilful will not discover it.

Be it as it may with regard to a criterion or criteria, there are methods of demonstration which, when applied to certain subjects, may lead to the discovery of unknown truths, bring to light relations hitherto unsuspected, and lift a paradox to the highest degree of certainty. In such a case, it is not by its novelty, nor even by its content, that a system should be judged, but by its method. The critic, then, should follow the example of the Supreme Court, which, in the cases which come before it, never examines the facts, but only the form of procedure. Now, what is the form of procedure? A method.

I then looked to see what philosophy, in the absence of a criterion, had accomplished by the aid of special methods, and I must say that I could not discover—in spite of the loudly-proclaimed pretensions of some—that it had produced any thing of real value; and, at last, wearied with the philosophical twaddle, I resolved to make a new search for the criterion. I confess it, to my shame, this folly lasted for two years, and I am not yet entirely rid of it. It was like seeking a needle in a haystack. I might have learned Chinese or Arabic in the time that I have lost in considering and reconsidering syllogisms, in rising to the summit of an induction as to the top of a ladder, in inserting a proposition between the horns of a dilemma, in decomposing, distinguishing, separating, denying, affirming, admitting, as if I could pass abstractions through a sieve.

I selected justice as the subject-matter of my experiments. Finally, after a thousand decompositions, recompositions, and double compositions, I found at the bottom of my analytical crucible, not the criterion of certainty, but a metaphysico-economico-political treatise, whose conclusions were such that I did not care to present them in a more artistic or, if you will, more intelligible form. The effect which this work produced upon all classes of minds gave me an idea of the spirit of our age, and did not cause me to regret the prudent and scientific obscurity of my style. How happens it that to-day I am obliged to defend my intentions, when my conduct bears the evident impress of such lofty morality?

You have read my work, sir, and you know the gist of my tedious and scholastic lucubrations. Considering the revolutions of humanity, the vicissitudes of empires, the transformations of property, and the innumerable forms of justice and of right, I asked, "Are the evils which afflict us inherent in our condition as men, or do they arise only from an error? This inequality of fortunes which all admit to be the cause of society's embarrassments, is it, as some assert, the effect of Nature; or, in the division of the products of labor and the soil, may there not have been some error in calculation? Does each laborer receive all that is due him, and only that which is due him? In short, in the present conditions of labor, wages, and exchange, is no one wronged?—are the accounts well kept?—is the social balance accurate?"

Then I commenced a most laborious investigation. It was necessary to arrange informal notes, to discuss contradictory titles, to reply to captious allegations, to refute absurd pretensions, and to describe fictitious debts, dishonest transactions, and fraudulent accounts. In order to triumph over quibblers, I had to deny the authority of custom, to examine the arguments of legislators, and to oppose science with science itself. Finally, all these operations completed, I had to give a judicial decision.

I therefore declared, my hand upon my heart, before God and men, that the causes of social inequality are three in number: 1. GRATUITOUS APPROPRIATION OF COLLECTIVE WEALTH; 2. INEQUALITY IN EXCHANGE; 3. THE RIGHT OF PROFIT OR INCREASE.

And since this threefold method of extortion is the very essence of the domain of property, I denied the legitimacy of property, and proclaimed its identity with robbery.

That is my only offence. I have reasoned upon property; I have searched for the criterion of justice; I have demonstrated, not the possibility, but the necessity, of equality of fortunes; I have allowed myself no attack upon persons, no assault upon the government, of which I, more than any one else, am a provisional adherent. If I have sometimes used the word PROPRIETOR, I have used it as the abstract name of a metaphysical being, whose reality breathes in every individual,—not alone in a privileged few.

Nevertheless, I acknowledge—for I wish my confession to be sincere—that the general tone of my book has been bitterly censured. They complain of an atmosphere of passion and invective unworthy of an honest man, and quite out of place in the treatment of so grave a subject.

If this reproach is well founded (which it is impossible for me either to deny or admit, because in my own cause I cannot be judge),—if, I say, I deserve this charge, I can only humble myself and acknowledge myself guilty of an involuntary wrong; the only excuse that I could offer being of such a nature that it ought not to be communicated to the public. All that I can say is, that I understand better than any one how the anger which injustice causes may render an author harsh and violent in his criticisms. When, after twenty years of labor, a man still finds himself on the brink of starvation, and then suddenly discovers in an equivocation, an error in calculation, the cause of the evil which torments him in common with so many millions of his fellows, he can scarcely restrain a cry of sorrow and dismay.

But, sir, though pride be offended by my rudeness, it is not to pride that I apologize, but to the proletaires, to the simple-minded, whom I perhaps have scandalized. My angry dialectics may have produced a bad effect on some peaceable minds. Some poor workingman—more affected by my sarcasm than by the strength of my arguments—may, perhaps, have concluded that property is the result of a perpetual Machiavelianism on the part of the governors against the governed,—a deplorable error of which my book itself is the best refutation. I devoted two chapters to showing how property springs from human personality and the comparison of individuals. Then I explained its perpetual limitation; and, following out the same idea, I predicted its approaching disappearance. How, then, could the editors of the "Revue Democratique," after having borrowed from me nearly the whole substance of their economical articles, dare to say: "The holders of the soil, and other productive capital, are more or less wilful accomplices in a vast robbery, they being the exclusive receivers and sharers of the stolen goods"?

The proprietors WILFULLY guilty of the crime of robbery! Never did that homicidal phrase escape my pen; never did my heart conceive the frightful thought. Thank Heaven! I know not how to calumniate my kind; and I have too strong a desire to seek for the reason of things to be willing to believe in criminal conspiracies. The millionnaire is no more tainted by property than the journeyman who works for thirty sous per day. On both sides the error is equal, as well as the intention. The effect is also the same, though positive in the former, and negative in the latter. I accused property; I did not denounce the proprietors, which would have been absurd: and I am sorry that there are among us wills so perverse and minds so shattered that they care for only so much of the truth as will aid them in their evil designs. Such is the only regret which I feel on account of my indignation, which, though expressed perhaps too bitterly, was at least honest, and legitimate in its source.

However, what did I do in this essay which I voluntarily submitted to the Academy of Moral Sciences? Seeking a fixed axiom amid social uncertainties, I traced back to one fundamental question all the secondary questions over which, at present, so keen and diversified a conflict is raging This question was the right of property. Then, comparing all existing theories with each other, and extracting from them that which is common to them all, I endeavored to discover that element in the idea of property which is necessary, immutable, and absolute; and asserted, after authentic verification, that this idea is reducible to that of INDIVIDUAL AND TRANSMISSIBLE POSSESSION; SUSCEPTIBLE OF EXCHANGE, BUT NOT OF ALIENATION; FOUNDED ON LABOR, AND NOT ON FICTITIOUS OCCUPANCY, OR IDLE CAPRICE. I said, further, that this idea was the result of our revolutionary movements,—the culminating point towards which all opinions, gradually divesting themselves of their contradictory elements, converge. And I tried to demonstrate this by the spirit of the laws, by political economy, by psychology and history.

A Father of the Church, finishing a learned exposition of the Catholic doctrine, cried, in the enthusiasm of his faith, *"Domine, si error est, a te decepti sumus* (if my religion is false, God is to blame)." I, as well as this theologian, can say, "If equality is a fable, God, through whom we act and think and are; God, who governs society by eternal laws, who rewards just nations, and punishes proprietors,—God alone is the author of evil; God has lied. The fault lies not with me."

But, if I am mistaken in my inferences, I should be shown my error, and led out of it. It is surely worth the trouble, and I think I deserve this honor. There is no ground for proscription.

For, in the words of that member of the Convention who did not like the guillotine, *to kill is not to reply*. Until then, I persist in regarding my work as useful, social, full of instruction for public officials,—worthy, in short, of reward and encouragement.

For there is one truth of which I am profoundly convinced,—nations live by absolute ideas, not by approximate and partial conceptions; therefore, men are needed who define principles, or at least test them in the fire of controversy. Such is the law,—the idea first, the pure idea, the understanding of the laws of God, the theory: practice follows with slow steps, cautious, attentive to the succession of events; sure to seize, towards this eternal meridian, the indications of supreme reason.

The co-operation of theory and practice produces in humanity the realization of order,—the absolute truth. 74

All of us, as long as we live, are called, each in proportion to his strength, to this sublime work. The only duty which it imposes upon us is to refrain from appropriating the truth to ourselves, either by concealing it, or by accommodating it to the temper of the century, or by using it for our own interests. This principle of conscience, so grand and so simple, has always been present in my thought.

Consider, in fact, sir, that which I might have done, but did not wish to do. I reason on the most honorable hypothesis. What hindered me from concealing, for some years to come, the abstract theory of the equality of fortunes, and, at the same time, from criticising constitutions and codes; from showing the absolute and the contingent, the immutable and the ephemeral, the eternal and the transitory, in laws present and past; from constructing a new system of legislation, and establishing on a solid foundation this social edifice, ever destroyed and as often rebuilt? Might I not, taking up the definitions of casuists, have clearly shown the cause of their contradictions and uncertainties, and supplied, at the same time, the inadequacies of their conclusions? Might I not have confirmed this labor by a vast historical exposition, in which the principle of exclusion, and of the accumulation of property, the appropriation of collective wealth, and the radical vice in exchanges, would have figured as the constant causes of tyranny, war, and revolution?

"It should have been done," you say. Do not doubt, sir, that such a task would have required more patience than genius. With the principles of social economy which I have analyzed, I would have had only to break the ground, and follow the furrow. The critic of laws finds nothing more difficult than to determine justice: the labor alone would have been longer. Oh, if I had pursued this glittering prospect, and, like the man of the burning bush, with inspired countenance and deep and solemn voice, had presented myself some day with new tables, there would have been found fools to admire, boobies to applaud, and cowards to offer me the dictatorship; for, in the way of popular infatuations, nothing is impossible.

But, sir, after this monument of insolence and pride, what should I have deserved in your opinion, at the tribunal of God, and in the judgment of free men? Death, sir, and eternal reprobation!

I therefore spoke the truth as soon as I saw it, waiting only long enough to give it proper expression. I pointed out error in order that each might reform himself, and render his labors more useful. I announced the existence of a new political element, in order that my associates in reform, developing it in concert, might arrive more promptly at that unity of principles which alone can assure to society a better day. I expected to receive, if not for my book, at least for my commendable conduct, a small republican ovation. And, behold! journalists denounce me, academicians curse me, political adventurers (great God!) think to make themselves tolerable by protesting that they are not like me! I give the formula by which the whole social edifice may be scientifically reconstructed, and the strongest minds reproach me for being able only to destroy. The rest despise me, because I am unknown. When the "Essay on Property" fell into the reformatory camp, some asked: "Who has spoken? Is it Arago? Is it Lamennais? Michel de Bourges or Garnier-Pages?"

And when they heard the name of a new man: "We do not know him," they would reply. Thus, the monopoly of thought, property in reason, oppresses the proletariat as well as the *bourgeoisie*. The worship of the infamous prevails even on the steps of the tabernacle.

But what am I saying? May evil befall me, if I blame the poor creatures! Oh! let us not despise those generous souls, who in the excitement of their patriotism are always prompt to identify the voice of their chiefs with the truth. Let us encourage rather their simple credulity, enlighten complacently and tenderly their precious sincerity, and reserve our shafts for those vain-glorious spirits who are always admiring their genius, and, in different tongues, caressing the people in order to govern them.

These considerations alone oblige me to reply to the strange and superficial conclusions of the "Journal du Peuple" (issue of Oct. 11, 1840), on the question of property. I leave, therefore, the journalist to address myself only to his readers. I hope that the self-love of the writer will not be offended, if, in the presence of the masses, I ignore an individual.

You say, proletaires of the "Peuple," "For the very reason that men and things exist, there always will be men who will possess things; nothing, therefore, can destroy property."

In speaking thus, you unconsciously argue exactly after the manner of M. Cousin, who always reasons from *possession* to PROPERTY. This coincidence, however, does not surprise me. M. Cousin is a philosopher of much mind, and you, proletaires, have still more. Certainly it is honorable, even for a philosopher, to be your companion in error.

Originally, the word PROPERTY was synonymous with PROPER or INDIVIDUAL POSSESSION. It designated each individual's special right to the use of a thing. But when this right of use, inert (if I may say so) as it was with regard to the other usufructuaries, became active and paramount,—that is, when the usufructuary converted his right to personally use the thing into the right to use it by his neighbor's labor,—then property changed its nature, and its idea became complex. The legists knew this very well, but instead of opposing, as they ought, this accumulation of profits, they accepted and sanctioned the whole. And as the right of farm-rent necessarily implies the right of use,—in other words, as the right to cultivate land by the labor of a slave supposes one's power to cultivate it himself, according to the principle that the greater includes the less,—the name property was reserved to designate this double right, and that of possession was adopted to designate the right of use.

Whence property came to be called the perfect right, the right of domain, the eminent right, the heroic or *quiritaire* right,—in Latin, *jus perfectum, jus optimum, jus quiritarium, jus dominii*,—while possession became assimilated to farm-rent.

Now, that individual possession exists of right, or, better, from natural necessity, all philosophers admit, and can easily e demonstrated; but when, in imitation of M. Cousin, we assume it to be the basis of the domain of property, we fall into the sophism called *sophisma amphiboliae vel ambiguitatis*, which consists in changing the meaning by a verbal equivocation.

People often think themselves very profound, because, by the aid of expressions of extreme generality, they appear to rise to the height of absolute ideas, and thus deceive inexperienced minds; and, what is worse, this is commonly called EXAMINING ABSTRACTIONS. But the abstraction formed by the comparison of identical facts is one thing, while that which is deduced from different acceptations of the same term is quite another. The first gives the universal idea, the axiom, the law; the second indicates the order of generation of ideas. All our errors arise from the constant confusion of these two kinds of abstractions. In this particular, languages and philosophies are alike deficient. The less common an idiom is, and the more obscure its terms, the more prolific is it as a source of error: a philosopher is sophistical in proportion to his ignorance of any method of neutralizing this imperfection in language. If the art of correcting the errors of speech by scientific methods is ever discovered, then philosophy will have found its criterion of certainty.

Now, then, the difference between property and possession being well established, and it being settled that the former, for the reasons which I have just given, must necessarily disappear, is it best, for the slight advantage of restoring an etymology, to retain the word PROPERTY? My opinion is that it would be very unwise to do so, and I will tell why. I quote from the "Journal du Peuple:"—

"To the legislative power belongs the right to regulate property, to prescribe the conditions of acquiring, possessing, and transmitting it... It cannot be denied that inheritance, assessment, commerce, industry, labor, and wages require the most important modifications."

You wish, proletaires, to REGULATE PROPERTY; that is, you wish to destroy it and reduce it to the right of possession. For to regulate property without the consent of the proprietors is to deny the right OF DOMAIN; to associate employees with proprietors is to destroy the EMINENT right; to suppress or even reduce farm-rent, house-rent, revenue, and increase generally, is to annihilate PERFECT property. Why, then, while laboring with such laudable enthusiasm for the establishment of equality, should you retain an expression whose equivocal meaning will always be an obstacle in the way of your success?

There you have the first reason—a wholly philosophical one—for rejecting not only the thing, but the name, property.

Here now is the political, the highest reason.

Every social revolution—M. Cousin will tell you—is effected only by the realization of an idea, either political, moral, or religious. When Alexander conquered Asia, his idea was to avenge Greek liberty against the insults of Oriental despotism; when Marius and Caesar overthrew the Roman patricians, their idea was to give bread to the people; when Christianity revolutionized the world, its idea was to emancipate mankind, and to substitute the worship of one God for the deities of Epicurus and Homer; when France rose in '89, her idea was liberty and equality before the law. There has been no true revolution, says M. Cousin, with out its idea; so that where an idea does not exist, or even fails of a formal expression, revolution is impossible. There are mobs, conspirators, rioters, regicides. There are no revolutionists. Society, devoid of ideas, twists and tosses about, and dies in the midst of its fruitless labor.

Nevertheless, you all feel that a revolution is to come, and that you alone can accomplish it. What, then, is the idea which governs you, proletaires of the nineteenth century?—for really I cannot call you revolutionists. What do you think?—what do you believe?—what do you want? Be guarded in your reply. I have read faithfully your favorite journals, your most esteemed authors. I find everywhere only vain and puerile *entites*; nowhere do I discover an idea.

I will explain the meaning of this word *entite*,—new, without doubt, to most of you.

By *entite* is generally understood a substance which the imagination grasps, but which is incognizable by the senses and the reason. Thus the SOPORIFIC POWER of opium, of which Sganarelle speaks, and the PECCANT HUMORS of ancient medicine, are *entites*. The *entite* is the support of those who do not wish to confess their ignorance. It is incomprehensible; or, as St. Paul says, the *argumentum non apparentium*. In philosophy, the *entite* is often only a repetition of words which add nothing to the thought.

For example, when M. Pierre Leroux—who says so many excellent things, but who is too fond, in my opinion, of his Platonic formulas—assures us that the evils of humanity are due to our IGNORANCE OF LIFE, M. Pierre Leroux utters an *entite;* for it is evident that if we are evil it is because we do not know how to live; but the knowledge of this fact is of no value to us.

When M. Edgar Quinet declares that France suffers and declines because there is an ANTAGONISM of men and of interests, he declares an *entite;* for the problem is to discover the cause of this antagonism.

When M. Lamennais, in thunder tones, preaches self-sacrifice and love, he proclaims two *entites;* for we need to know on what conditions self-sacrifice and love can spring up and exist.

So also, proletaires, when you talk of LIBERTY, PROGRESS, and THE SOVEREIGNTY OF THE PEOPLE, you make of these naturally intelligible things so many *entites* in space: for, on the one hand, we need a new definition of liberty, since that of '89 no longer suffices; and, on the other, we must know in what direction society should proceed in order to be in progress. As for the sovereignty of the people, that is a grosser *entite* than the sovereignty of reason; it is the *entite* of *entites*. In fact, since sovereignty can no more be conceived of outside of the people than outside of reason, it remains to be ascertained who, among the people, shall exercise the sovereignty; and, among so many minds, which shall be the sovereigns. To say that the people should elect their representatives is to say that the people should recognize their sovereigns, which does not remove the difficulty at all.

But suppose that, equal by birth, equal before the law, equal in personality, equal in social functions, you wish also to be equal in conditions.

Suppose that, perceiving all the mutual relations of men, whether they produce or exchange or consume, to be relations of commutative justice,—in a word, social relations; suppose, I say, that, perceiving this, you wish to give this natural society a legal existence, and to establish the fact by law,—

I say that then you need a clear, positive, and exact expression of your whole idea,—that is, an expression which states at once the principle, the means, and the end; and I add that that expression is ASSOCIATION.

And since the association of the human race dates, at least rightfully, from the beginning of the world, and has gradually established and perfected itself by successively divesting itself of its negative elements, slavery, nobility, despotism, aristocracy, and feudalism,—I say that, to eliminate the last negation of society, to formulate the last revolutionary idea, you must change your old rallying-cries, NO MORE ABSOLUTISM, NO MORE NOBILITY, NO MORE SLAVES! into that of NO MORE PROPERTY!...

But I know what astonishes you, poor souls, blasted by the wind of poverty, and crushed by your patrons' pride: it is EQUALITY, whose consequences frighten you. How, you have said in your journal,—how can we "dream of a level which, being unnatural, is therefore unjust? How shall we pay the day's labor of a Cormenin or a Lamennais?"

Plebeians, listen! When, after the battle of Salamis, the Athenians assembled to award the prizes for courage, after the ballots had been collected, it was found that each combatant had one vote for the first prize, and Themistocles all the votes for the second. The people of Minerva were crowned by their own hands. Truly heroic souls! all were worthy of the olive-branch, since all had ventured to claim it for themselves. Antiquity praised this sublime spirit. Learn, proletaires, to esteem yourselves, and to respect your dignity. You wish to be free, and you know not how to be citizens. Now, whoever says "citizens" necessarily says equals.

If I should call myself Lamennais or Cormenin, and some journal, speaking of me, should burst forth with these hyperboles, INCOMPARABLE GENIUS, SUPERIOR MIND, CONSUMMATE VIRTUE, NOBLE CHARACTER, I should not like it, and should complain,—first, because such eulogies are never deserved; and, second, because they furnish a bad example. But I wish, in order to reconcile you to equality, to measure for you the greatest literary personage of our century. Do not accuse me of envy, proletaires, if I, a defender of equality, estimate at their proper value talents which are universally admired, and which I, better than any one, know how to recognize. A dwarf can always measure a giant: all that he needs is a yardstick.

You have seen the pretentious announcements of "L'Esquisse d'une Philosophie," and you have admired the work on trust; for either you have not read it, or, if you have, you are incapable of judging it. Acquaint yourselves, then, with this speculation more brilliant than sound; and, while admiring the enthusiasm of the author, cease to pity those useful labors which only habit and the great number of the persons engaged in them render contemptible. I shall be brief; for, notwithstanding the importance of the subject and the genius of the author, what I have to say is of but little moment.

M. Lamennais starts with the existence of God. How does he demonstrate it? By Cicero's argument,—that is, by the consent of the human race. There is nothing new in that. We have still to find out whether the belief of the human race is legitimate; or, as Kant says, whether our subjective certainty of the existence of God corresponds with the objective truth. This, however, does not trouble M. Lamennais. He says that, if the human race believes, it is because it has a reason for believing.

Then, having pronounced the name of God, M. Lamennais sings a hymn; and that is his demonstration!

This first hypothesis admitted, M. Lamennais follows it with a second; namely, that there are three persons in God. But, while Christianity teaches the dogma of the Trinity only on the authority of revelation, M. Lamennais pretends to arrive at it by the sole force of argument; and he does not perceive that his pretended demonstration is, from beginning to end, anthropomorphism,—that is, an ascription of the faculties of the human mind and the powers of nature to the Divine substance. New songs, new hymns!

God and the Trinity thus DEMONSTRATED, the philosopher passes to the creation,—a third hypothesis, in which M. Lamennais, always eloquent, varied, and sublime, DEMONSTRATES that God made the world neither of nothing, nor of something, nor of himself; that he was free in creating, but that nevertheless he could not but create; that there is in matter a matter which is not matter; that the archetypal ideas of the world are separated from each other, in the Divine mind, by a division which is obscure and unintelligible, and yet substantial and real, which involves intelligibility, &c. We meet with like contradictions concerning the origin of evil. To explain this problem,—one of the profoundest in philosophy,—M. Lamennais at one time denies evil, at another makes God the author of evil, and at still another seeks outside of God a first cause which is not God,—an amalgam of *entites* more or less incoherent, borrowed from Plato, Proclus, Spinoza, I might say even from all philosophers.

Having thus established his trinity of hypotheses, M. Lamennais deduces therefrom, by a badly connected chain of analogies, his whole philosophy. And it is here especially that we notice the syncretism which is peculiar to him. The theory of M. Lamennais embraces all systems, and supports all opinions. Are you a materialist? Suppress, as useless *entites*, the three persons in God; then, starting directly from heat, light, and electro-magnetism,—which, according to the author, are the three original fluids, the three primary external manifestations of Will, Intelligence, and Love,—you have a materialistic and atheistic cosmogony. On the contrary, are you wedded to spiritualism? With the theory of the immateriality of the body, you are able to see everywhere nothing but spirits. Finally, if you incline to pantheism, you will be satisfied by M. Lamennais, who formally teaches that the world is not an EMANATION from Divinity,—which is pure pantheism,—but a FLOW of Divinity.

I do not pretend, however, to deny that "L'Esquisse" contains some excellent things; but, by the author's declaration, these things are not original with him; it is the system which is his. That is undoubtedly the reason why M. Lamennais speaks so contemptuously of his predecessors in philosophy, and disdains to quote his originals. He thinks that, since "L'Esquisse" contains all true philosophy, the world will lose nothing when the names and works of the old philosophers perish. M. Lamennais, who renders glory to God in beautiful songs, does not know how as well to render justice to his fellows. His fatal fault is this appropriation of knowledge, which the theologians call the PHILOSOPHICAL SIN, or the SIN AGAINST THE HOLY GHOST—a sin which will not damn you, proletaires, nor me either.

In short, "L'Esquisse," judged as a system, and divested of all which its author borrows from previous systems, is a commonplace work, whose method consists in constantly explaining the known by the unknown, and in giving entites for abstractions, and tautologies for proofs. Its whole theodicy is a work not of genius but of imagination, a patching up of neo-Platonic ideas. The psychological portion amounts to nothing, M. Lamennais openly ridiculing labors of this character, without which, however, metaphysics is impossible. The book, which treats of logic and its methods, is weak, vague, and shallow. Finally, we find in the physical and physiological speculations which M. Lamennais deduces from his trinitarian cosmogony grave errors, the preconceived design of accommodating facts to theory, and the substitution in almost every case of hypothesis for reality. The third volume on industry and art is the most interesting to read, and the best. It is true that M. Lamennais can boast of nothing but his style. As a philosopher, he has added not a single idea to those which existed before him.

Why, then, this excessive mediocrity of M. Lamennais considered as a thinker, a mediocrity which disclosed itself at the time of the publication of the "Essai sur l'Indifference!"? It is because (remember this well, proletaires!) Nature makes no man truly complete, and because the development of certain faculties almost always excludes an equal development of the opposite faculties; it is because M. Lamennais is preeminently a poet, a man of feeling and sentiment. Look at his style,—exuberant, sonorous, picturesque, vehement, full of exaggeration and invective,—and hold it for certain that no man possessed of such a style was ever a true metaphysician. This wealth of expression and illustration, which everybody admires, becomes in M Lamennais the incurable cause of his philosophical impotence. His flow of language, and his sensitive nature misleading his imagination, he thinks that he is reasoning when he is only repeating himself, and readily takes a description for a logical deduction. Hence his horror of positive ideas, his feeble powers of analysis, his pronounced taste for indefinite analogies, verbal abstractions, hypothetical generalities, in short, all sorts of entites.

Further, the entire life of M. Lamennais is conclusive proof of his anti-philosophical genius. Devout even to mysticism, an ardent ultramontane, an intolerant theocrat, he at first feels the double influence of the religious reaction and the literary theories which marked the beginning of this century, and falls back to the middle ages and Gregory VII.; then, suddenly becoming a progressive Christian and a democrat, he gradually leans towards rationalism, and finally falls into deism. At present, everybody waits at the trap-door. As for me, though I would not swear to it, I am inclined to think that M. Lamennais, already taken with scepticism, will die in a state of indifference. He owes to individual reason and methodical doubt this expiation of his early essays.

It has been pretended that M. Lamennais, preaching now a theocracy, now universal democracy, has been always consistent; that, under different names, he has sought invariably one and the same thing,—unity. Pitiful excuse for an author surprised in the very act of contradiction! What would be thought of a man who, by turns a servant of despotism under Louis XVI, a demagogue with Robespierre, a courtier of the Emperor, a bigot during fifteen years of the Restoration, a conservative since 1830, should dare to say that he ever had wished for but one thing,—public order? Would he be regarded as any the less a renegade from all parties? Public order, unity, the world's welfare, social harmony, the union of the nations,—concerning each of these things there is no possible difference of opinion. Everybody wishes them; the character of the publicist depends only upon the means by which he proposes to arrive at them. But why look to M. Lamennais for a steadfastness of opinion, which he himself repudiates? Has he not said, "The mind has no law; that which I believe to-day, I did not believe yesterday; I do not know that I shall believe it to-morrow"?

No; there is no real superiority among men, since all talents and capacities are combined never in one individual. This man has the power of thought, that one imagination and style, still another industrial and commercial capacity. By our very nature and education, we possess only special aptitudes which are limited and confined, and which become consequently more necessary as they gain in depth and strength. Capacities are to each other as functions and persons; who would dare to classify them in ranks? The finest genius is, by the laws of his existence and development, the most dependent upon the society which creates him. Who would dare to make a god of the glorious child?

"It is not strength which makes the man," said a Hercules of the market-place to the admiring crowd; "it is character." That man, who had only his muscles, held force in contempt. The lesson is a good one, proletaires; we should profit by it. It is not talent (which is also a force), it is not knowledge, it is not beauty which makes the man. It is heart, courage, will, virtue. Now, if we are equal in that which makes us men, how can the accidental distribution of secondary faculties detract from our manhood?

Remember that privilege is naturally and inevitably the lot of the weak; and do not be misled by the fame which accompanies certain talents whose greatest merit consists in their rarity, and a long and toilsome apprenticeship. It is easier for M. Lamennais to recite a philippic, or sing a humanitarian ode after the Platonic fashion, than to discover a single useful truth; it is easier for an economist to apply the laws of production and distribution than to write ten lines in the style of M. Lamennais; it is easier for both to speak than to act. You, then, who put your hands to the work, who alone truly create, why do you wish me to admit your inferiority? But, what am I saying?

Yes, you are inferior, for you lack virtue and will! Ready for labor and for battle, you have, when liberty and equality are in question, neither courage nor character!

In the preface to his pamphlet on "Le Pays et le Gouvernement," as well as in his defence before the jury, M. Lamennais frankly declared himself an advocate of property. Out of regard for the author and his misfortune, I shall abstain from characterizing this declaration, and from examining these two sorrowful performances. M. Lamennais seems to be only the tool of a quasi-radical party, which flatters him in order to use him, without respect for a glorious, but henceforth powerless, old age. What means this profession of faith? From the first number of "L'Avenir" to "L'Esquisse d'une Philosophie," M. Lamennais always favors equality, association, and even a sort of vague and indefinite communism. M. Lamennais, in recognizing the right of property, gives the lie to his past career, and renounces his most generous tendencies. Can it, then, be true that in this man, who has been too roughly treated, but who is also too easily flattered, strength of talent has already outlived strength of will?

It is said that M. Lamennais has rejected the offers of several of his friends to try to procure for him a commutation of his sentence. M. Lamennais prefers to serve out his time. May not this affectation of a false stoicism come from the same source as his recognition of the right of property? The Huron, when taken prisoner, hurls insults and threats at his conqueror,—that is the heroism of the savage; the martyr prays for his executioners, and is willing to receive from them his life,—that is the heroism of the Christian. Why has the apostle of love become an apostle of anger and revenge? Has, then, the translator of "L'Imitation" forgotten that he who offends charity cannot honor virtue? Galileo, retracting on his knees before the tribunal of the inquisition his heresy in regard to the movement of the earth, and recovering at that price his liberty, seems to me a hundred times grander than M. Lamennais. What! if we suffer for truth and justice, must we, in retaliation, thrust our persecutors outside the pale of human society; and, when sentenced to an unjust punishment, must we decline exemption if it is offered to us, because it pleases a few base satellites to call it a pardon? Such is not the wisdom of Christianity. But I forgot that in the presence of M. Lamennais this name is no longer pronounced. May the prophet of "L'Avenir" be soon restored to liberty and his friends; but, above all, may he henceforth derive his inspiration only from his genius and his heart!

O proletaires, proletaires! how long are you to be victimized by this spirit of revenge and implacable hatred which your false friends kindle, and which, perhaps, has done more harm to the development of reformatory ideas than the corruption, ignorance, and malice of the government? Believe me, at the present time everybody is to blame. In fact, in intention, or in example, all are found wanting; and you have no right to accuse any one. The king himself (God forgive me! I do not like to justify a king),—the king himself is, like his predecessors, only the personification of an idea, and an idea, proletaires, which possesses you yet. His greatest wrong consists in wishing for its complete realization, while you wish it realized only partially,—consequently, in being logical in his government; while you, in your complaints, are not at all so. You clamor for a second regicide. He that is without sin among you,—let him cast at the prince of property the first stone!

How successful you would have been if, in order to influence men, you had appealed to the self-love of men,—if, in order to alter the constitution and the law, you had placed yourselves within the constitution and the law! Fifty thousand laws, they say, make up our political and civil codes. Of these fifty thousand laws, twenty-five thousand are for you, twenty-five thousand against you. Is it not clear that your duty is to oppose the former to the latter, and thus, by the argument of contradiction, drive privilege into its last ditch? This method of action is henceforth the only useful one, being the only moral and rational one.

For my part, if I had the ear of this nation, to which I am attached by birth and predilection, with no intention of playing the leading part in the future republic, I would instruct the laboring masses to conquer property through institutions and judicial pleadings; to seek auxiliaries and accomplices in the highest ranks of society, and to ruin all privileged classes by taking advantage of their common desire for power and popularity.

The petition for the electoral reform has already received two hundred thousand signatures, and the illustrious Arago threatens us with a million. Surely, that will be well done; but from this million of citizens, who are as willing to vote for an emperor as for equality, could we not select ten thousand signatures—I mean bona fide signatures—whose authors can read, write, cipher, and even think a little, and whom we could invite, after due perusal and verbal explanation, to sign such a petition as the following:—

"TO HIS EXCELLENCY THE MINISTER OF THE INTERIOR:—

"MONSIEUR LE MINISTRE,—On the day when a royal ordinance, decreeing the establishment of model national workshops, shall appear in the 'Moniteur,' the undersigned, to the number of TEN THOUSAND, will repair to the Palace of the Tuileries, and there, with all the power of their lungs, will shout, 'Long live Louis Philippe!'

"On the day when the 'Moniteur' shall inform the public that this petition is refused, the undersigned, to the number of TEN THOUSAND, will say secretly in their hearts, 'Down with Louis Philippe!'"

If I am not mistaken, such a petition would have some effect.[75] The pleasure of a popular ovation would be well worth the sacrifice of a few millions. They sow so much to reap unpopularity! Then, if the nation, its hopes of 1830 restored, should feel it its duty to keep its promise,—and it would keep it, for the word of the nation is, like that of God, sacred,—if, I say, the nation, reconciled by this act with the public-spirited monarchy, should bear to the foot of the throne its cheers and its vows, and should at that solemn moment choose me to speak in its name, the following would be the substance of my speech:—

"SIRE,—This is what the nation wishes to say to your Majesty:—

"O King! you see what it costs to gain the applause of the citizens. Would you like us henceforth to take for our motto: 'Let us help the King, the King will help us'? Do you wish the people to cry: 'THE KING AND THE FRENCH NATION'? Then abandon these grasping bankers, these quarrelsome lawyers, these miserable bourgeois, these infamous writers, these dishonored men. All these, Sire, hate you, and continue to support you only because they fear us. Finish the work of our kings; wipe out aristocracy and privilege; consult with these faithful proletaires, with the nation, which alone can honor a sovereign and sincerely shout, 'Long live the king!'"

The rest of what I have to say, sir, is for you alone; others would not understand me. You are, I perceive, a republican as well as an economist, and your patriotism revolts at the very idea of addressing to the authorities a petition in which the government of Louis Philippe should be tacitly recognized. "National workshops! it were well to have such institutions established," you think; "but patriotic hearts never will accept them from an aristocratic ministry, nor by the courtesy of a king." Already, undoubtedly, your old prejudices have returned, and you now regard me only as a sophist, as ready to flatter the powers that be as to dishonor, by pushing them to an extreme, the principles of equality and universal fraternity.

What shall I say to you?... That I should so lightly compromise the future of my theories, either this clever sophistry which is attributed to me must be at bottom a very trifling affair, or else my convictions must be so firm that they deprive me of free-will.

But, not to insist further on the necessity of a compromise between the executive power and the people, it seems to me, sir, that, in doubting my patriotism, you reason very capriciously, and that your judgments are exceedingly rash. You, sir, ostensibly defending government and property, are allowed to be a republican, reformer, phalansterian, any thing you wish; I, on the contrary, demanding distinctly enough a slight reform in public economy, am foreordained a conservative, and likewise a friend of the dynasty. I cannot explain myself more clearly. So firm a believer am I in the philosophy of accomplished facts and the *statu quo* of governmental forms that, instead of destroying that which exists and beginning over again the past, I prefer to render every thing legitimate by correcting it. It is true that the corrections which I propose, though respecting the form, tend to finally change the nature of the things corrected. Who denies it? But it is precisely that which constitutes my system of *statu quo*. I make no war upon symbols, figures, or phantoms. I respect scarecrows, and bow before bugbears. I ask, on the one hand, that property be left as it is, but that interest on all kinds of capital be gradually lowered and finally abolished; on the other hand, that the charter be maintained in its present shape, but that method be introduced into administration and politics. That is all. Nevertheless, submitting to all that is, though not satisfied with it, I endeavor to conform to the established order, and to render unto Caesar the things that are Caesar's. Is it thought, for instance, that I love property?... Very well; I am myself a proprietor and do homage to the right of increase, as is proved by the fact that I have creditors to whom I faithfully pay, every year, a large amount of interest. The same with politics. Since we are a monarchy, I would cry, "LONG LIVE THE KING," rather than suffer death; which does not prevent me, however, from demanding that the irremovable, inviolable, and hereditary representative of the nation shall act with the proletaires against the privileged classes; in a word, that the king shall become the leader of the radical party. Thereby we proletaires would gain every thing; and I am sure that, at this price, Louis Philippe might secure to his family the perpetual presidency of the republic. And this is why I think so.

If there existed in France but one great functional inequality, the duty of the functionary being, from one end of the year to the other, to hold full court of savants, artists, soldiers, deputies, inspectors, &c., it is evident that the expenses of the presidency then would be the national expenses; and that, through the reversion of the civil list to the mass of consumers, the great inequality of which I speak would form an exact equation with the whole nation. Of this no economist needs a demonstration. Consequently, there would be no more fear of cliques, courtiers, and appanages, since no new inequality could be established. The king, as king, would have friends (unheard-of thing), but no family. His relatives or kinsmen, —*agnats et cognats*,—if they were fools, would be nothing to him; and in no case, with the exception of the heir apparent, would they have, even in court, more privileges than others. No more nepotism, no more favor, no more baseness. No one would go to court save when duty required, or when called by an honorable distinction; and as all conditions would be equal and all functions equally honored, there would be no other emulation than that of merit and virtue. I wish the king of the French could say without shame, "My brother the gardener, my sister-in-law the milk-maid, my son the prince-royal, and my son the blacksmith." His daughter might well be an artist. That would be beautiful, sir; that would be royal; no one but a buffoon could fail to understand it.

In this way, I have come to think that the forms of royalty may be made to harmonize with the requirements of equality, and have given a monarchical form to my republican spirit. I have seen that France contains by no means as many democrats as is generally supposed, and I have compromised with the monarchy. I do not say, however, that, if France wanted a republic, I could not accommodate myself equally well, and perhaps better. By nature, I hate all signs of distinction, crosses of honor, gold lace, liveries, costumes, honorary titles, &c., and, above all, parades. If I had my way, no general should be distinguished from a soldier, nor a peer of France from a peasant. Why have I never taken part in a review? for I am happy to say, sir, that I am a national guard; I have nothing else in the world but that. Because the review is always held at a place which I do not like, and because they have fools for officers whom I am compelled to obey. You see, —and this is not the best of my history,—that, in spite of my conservative opinions, my life is a perpetual sacrifice to the republic.

Nevertheless, I doubt if such simplicity would be agreeable to French vanity, to that inordinate love of distinction and flattery which makes our nation the most frivolous in the world. M. Lamartine, in his grand "Meditation on Bonaparte," calls the French A NATION OF BRUTUSES. We are merely a nation of Narcissuses. Previous to '89, we had the aristocracy of blood; then every bourgeois looked down upon the commonalty, and wished to be a nobleman. Afterwards, distinction was based on wealth, and the bourgeoisie jealous of the nobility, and proud of their money, used 1830 to promote, not liberty by any means, but the aristocracy of wealth. When, through the force of events, and the natural laws of society, for the development of which France offers such free play, equality shall be established in functions and fortunes, then the beaux and the belles, the savants and the artists, will form new classes. There is a universal and innate desire in this Gallic country for fame and glory. We must have distinctions, be they what they may,—nobility, wealth, talent, beauty, or dress. I suspect MM. Arage and Garnier-Pages of having aristocratic manners, and I picture to myself our great journalists, in their columns so friendly to the people, administering rough kicks to the compositors in their printing offices.

"This man," once said "Le National" in speaking of Carrel, "whom we had proclaimed FIRST CONSUL!... Is it not true that the monarchical principle still lives in the hearts of our democrats, and that they want universal suffrage in order to make themselves kings? Since "Le National" prides itself on holding more fixed opinions than "Le Journal des Debats," I presume that, Armand Carrel being dead, M. Armand Marrast is now first consul, and M. Garnier-Pages second consul. In every thing the deputy must give way to the journalist. I do not speak of M. Arago, whom I believe to be, in spite of calumny, too learned for the consulship. Be it so. Though we have consuls, our position is not much altered. I am ready to yield my share of sovereignty to MM. Armand Marrast and Garnier-Pages, the appointed consuls, provided they will swear on entering upon the duties of their office, to abolish property and not be haughty.

Forever promises! Forever oaths! Why should the people trust in tribunes, when kings perjure themselves? Alas! truth and honesty are no longer, as in the days of King John, in the mouth of princes. A whole senate has been convicted of felony, and, the interest of the governors always being, for some mysterious reason, opposed to the interest of the governed, parliaments follow each other while the nation dies of hunger. No, no! No more protectors, no more emperors, no more consuls. Better manage our affairs ourselves than through agents. Better associate our industries than beg from monopolies; and, since the republic cannot dispense with virtues, we should labor for our reform.

This, therefore, is my line of conduct. I preach emancipation to the proletaires; association to the laborers; equality to the wealthy. I push forward the revolution by all means in my power,—the tongue, the pen, the press, by action, and example. My life is a continual apostleship.

Yes, I am a reformer; I say it as I think it, in good faith, and that I may be no longer reproached for my vanity. I wish to convert the world. Very likely this fancy springs from an enthusiastic pride which may have turned to delirium; but it will be admitted at least that I have plenty of company, and that my madness is not monomania. At the present day, everybody wishes to be reckoned among the lunatics of Beranger. To say nothing of the Babeufs, the Marats, and the Robespierres, who swarm in our streets and workshops, all the great reformers of antiquity live again in the most illustrious personages of our time. One is Jesus Christ, another Moses, a third Mahomet; this is Orpheus, that Plato, or Pythagoras. Gregory VII., himself, has risen from the grave together with the evangelists and the apostles; and it may turn out that even I am that slave who, having escaped from his master's house, was forthwith made a bishop and a reformer by St. Paul. As for the virgins and holy women, they are expected daily; at present, we have only Aspasias and courtesans.

Now, as in all diseases, the diagnostic varies according to the temperament, so my madness has its peculiar aspects and distinguishing characteristic.

Reformers, as a general thing, are jealous of their role; they suffer no rivals, they want no partners; they have disciples, but no co-laborers. It is my desire, on the contrary, to communicate my enthusiasm, and to make it, as far as I can, epidemic. I wish that all were, like myself, reformers, in order that there might be no more sects; and that Christs, Anti-Christs, and false Christs might be forced to understand and agree with each other.

Again, every reformer is a magician, or at least desires to become one. Thus Moses, Jesus Christ, and the apostles, proved their mission by miracles. Mahomet ridiculed miracles after having endeavored to perform them. Fourier, more cunning, promises us wonders when the globe shall be covered with phalansteries. For myself, I have as great a horror of miracles as of authorities, and aim only at logic. That is why I continually search after the criterion of certainty. I work for the reformation of ideas. Little matters it that they find me dry and austere. I mean to conquer by a bold struggle, or die in the attempt; and whoever shall come to the defence of property, I swear that I will force him to argue like M. Considerant, or philosophize like M. Troplong.

Finally,—and it is here that I differ most from my compeers,—I do not believe it necessary, in order to reach equality, to turn every thing topsy-turvy. To maintain that nothing but an overturn can lead to reform is, in my judgment, to construct a syllogism, and to look for the truth in the regions of the unknown. Now, I am for generalization, induction, and progress. I regard general disappropriation as impossible: attacked from that point, the problem of universal association seems to me insolvable. Property is like the dragon which Hercules killed: to destroy it, it must be taken, not by the head, but by the tail,—that is, by profit and interest.

I stop. I have said enough to satisfy any one who can read and understand. The surest way by which the government can baffle intrigues and break up parties is to take possession of science, and point out to the nation, at an already appreciable distance, the rising oriflamme of equality; to say to those politicians of the tribune and the press, for whose fruitless quarrels we pay so dearly, "You are rushing forward, blind as you are, to the abolition of property; but the government marches with its eyes open. You hasten the future by unprincipled and insincere controversy; but the government, which knows this future, leads you thither by a happy and peaceful transition. The present generation will not pass away before France, the guide and model of civilized nations, has regained her rank and legitimate influence."

But, alas! the government itself,—who shall enlighten it? Who can induce it to accept this doctrine of equality, whose terrible but decisive formula the most generous minds hardly dare to acknowledge?... I feel my whole being tremble when I think that the testimony of three men—yes, of three men who make it their business to teach and define—would suffice to give full play to public opinion, to change beliefs, and to fix destinies. Will not the three men be found?...

May we hope, or not? What must we think of those who govern us? In the world of sorrow in which the proletaire moves, and where nothing is known of the intentions of power, it must be said that despair prevails. But you, sir,—you, who by function belong to the official world; you, in whom the people recognize one of their noblest friends, and property its most prudent adversary,—what say you of our deputies, our ministers, our king? Do you believe that the authorities are friendly to us? Then let the government declare its position; let it print its profession of faith in equality, and I am dumb. Otherwise, I shall continue the war; and the more obstinacy and malice is shown, the oftener will I redouble my energy and audacity. I have said before, and I repeat it,—I have sworn, not on the dagger and the death's-head, amid the horrors of a catacomb, and in the presence of men besmeared with blood; but I have sworn on my conscience to pursue property, to grant it neither peace nor truce, until I see it everywhere execrated. I have not yet published half the things that I have to say concerning the right of domain, nor the best things. Let the knights of property, if there are any who fight otherwise than by retreating, be prepared every day for a new demonstration and accusation; let them enter the arena armed with reason and knowledge, not wrapped up in sophisms, for justice will be done.

"To become enlightened, we must have liberty. That alone suffices; but it must be the liberty to use the reason in regard to all public matters.

"And yet we hear on every hand authorities of all kinds and degrees crying: 'Do not reason!'

"If a distinction is wanted, here is one:—

"The PUBLIC use of the reason always should be free, but the PRIVATE use ought always to be rigidly restricted. By public use, I mean the scientific, literary use; by private, that which may be taken advantage of by civil officials and public functionaries. Since the governmental machinery must be kept in motion, in order to preserve unity and attain our object, we must not reason; we must obey. But the same individual who is bound, from this point of view, to passive obedience, has the right to speak in his capacity of citizen and scholar. He can make an appeal to the public, submit to it his observations on events which occur around him and in the ranks above him, taking care, however, to avoid offences which are punishable.

"Reason, then, as much as you like; only, obey."—Kant: Fragment on the Liberty of Thought and of the Press. Tissot's Translation.

These words of the great philosopher outline for me my duty. I have delayed the reprint of the work entitled "What is Property?" in order that I might lift the discussion to the philosophical height from which ridiculous clamor has dragged it down; and that, by a new presentation of the question, I might dissipate the fears of good citizens. I now reenter upon the public use of my reason, and give truth full swing. The second edition of the First Memoir on Property will immediately follow the publication of this letter. Before issuing any thing further, I shall await the observations of my critics, and the co-operation of the friends of the people and of equality.

Hitherto, I have spoken in my own name, and on my own personal responsibility. It was my duty. I was endeavoring to call attention to principles which antiquity could not discover, because it knew nothing of the science which reveals them,—political economy. I have, then, testified as to FACTS; in short, I have been a WITNESS. Now my role changes. It remains for me to deduce the practical consequences of the facts proclaimed. The position of PUBLIC PROSECUTOR is the only one which I am henceforth fitted to fill, and I shall sum up the case in the name of the PEOPLE.

I am, sir, with all the consideration that I owe to your talent and your character,

Your very humble and most obedient servant,

P. J. PROUDHON,

Pensioner of the Academy of Besancon.

P.S. During the session of April 2, the Chamber of Deputies rejected, by a very large majority, the literary-property bill, BECAUSE IT DID NOT UNDERSTAND IT. Nevertheless, literary property is only a special form of the right of property, which everybody claims to understand. Let us hope that this legislative precedent will not be fruitless for the cause of equality. The consequence of the vote of the Chamber is the abolition of capitalistic property,—property incomprehensible, contradictory, impossible, and absurd.

FOOTNOTES:

1 (return)
[In the French edition of Proudhon's works, the above sketch of his life is prefixed to the first volume of his correspondence, but the translator prefers to insert it here as the best method of introducing the author to the American public.]

2 (return)
["An Inquiry into Grammatical Classifications." By P. J. Proudhon. A treatise which received honorable mention from the Academy of Inscriptions, May 4, 1839. Out of print.]

3 (return)
["The Utility of the Celebration of Sunday," &c. By P. J. Proudhon. Besancon, 1839, 12mo; 2d edition, Paris, 1841, 18mo.]

4 (return)
[Charron, on "Wisdom," Chapter xviii.]

5 (return)
[M. Vivien, Minister of Justice, before commencing proceedings against the "Memoir upon Property," asked the opinion of M. Blanqui; and it was on the strength of the observations of this honorable academician that he spared a book which had already excited the indignation of the magistrates. M. Vivien is not the only official to whom I have been indebted, since my first publication, for assistance and protection; but such generosity in the political arena is so rare that one may acknowledge it graciously and freely. I have always thought, for my part, that bad institutions made bad magistrates; just as the cowardice and hypocrisy of certain bodies results solely from the spirit which governs them. Why, for instance, in spite of the virtues and talents for which they are so noted, are the academies generally centres of intellectual repression, stupidity, and base intrigue? That question ought to be proposed by an academy: there would be no lack of competitors.]

6 (return)
[In Greek, {GREEK e ncg } examiner; a philosopher whose business is to seek the truth.]

7 (return)
[Religion, laws, marriage, were the privileges of freemen, and, in the beginning, of nobles only. Dii majorum gentium—gods of the patrician families; jus gentium—right of nations; that is, of families or nobles. The slave and the plebeian had no families; their children were treated as the offspring of animals. BEASTS they were born, BEASTS they must live.]

8 (return)
[If the chief of the executive power is responsible, so must the deputies be also. It is astonishing that this idea has never occurred to any one; it might be made the subject of an interesting essay. But I declare that I would not, for all the world, maintain it; the people are yet much too logical for me to furnish them with arguments.]

9 (return)
[See De Tocqueville, "Democracy in the United States;" and Michel Chevalier, "Letters on North America." Plutarch tells us, "Life of Pericles," that in Athens honest people were obliged to conceal themselves while studying, fearing they would be regarded as aspirants for office.]

10 (return)
["Sovereignty," according to Toullier, "is human omnipotence." A materialistic definition: if sovereignty is any thing, it is a RIGHT not a FORCE or a faculty. And what is human omnipotence?]

11 (return)
[The Proudhon here referred to is J. B. V. Proudhon; a distinguished French jurist, and distant relative of the Translator.]

12 (return)
[Here, especially, the simplicity of our ancestors appears in all its rudeness. After having made first cousins heirs, where there were no legitimate children, they could not so divide the property between two different branches as to prevent the simultaneous existence of extreme wealth and extreme poverty in the same family. For example:— James, dying, leaves two sons, Peter and John, heirs of his fortune: James's property is divided equally between them. But Peter has only one daughter, while John, his brother, leaves six sons. It is clear that, to be true to the principle of equality, and at the same time to that of heredity, the two estates must be divided in seven equal portions among the children of Peter and John; for otherwise a stranger might marry Peter's daughter, and by this

alliance half of the property of James, the grandfather, would be transferred to another family, which is contrary to the principle of heredity. Furthermore, John's children would be poor on account of their number, while their cousin, being an only child, would be rich, which is contrary to the principle of equality. If we extend this combined application of two principles apparently opposed to each other, we shall become convinced that the right of succession, which is assailed with so little wisdom in our day, is no obstacle to the maintenance of equality.]

13 (return)
[*Zeus klesios*.]

14 (return)
[Giraud, "Investigations into the Right of Property among the Romans."]

15 (return)
[Precarious, from precor, "I pray;" because the act of concession expressly signified that the lord, in answer to the prayers of his men or slaves, had granted them permission to labor.]

16 (return)
[I cannot conceive how any one dares to justify the inequality of conditions, by pointing to the base inclinations and propensities of certain men. Whence comes this shameful degradation of heart and mind to which so many fall victims, if not from the misery and abjection into which property plunges them?]

17 (return)
[How many citizens are needed to support a professor of philosophy?—Thirty-five millions. How many for an economist?—Two billions. And for a literary man, who is neither a savant, nor an artist, nor a philosopher, nor an economist, and who writes newspaper novels?—None.]

18 (return)
[There is an error in the author's calculation here; but the translator, feeling sure that the reader will understand Proudhon's meaning, prefers not to alter his figures.—Translator.]

19 (return)
[*Hoc inter se differunt onanismus et manuspratio, nempe quod haec a solitario exercetur, ille autem a duobus reciprocatur, masculo scilicet et faemina. Porro foedam hanc onanismi venerem ludentes uxoria mariti habent nunc omnigm suavissimam*]

20 (return)
[Polyandry,—plurality of husbands.]

21 (return)
[Infanticide has just been publicly advocated in England, in a pamphlet written by a disciple of Malthus. He proposes an ANNUAL MASSACRE OF THE INNOCENTS in all families containing more children than the law allows; and he asks that a magnificent cemetery, adorned with statues, groves, fountains, and flowers, be set apart as a special burying-place for the superfluous children. Mothers would resort to this delightful spot to dream of the happiness of these little angels, and would return, quite comforted, to give birth to others, to be buried in their turn.]

22 (return)
[To perform an act of benevolence towards one's neighbor is called, in Hebrew, to do justice; in Greek, to take compassion or pity ({GREEK n n f e },from which is derived the French *aumone*); in Latin, to perform an act of love or charity; in French, give alms. We can trace the degradation of this principle through these various expressions: the first signifies duty; the second only sympathy; the third, affection, a matter of choice, not an obligation; the fourth, caprice.]

23 (return)
[I mean here by equite what the Latins called humanitas,— that is, the kind of sociability which is peculiar to man. Humanity, gentle and courteous to all, knows how to distinguish ranks, virtues, and capacities without injury to any.]

24 (return)
[Justice and equite never have been understood.]

25 (return)
[Between woman and man there may exist love, passion, ties of custom, and the like; but there is no real society. Man and woman are not companions. The difference of the sexes places a barrier between them, like that placed between animals by a difference of race. Consequently, far from advocating what is now called the emancipation of woman, I should incline, rather, if there were no other alternative, to exclude her from society.]

26 (return)
["The strong-box of Cosmo de Medici was the grave of Florentine liberty," said M. Michelet to the College of France.]

27 (return)
["My right is my lance and my buckler." General de Brossard said, like Achilles: "I get wine, gold, and women with my lance and my buckler."]

28 (return)

[It would be interesting and profitable to review the authors who have written on usury, or, to use the gentler expression which some prefer, lending at interest. The theologians always have opposed usury; but, since they have admitted always the legitimacy of rent, and since rent is evidently identical with interest, they have lost themselves in a labyrinth of subtle distinctions, and have finally reached a pass where they do not know what to think of usury. The Church—the teacher of morality, so jealous and so proud of the purity of her doctrine—has always been ignorant of the real nature of property and usury. She even has proclaimed through her pontiffs the most deplorable errors. *Non potest mutuum,* said Benedict XIV., *locationi ullo pacto comparari.* "Rent," says Bossuet, "is as far from usury as heaven is from the earth." How, on{sic} such a doctrine, condemn lending at interest? how justify the Gospel, which expressly forbids usury? The difficulty of theologians is a very serious one. Unable to refute the economical demonstrations, which rightly assimilate interest to rent, they no longer dare to condemn interest, and they can say only that there must be such a thing as usury, since the Gospel forbids it.]

29 (return)

["I preach the Gospel, I live by the Gospel," said the Apostle; meaning thereby that he lived by his labor. The Catholic clergy prefer to live by property. The struggles in the communes of the middle ages between the priests and bishops and the large proprietors and seigneurs are famous. The papal excommunications fulminated in defence of ecclesiastical revenues are no less so. Even to-day, the official organs of the Gallican clergy still maintain that the pay received by the clergy is not a salary, but an indemnity for goods of which they were once proprietors, and which were taken from them in '89 by the Third Estate. The clergy prefer to live by the right of increase rather than by labor.]

30 (return)

[The meaning ordinarily attached to the word "anarchy" is absence of principle, absence of rule; consequently, it has been regarded as synonymous with "disorder."]

31 (return)

[If such ideas are ever forced into the minds of the people, it will be by representative government and the tyranny of talkers. Once science, thought, and speech were characterized by the same expression. To designate a thoughtful and a learned man, they said, "a man quick to speak and powerful in discourse." For a long time, speech has been abstractly distinguished from science and reason. Gradually, this abstraction is becoming realized, as the logicians say, in society; so that we have to-day savants of many kinds who talk but little, and TALKERS who are not even savants in the science of speech. Thus a philosopher is no longer a savant: he is a talker. Legislators and poets were once profound and sublime characters: now they are talkers. A talker is a sonorous bell, whom the least shock suffices to set in perpetual motion. With the talker, the flow of speech is always directly proportional to the poverty of thought. Talkers govern the world; they stun us, they bore us, they worry us, they suck our blood, and laugh at us. As for the savants, they keep silence: if they wish to say a word, they are cut short. Let them write.]

32 (return)

[*libertas, librare, libratio, libra,*—liberty, to liberate, libration, balance (pound),—words which have a common derivation. Liberty is the balance of rights and duties. To make a man free is to balance him with others,—that is, to put him or their level.]

33 (return)

[In a monthly publication, the first number of which has just appeared under the name of "L'Egalitaire," self-sacrifice is laid down as a principle of equality. This is a confusion of ideas. Self-sacrifice, taken alone, is the last degree of inequality. To seek equality in self-sacrifice is to confess that equality is against nature. Equality must be based upon justice, upon strict right, upon the principles invoked by the proprietor himself; otherwise it will never exist. Self-sacrifice is superior to justice; but it cannot be imposed as law, because it is of such a nature as to admit of no reward. It is, indeed, desirable that everybody shall recognize the necessity of self-sacrifice, and the idea of "L'Egalitaire" is an excellent example. Unfortunately, it can have no effect. What would you reply, indeed, to a man who should say to you, "I do not want to sacrifice myself"? Is he to be compelled to do so? When self-sacrifice is forced, it becomes oppression, slavery, the exploitation of man by man. Thus have the proletaires sacrificed themselves to property.]

34 (return)

[The disciples of Fourier have long seemed to me the most advanced of all modern socialists, and almost the only ones worthy of the name. If they had understood the nature of their task, spoken to the people, awakened their sympathies, and kept silence when they did not understand; if they had made less extravagant pretensions, and had shown more respect for public intelligence,—perhaps the reform would now, thanks to them, be in progress. But why are these earnest reformers continually bowing to power and wealth,—that is, to all that is anti- reformatory? How, in a thinking age, can they fail to see that the world must be converted by DEMONSTRATION, not by myths and allegories? Why do they, the deadly enemies of civilization, borrow from it, nevertheless, its most pernicious fruits,—property, inequality of fortune and rank, gluttony, concubinage, prostitution, what do I know? theurgy, magic, and sorcery? Why these endless denunciations of morality, metaphysics, and psychology, when the abuse of these sciences, which they do not understand, constitutes their whole system? Why this mania for deifying a man whose principal merit consisted in talking nonsense about things whose names, even, he did not know, in the strongest language ever put upon paper? Whoever admits the infallibility of a man becomes thereby incapable of instructing others. Whoever denies his own reason will soon proscribe free thought. The phalansterians would not fail to do it if they had the power. Let them condescend to reason, let them proceed systematically, let them give us demonstrations instead of revelations, and we will listen willingly. Then let them organize manufactures, agriculture, and commerce; let them make labor attractive, and the most humble functions honorable, and our praise shall be theirs. Above all, let them throw off that Illuminism which gives them the appearance of impostors or dupes, rather than believers and apostles.]

35 (return)

[Individual possession is no obstacle to extensive cultivation and unity of exploitation. If I have not spoken of the drawbacks arising from small estates, it is because I thought it useless to repeat what so many others have said, and what by this time all the world must know. But I am surprised that the economists, who have so clearly shown the disadvantages of spade-husbandry, have failed to see that it is caused entirely by property; above all, that they have not perceived that their plan for mobilizing the soil is a first step towards the abolition of property.]

36 (return)

[In the Chamber of Deputies, during the session of the fifth of January, 1841, M. Dufaure moved to renew the expropriation bill, on the ground of public utility.]

37 (return)

["What is Property?" Chap. IV., Ninth Proposition.]

38 (return)

[*Tu cognovisti sessionem meam et resurrectionem meam.* Psalm 139.]

39 (return)

[The emperor Nicholas has just compelled all the manufacturers in his empire to maintain, at their own expense, within their establishments, small hospitals for the reception of sick workmen,—the number of beds in each being proportional to the number of laborers in the factory. "You profit by man's labor," the Czar could have said to his proprietors; "you shall be responsible for man's life." M. Blanqui has said that such a measure could not succeed in France. It would be an attack upon property,—a thing hardly conceivable even in Russia, Scythia, or among the Cossacks; but among us, the oldest sons of civilization!... I fear very much that this quality of age may prove in the end a mark of decrepitude.]

40 (return)

[Course of M. Blanqui. Lecture of Nov. 27, 1840.]

41 (return)

[In "Mazaniello," the Neapolitan fisherman demands, amid the applause of the galleries, that a tax be levied upon luxuries.]

42 (return)

[*Seme le champ, proletaire; C'est l l'oisif qui recoltera.*]

43 (return)

["In some countries, the enjoyment of certain political rights depends upon the amount of property. But, in these same countries, property is expressive, rather than attributive, of the qualifications necessary to the exercise of these rights. It is rather a conjectural proof than the cause of these qualifications."—Rossi: Treatise on Penal Law.]

44 (return)

[Lecture of December 22.]

45 (return)

[Lecture of Jan. 15, 1841.]

46 (return)

[Lecture of Jan. 15, 1841.]

47 (return)

[MM. Blanqui and Wolowski.]

48 (return)

[Subject proposed by the Fourth Class of the Institute, the Academy of Moral and Political Sciences: "What would be the effect upon the working-class of the organization of labor, according to the modern ideas of association?"]

49 (return)
[Subject proposed by the Academy of Besancon: "The economical and moral consequences in France, up to the present time, and those which seem likely to appear in future, of the law concerning the equal division of hereditary property between the children."]

50 (return)
[{GREEK, ?n n '},—greater property. The Vulgate translates it avaritia.]

51 (return)
[Similar or analogous customs have existed among all nations. Consult, among other works, "Origin of French Law," by M. Michelet; and "Antiquities of German Law," by Grimm.]

52 (return)
[*Dees hominesque testamur, nos arma neque contra patriam cepisse neque quo periculum aliis faceremus, sed uti corpora nostra ab injuria tuta forent, qui miseri, egentes, violentia atque crudelitate foeneraterum, plerique patriae, sed omnesfarna atque fortunis expertes sumus; neque cuiquam nostrum licuit, more majorum, lege uti, neque, amisso patrimonio, libferum corpus habere.*—Sallus: Bellum Catilinarium.]

53 (return)
[Fifty, sixty, and eighty per cent.—Course of M. Blanqui.]

54 (return)
[*Episcopi plurimi, quos et hortamento esse oportet caeteris et exemplo, divina prouratione contempta, procuratores rerum saeularium fieri, derelicta cathedra, plebeleserta, per alienas provincias oberrantes, negotiationis quaestuosae nundinas au uucu-, pari, esurientibus in ecclesia fratribus habere argentum largitur velle, fundos insidi.sis fraudibus rapere, usuris multiplicantibus faenus augere.*—Cyprian: De Lapsis. {—NOTE: what does this refer to? This is at bottom of pg 341 in MS} In this passage, St. Cyprian alludes to lending on mortgages and to compound interest.]

55 (return)
["Inquiries concerning Property among the Romans."]

56 (return)
["Its acquisitive nature works rapidly in the sleep of the law. It is ready, at the word, to absorb every thing. Witness the famous equivocation about the ox-hide which, when cut up into thongs, was large enough to enclose the site of Carthage.... The legend has reappeared several times since Dido.... Such is the love of man for the land. Limited by tombs, measured by the members of the human body, by the thumb, the foot, and the arm, it harmonizes, as far as possible, with the very proportions of man. Nor is he satisfied yet: he calls Heaven to witness that it is his; he tries to or his land, to give it the form of heaven.... In his titanic intoxication, he describes property in the very terms which he employs in describing the Almighty—*fundus optimus maximus*.... He shall make it his couch, and they shall be separated no more,—{GREEK, ' nf g h g g."}—Michelet:Origin of French Law.]

57 (return)
[M. Guizot denies that Christianity alone is entitled to the glory of the abolition of slavery. "To this end," he says, "many causes were necessary,—the evolution of other ideas and other principles of civilization." So general an assertion cannot be refuted. Some of these ideas and causes should have been pointed out, that we might judge whether their source was not wholly Christian, or whether at least the Christian spirit had not penetrated and thus fructified them. Most of the emancipation charters begin with these words: "For the love of God and the salvation of my soul."]

58 (return)
[*Weregild*,—the fine paid for the murder of a man. So much for a count, so much for a baron, so much for a freeman, so much for a priest; for a slave, nothing. His value was restored to the proprietor.]

59 (return)
[The spirit of despotism and monopoly which animated the communes has not escaped the attention of historians. "The formation of the commoners' associations," says Meyer, "did not spring from the true spirit of liberty, but from the desire for exemption from the charges of the seigniors, from individual interests, and jealousy of the welfare of others.... Each commune or corporation opposed the creation of every other; and this spirit increased to such an extent that the King of England, Henry V., having established a university at Caen, in 1432, the city and university of Paris opposed the registration of the edict."]

60 (return)
[Feudalism was, in spirit and in its providential destiny, a long protest of the human personality against the monkish communism with which Europe, in the middle ages, was overrun. After the orgies of Pagan selfishness, society—carried to the opposite extreme by the Christian religion—risked its life by unlimited self-denial and absolute indifference to the pleasures of the world. Feudalism was the balance-weight which saved Europe from the combined influence of the

religious communities and the Manlchean sects which had sprung up since the fourth century under different names and in different countries. Modern civilization is indebted to feudalism for the definitive establishment of the person, of marriage, of the family, and of country. (See, on this subject, Guizot, "History of Civilization in Europe.")]

61 (return)
[This was made evident in July, 1830, and the years which followed it, when the electoral bourgeoisie effected a revolution in order to get control over the king, and suppressed the emeutes in order to restrain the people. The bourgeoisie, through the jury, the magistracy, its position in the army, and its municipal despotism, governs both royalty and the people. It is the bourgeoisie which, more than any other class, is conservative and retrogressive. It is the bourgeoisie which makes and unmakes ministries. It is the bourgeoisie which has destroyed the influence of the Upper Chamber, and which will dethrone the King whenever he shall become unsatisfactory to it. It is to please the bourgeoisie that royalty makes itself unpopular. It is the bourgeoisie which is troubled at the hopes of the people, and which hinders reform. The journals of the bourgeoisie are the ones which preach morality and religion to us, while reserving scepticism and indifference for themselves; which attack personal government, and favor the denial of the electoral privilege to those who have no property. The bourgeoisie will accept any thing rather than the emancipation of the proletariat. As soon as it thinks its privileges threatened, it will unite with royalty; and who does not know that at this very moment these two antagonists have suspended their quarrels?... It has been a question of property.]

62 (return)
[The same opinion was recently expressed from the tribune by one of our most honorable Deputies, M. Gauguier. "Nature," said he, "has not endowed man with landed property." Changing the adjective LANDED, which designates only a species into CAPITALISTIC, which denotes the genus,—M. Gauguier made an egalitaire profession of faith.]

63 (return)
[A professor of comparative legislation, M. Lerminier, has gone still farther. He has dared to say that the nation took from the clergy all their possessions, not because of IDLENESS, but because of UNWORTHINESS. "You have civilized the world," cries this apostle of equality, speaking to the priests; "and for that reason your possessions were given you. In your hands they were at once an instrument and a reward. But you do not now deserve them, for you long since ceased to civilize any thing whatever...."]

64 (return)
["Treatise on Prescription."]

65 (return)
["Origin of French Law."]

66 (return)
[To honor one's parents, to be grateful to one's benefactors, to neither kill nor steal,—truths of inward sensation. To obey God rather than men, to render to each that which is his; the whole is greater than a part, a straight line is the shortest road from one point to another,—truths of intuition. All are a priori but the first are felt by the conscience, and imply only a simple act of the soul; the second are perceived by the reason, and imply comparison and relation. In short, the former are sentiments, the latter are ideas.]

67 (return)
[Armand Carrel would have favored the fortification of the capital. "Le National" has said, again and again, placing the name of its old editor by the side of the names of Napoleon and Vauban. What signifies this exhumation of an anti-popular politician? It signifies that Armand Carrel wished to make government an individual and irremovable, but elective, property, and that he wished this property to be elected, not by the people, but by the army. The political system of Carrel was simply a reorganization of the pretorian guards. Carrel also hated the *pequins*. That which he deplored in the revolution of July was not, they say, the insurrection of the people, but the victory of the people over the soldiers. That is the reason why Carrel, after 1830, would never support the patriots. "Do you answer me with a few regiments?" he asked. Armand Carrel regarded the army—the military power—as the basis of law and government. This man undoubtedly had a moral sense within him, but he surely had no sense of justice. Were he still in this world, I declare it boldly, liberty would have no greater enemy than Carrel.]

68 (return)
[In a very short article, which was read by M. Wolowski, M. Louis Blanc declares, in substance, that he is not a communist (which I easily believe); that one must be a fool to attack property (but he does not say why); and that it is very necessary to guard against confounding property with its abuses. When Voltaire overthrew Christianity, he repeatedly avowed that he had no spite

against religion, but only against its abuses.]

69 (return)

[The property fever is at its height among writers and artists, and it is curious to see the complacency with which our legislators and men of letters cherish this devouring passion. An artist sells a picture, and then, the merchandise delivered, assumes to prevent the purchaser from selling engravings, under his DESIGN. A dispute arises between the amateur and the artist in regard to both the fact and the law. M. Villemain, the Minister of Public Instruction, being consulted as to this particular case, finds that the painter is right; only the property in the design should have been specially reserved in the contract: so that, in reality, M. Villemain recognizes in the artist a power to surrender his work and prevent its communication; thus contradicting the legal axiom, One CANNOT GIVE AND KEEP AT THE SAME TIME. A strange reasoner is M. Villemain! An ambiguous principle leads to a false conclusion. Instead of rejecting the principle, M. Villemain hastens to admit the conclusion. With him the *reductio ad absurdum* is a convincing argument. Thus he is made official defender of literary property, sure of being understood and sustained by a set of loafers, the disgrace of literature and the plague of public morals. Why, then, does M. Villemain feel so strong an interest in setting himself up as the chief of the literary classes, in playing for their benefit the role of Trissotin in the councils of the State, and in becoming the accomplice and associate of a band of profligates,—*soi-disant* men of letters,—who for more than ten years have labored with such deplorable success to ruin public spirit, and corrupt the heart by warping the mind?]

70 (return)

[M. Leroux has been highly praised in a review for having defended property. I do not know whether the industrious encyclopedist is pleased with the praise, but I know very well that in his place I should mourn for reason and for truth.]

71 (return)

["Impartial," of Besancon.]

72 (return)

[The Arians deny the divinity of Christ. The Semi-Arians differ from the Arians only by a few subtle distinctions. M. Pierre Leroux, who regards Jesus as a man, but claims that the Spirit of God was infused into him, is a true Semi-Arian.

The Manicheans admit two co-existent and eternal principles,—God and matter, spirit and flesh, light and darkness, good and evil; but, unlike the Phalansterians, who pretend to reconcile the two, the Manicheans make war upon matter, and labor with all their might for the destruction of the flesh, by condemning marriage and forbidding reproduction,—which does not prevent them, however, from indulging in all the carnal pleasures which the intensest lust can conceive of. In this last particular, the tendency of the Fourieristic morality is quite Manichean.

The Gnostics do not differ from the early Christians. As their name indicates, they regarded themselves as inspired. Fourier, who held peculiar ideas concerning the visions of somnambulists, and who believed in the possibility of developing the magnetic power to such an extent as to enable us to commune with invisible beings, might, if he were living, pass also for a Gnostic.

The Adamites attend mass entirely naked, from motives of chastity. Jean Jacques Rousseau, who took the sleep of the senses for chastity, and who saw in modesty only a refinement of pleasure, inclined towards Adamism. I know such a sect, whose members usually celebrate their mysteries in the costume of Venus coming from the bath.

The Pre-Adamites believe that men existed before the first man. I once met a Pre-Adamite. True, he was deaf and a Fourierist.

The Pelagians deny grace, and attribute all the merit of good works to liberty. The Fourierists, who teach that man's nature and passions are good, are reversed Pelagians; they give all to grace, and nothing to liberty.

The Socinians, deists in all other respects, admit an original revelation. Many people are Socinians to-day, who do not suspect it, and who regard their opinions as new.

The Neo-Christians are those simpletons who admire Christianity because it has produced bells and cathedrals. Base in soul, corrupt in heart, dissolute in mind and senses, the Neo-Christians seek especially after the external form, and admire religion, as they love women, for its physical beauty. They believe in a coming revelation, as well as a transfiguration of Catholicism. They will sing masses at the grand spectacle in the phalanstery.]

73 (return)

[It should be understood that the above refers only to the moral and political doctrines of Fourier,—doctrines which, like all philosophical and religious systems, have their root and *raison d'existence* in society itself, and for this reason deserve to be examined. The peculiar speculations of Fourier and his sect concerning cosmogony, geology, natural history, physiology, and psychology, I leave to the attention of those who would think it their duty to seriously refute the fables of Blue Beard and the Ass's Skin.]

74 (return)

[A writer for the radical press, M. Louis Raybaud, said, in the preface to his "Studies of Contemporary Reformers:" "Who does not know that morality is relative? Aside from a few grand sentiments which are strikingly instinctive, the measure of human acts varies with nations and climates, and only civilization— the progressive education of the race—can lead to a universal morality.... The absolute escapes our contingent and finite nature; the absolute is the secret of

God." God keep from evil M. Louis Raybaud! But I cannot help remarking that all political apostates begin by the negation of the absolute, which is really the negation of truth. What can a writer, who professes scepticism, have in common with radical views? What has he to say to his readers? What judgment is he entitled to pass upon contemporary reformers? M. Raybaud thought it would seem wise to repeat an old impertinence of the legist, and that may serve him for an excuse. We all have these weaknesses. But I am surprised that a man of so much intelligence as M. Raybaud, who STUDIES SYSTEMS, fails to see the very thing he ought first to recognize,—namely, that systems are the progress of the mind towards the absolute.]

75 (return)

[The electoral reform, it is continually asserted, is not an END, but a MEANS. Undoubtedly; but what, then, is the end? Why not furnish an unequivocal explanation of its object? How can the people choose their representatives, unless they know in advance the purpose for which they choose them, and the object of the commission which they entrust to them? But, it is said, the very business of those chosen by the people is to find out the object of the reform. That is a quibble. What is to hinder these persons, who are to be elected in future, from first seeking for this object, and then, when they have found it, from communicating it to the people? The reformers have well said, that, while the object of the electoral reform remains in the least indefinite, it will be only a means of transferring power from the hands of petty tyrants to the hands of other tyrants. We know already how a nation may be oppressed by being led to believe that it is obeying only its own laws. The history of universal suffrage, among all nations, is the history of the restrictions of liberty by and in the name of the multitude. Still, if the electoral reform, in its present shape, were rational, practical, acceptable to clean consciences and upright minds, perhaps one might be excused, though ignorant of its object, for supporting it. But, no; the text of the petition determines nothing, makes no distinctions, requires no conditions, no guarantee; it establishes the right without the duty. "Every Frenchman is a voter, and eligible to office." As well say: "Every bayonet is intelligent, every savage is civilized, every slave is free." In its vague generality, the reformatory petition is the weakest of abstractions, or the highest form of political treason. Consequently, the enlightened patriots distrust and despise each other. The most radical writer of the time,—he whose economical and social theories are, without comparison, the most advanced,—M. Leroux, has taken a bold stand against universal suffrage and democratic government, and has written an exceedingly keen criticism of J. J. Rousseau. That is undoubtedly the reason why M. Leroux is no longer the philosopher of "Le National." That journal, like Napoleon, does not like men of ideas. Nevertheless, "Le National" ought to know that he who fights against ideas will perish by ideas.]

CPSIA information can be obtained
at www.ICGtesting.com
Printed in the USA
LVHW060104291019
635656LV00003B/92/P

9 780368 259364